Vampire Game

JUDAL

Vampire Game Vol. 10
Created by Judal

Translation - Patrick Coffman
English Adaptation - Jason Deitrich
Copy Editor - Troy Lewter
Retouch and Lettering - JUNEMOON Studios
Production Artist - Vicente Rivera, Jr.
Cover Design - Anna Kernbaum

Editor - Tim Beedle
Digital Imaging Manager - Chris Buford
Pre-Press Manager - Antonio DePietro
Production Managers - Jennifer Miller and Mutsumi Miyazaki
Art Director - Matt Alford
Managing Editor - Jill Freshney
VP of Production - Ron Klamert
Editor-in-Chief - Mike Kiley
President and C.O.O. - John Parker
Publisher and C.E.O. - Stuart Levy

A  Manga

TOKYOPOP Inc.
5900 Wilshire Blvd. Suite 2000
Los Angeles, CA 90036

E-mail: info@TOKYOPOP.com
Come visit us online at www.TOKYOPOP.com

ISBN: 1-59532-440-2

First TOKYOPOP printing: February 2005
10 9 8 7 6 5 4 3 2 1
Printed in the USA

VAMPIRE GAME

Volume 10

by

JUDAL

HAMBURG // LONDON // LOS ANGELES // TOKYO

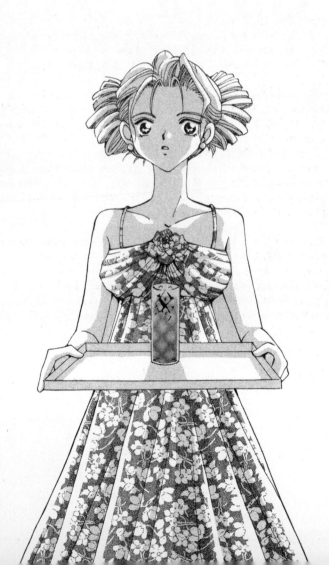

VAMPIRE GAME

The Story Thus Far...

This is the tale of the Vampire King Duzell and his quest for revenge against the good King Phelios, a valiant warrior who slew the vampire a century ago. Now Duzell has returned, reincarnated as a feline foe to deliver woe to... well, that's the problem. Who is the reincarnation of King Phelios?

Ishtar, Duzell and the rest of her royal regulars have journeyed to Zi Alda to visit Ishtar's sick aunt and to test the familial waters, murky as they may be, for any sign of Phelios' reincarnation. So far the sneaky little king hasn't shown up, but Ishtar and Duzell have found a scheming little military wife named Leene, who would like nothing more than to ensure that Ishtar never again breathes that fresh Pheliostan air. Or any air, for that matter. Though married to Ashley, the General of the Zi Alda army, Leene has a thing for Yuujel, the highly-desired prince of Zi Alda, who was recently revealed to be none other than Yujinn, Princess Ishtar's magic teacher.

Now, Ishtar doesn't love Yuujel, she loves Darres, but Leene doesn't realize this, and fearing that the princess may be in town to snatch up her favorite free prince, she's made a decision to use poison to permanently end Ishtar's prince-stealing ways. However, someone has gotten the better of our little Leene. Someone with a sick sense of humor. They've leaked word of Leene's plot to the public, leaving poor Leene stuck in the Zi Alda ballroom with what may be a glass of very cruel intentions in her hand.

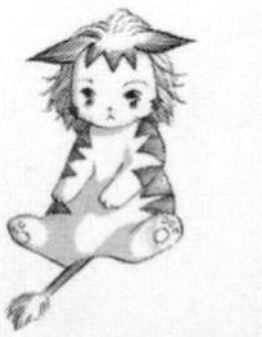

Table of Contents

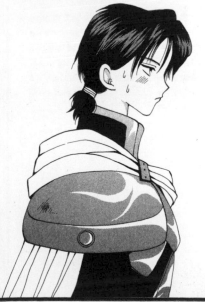
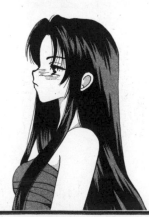

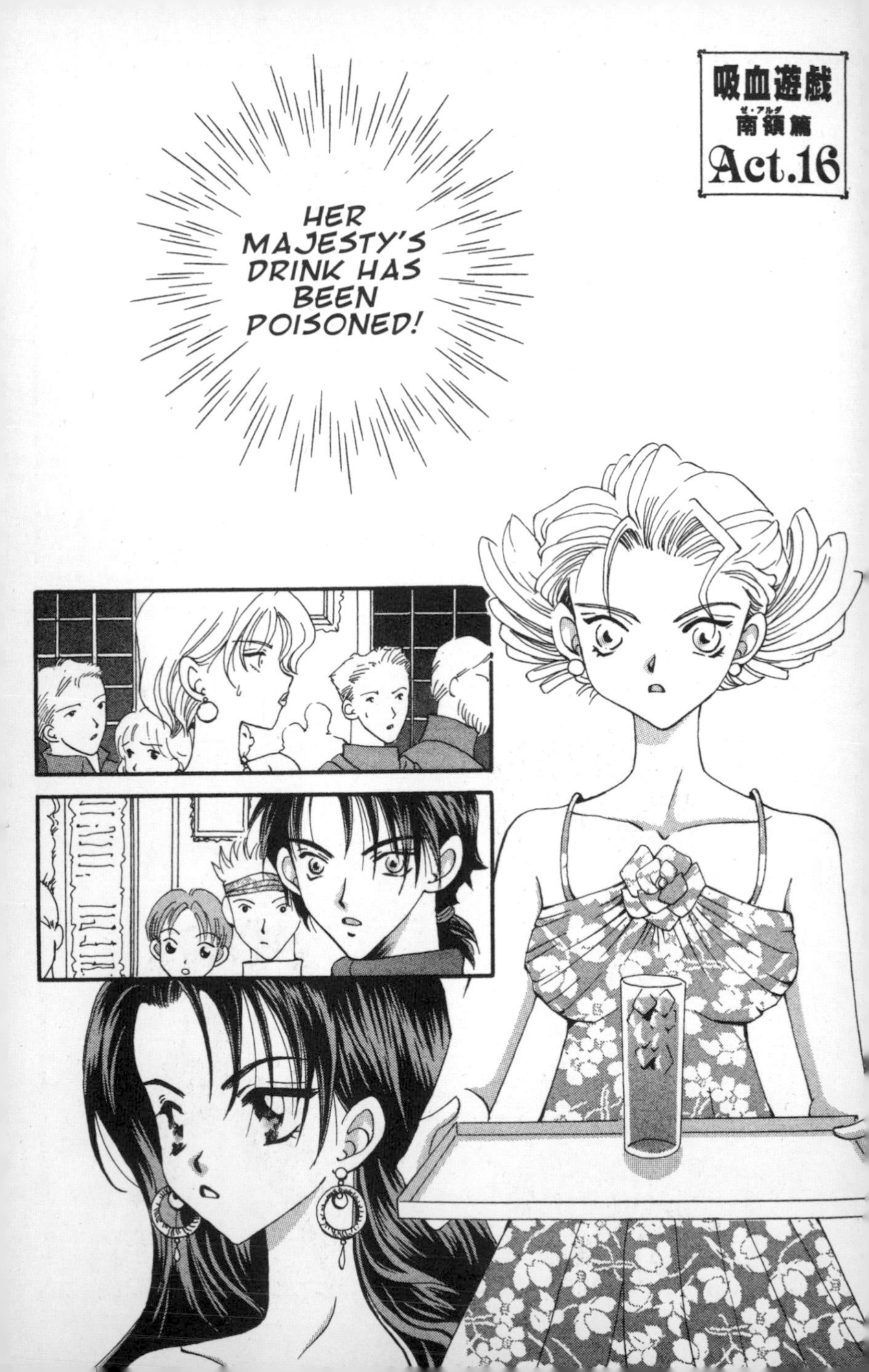
吸血遊戯
南領篇
Act.16
HER MAJESTY'S DRINK HAS BEEN POISONED!

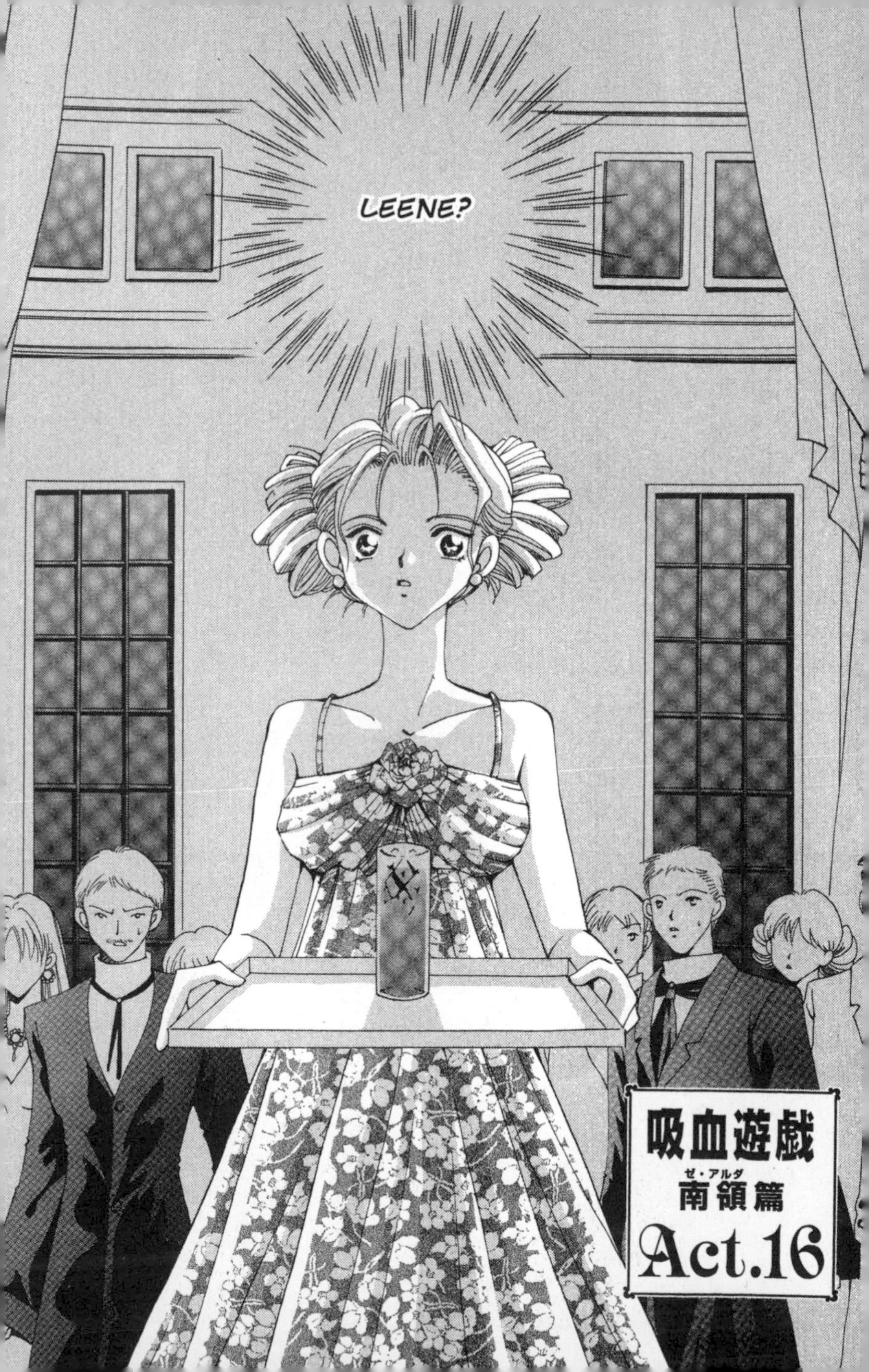
LEENE?
吸血遊戯
ゼ・アルダ
南領篇
Act.16

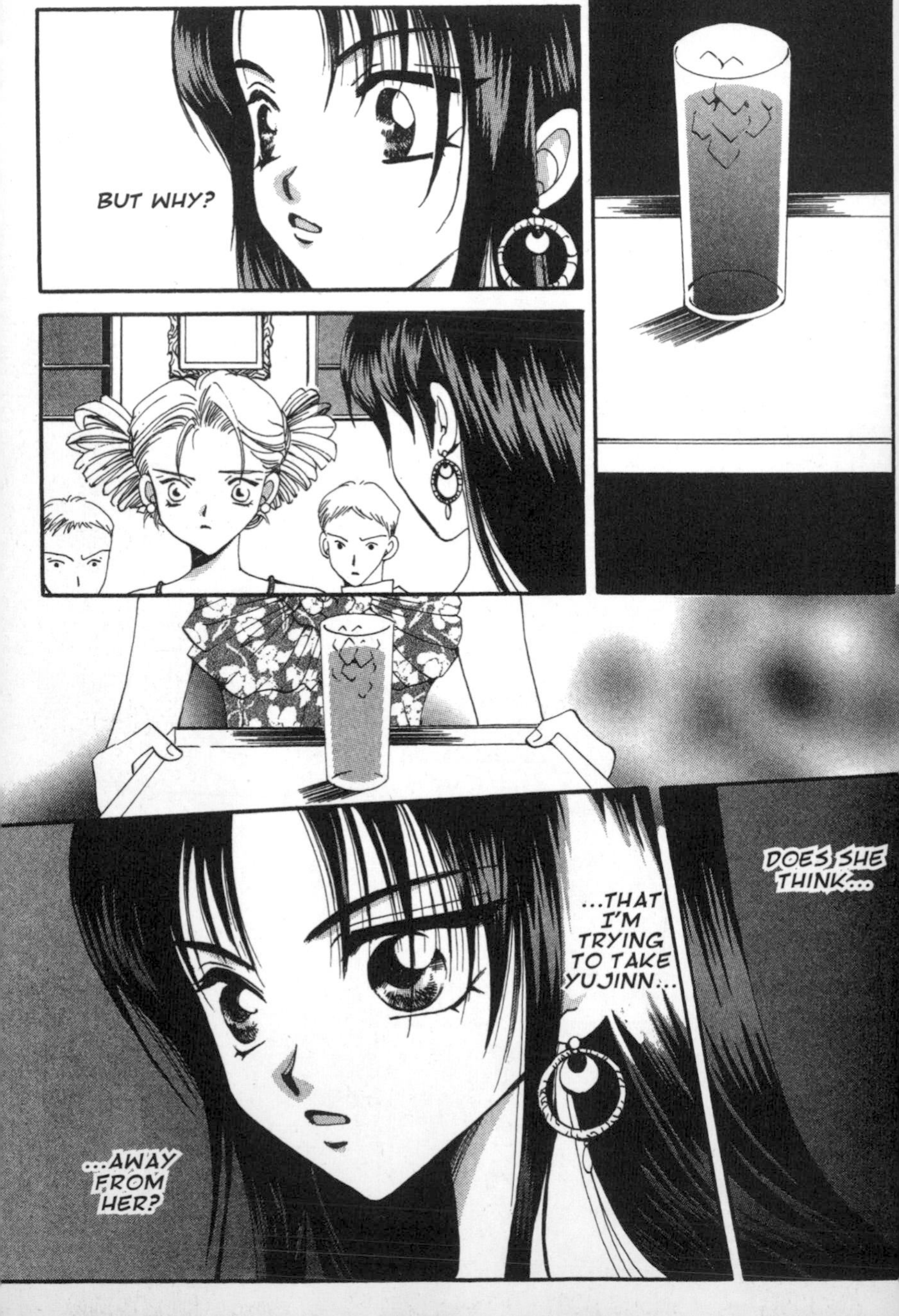
BUT WHY?
DOES SHE THINK...
...THAT I'M TRYING TO TAKE YUJINN...
...AWAY FROM HER?

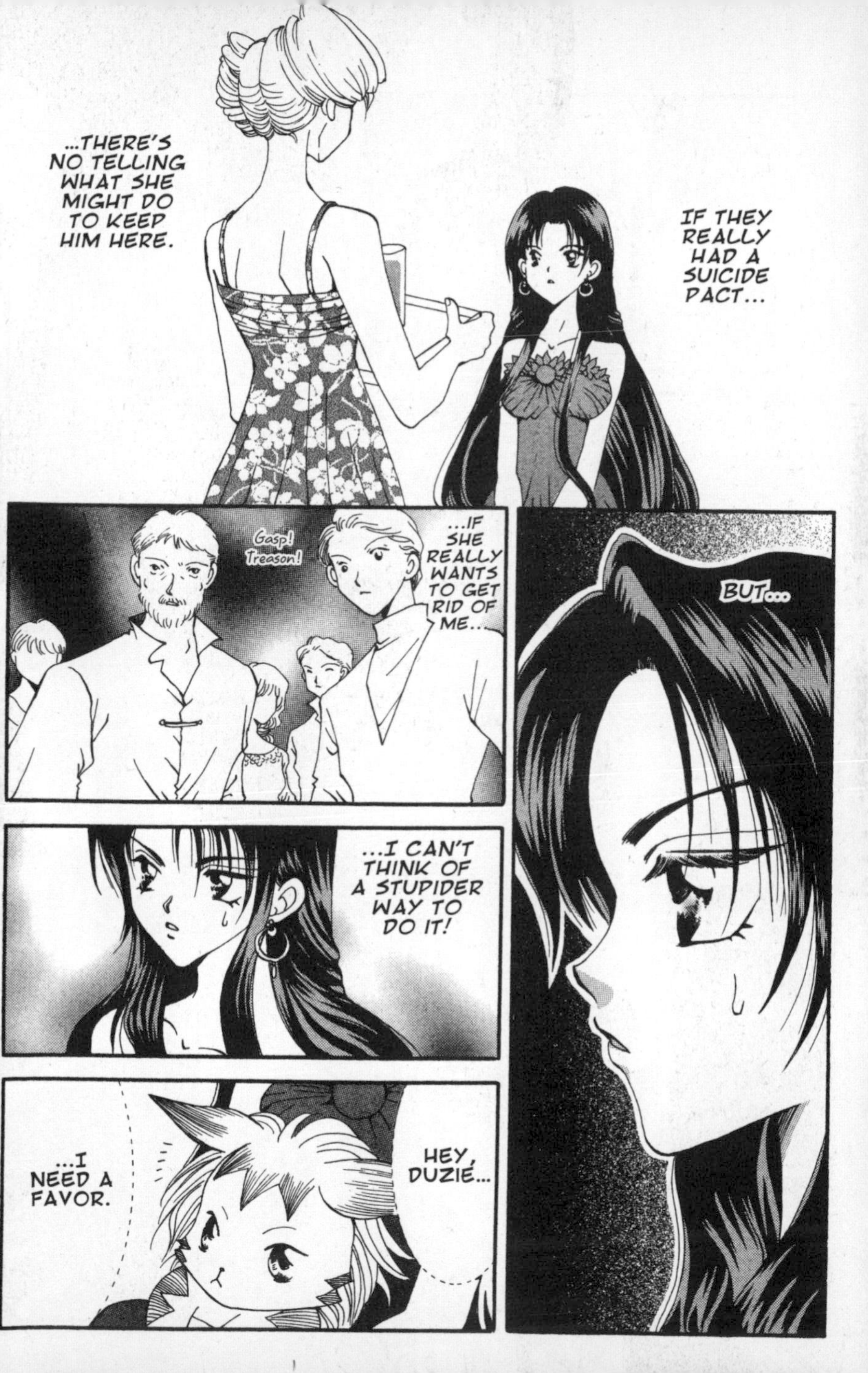
IF THEY REALLY HAD A SUICIDE PACT...
...THERE'S NO TELLING WHAT SHE MIGHT DO TO KEEP HIM HERE.
BUT...
...IF SHE REALLY WANTS TO GET RID OF ME...
Gasp! Treason!
...I CAN'T THINK OF A STUPIDER WAY TO DO IT!
HEY, DUZIE...
...I NEED A FAVOR.

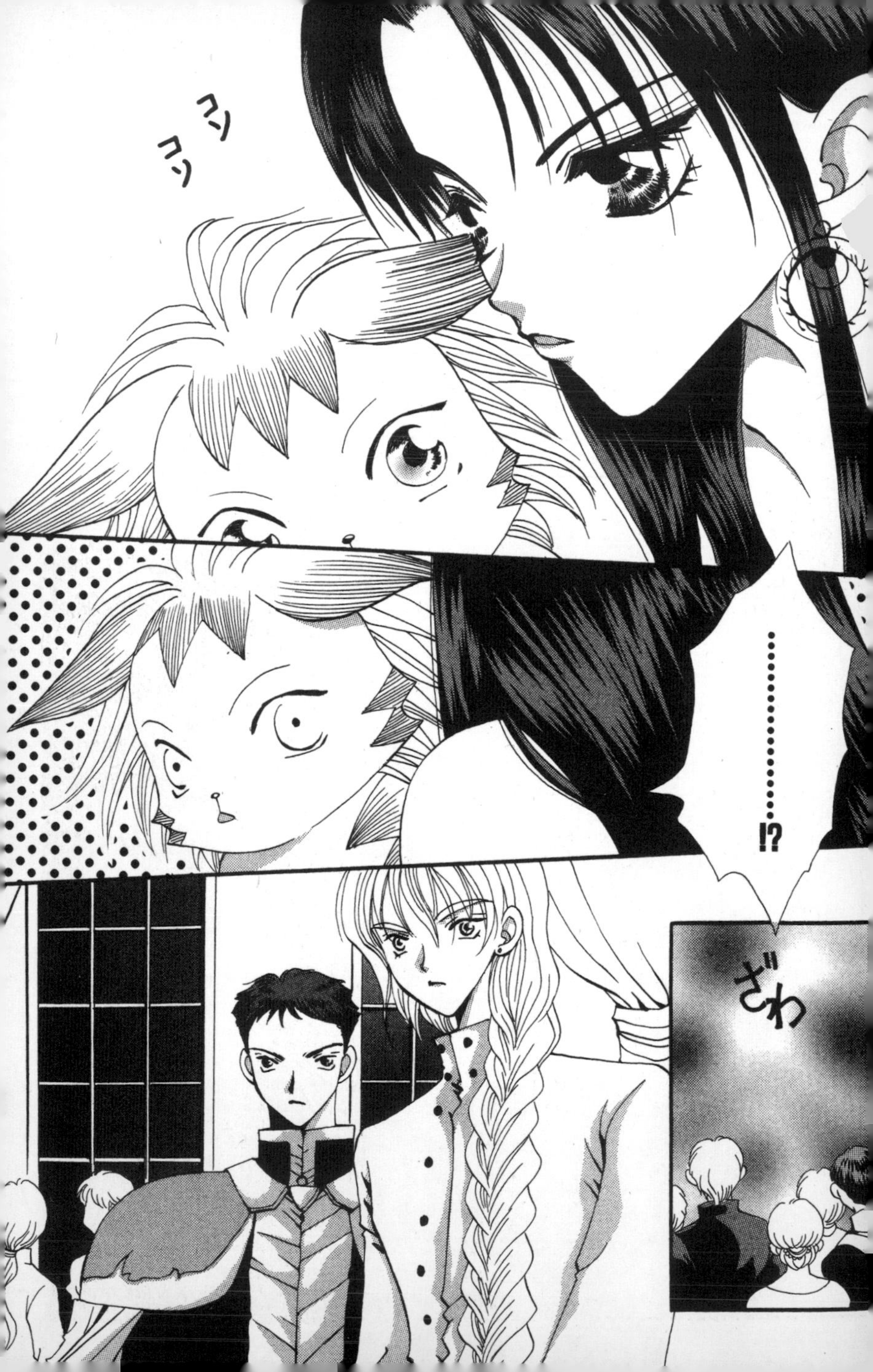
コツ
コツ
……!?
ざわ

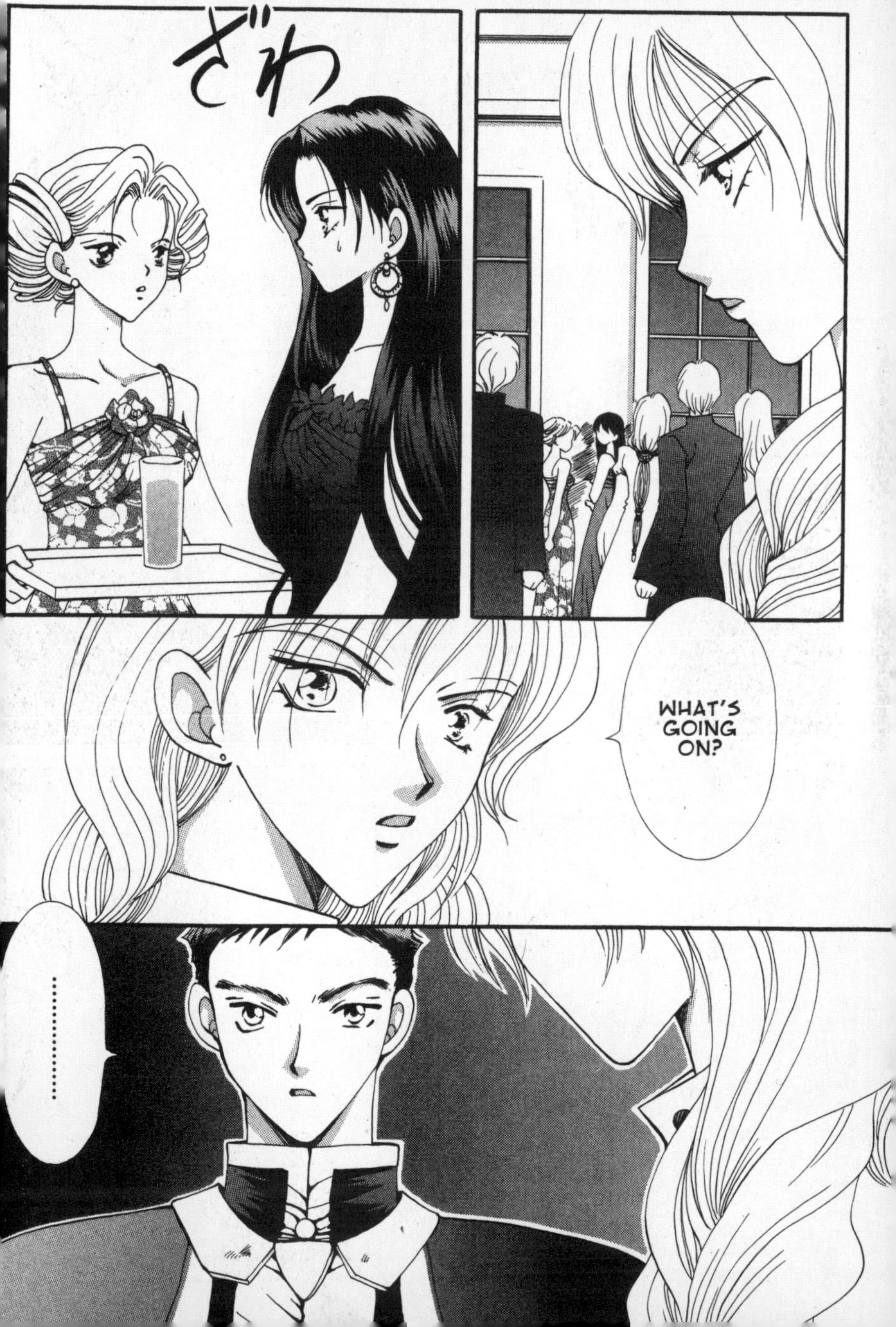
ざわ
WHAT'S GOING ON?
....

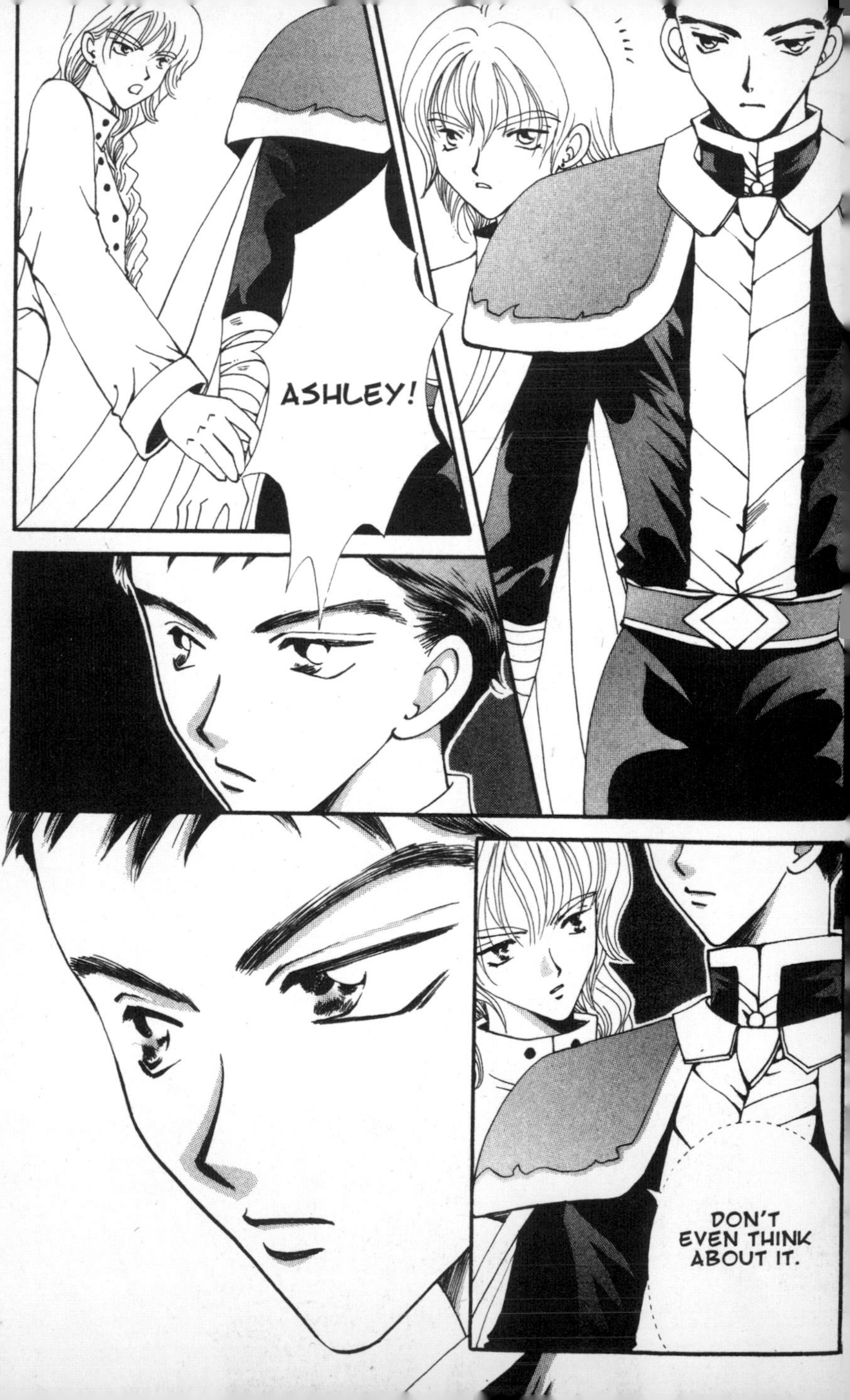
ASHLEY!
DON'T EVEN THINK ABOUT IT.

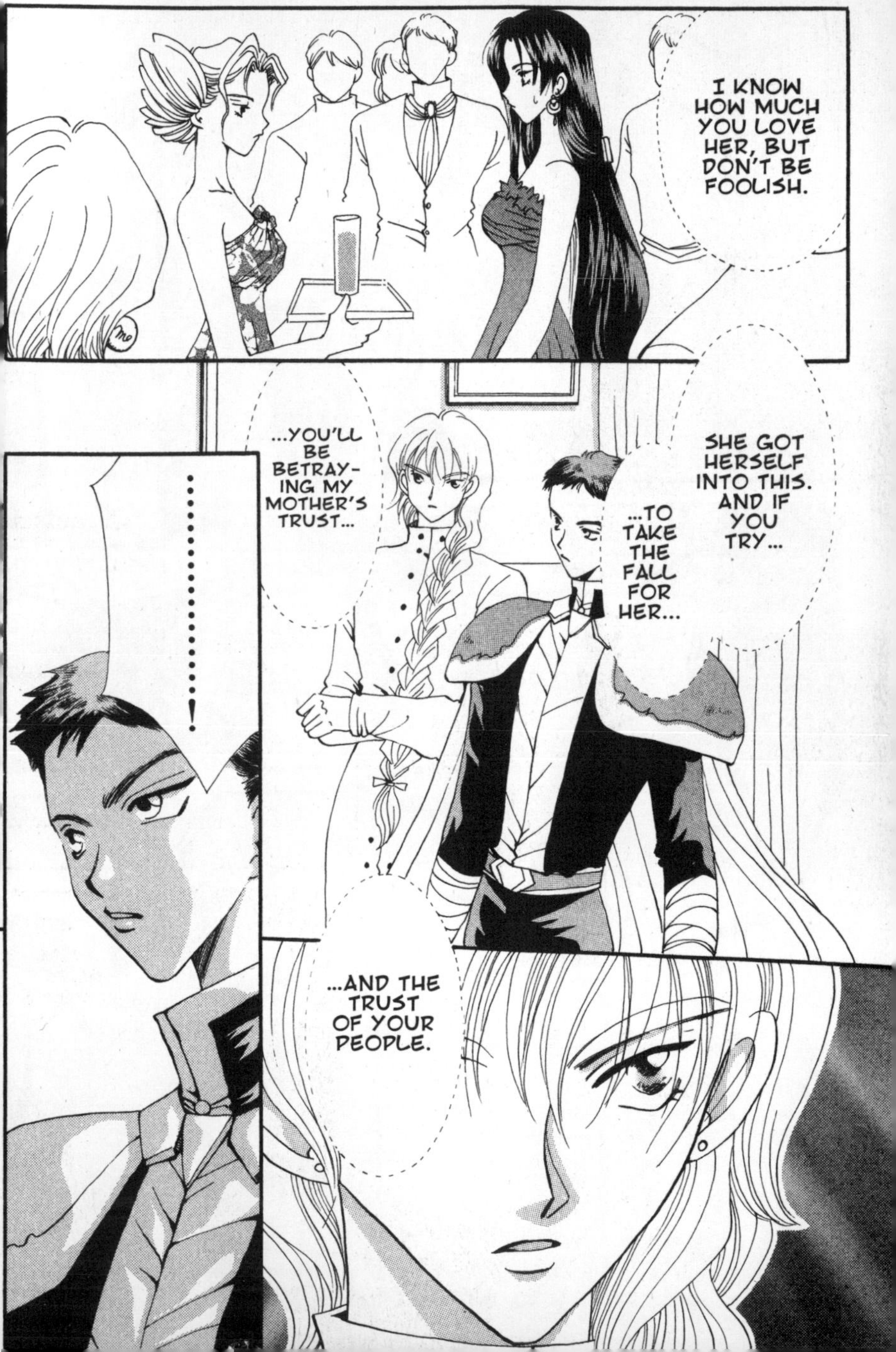
I KNOW HOW MUCH YOU LOVE HER, BUT DON'T BE FOOLISH.
SHE GOT HERSELF INTO THIS. AND IF YOU TRY...
...TO TAKE THE FALL FOR HER...
...YOU'LL BE BETRAY-ING MY MOTHER'S TRUST...
...AND THE TRUST OF YOUR PEOPLE.
..............!

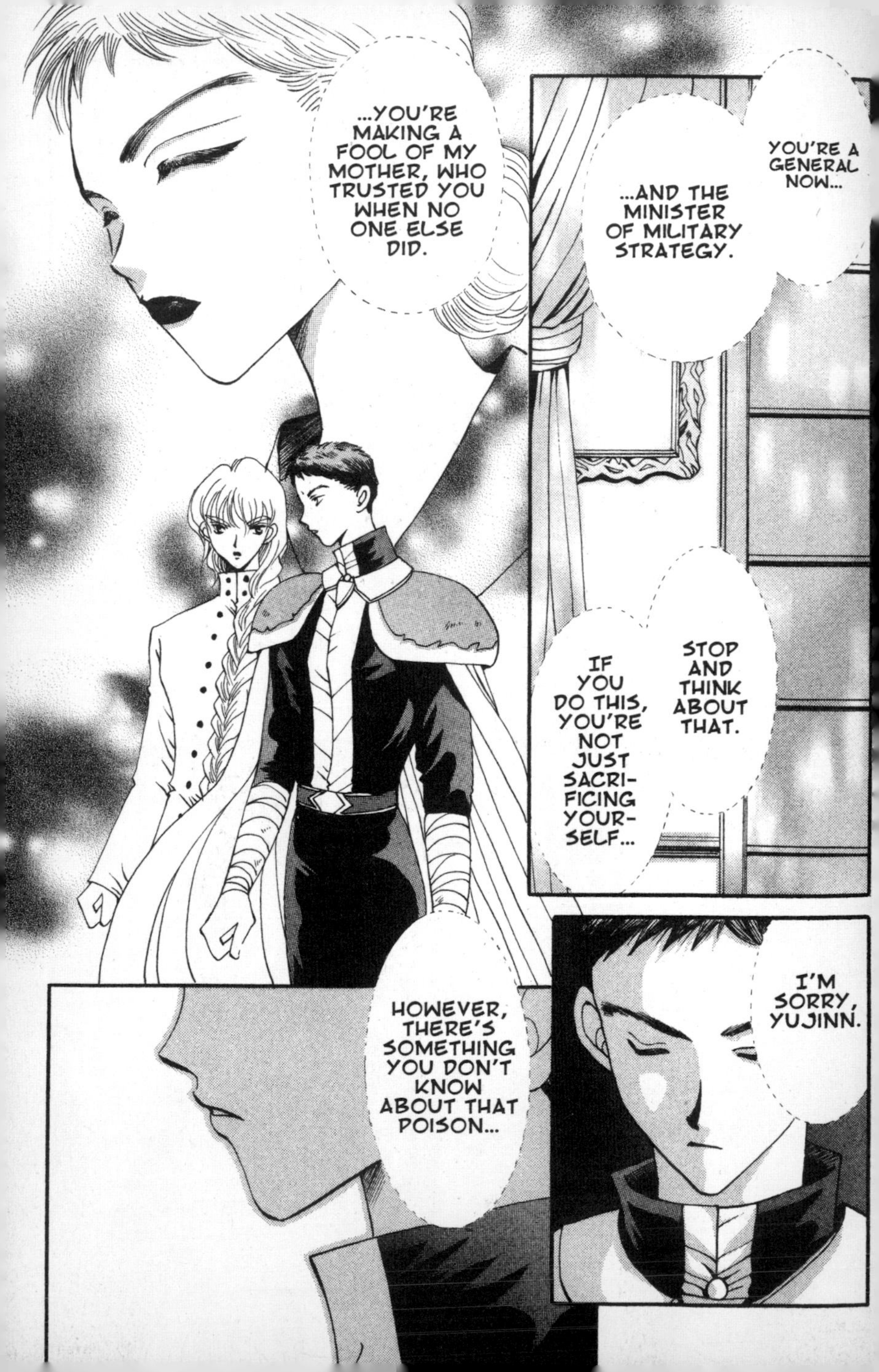
YOU'RE A GENERAL NOW...
...AND THE MINISTER OF MILITARY STRATEGY.
STOP AND THINK ABOUT THAT.
IF YOU DO THIS, YOU'RE NOT JUST SACRIFICING YOURSELF...
...YOU'RE MAKING A FOOL OF MY MOTHER, WHO TRUSTED YOU WHEN NO ONE ELSE DID.
I'M SORRY, YUJINN.
HOWEVER, THERE'S SOMETHING YOU DON'T KNOW ABOUT THAT POISON...

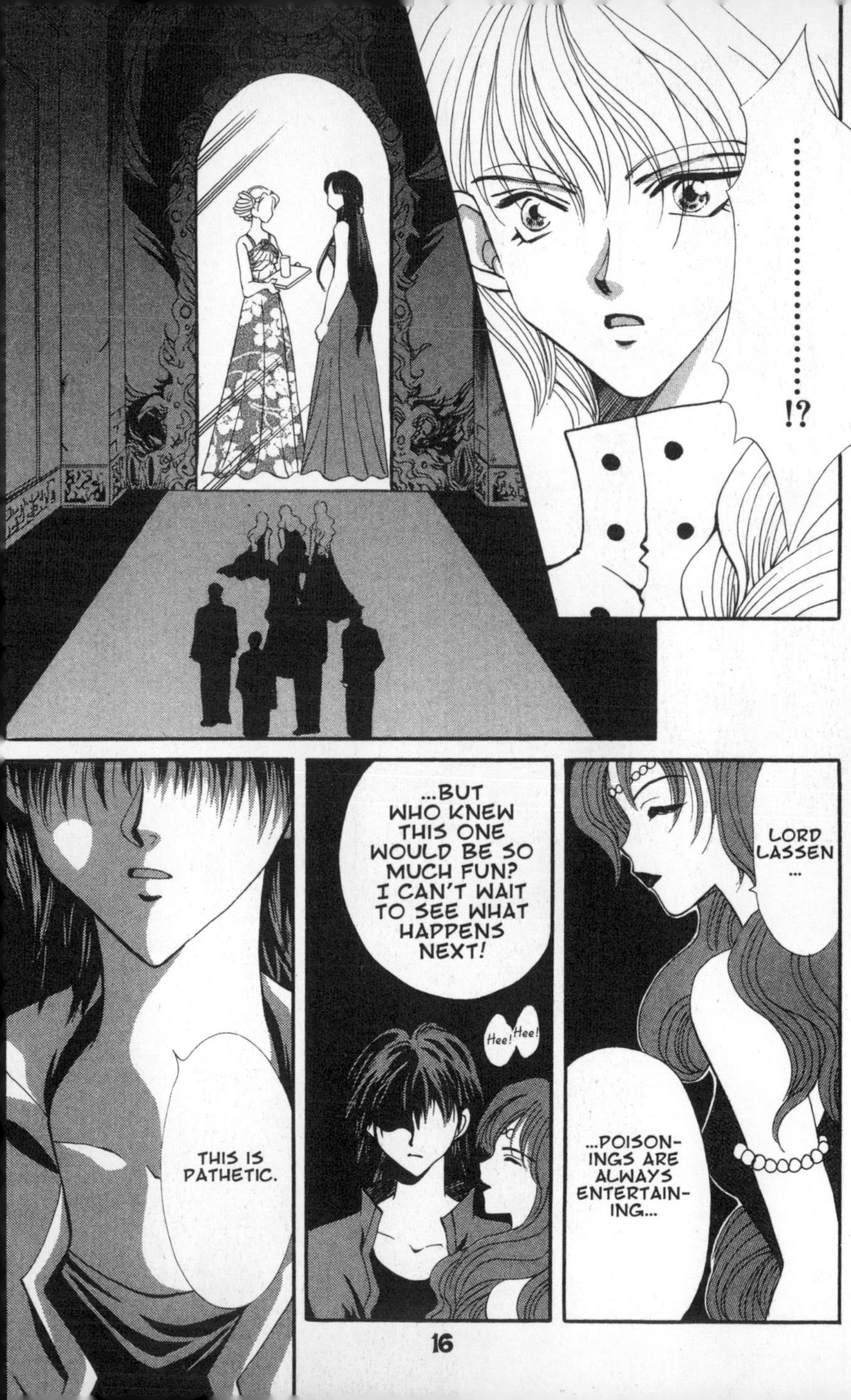

......!?
LORD LASSEN ...
...POISON-INGS ARE ALWAYS ENTERTAIN-ING...
...BUT WHO KNEW THIS ONE WOULD BE SO MUCH FUN? I CAN'T WAIT TO SEE WHAT HAPPENS NEXT!
Hee! Hee!
THIS IS PATHETIC.

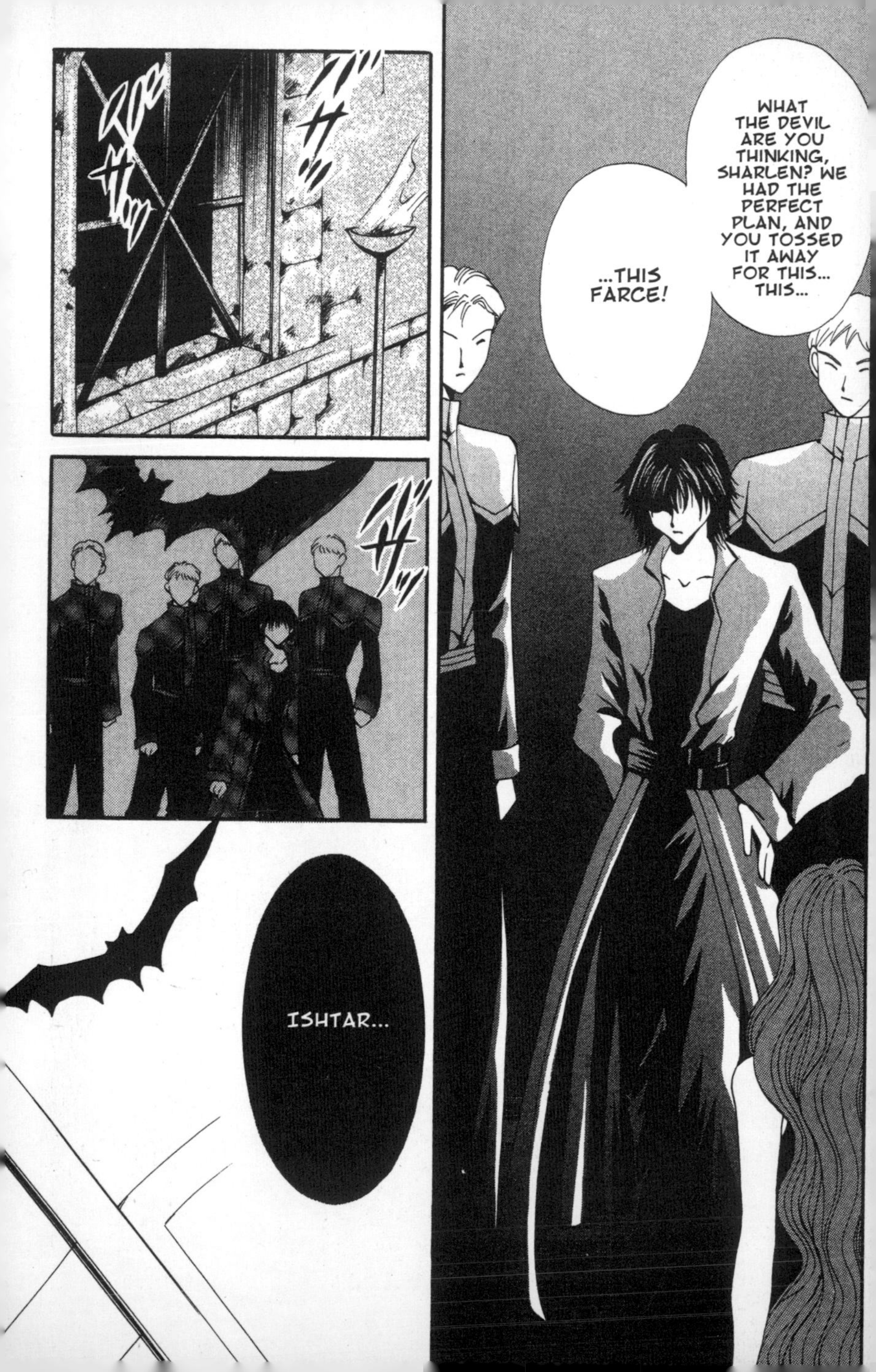
WHAT THE DEVIL ARE YOU THINKING, SHARLEN? WE HAD THE PERFECT PLAN, AND YOU TOSSED IT AWAY FOR THIS... THIS...
...THIS FARCE!
ISHTAR...

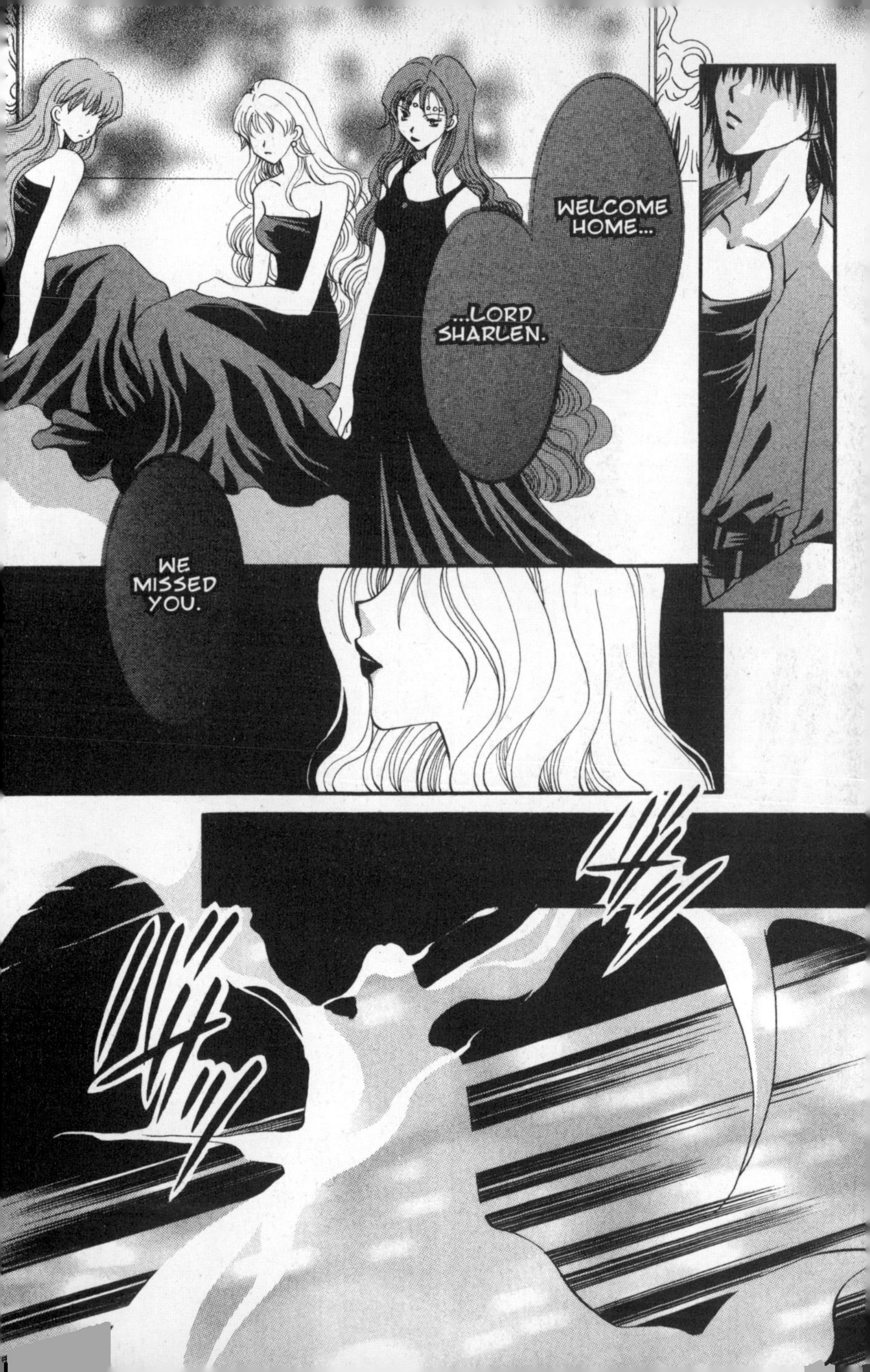
WELCOME HOME...
...LORD SHARLEN.
WE MISSED YOU.

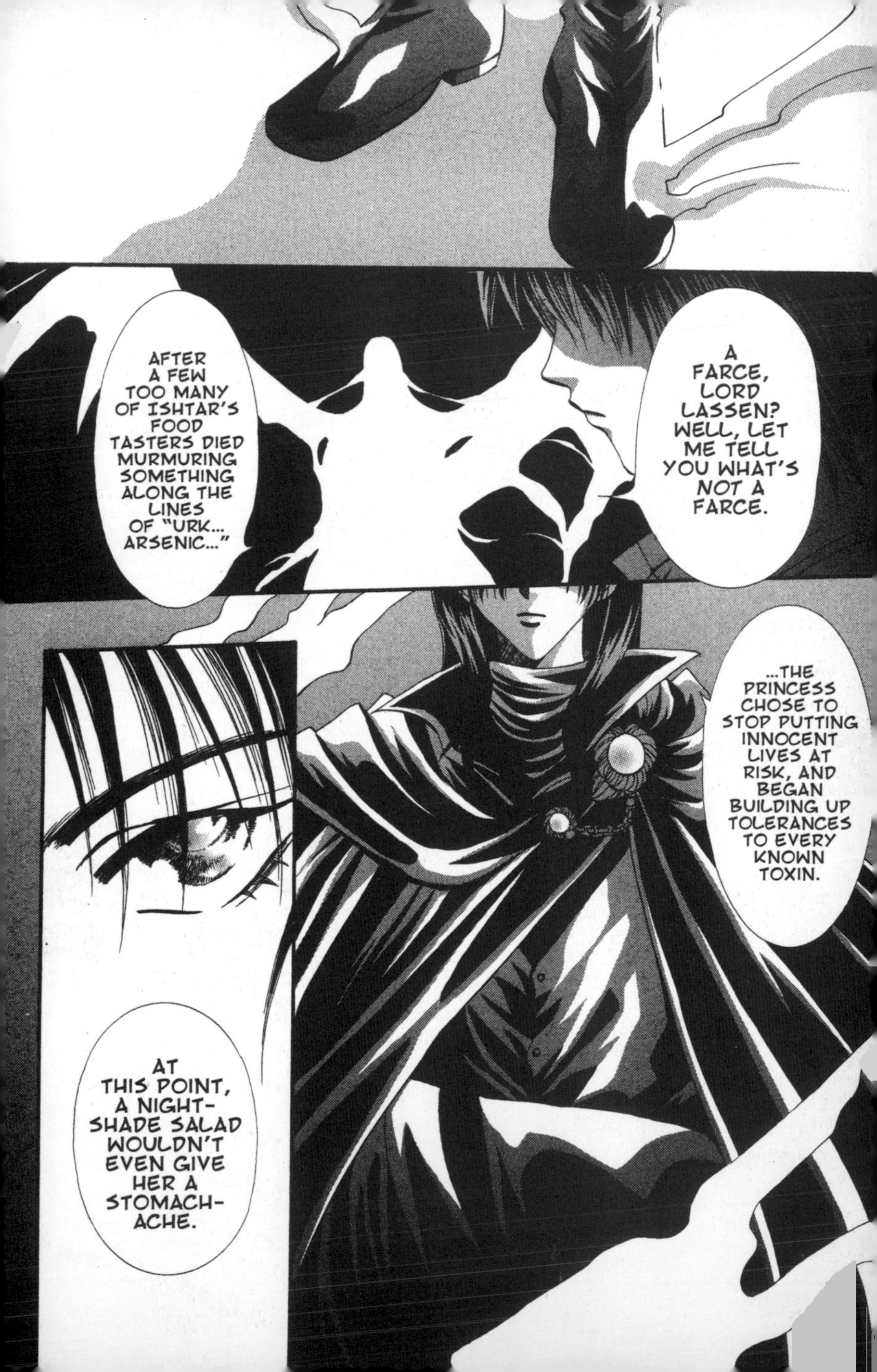
A FARCE, LORD LASSEN? WELL, LET ME TELL YOU WHAT'S NOT A FARCE.
AFTER A FEW TOO MANY OF ISHTAR'S FOOD TASTERS DIED MURMURING SOMETHING ALONG THE LINES OF "URK... ARSENIC..."
...THE PRINCESS CHOSE TO STOP PUTTING INNOCENT LIVES AT RISK, AND BEGAN BUILDING UP TOLERANCES TO EVERY KNOWN TOXIN.
AT THIS POINT, A NIGHT-SHADE SALAD WOULDN'T EVEN GIVE HER A STOMACH-ACHE.

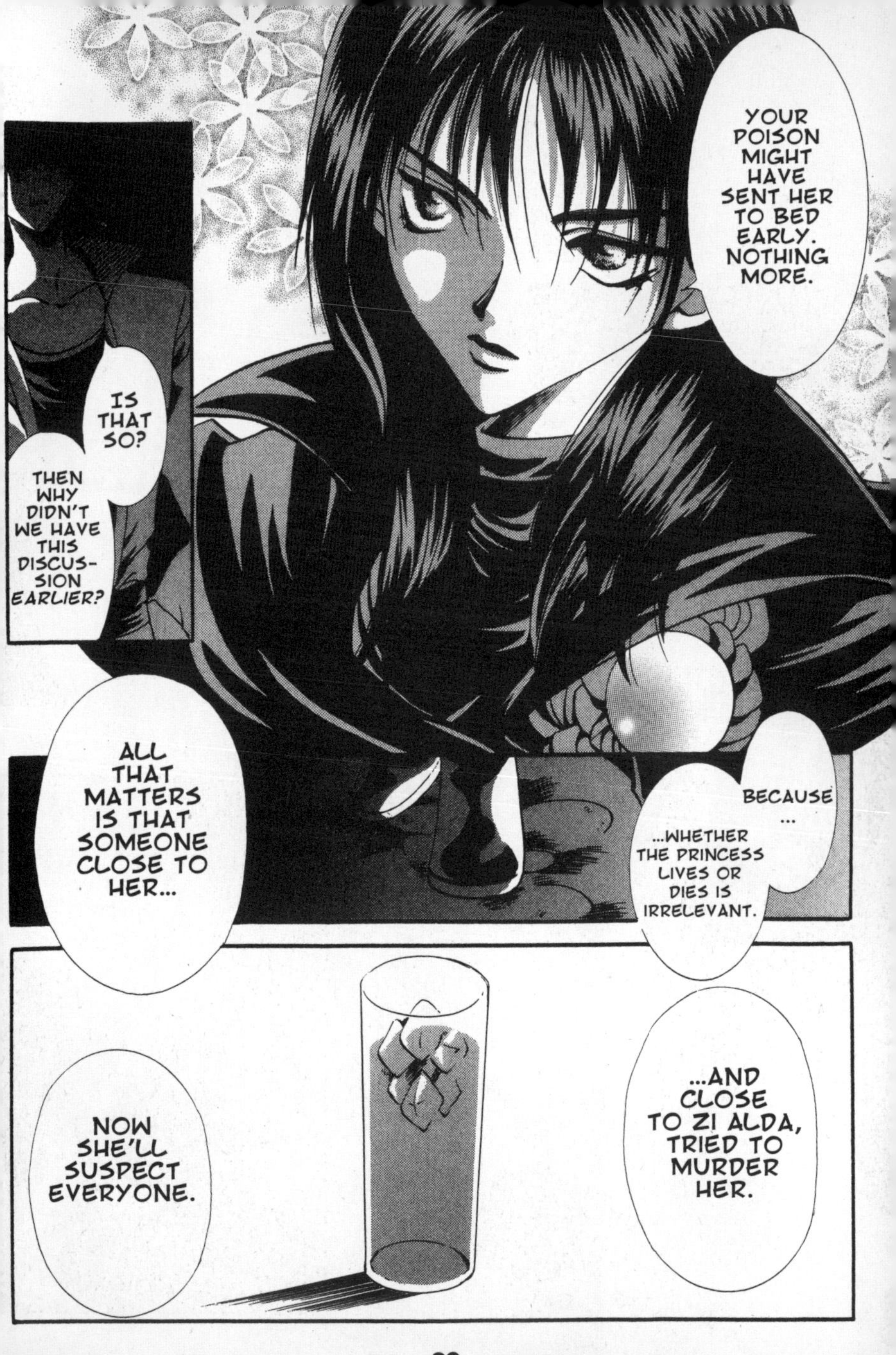
YOUR POISON MIGHT HAVE SENT HER TO BED EARLY. NOTHING MORE.
IS THAT SO?
THEN WHY DIDN'T WE HAVE THIS DISCUS-SION EARLIER?
BECAUSE ...
...WHETHER THE PRINCESS LIVES OR DIES IS IRRELEVANT.
ALL THAT MATTERS IS THAT SOMEONE CLOSE TO HER...
...AND CLOSE TO ZI ALDA, TRIED TO MURDER HER.
NOW SHE'LL SUSPECT EVERYONE.

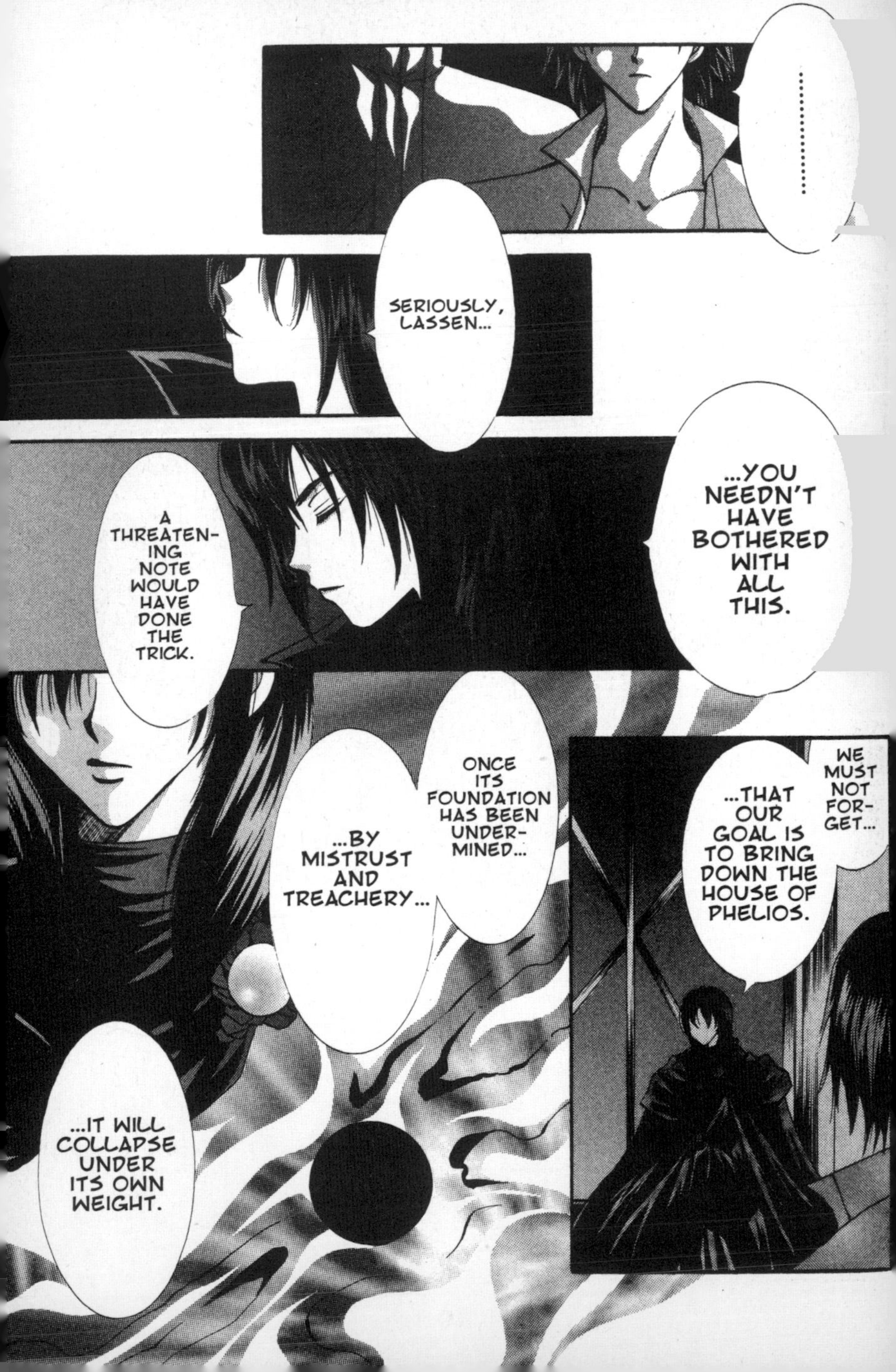

......
SERIOUSLY, LASSEN...
...YOU NEEDN'T HAVE BOTHERED WITH ALL THIS.
A THREATEN-ING NOTE WOULD HAVE DONE THE TRICK.
WE MUST NOT FOR-GET...
...THAT OUR GOAL IS TO BRING DOWN THE HOUSE OF PHELIOS.
ONCE ITS FOUNDATION HAS BEEN UNDER-MINED...
...BY MISTRUST AND TREACHERY...
...IT WILL COLLAPSE UNDER ITS OWN WEIGHT.

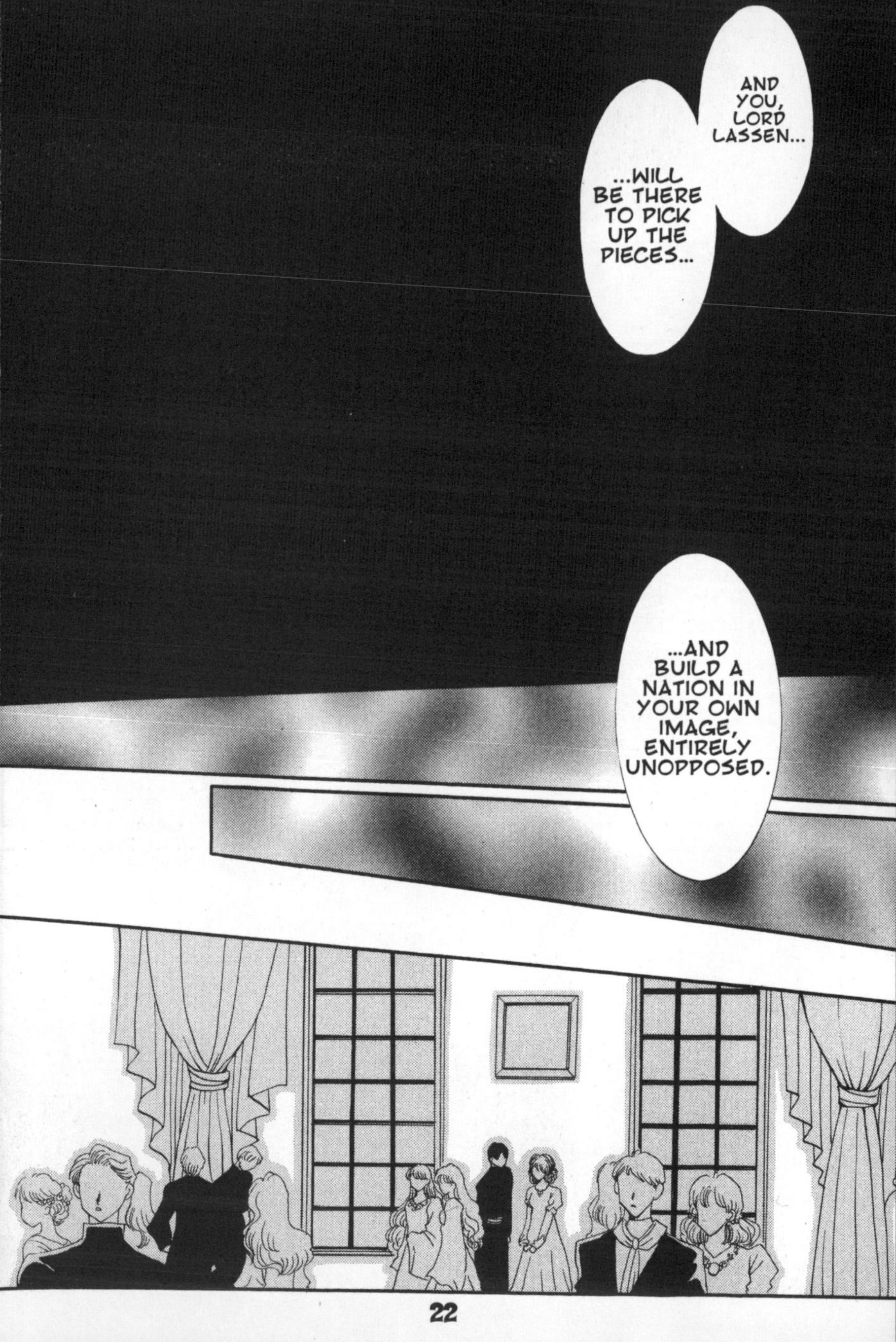
AND YOU, LORD LASSEN...
...WILL BE THERE TO PICK UP THE PIECES...
...AND BUILD A NATION IN YOUR OWN IMAGE, ENTIRELY UNOPPOSED.

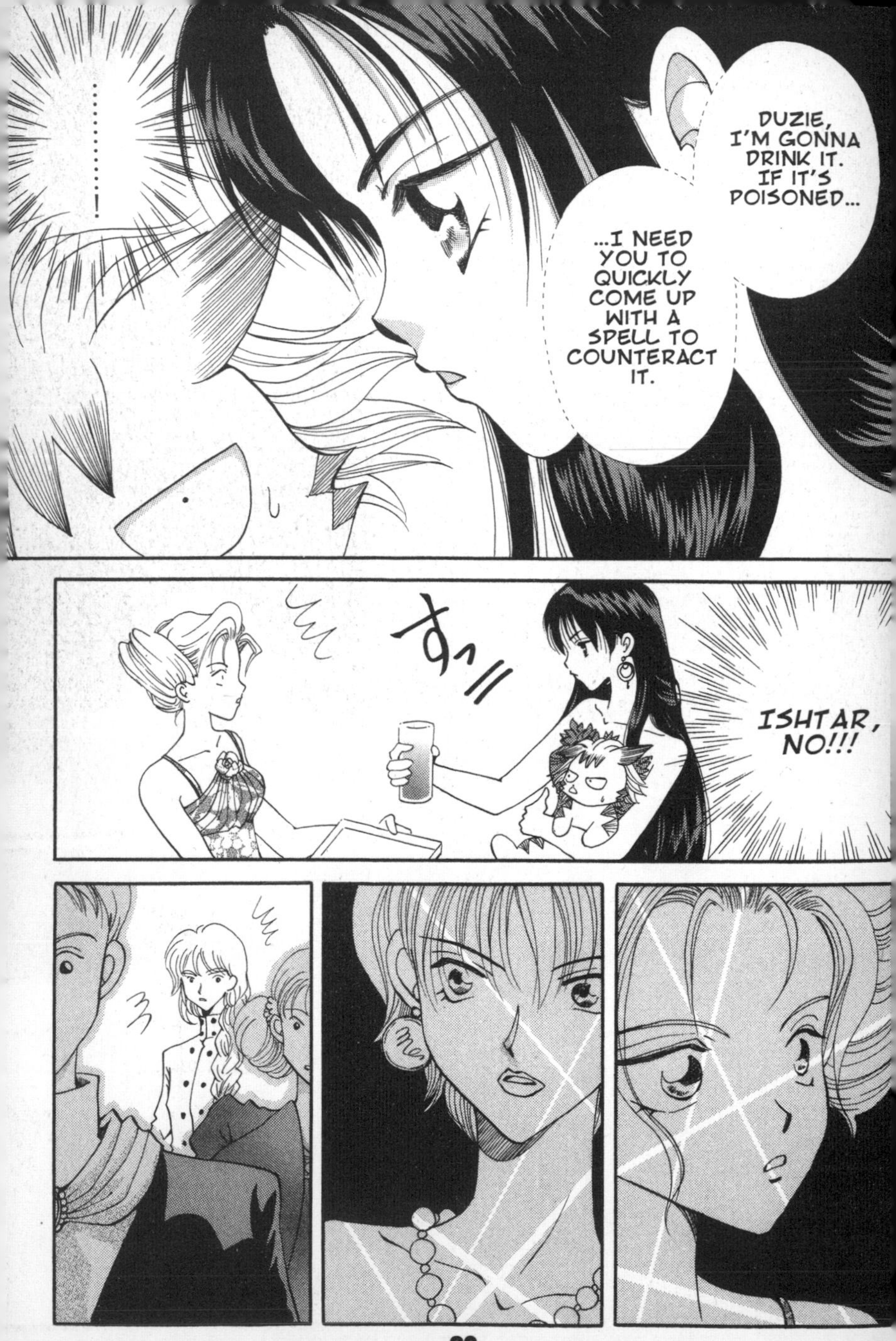
DUZIE, I'M GONNA DRINK IT. IF IT'S POISONED...
...I NEED YOU TO QUICKLY COME UP WITH A SPELL TO COUNTERACT IT.
......!
ISHTAR, NO!!!
すっ

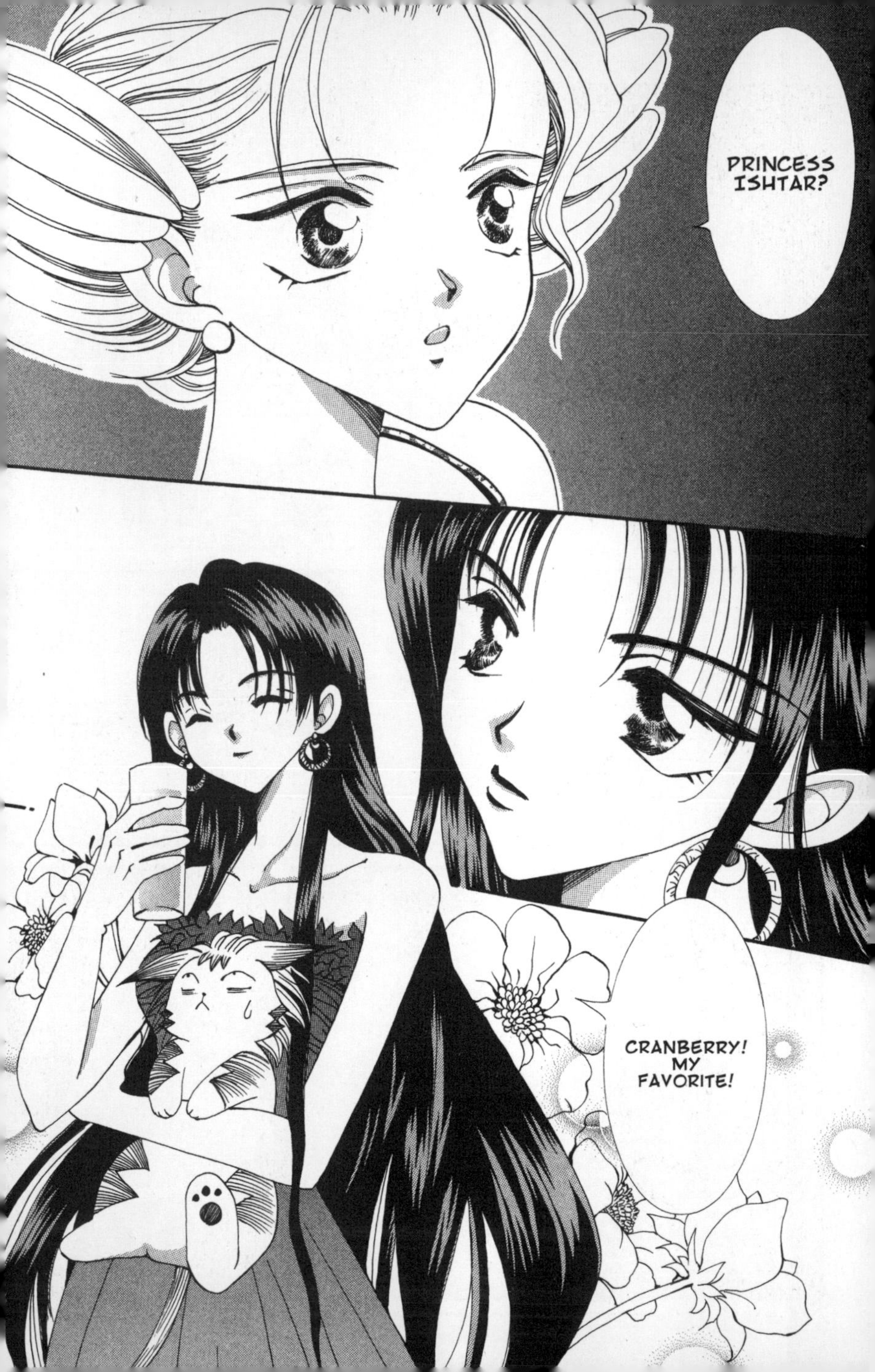
PRINCESS ISHTAR?
CRANBERRY! MY FAVORITE!

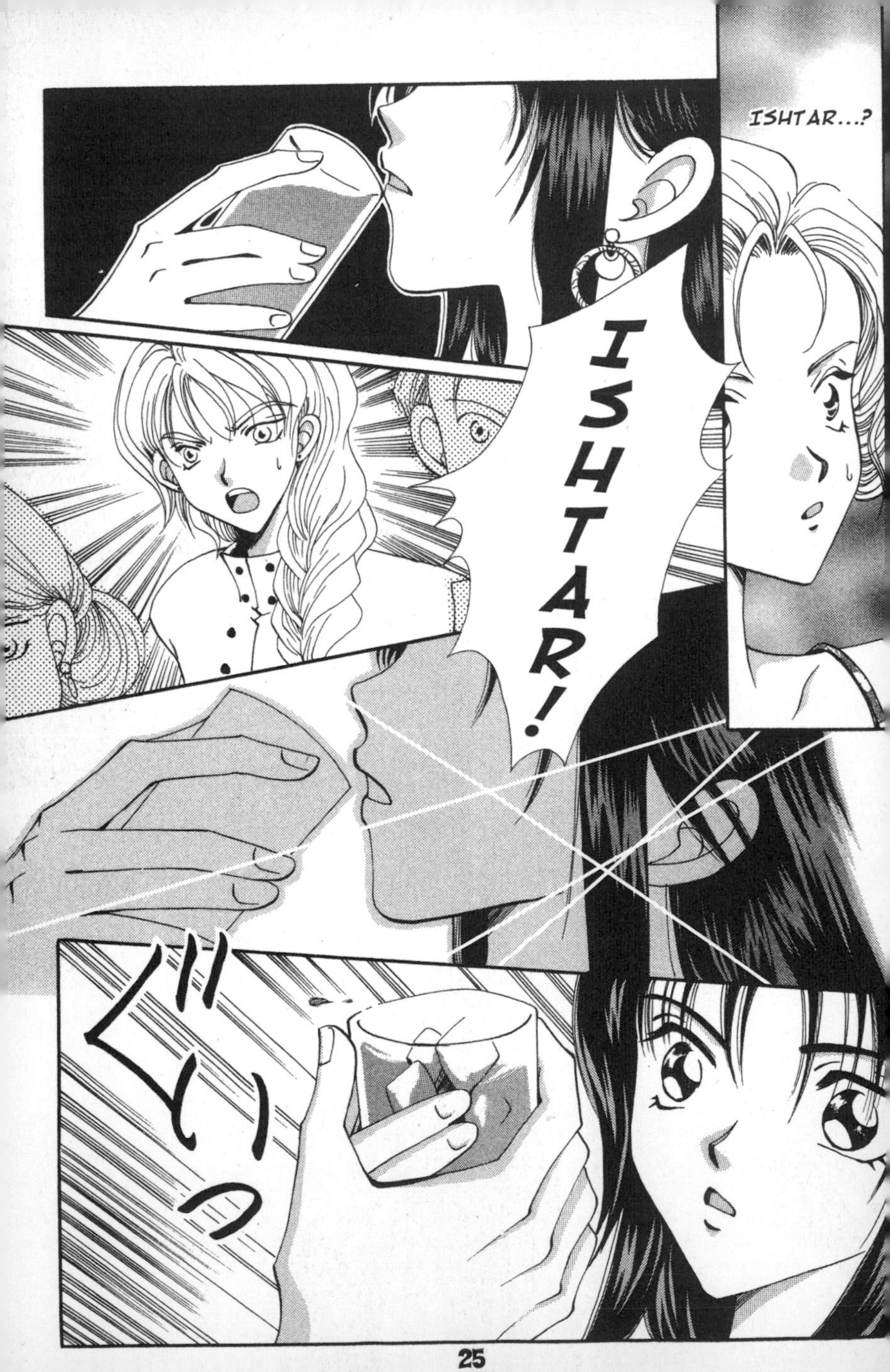
ISHTAR...?
ISHTAR!
ぐいっ

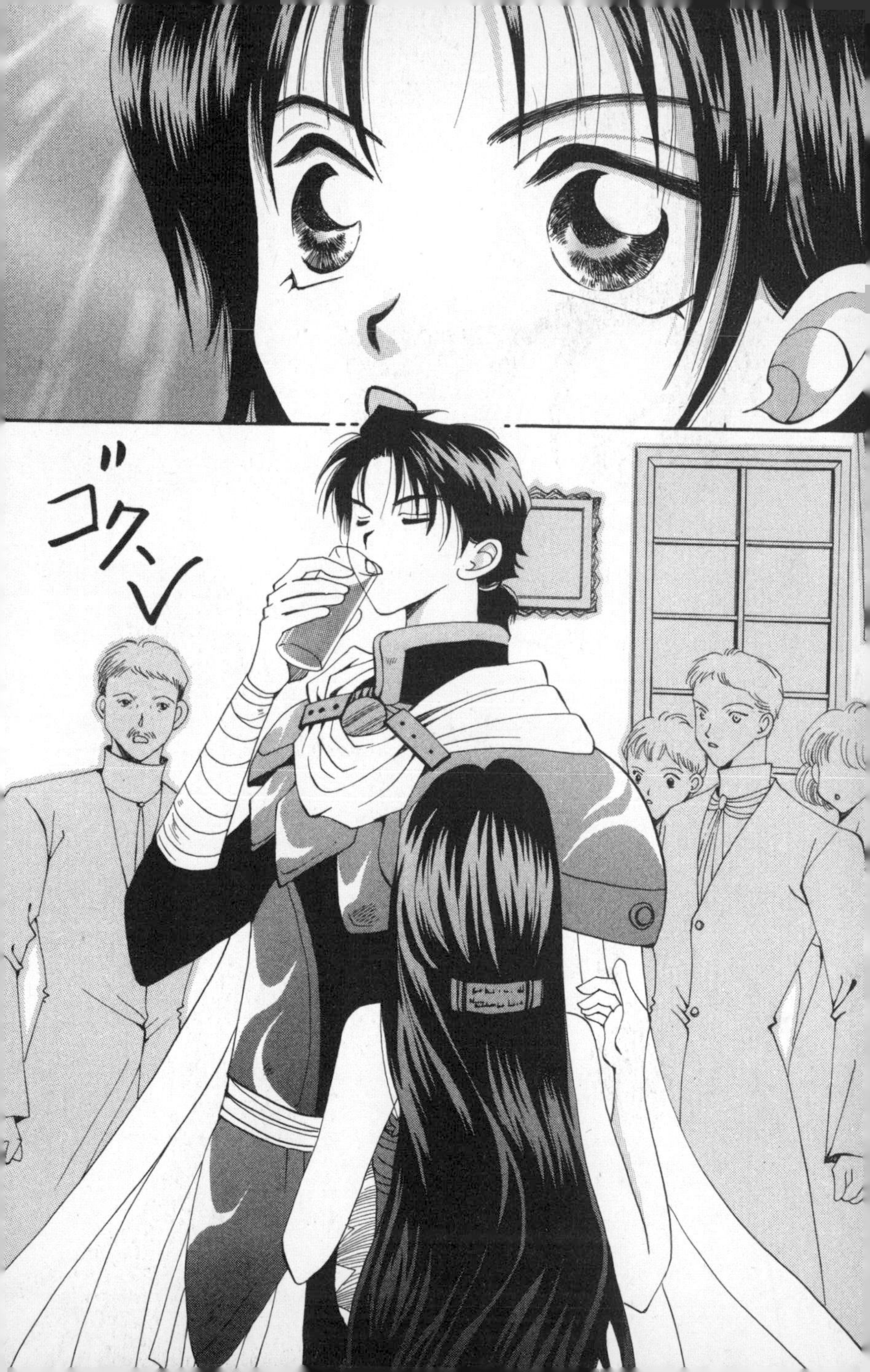
ゴクッ

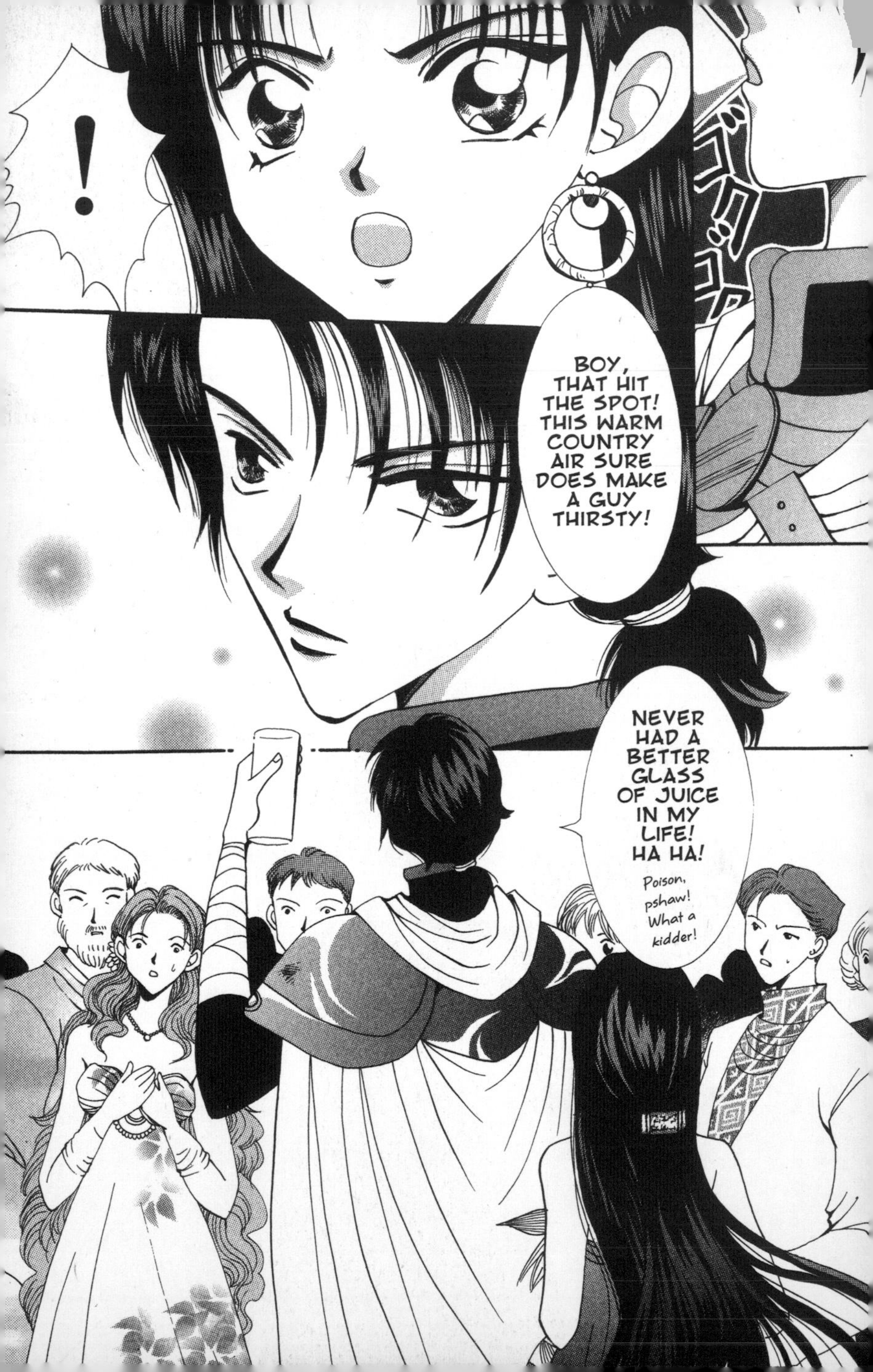
!
BOY, THAT HIT THE SPOT! THIS WARM COUNTRY AIR SURE DOES MAKE A GUY THIRSTY!
NEVER HAD A BETTER GLASS OF JUICE IN MY LIFE! HA HA!
Poison, pshaw! What a kidder!

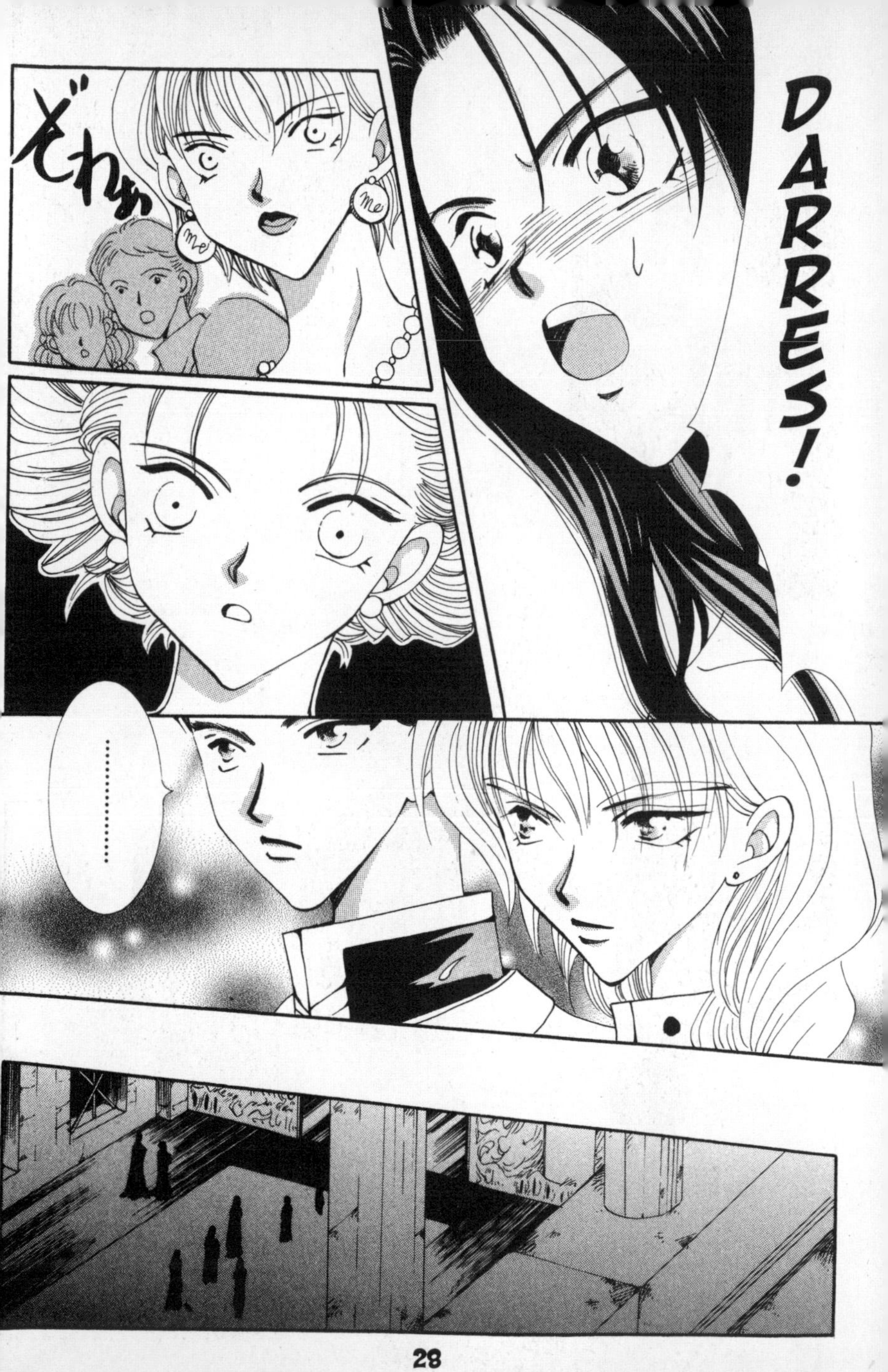
DARRES!
ざわぁ
....

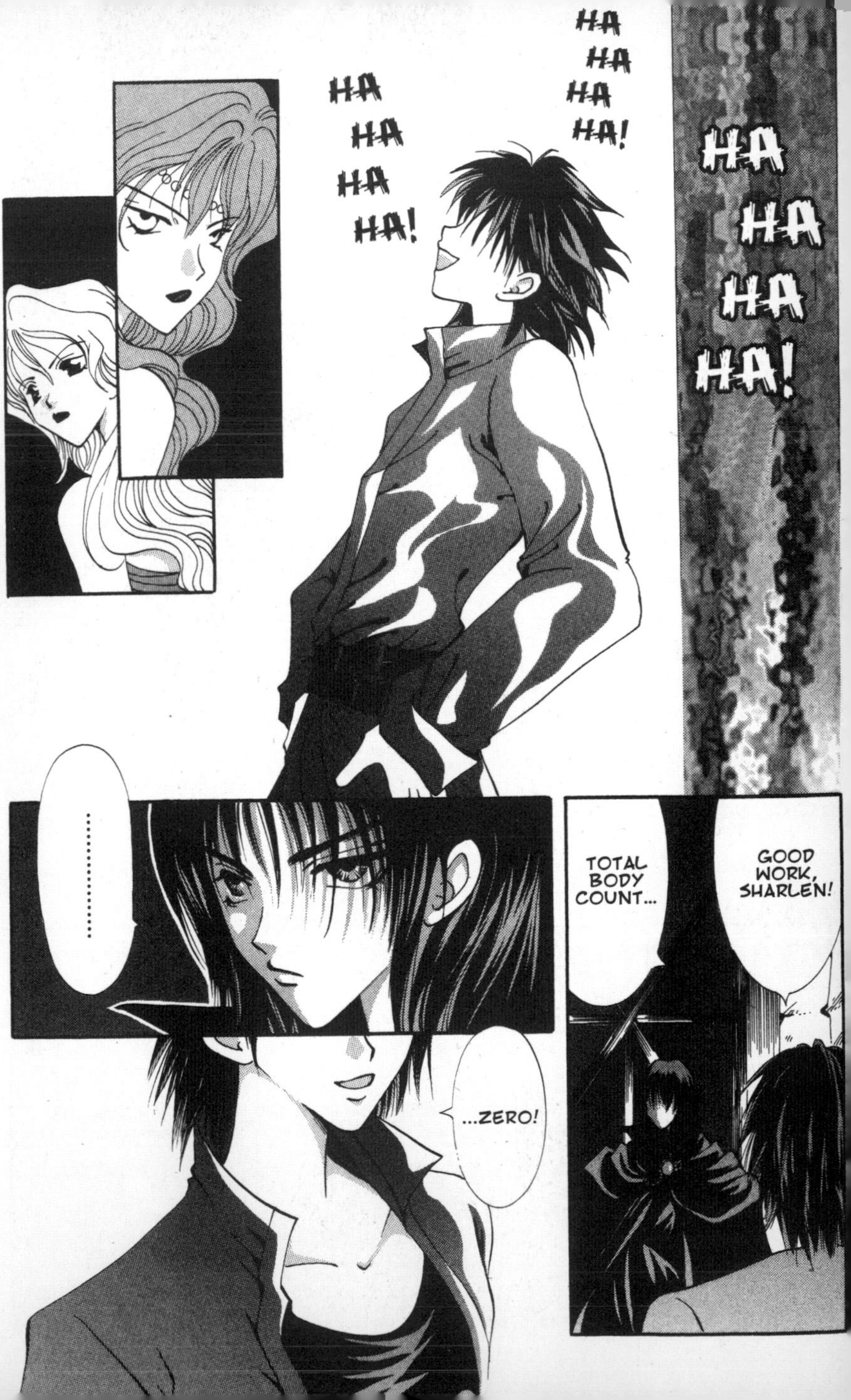
HA HA HA HA!
HA HA HA HA!
HA HA HA HA!
GOOD WORK, SHARLEN!
TOTAL BODY COUNT...
......
...ZERO!

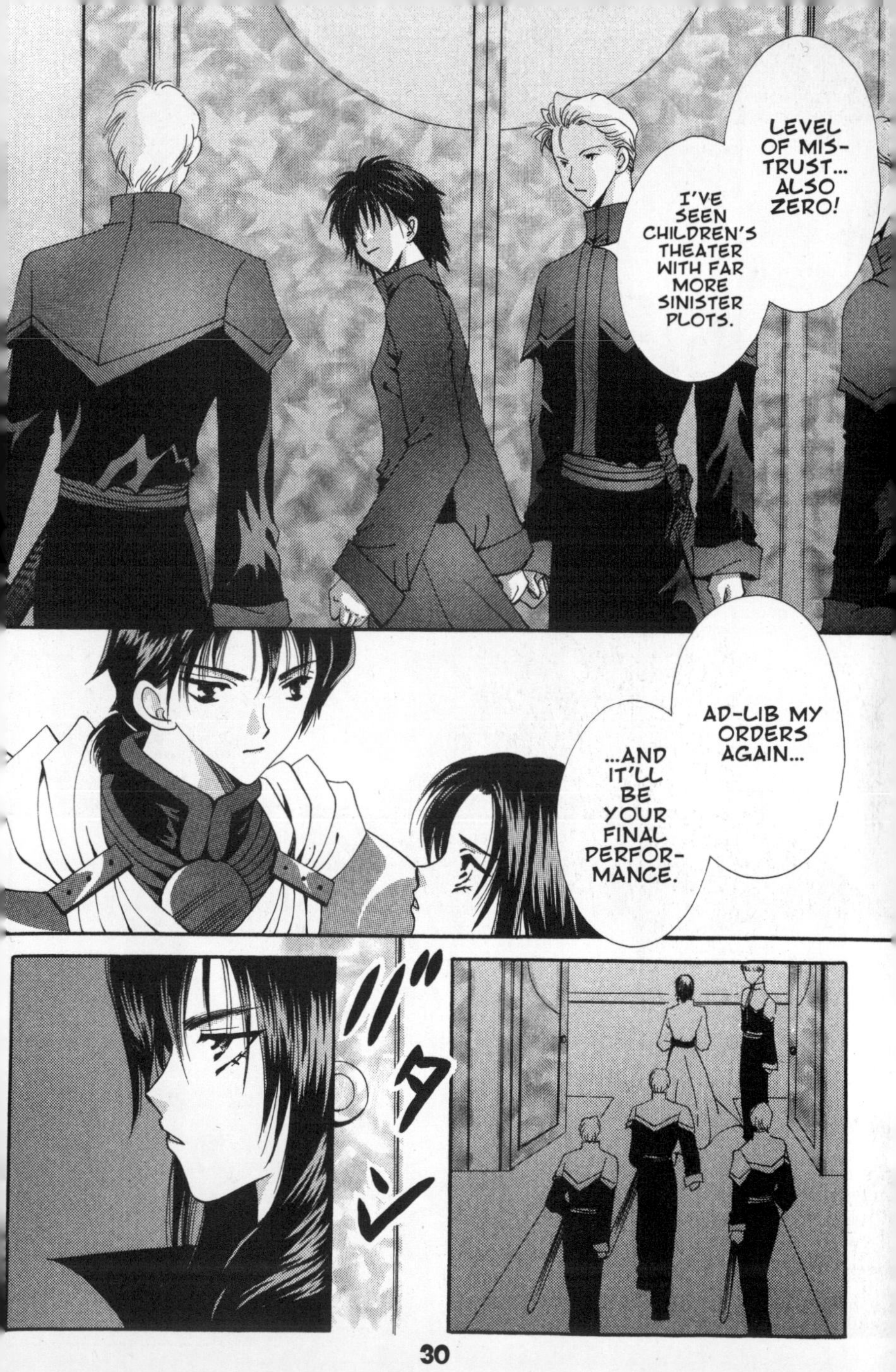
LEVEL OF MIS-TRUST... ALSO ZERO!
I'VE SEEN CHILDREN'S THEATER WITH FAR MORE SINISTER PLOTS.
AD-LIB MY ORDERS AGAIN...
...AND IT'LL BE YOUR FINAL PERFORMANCE.
バタン

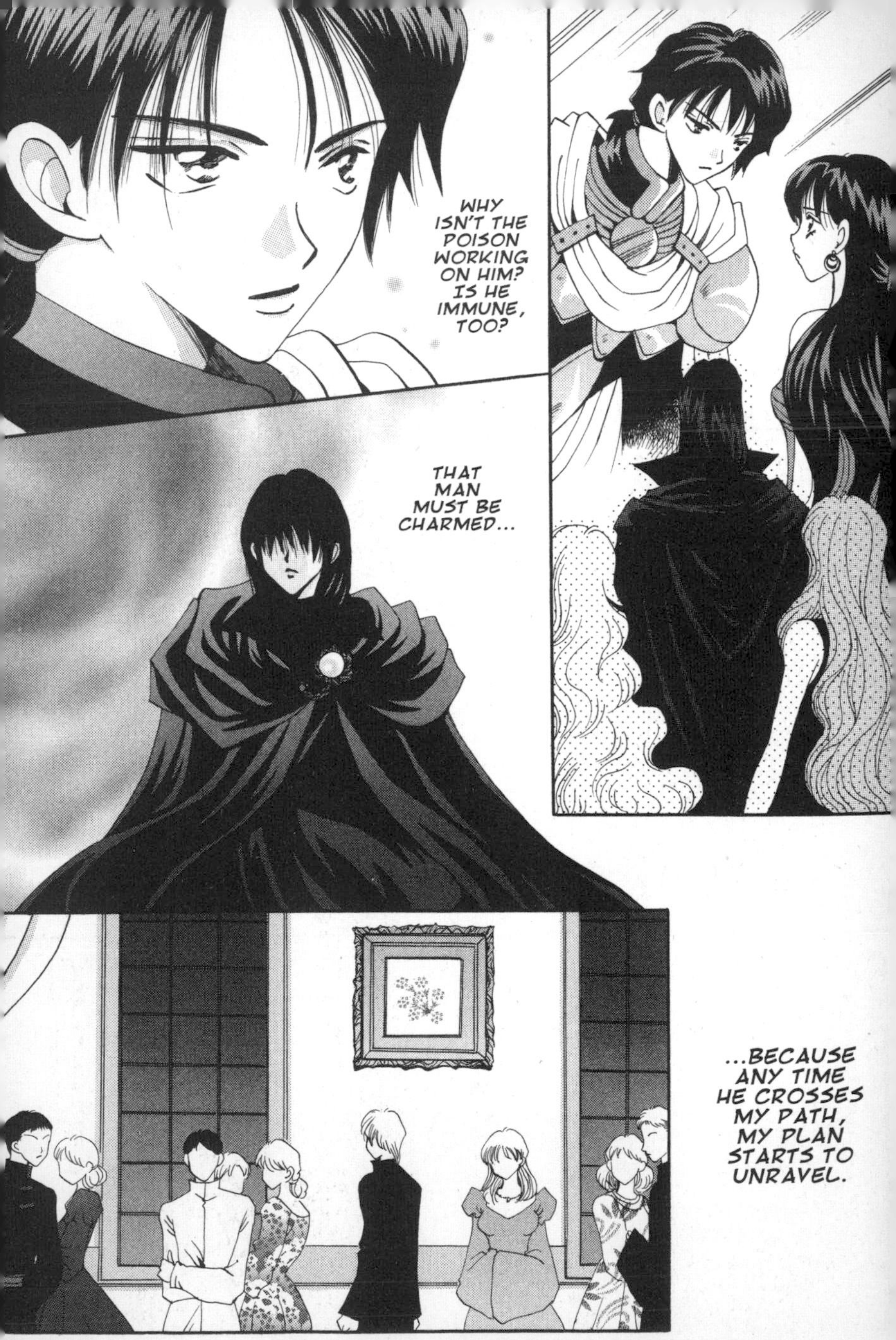
WHY ISN'T THE POISON WORKING ON HIM? IS HE IMMUNE, TOO?
THAT MAN MUST BE CHARMED...
...BECAUSE ANY TIME HE CROSSES MY PATH, MY PLAN STARTS TO UNRAVEL.

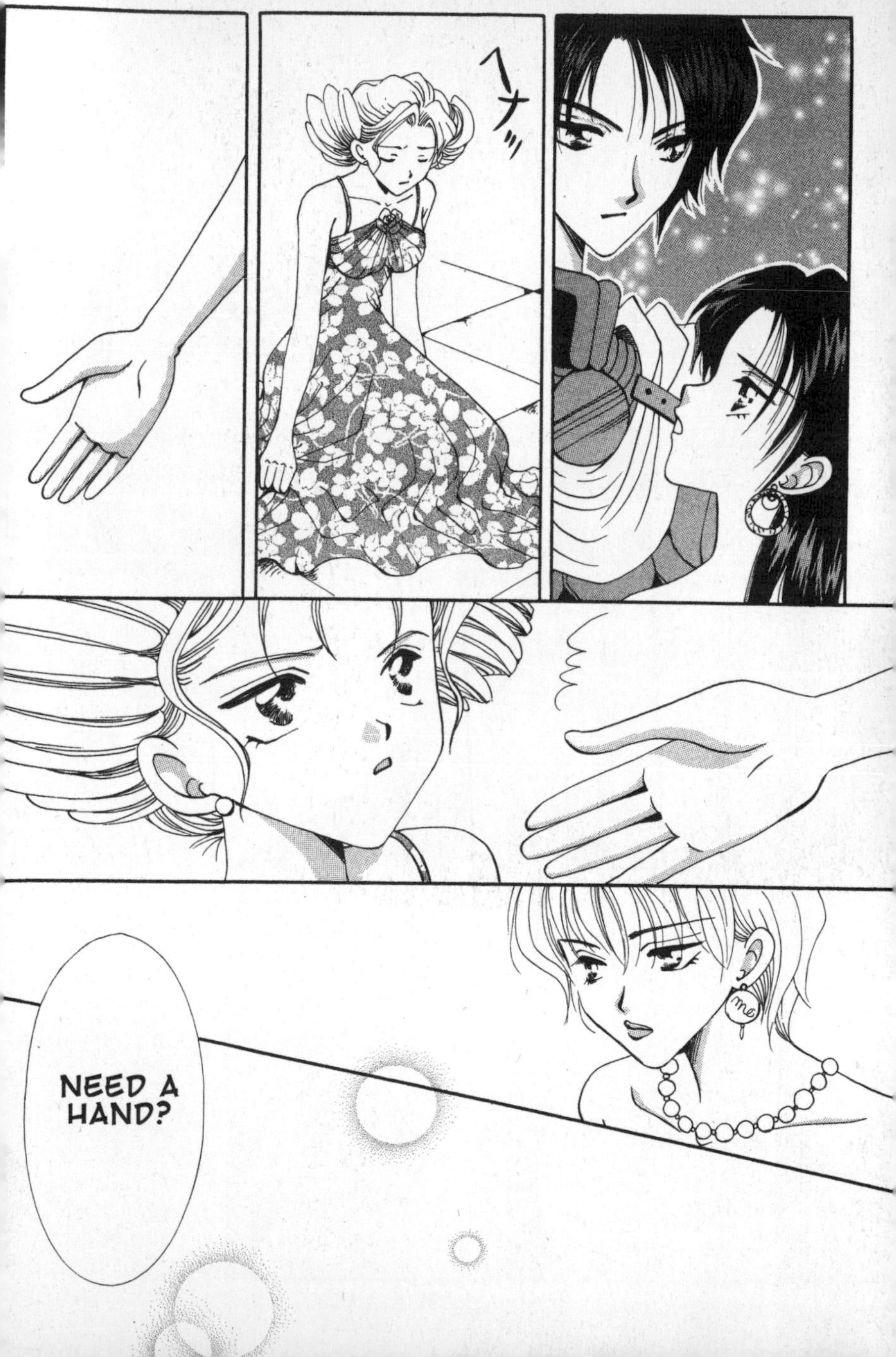
ヘナッ
NEED A HAND?

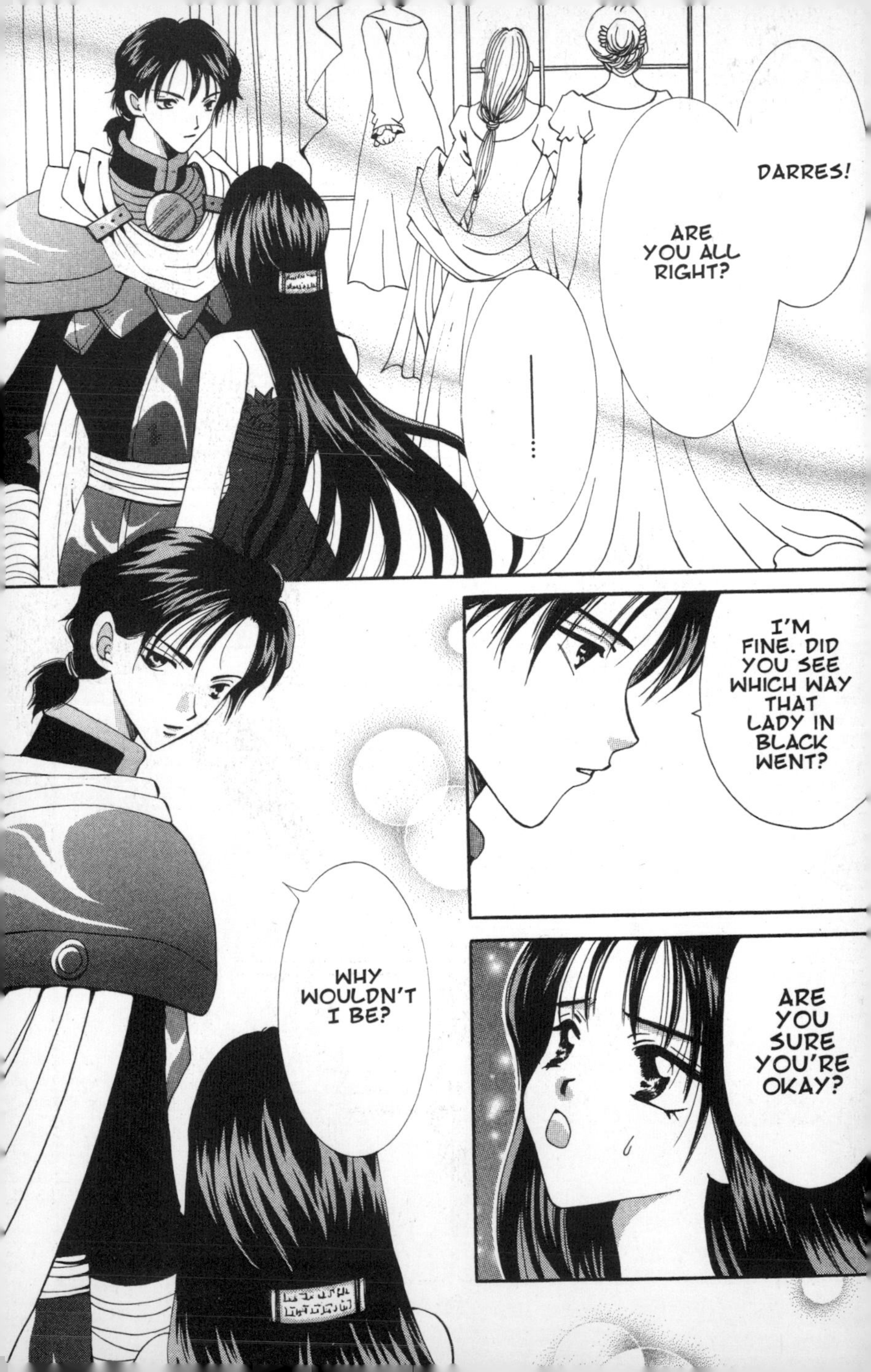
DARRES!
ARE YOU ALL RIGHT?
......
I'M FINE. DID YOU SEE WHICH WAY THAT LADY IN BLACK WENT?
ARE YOU SURE YOU'RE OKAY?
WHY WOULDN'T I BE?

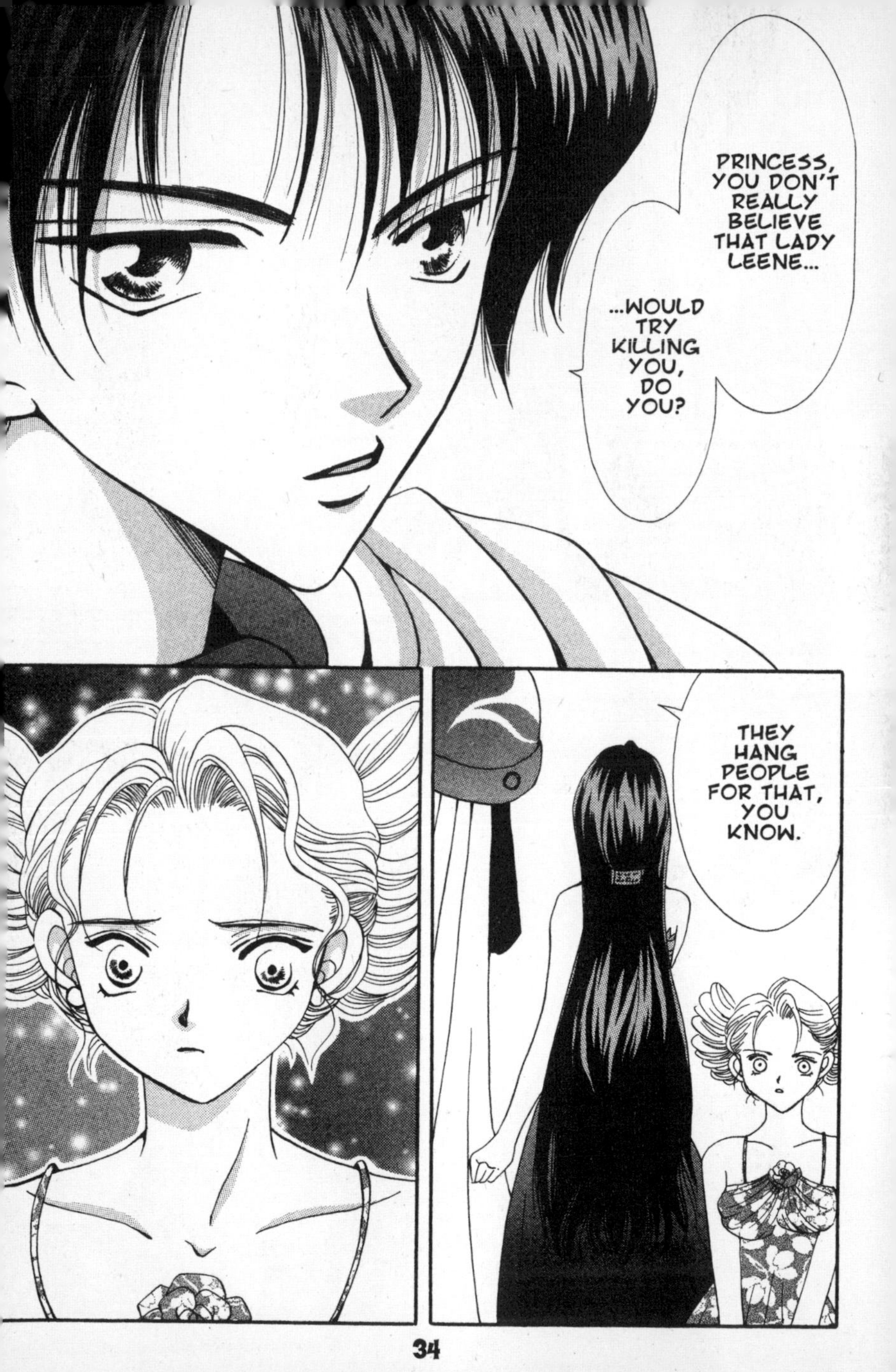
PRINCESS, YOU DON'T REALLY BELIEVE THAT LADY LEENE...
...WOULD TRY KILLING YOU, DO YOU?
THEY HANG PEOPLE FOR THAT, YOU KNOW.

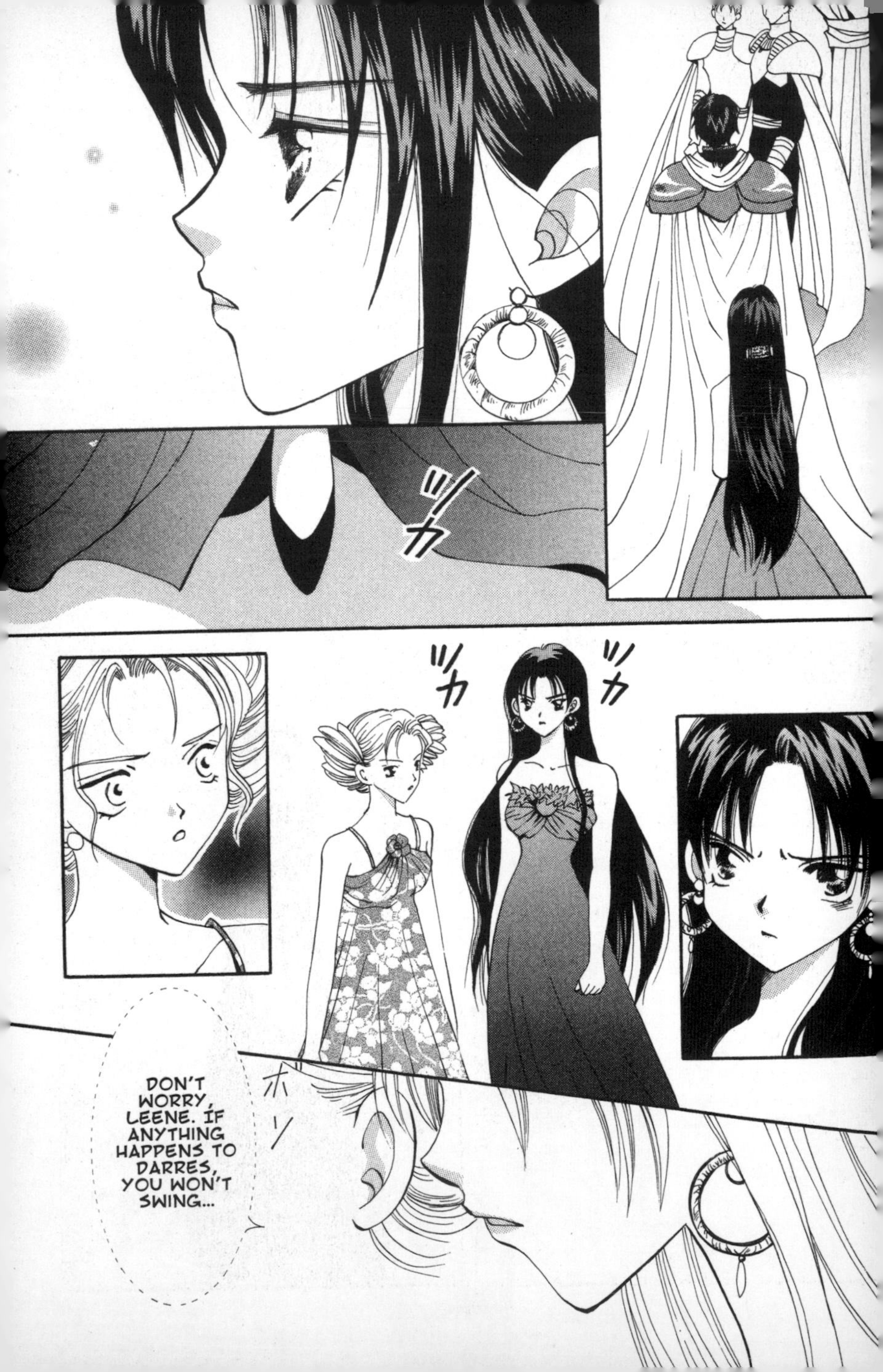
ツカ
ツカ
ツカ
DON'T WORRY, LEENE. IF ANYTHING HAPPENS TO DARRES, YOU WON'T SWING...
ホー

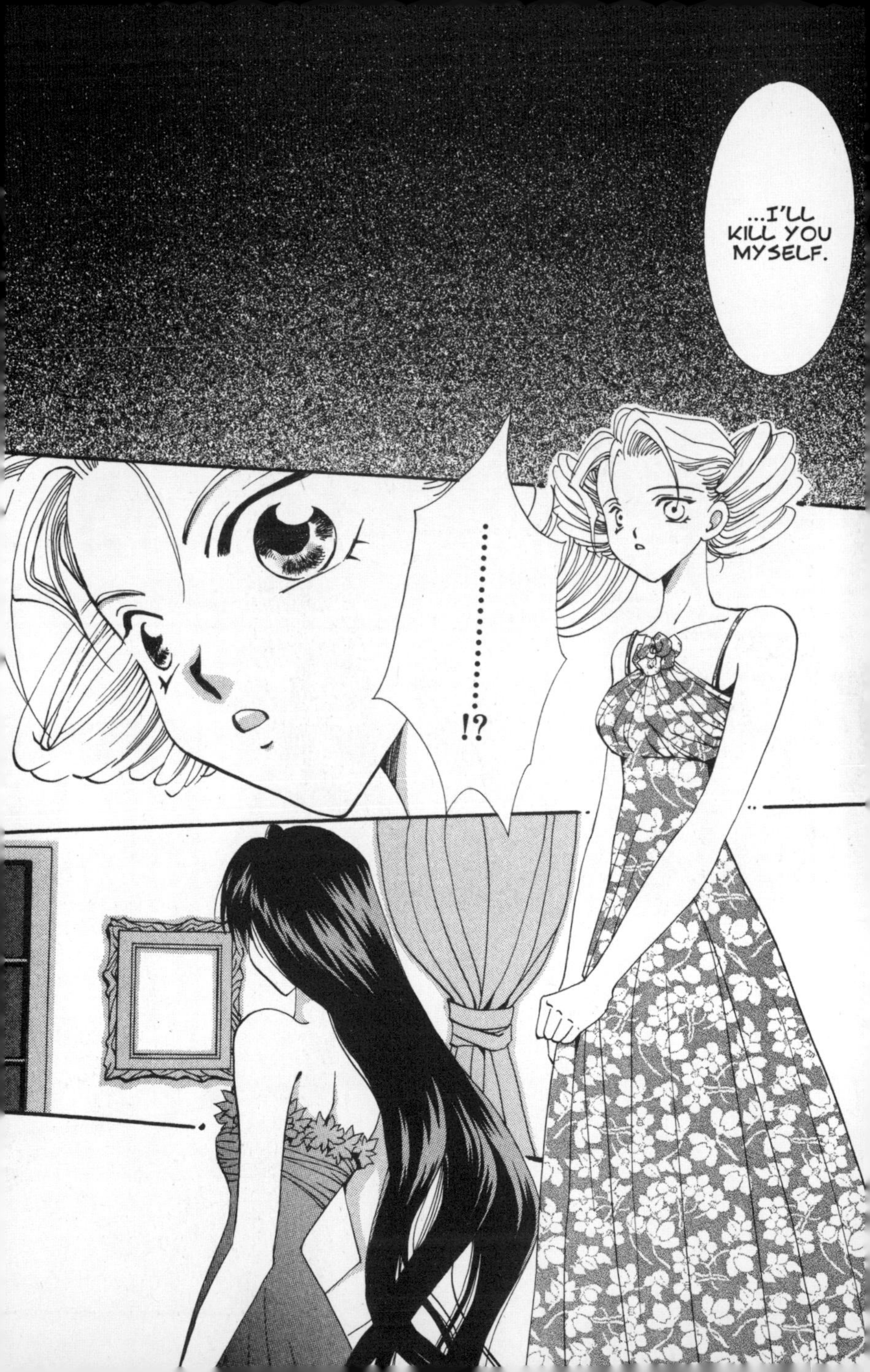
...I'LL KILL YOU MYSELF.
......!?

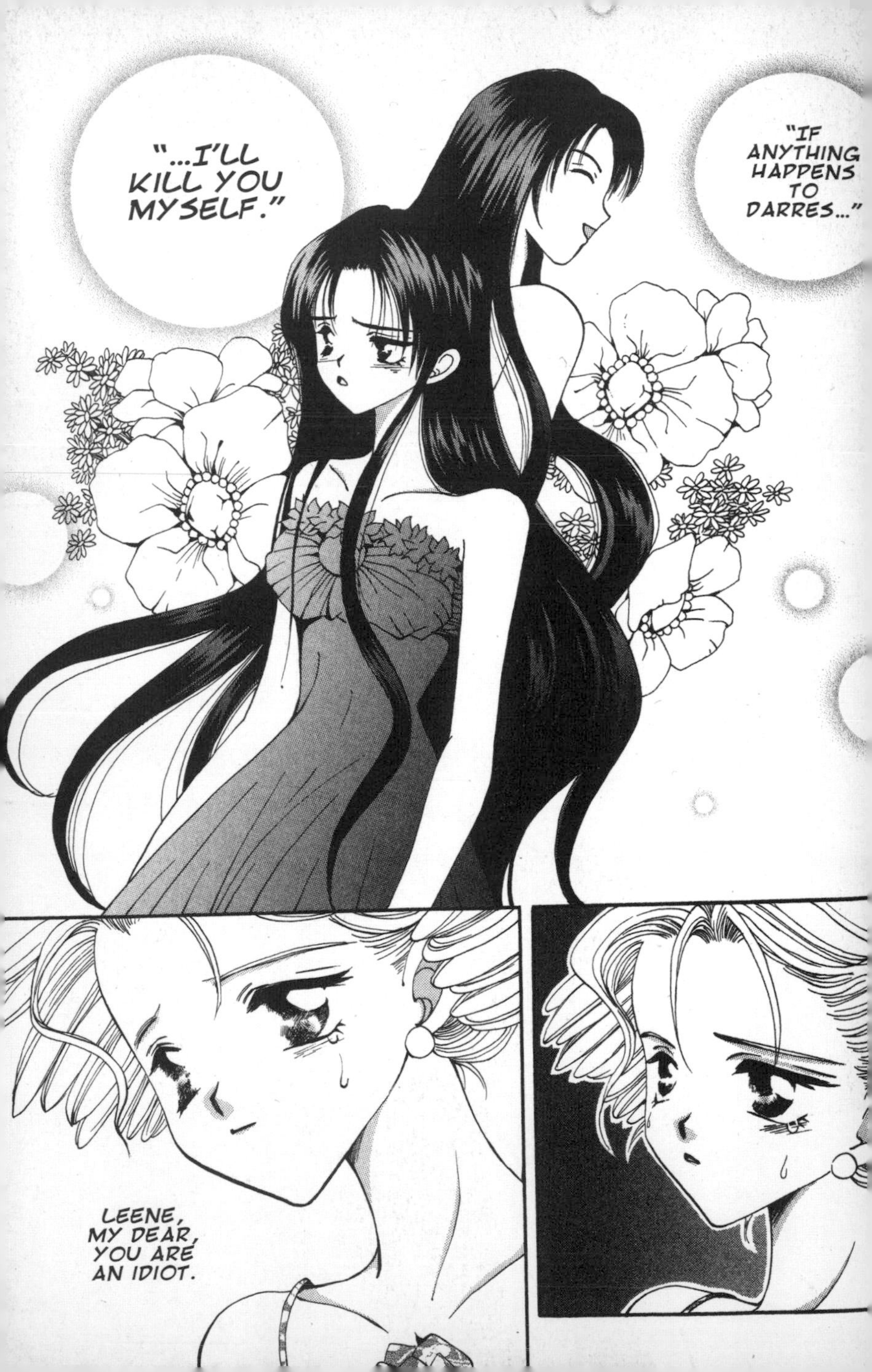
"IF ANYTHING HAPPENS TO DARRES..."
"...I'LL KILL YOU MYSELF."
LEENE, MY DEAR, YOU ARE AN IDIOT.

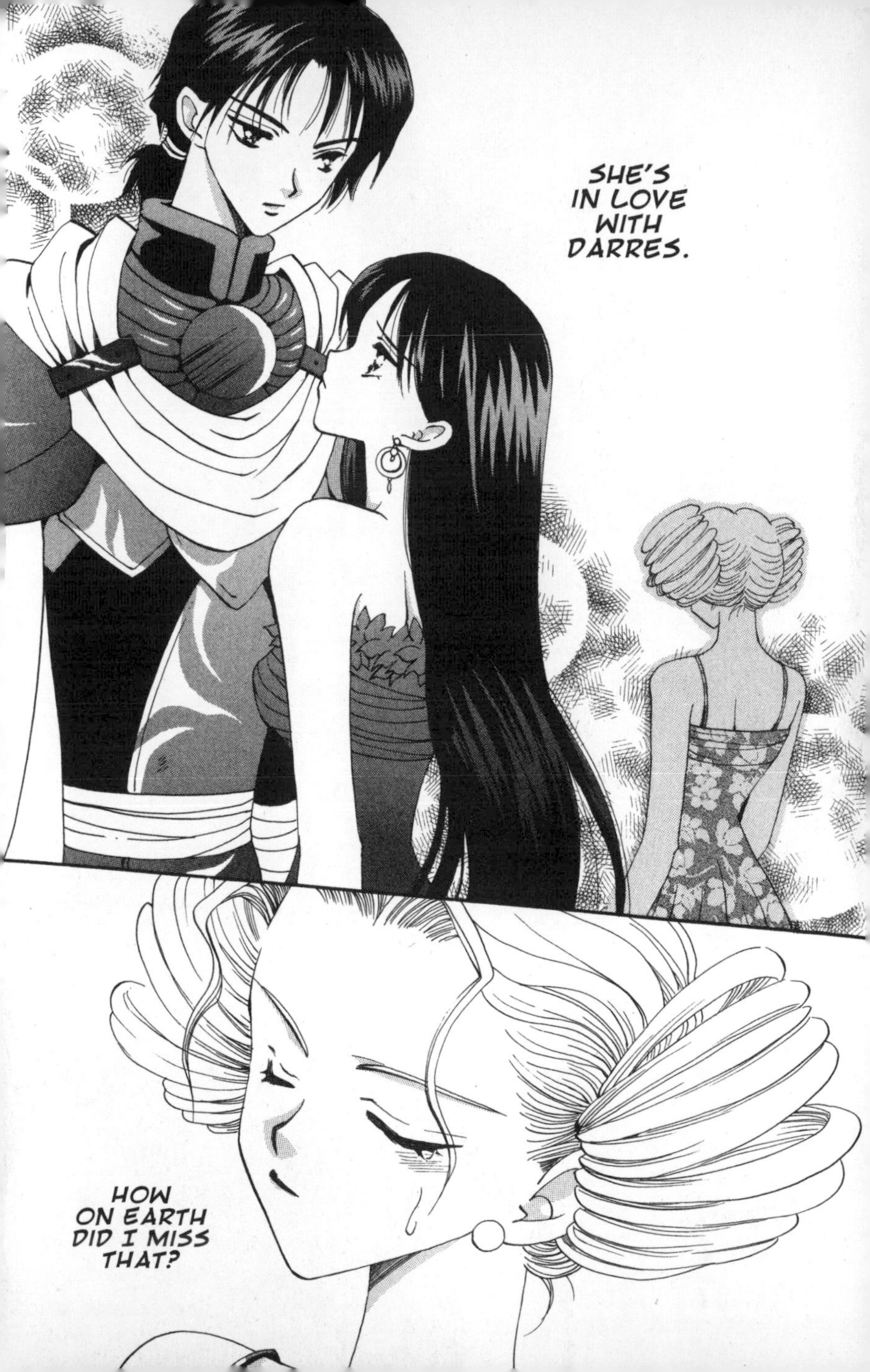
SHE'S IN LOVE WITH DARRES.
HOW ON EARTH DID I MISS THAT?

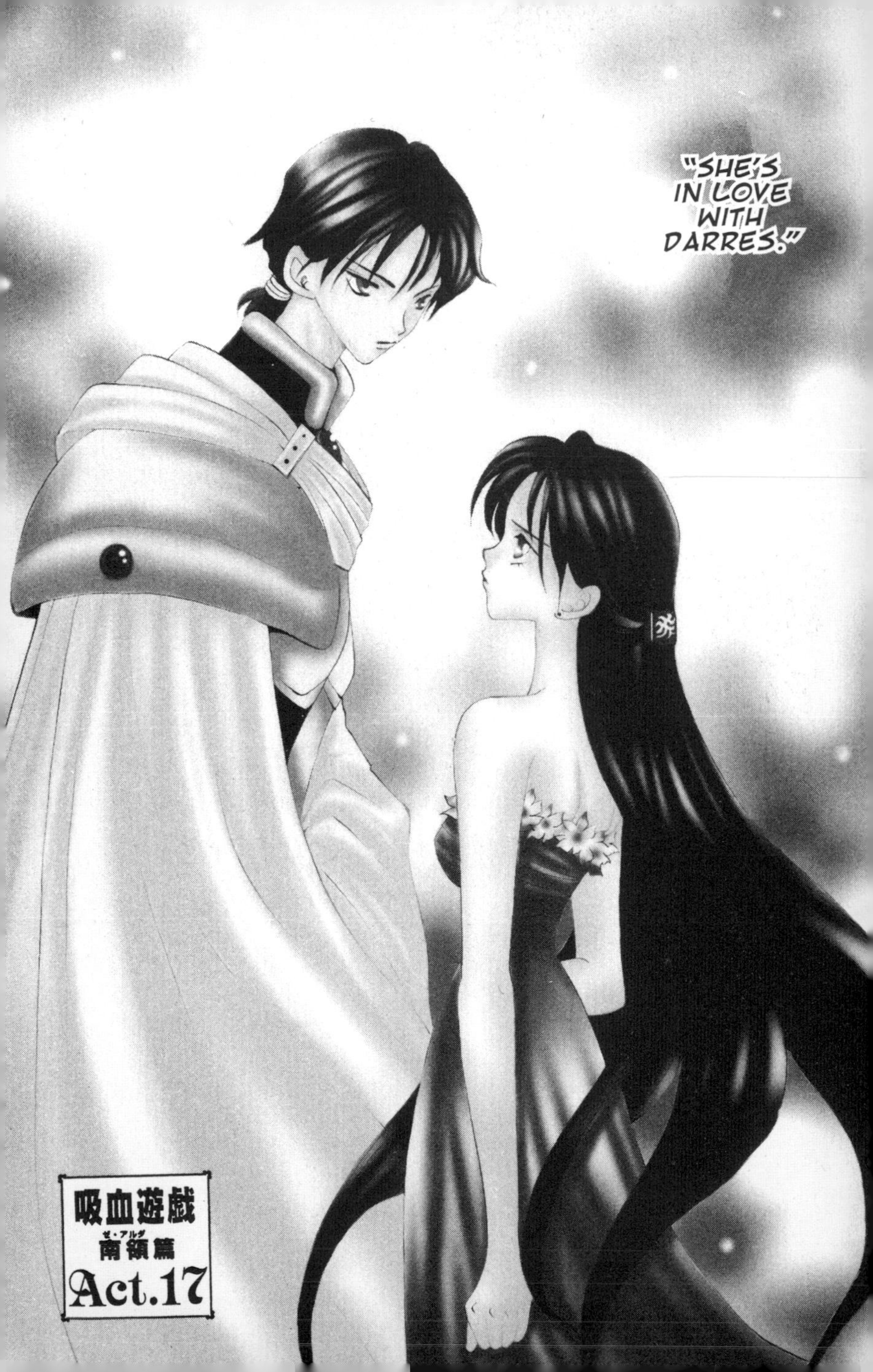
"SHE'S IN LOVE WITH DARRES."
吸血遊戯
ゼ・アルダ
南領篇
Act.17

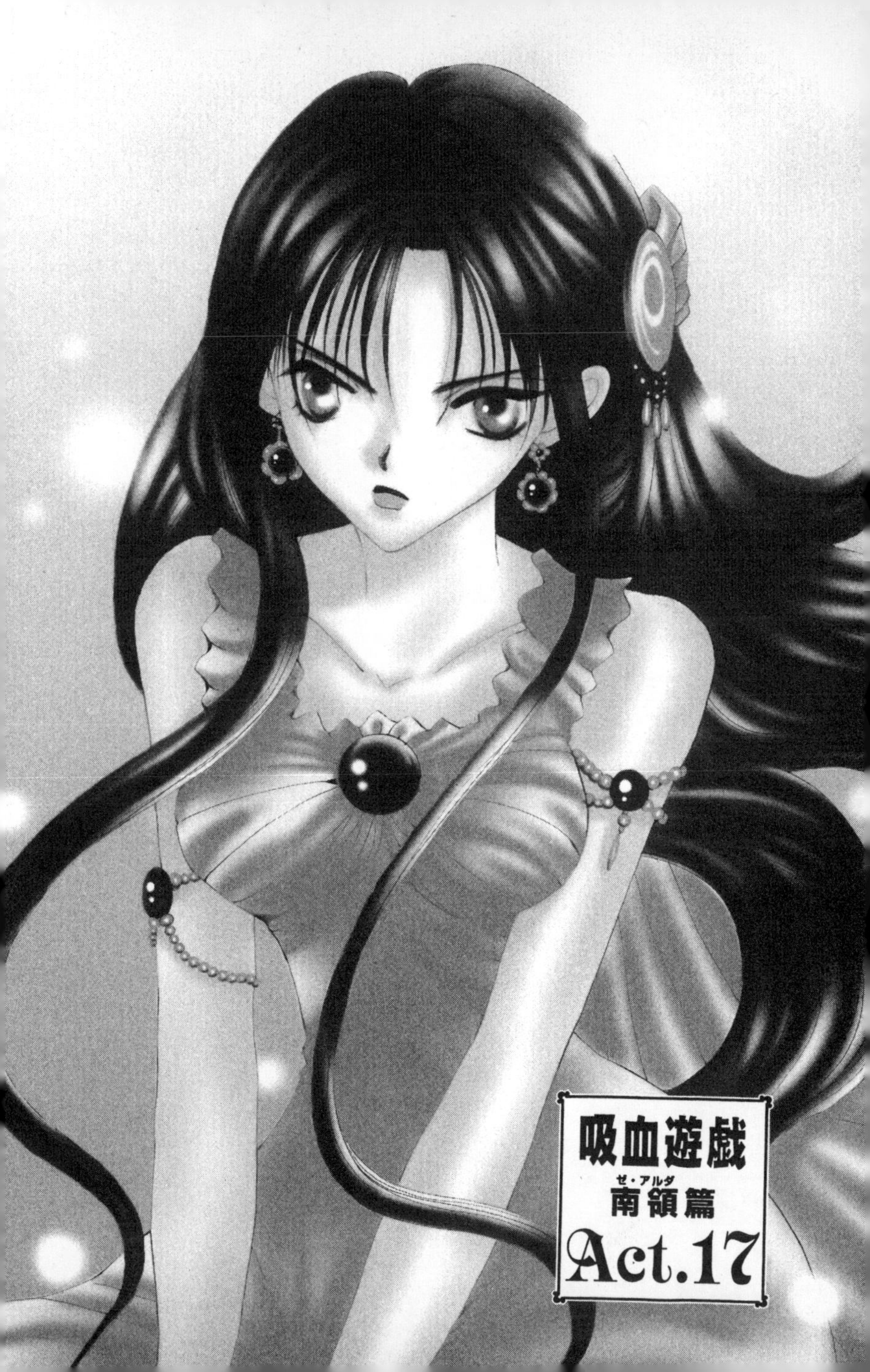
吸血遊戯
ゼ・アルダ
南領篇
Act.17

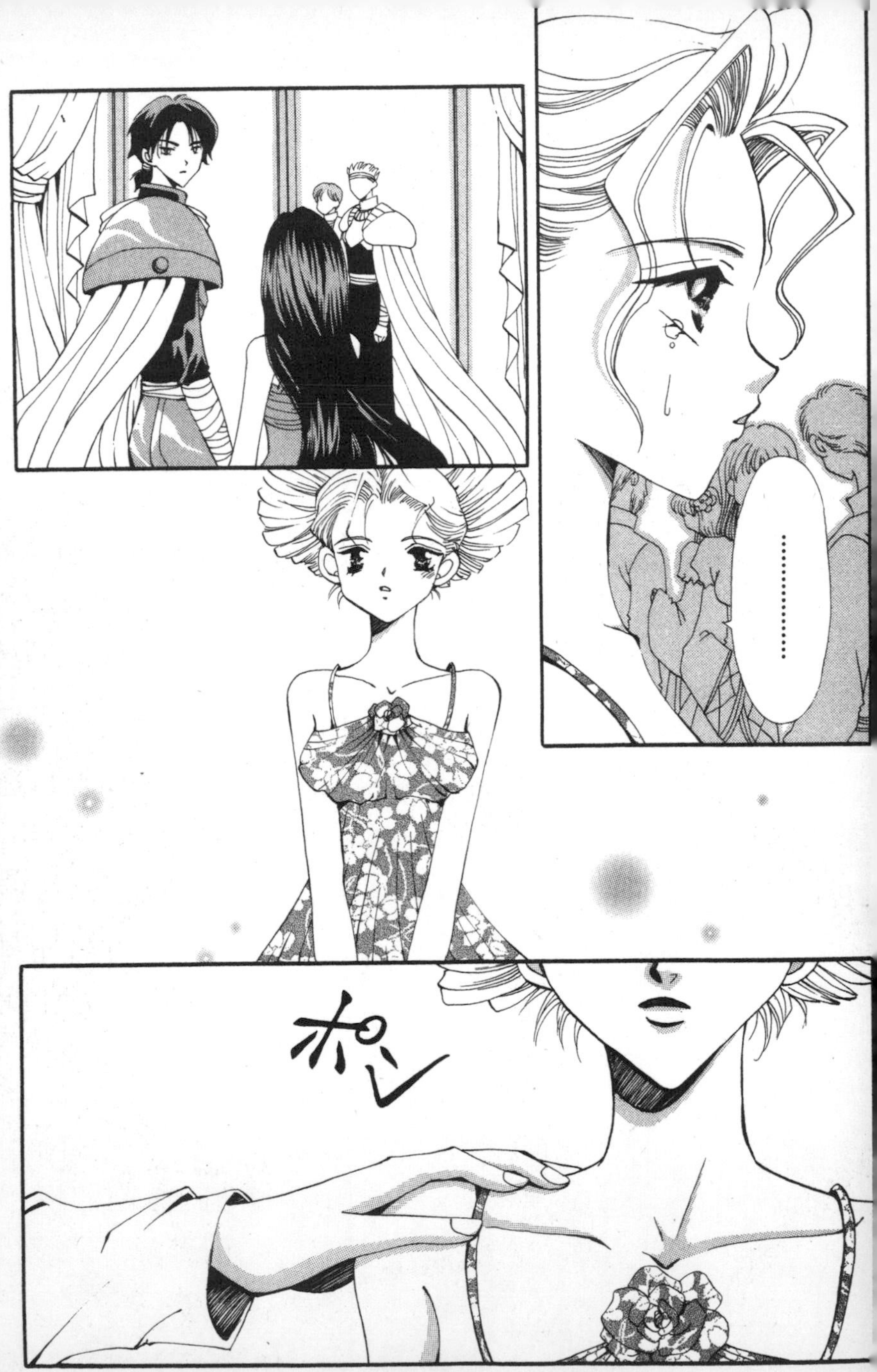
……
ポン

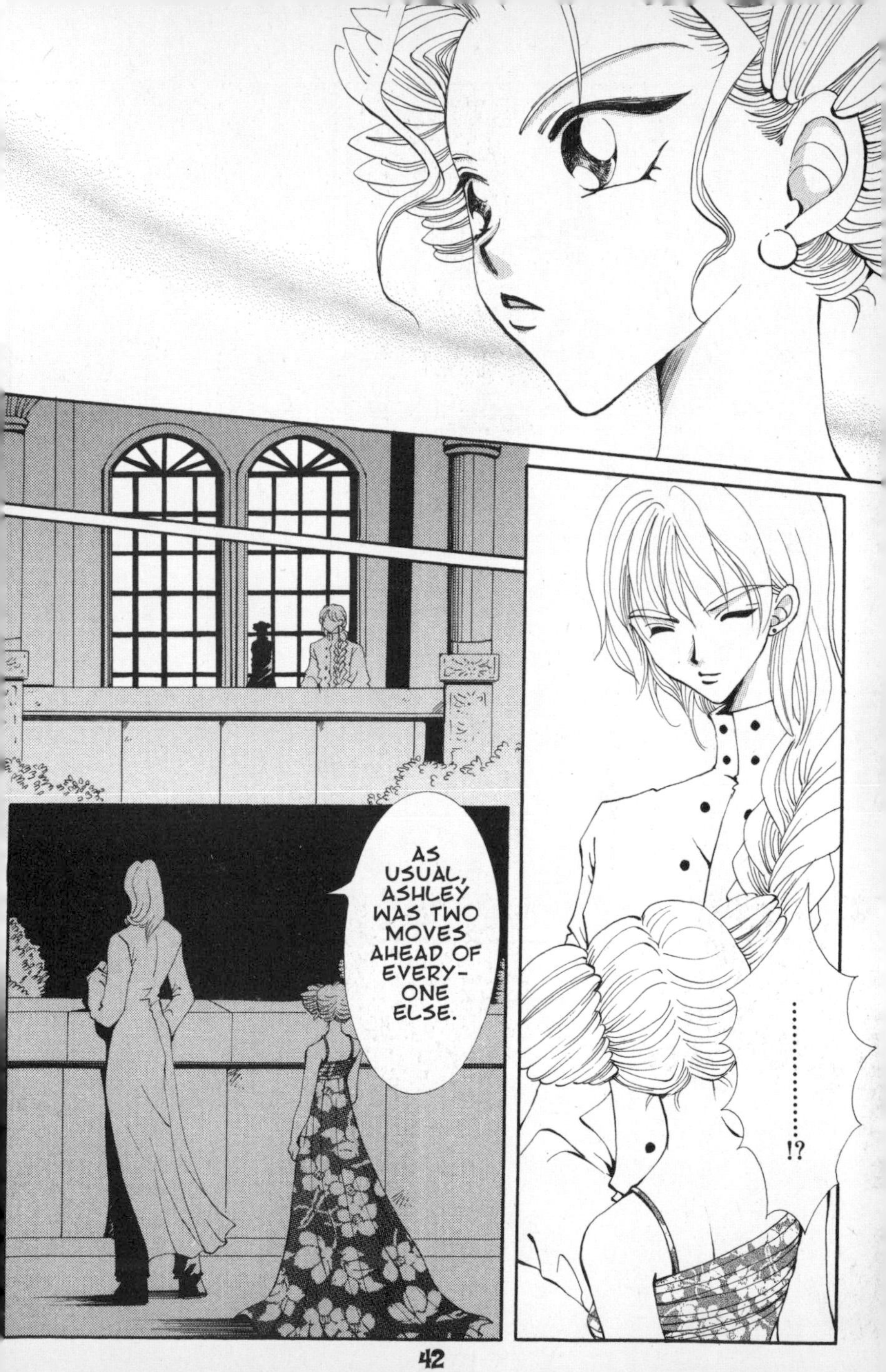
..........!?
AS USUAL, ASHLEY WAS TWO MOVES AHEAD OF EVERY-ONE ELSE.

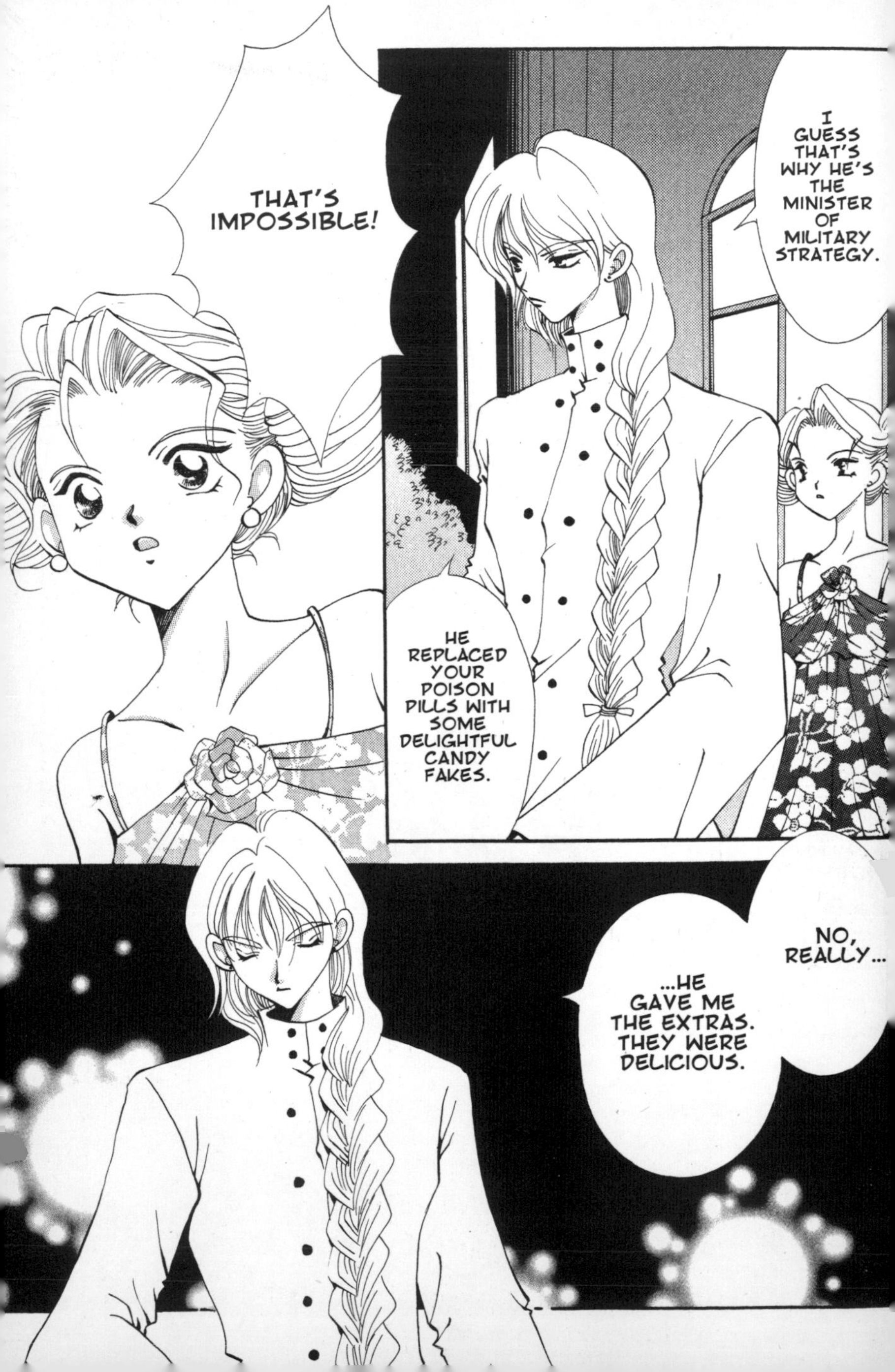
I GUESS THAT'S WHY HE'S THE MINISTER OF MILITARY STRATEGY.
HE REPLACED YOUR POISON PILLS WITH SOME DELIGHTFUL CANDY FAKES.
THAT'S IMPOSSIBLE!
NO, REALLY...
...HE GAVE ME THE EXTRAS. THEY WERE DELICIOUS.

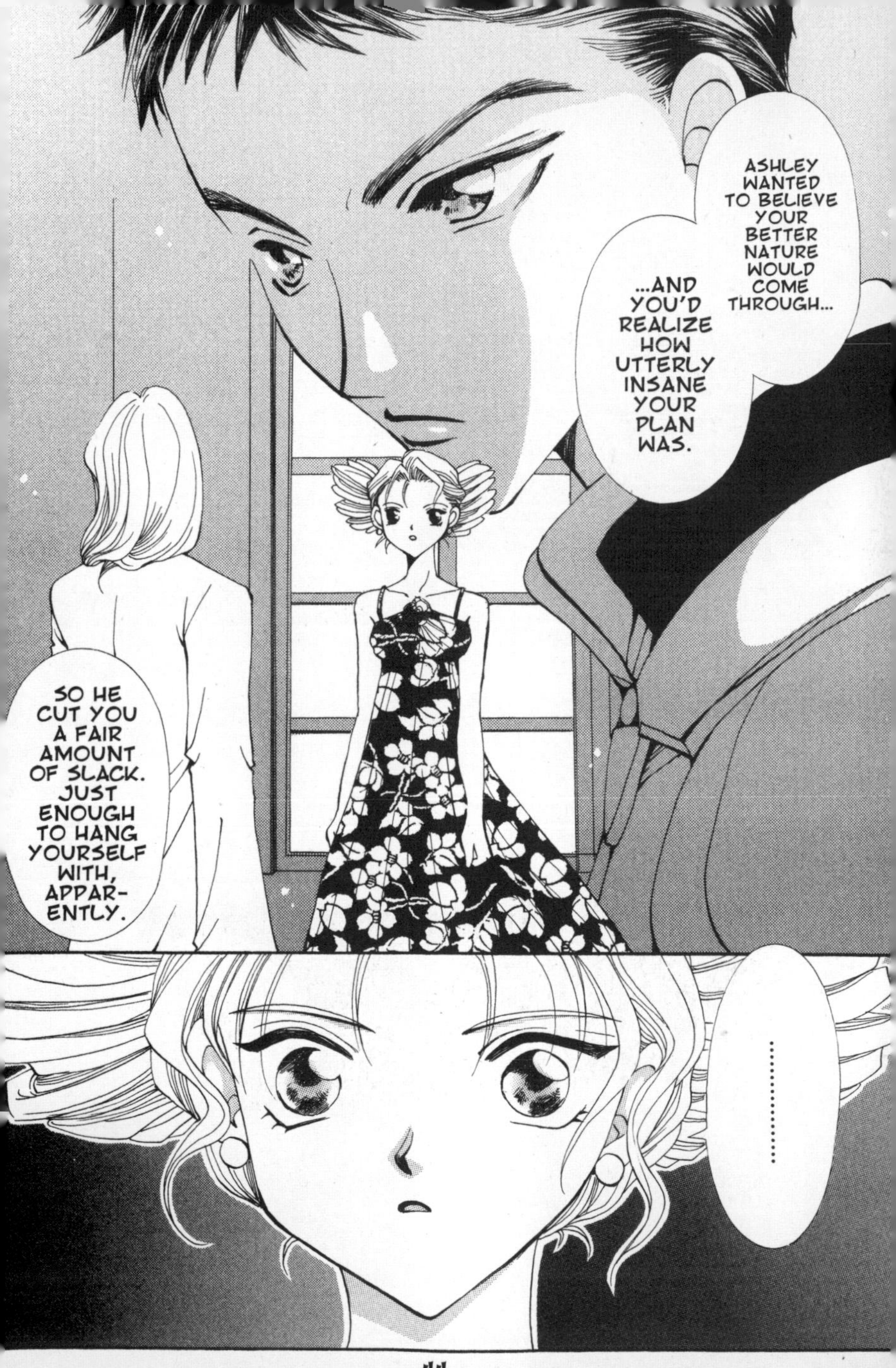
ASHLEY WANTED TO BELIEVE YOUR BETTER NATURE WOULD COME THROUGH...
...AND YOU'D REALIZE HOW UTTERLY INSANE YOUR PLAN WAS.
SO HE CUT YOU A FAIR AMOUNT OF SLACK. JUST ENOUGH TO HANG YOURSELF WITH, APPAR-ENTLY.
....

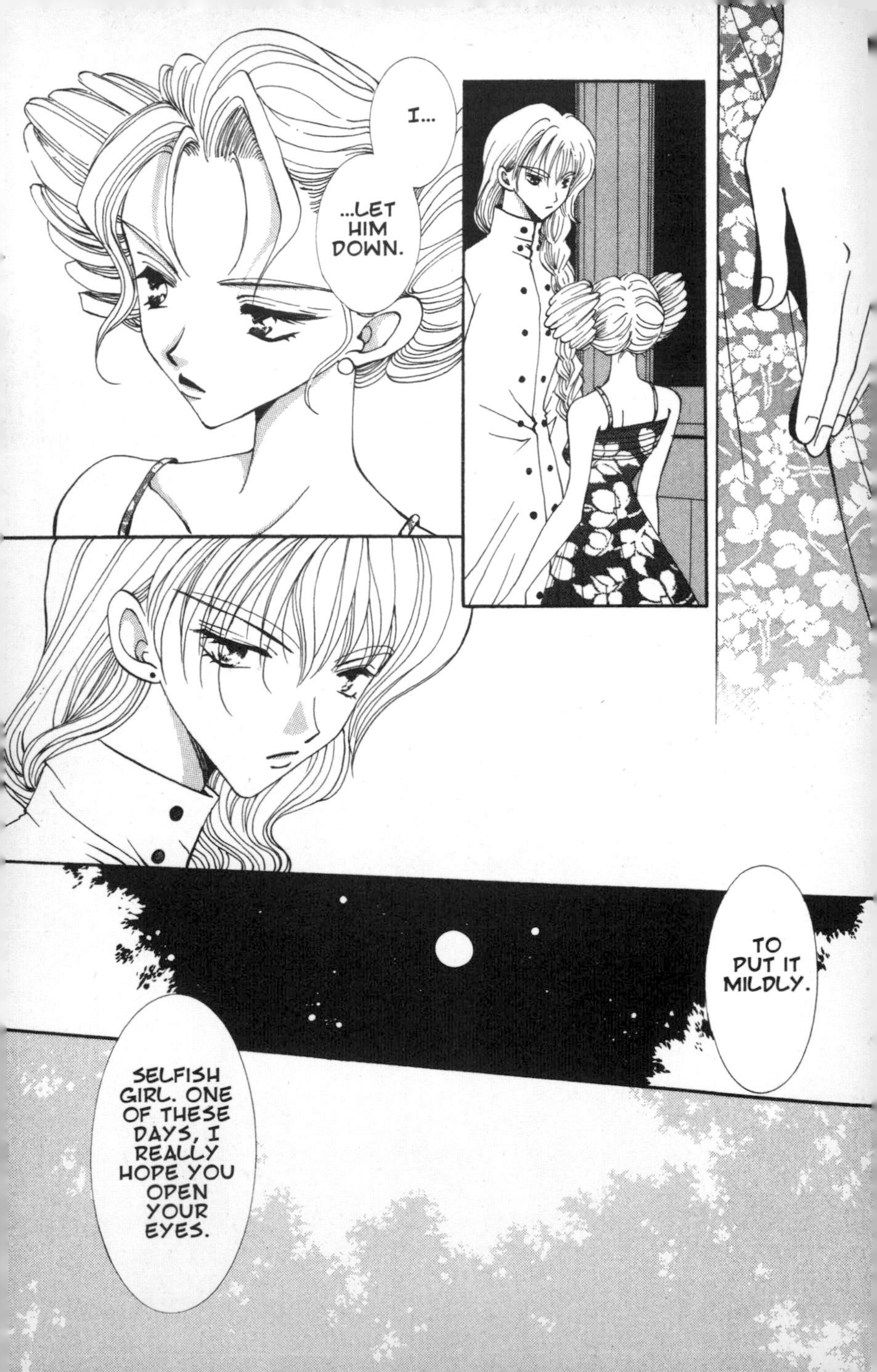
I...
...LET HIM DOWN.
TO PUT IT MILDLY.
SELFISH GIRL. ONE OF THESE DAYS, I REALLY HOPE YOU OPEN YOUR EYES.

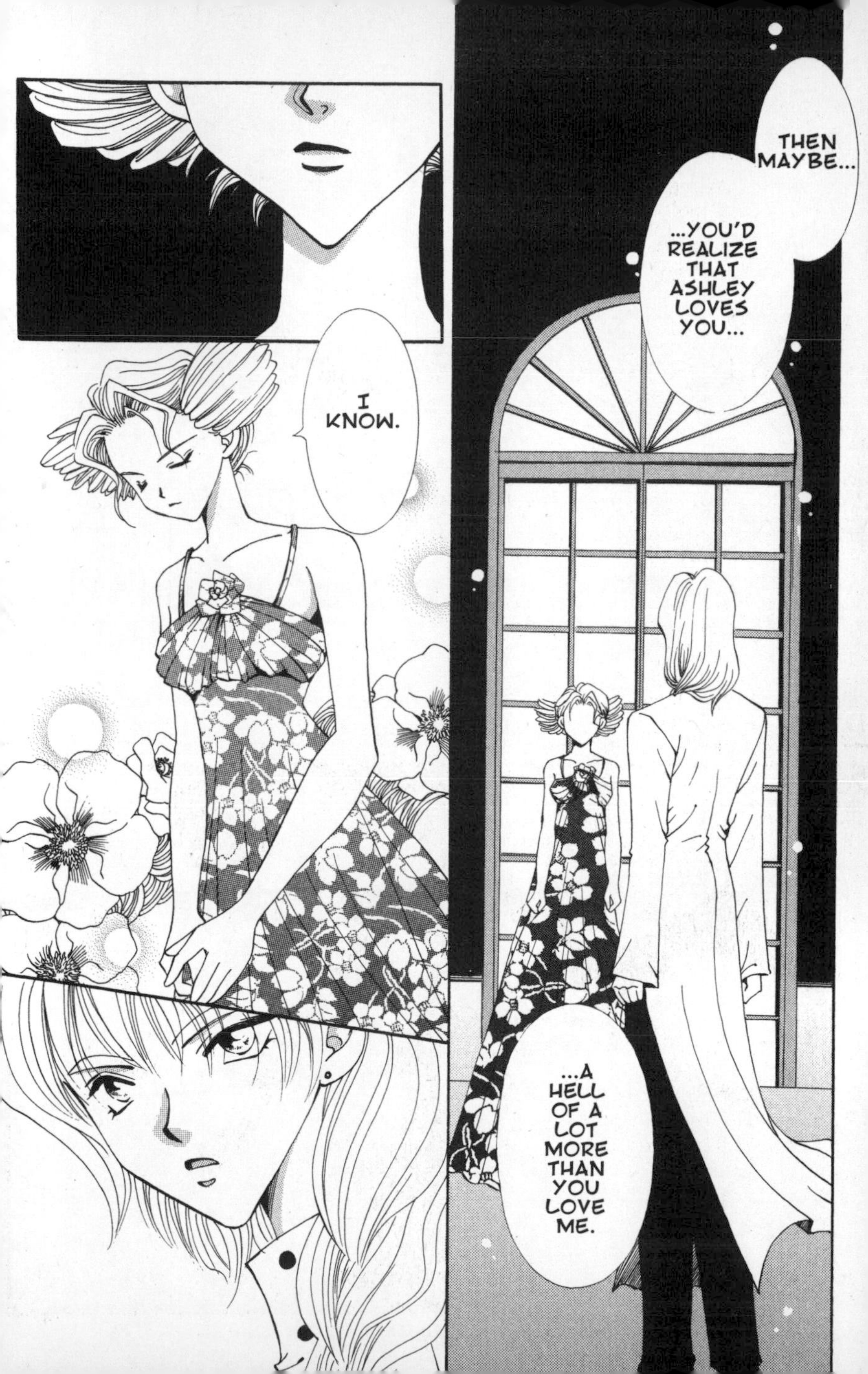
THEN MAYBE...
...YOU'D REALIZE THAT ASHLEY LOVES YOU...
...A HELL OF A LOT MORE THAN YOU LOVE ME.
I KNOW.

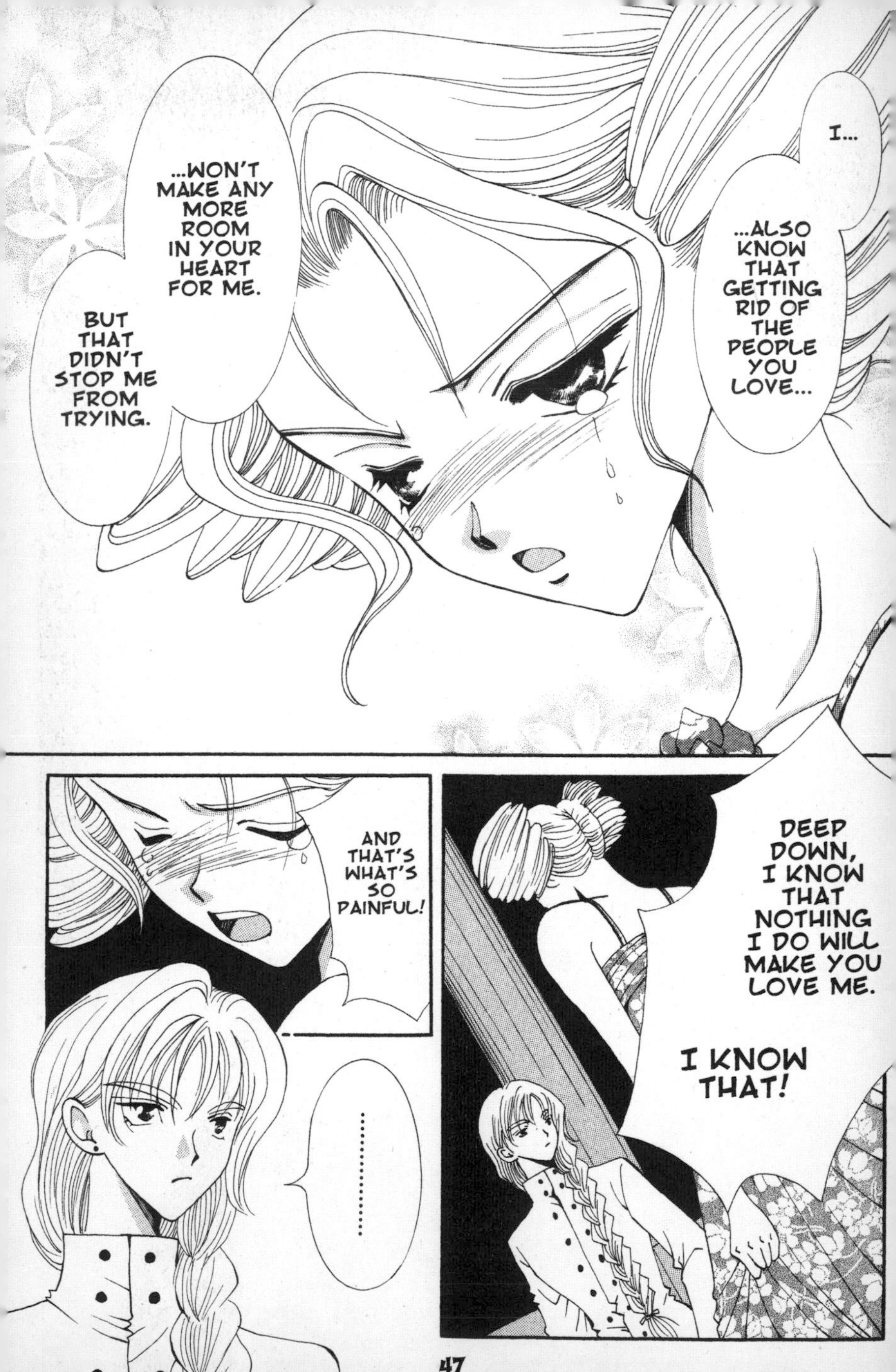
I...
...ALSO KNOW THAT GETTING RID OF THE PEOPLE YOU LOVE...
...WON'T MAKE ANY MORE ROOM IN YOUR HEART FOR ME.
BUT THAT DIDN'T STOP ME FROM TRYING.
DEEP DOWN, I KNOW THAT NOTHING I DO WILL MAKE YOU LOVE ME.
I KNOW THAT!
AND THAT'S WHAT'S SO PAINFUL!
....

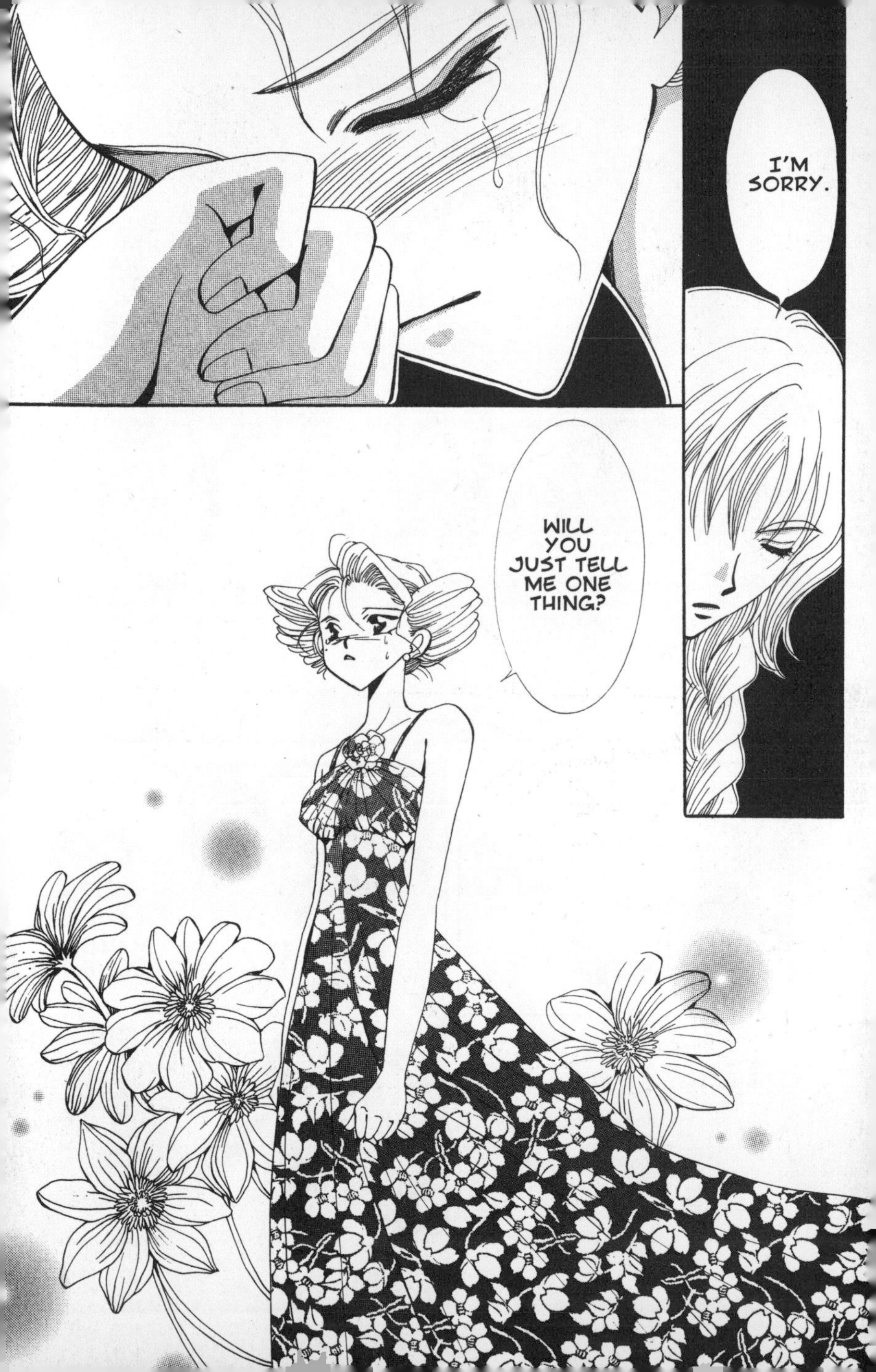
I'M SORRY.
WILL YOU JUST TELL ME ONE THING?

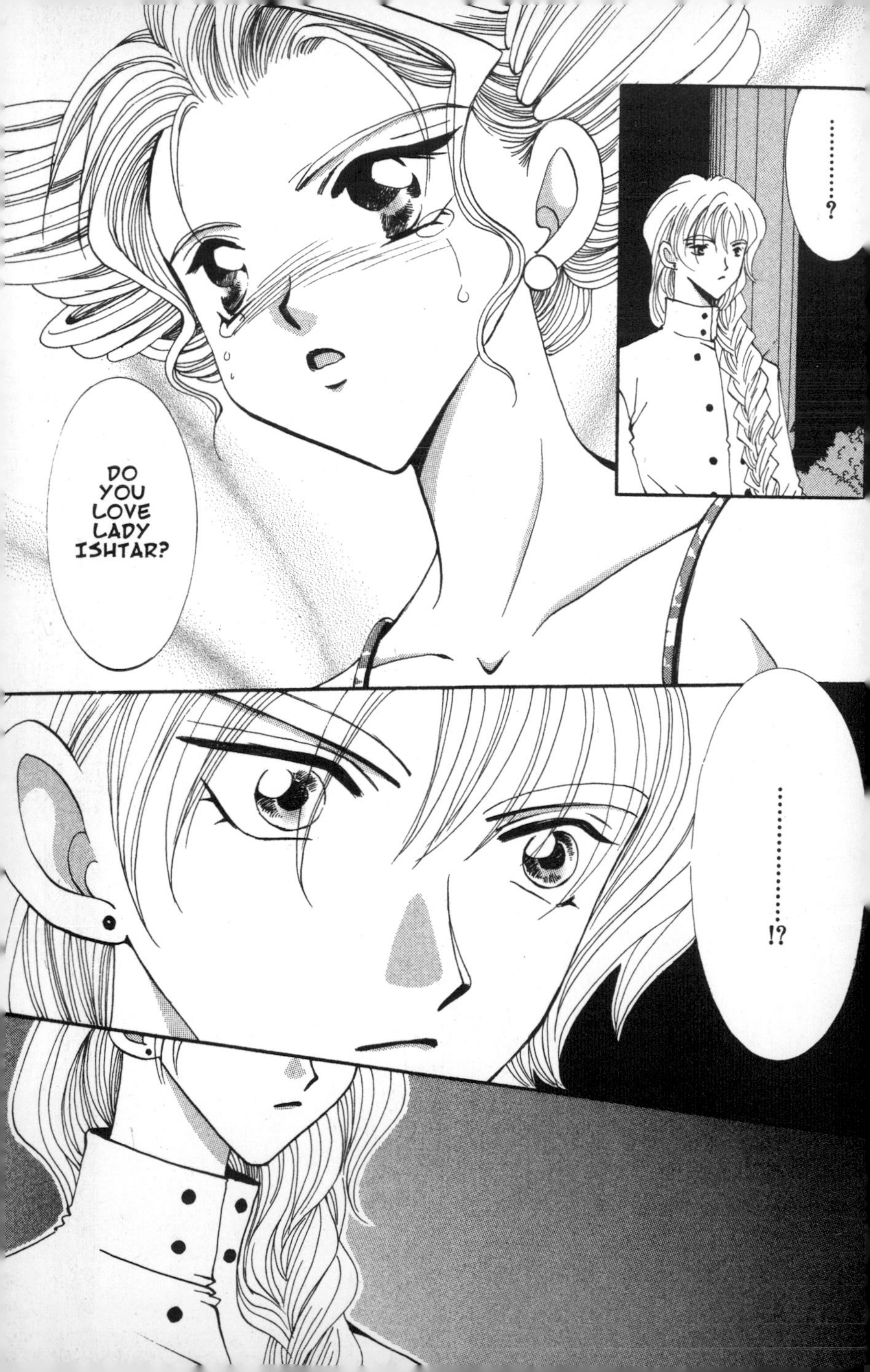

........?
DO YOU LOVE LADY ISHTAR?
..........!?

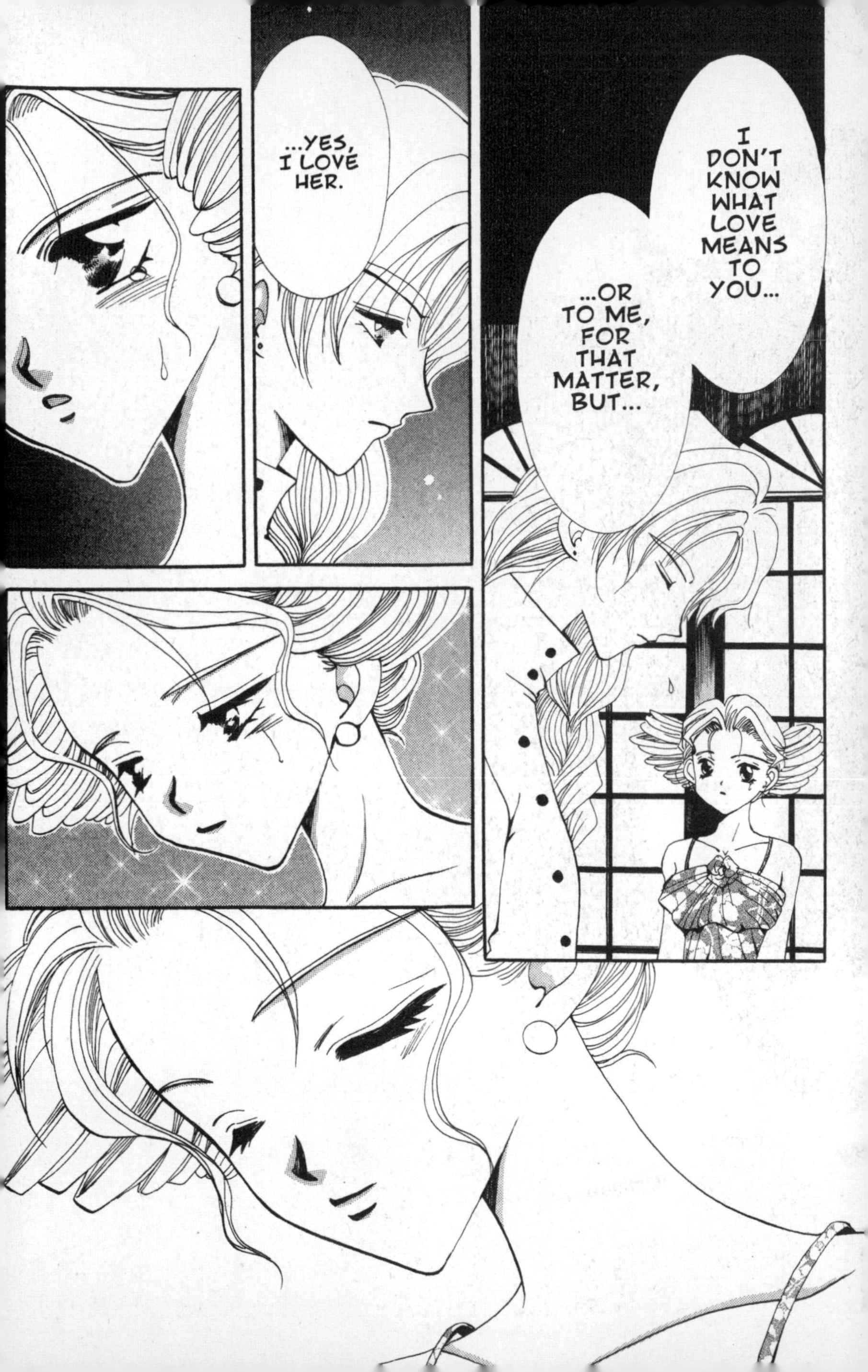
I DON'T KNOW WHAT LOVE MEANS TO YOU...
...OR TO ME, FOR THAT MATTER, BUT...
...YES, I LOVE HER.

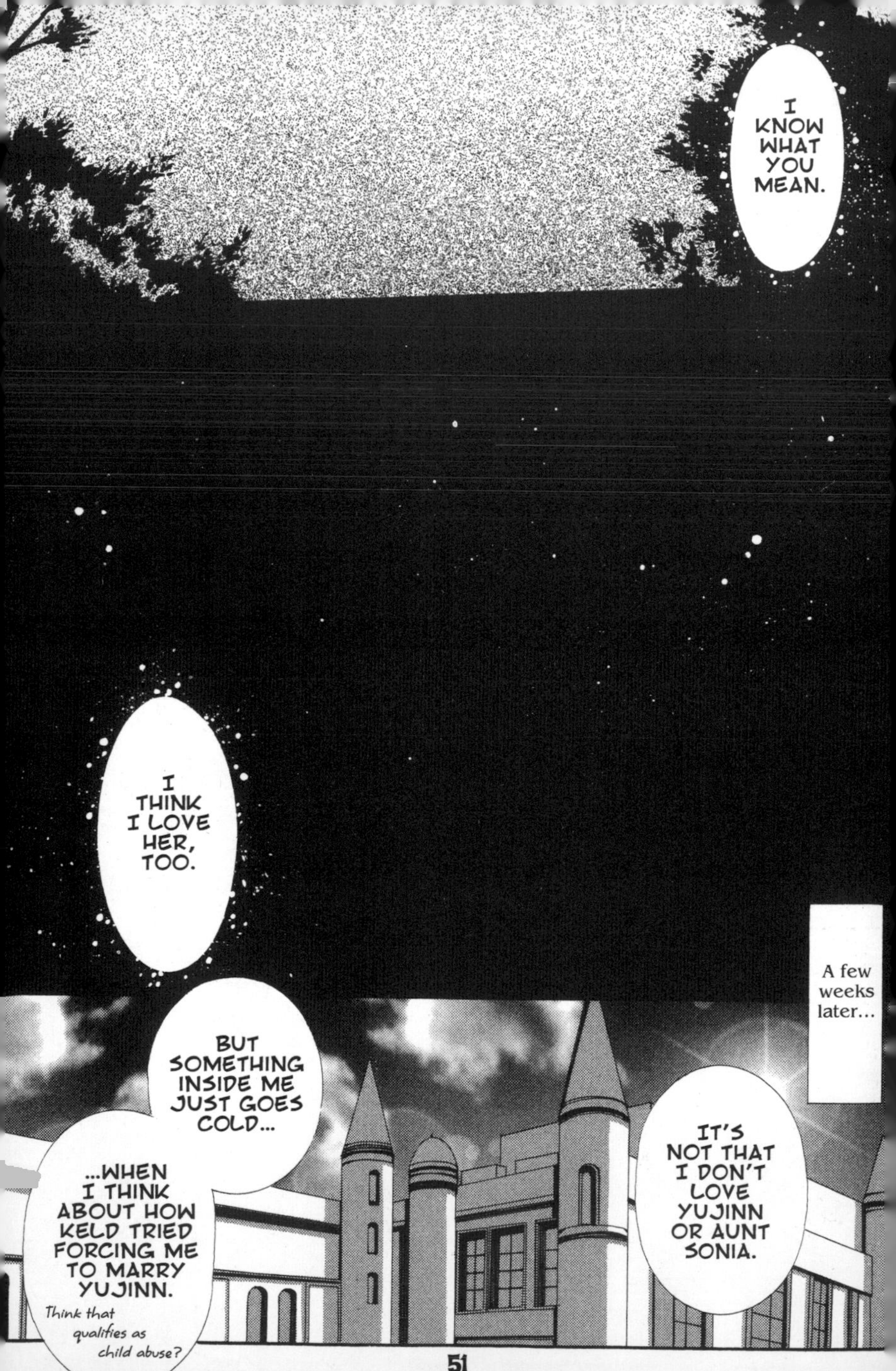
I KNOW WHAT YOU MEAN.
I THINK I LOVE HER, TOO.
A few weeks later...
IT'S NOT THAT I DON'T LOVE YUJINN OR AUNT SONIA.
BUT SOMETHING INSIDE ME JUST GOES COLD...
...WHEN I THINK ABOUT HOW KELD TRIED FORCING ME TO MARRY YUJINN.
Think that qualifies as child abuse?

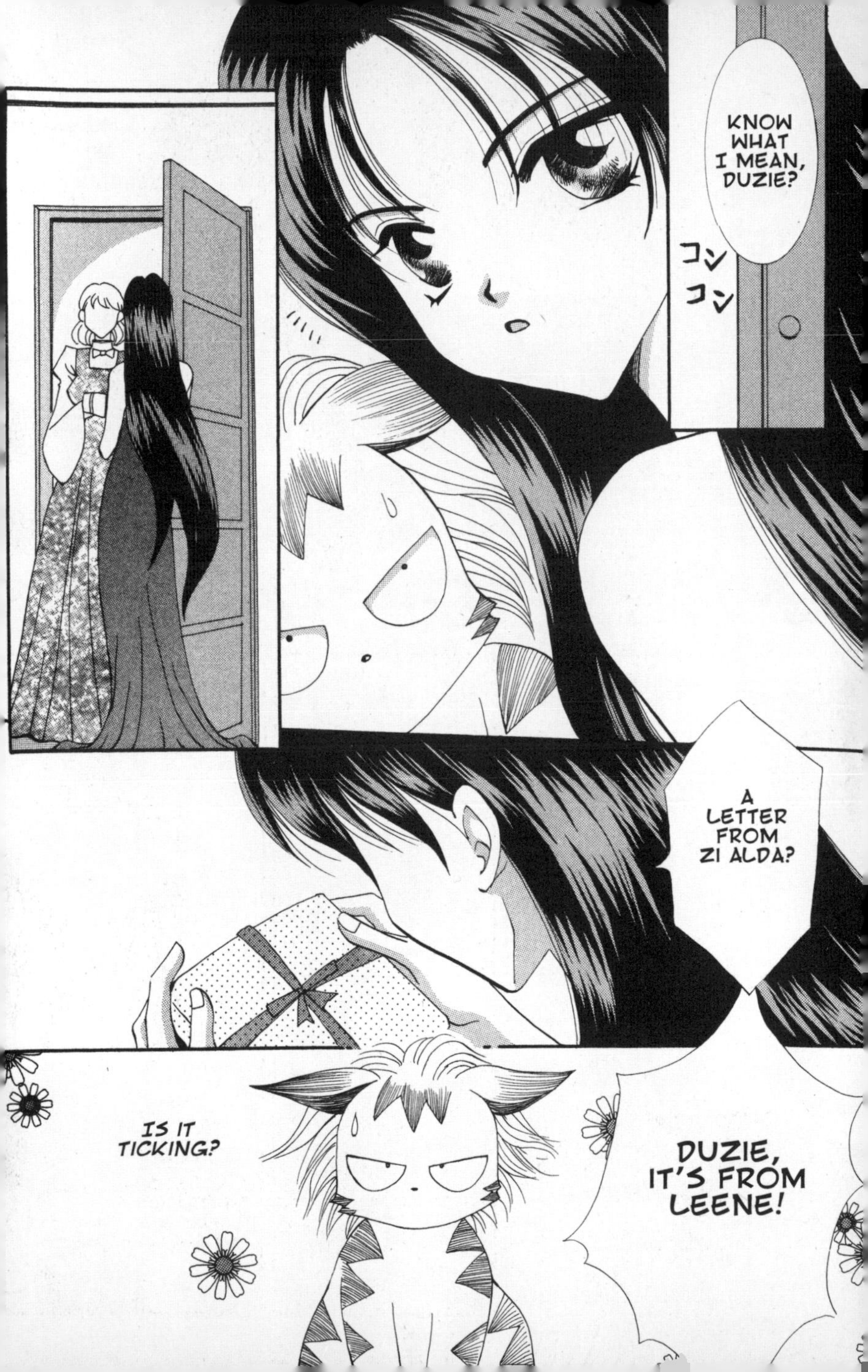
KNOW WHAT I MEAN, DUZIE?
コン
コン
A LETTER FROM ZI ALDA?
DUZIE, IT'S FROM LEENE!
IS IT TICKING?

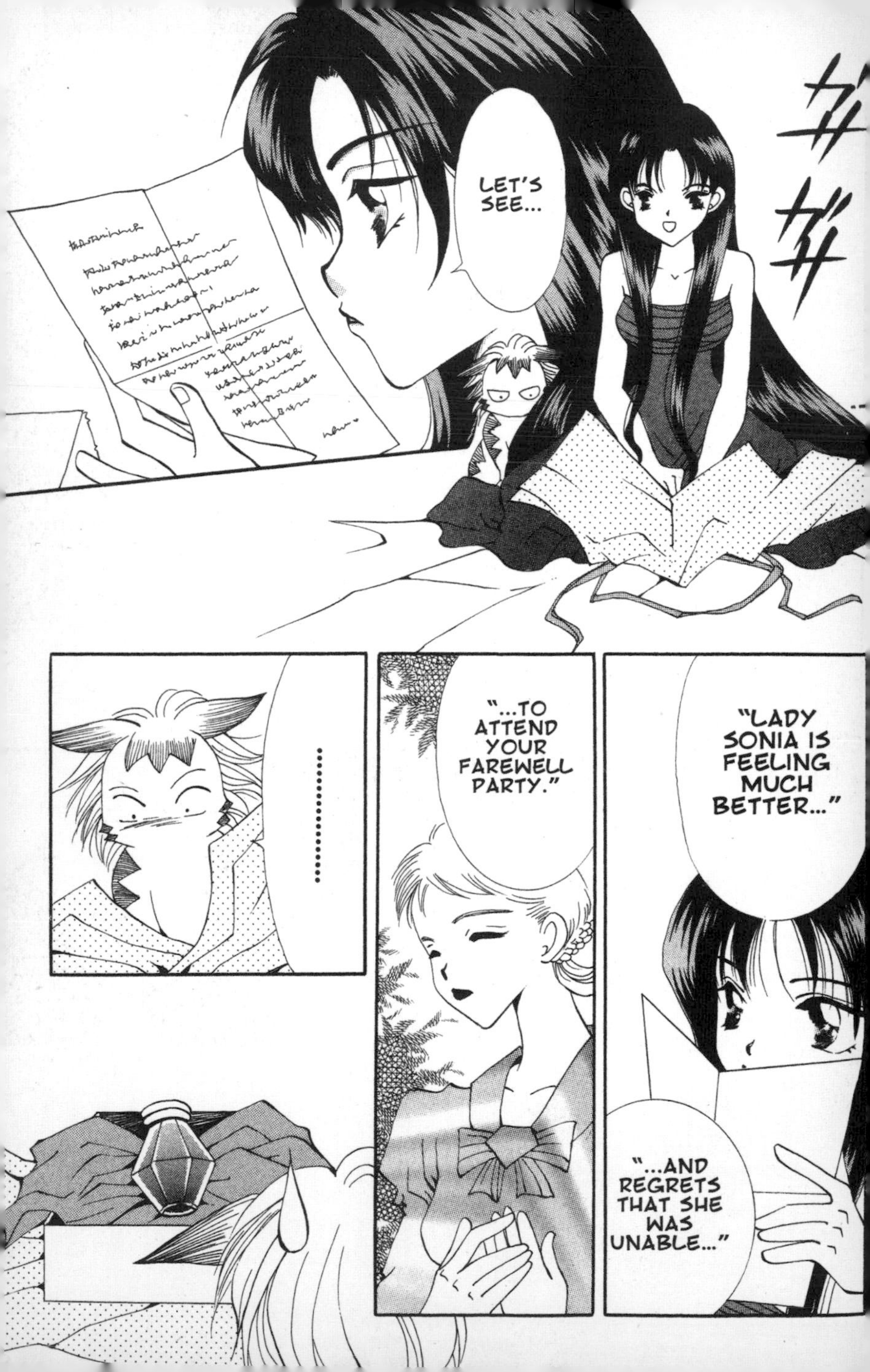
LET'S SEE...
"LADY SONIA IS FEELING MUCH BETTER..."
"...AND REGRETS THAT SHE WAS UNABLE..."
"...TO ATTEND YOUR FAREWELL PARTY."
....

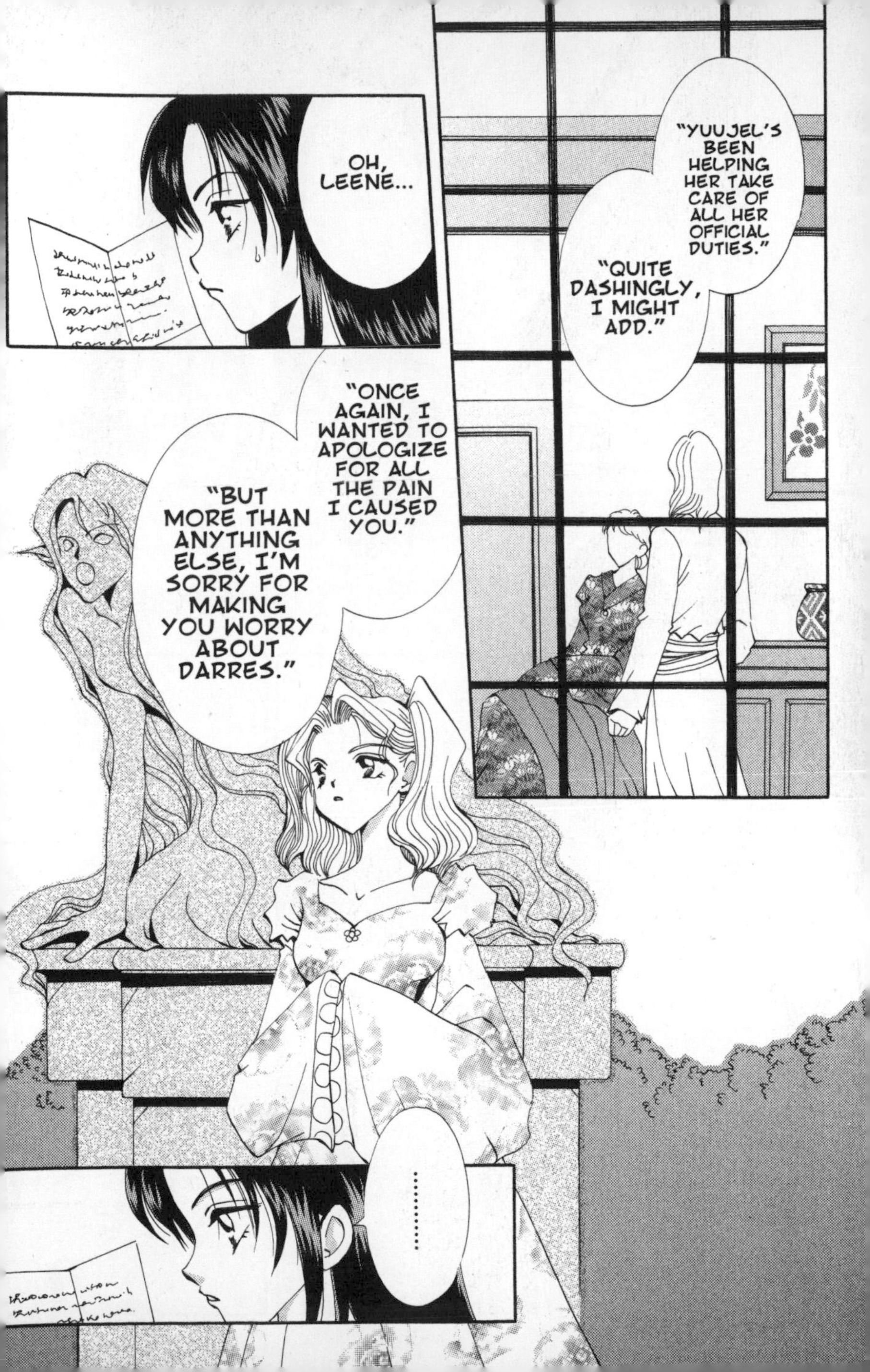
"YUUJEL'S BEEN HELPING HER TAKE CARE OF ALL HER OFFICIAL DUTIES."
"QUITE DASHINGLY, I MIGHT ADD."
OH, LEENE...
"ONCE AGAIN, I WANTED TO APOLOGIZE FOR ALL THE PAIN I CAUSED YOU."
"BUT MORE THAN ANYTHING ELSE, I'M SORRY FOR MAKING YOU WORRY ABOUT DARRES."
....

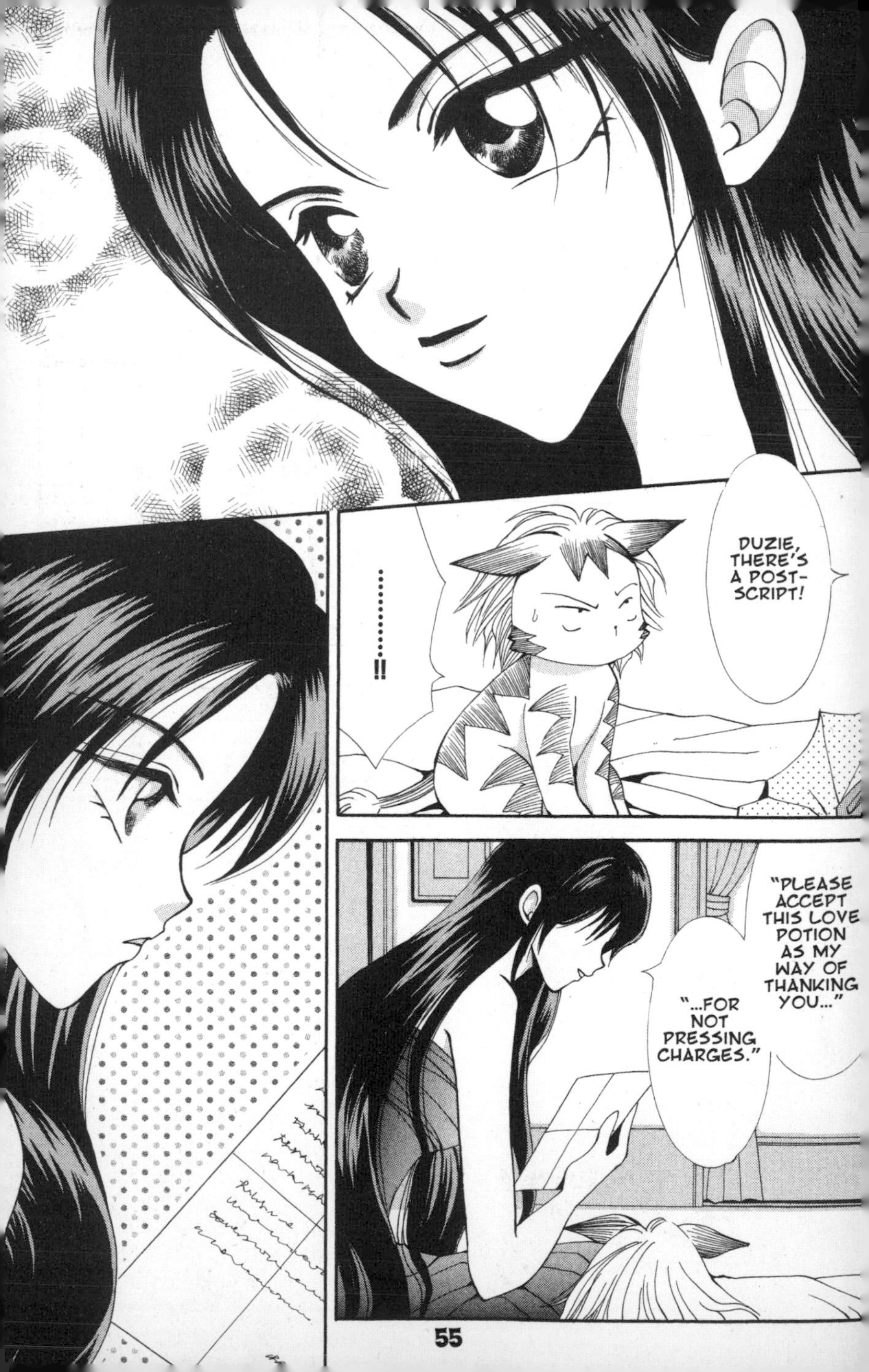
DUZIE, THERE'S A POST-SCRIPT!
......!!
"PLEASE ACCEPT THIS LOVE POTION AS MY WAY OF THANKING YOU..."
"...FOR NOT PRESSING CHARGES."

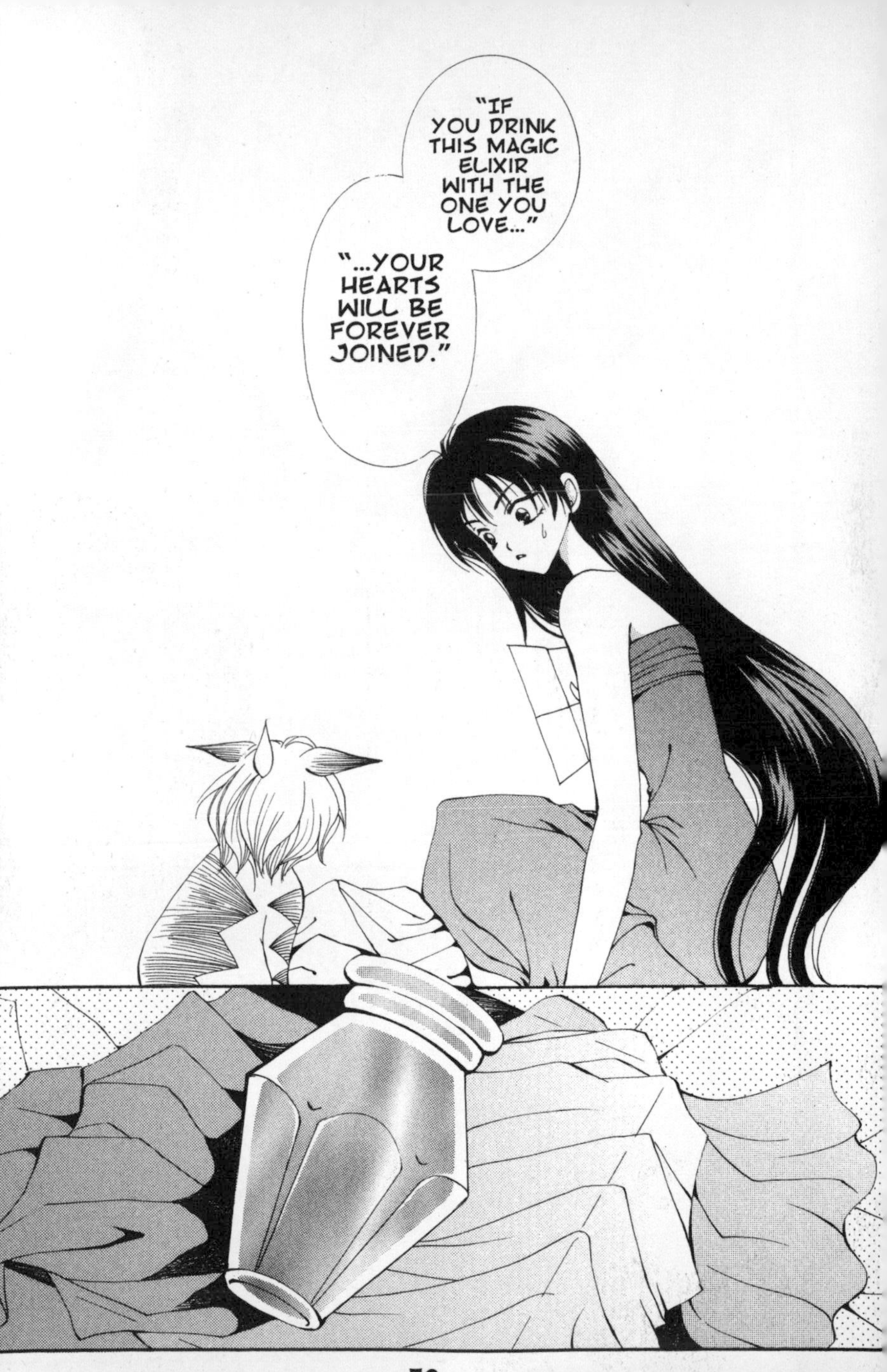
"IF YOU DRINK THIS MAGIC ELIXIR WITH THE ONE YOU LOVE..."
"...YOUR HEARTS WILL BE FOREVER JOINED."

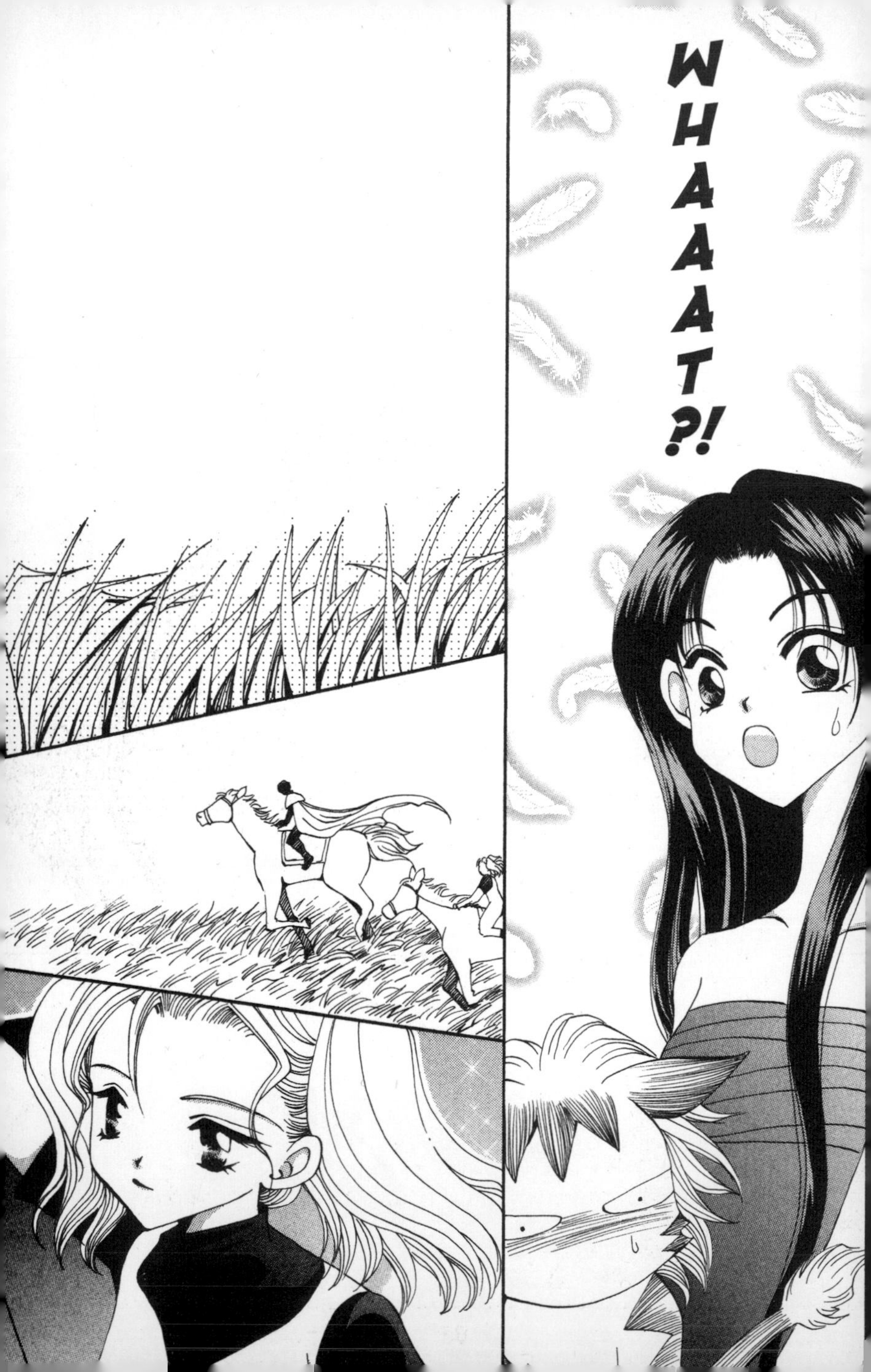
WHAAAAT?!

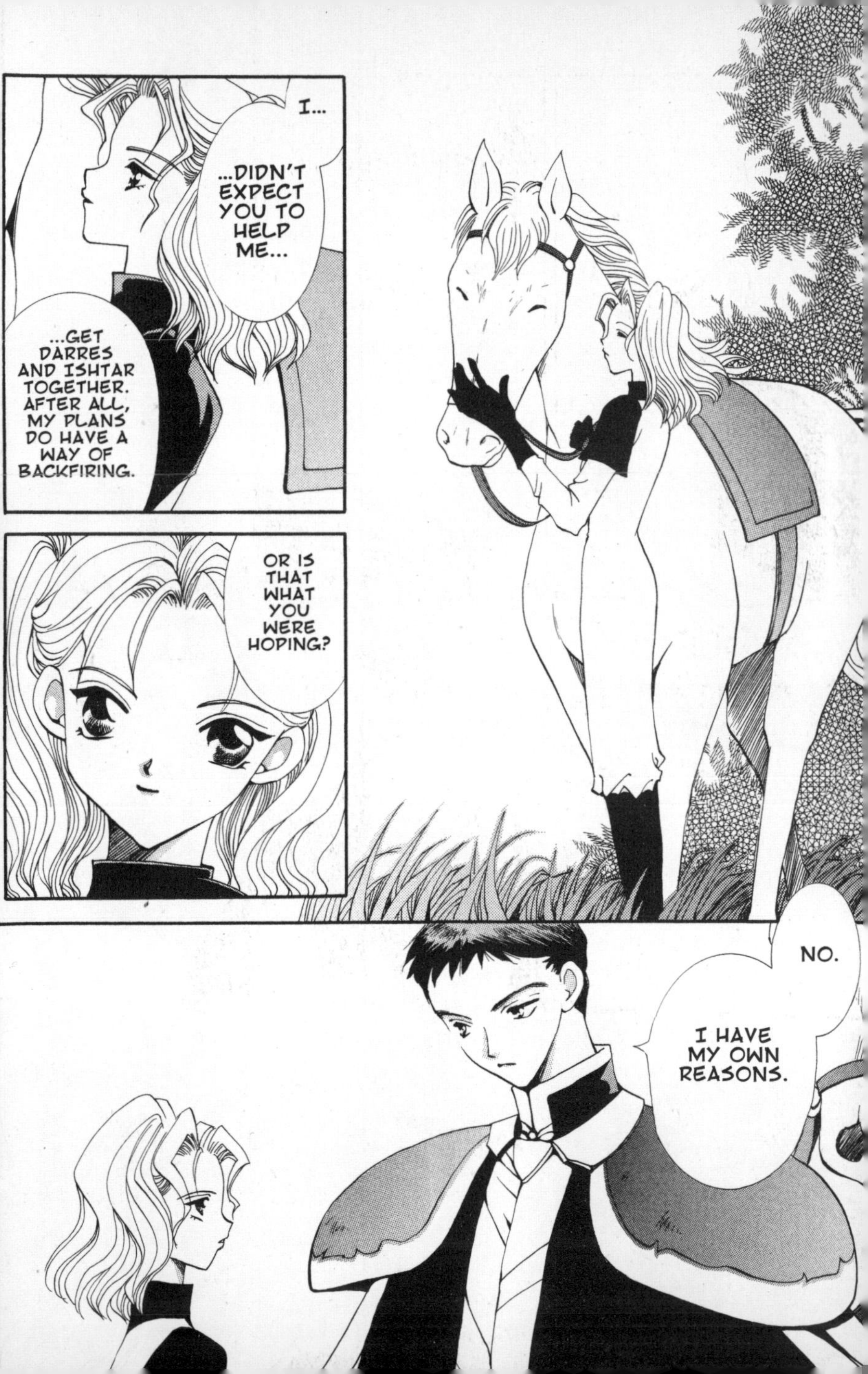
I...
...DIDN'T EXPECT YOU TO HELP ME...
...GET DARRES AND ISHTAR TOGETHER. AFTER ALL, MY PLANS DO HAVE A WAY OF BACKFIRING.
OR IS THAT WHAT YOU WERE HOPING?
NO.
I HAVE MY OWN REASONS.

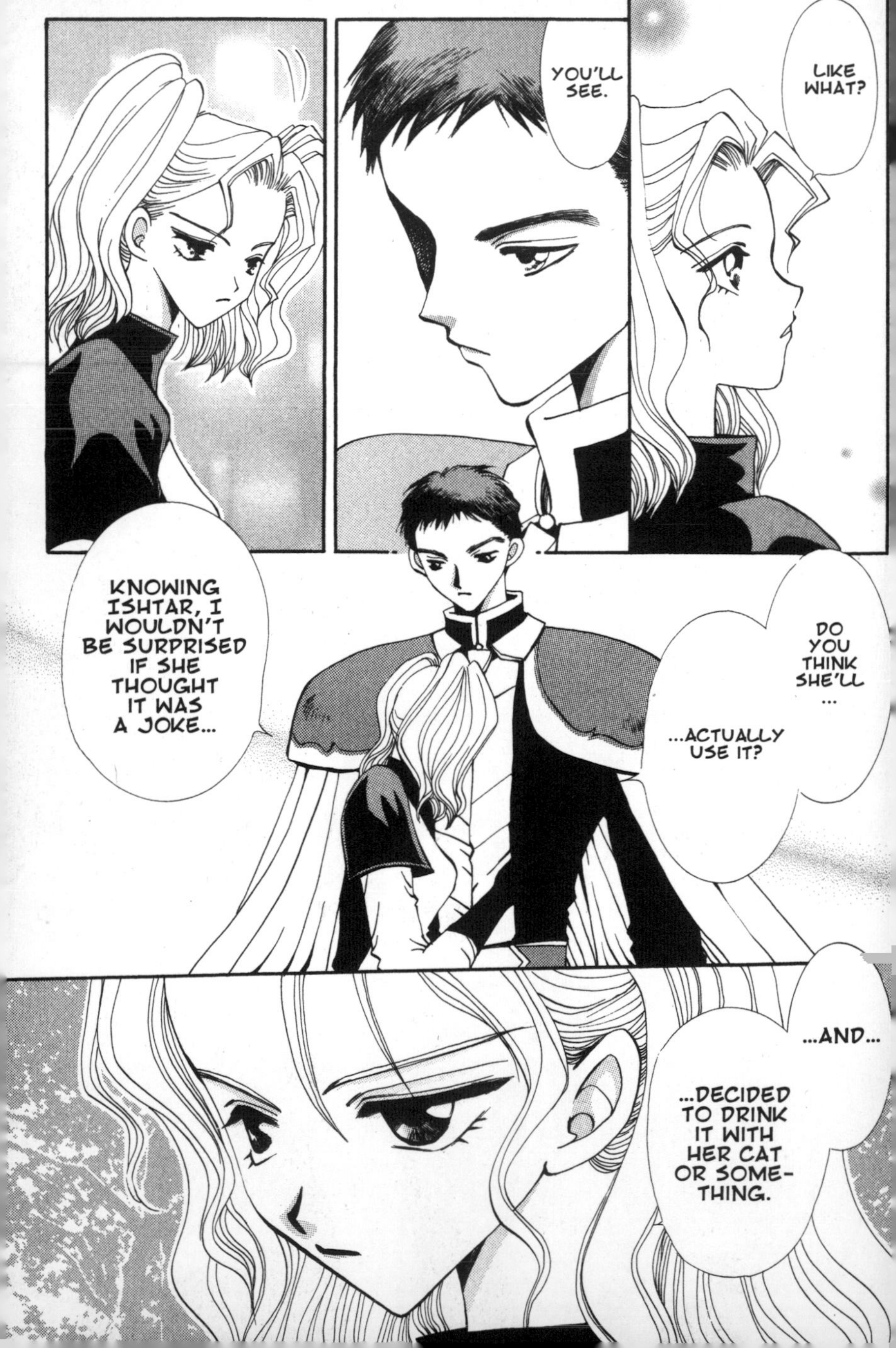
LIKE WHAT?
YOU'LL SEE.
DO YOU THINK SHE'LL ...
...ACTUALLY USE IT?
KNOWING ISHTAR, I WOULDN'T BE SURPRISED IF SHE THOUGHT IT WAS A JOKE...
...AND...
...DECIDED TO DRINK IT WITH HER CAT OR SOME-THING.

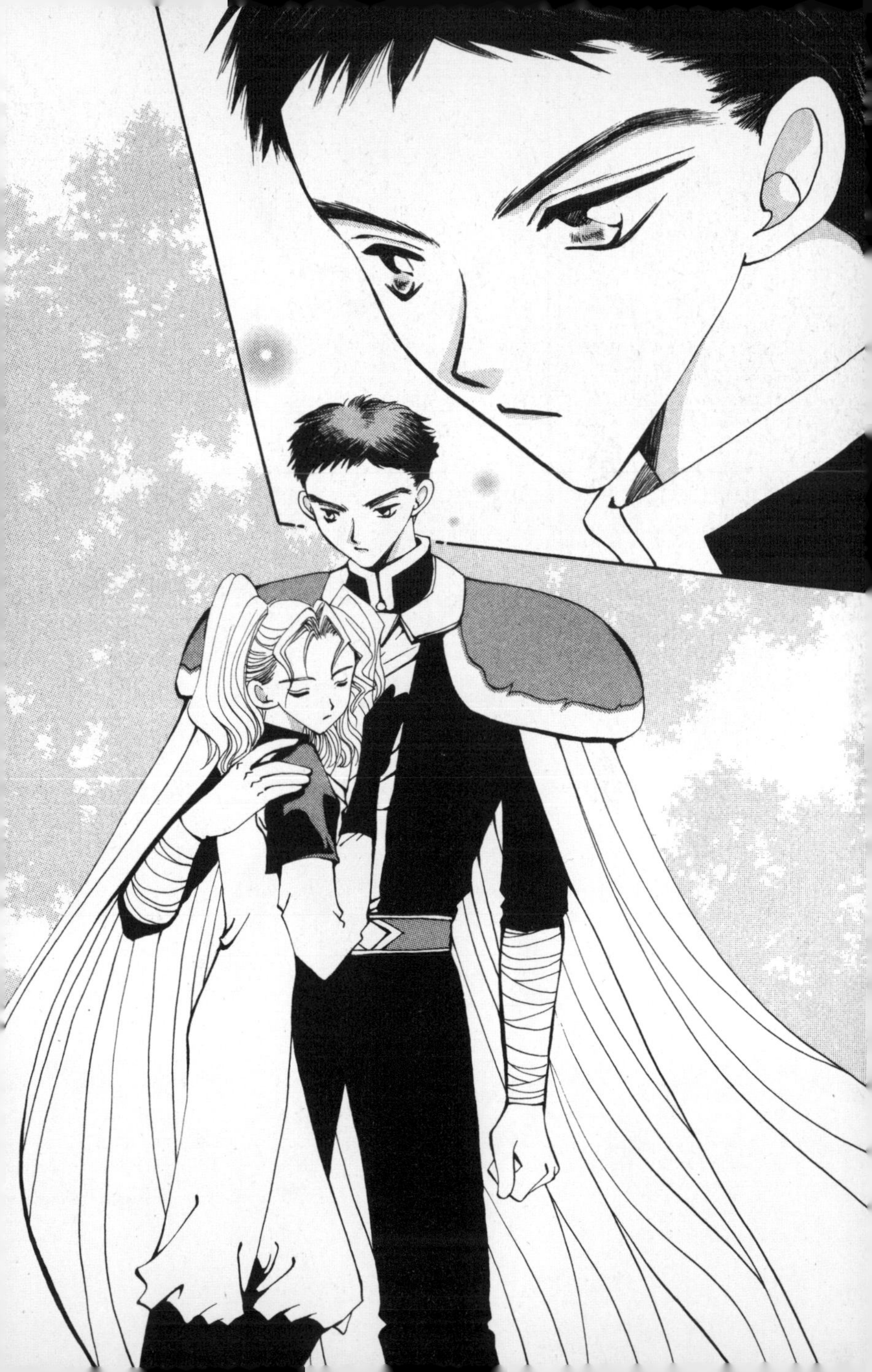

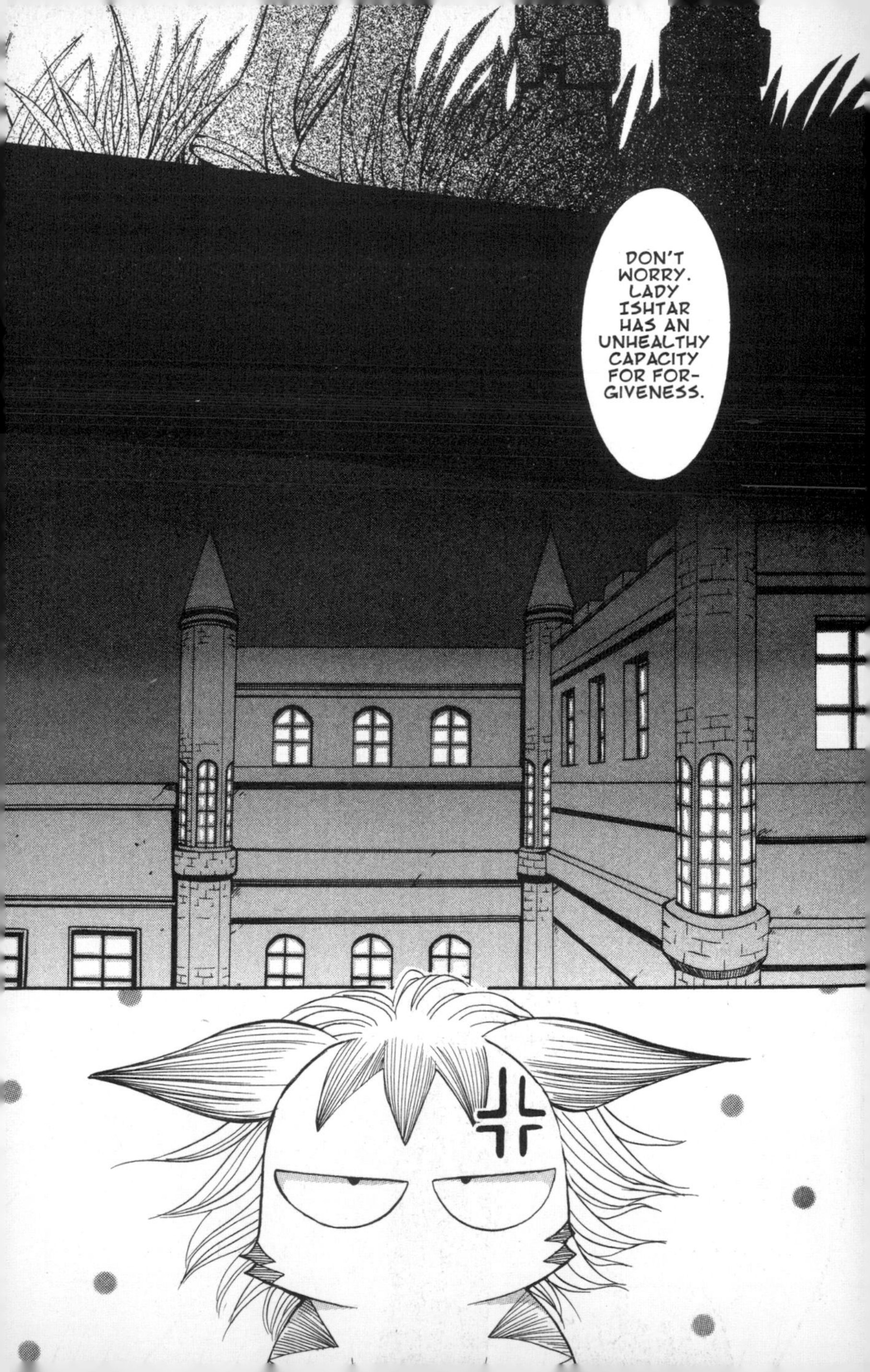
DON'T WORRY. LADY ISHTAR HAS AN UNHEALTHY CAPACITY FOR FOR-GIVENESS.

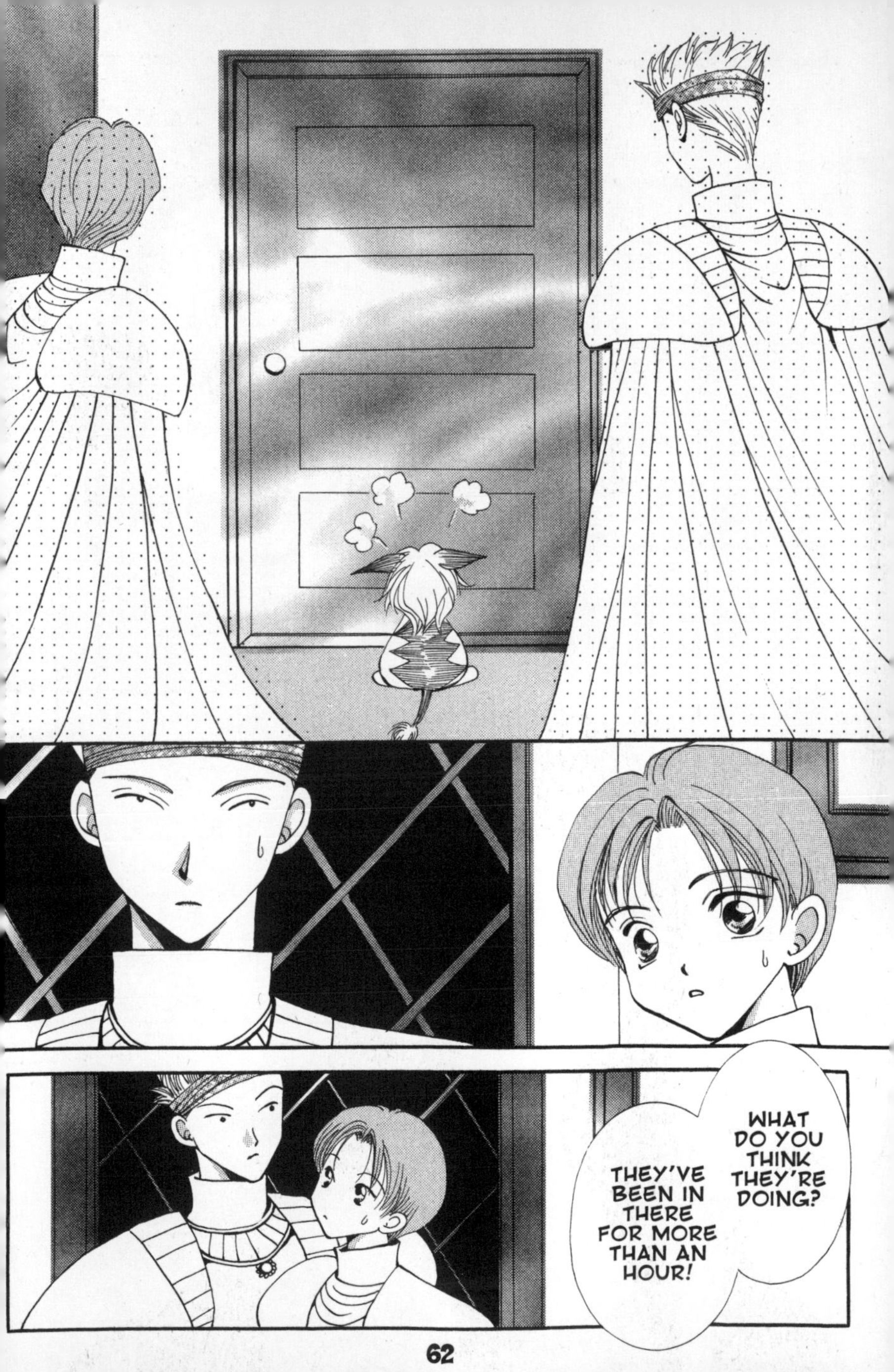
WHAT DO YOU THINK THEY'RE DOING?
THEY'VE BEEN IN THERE FOR MORE THAN AN HOUR!

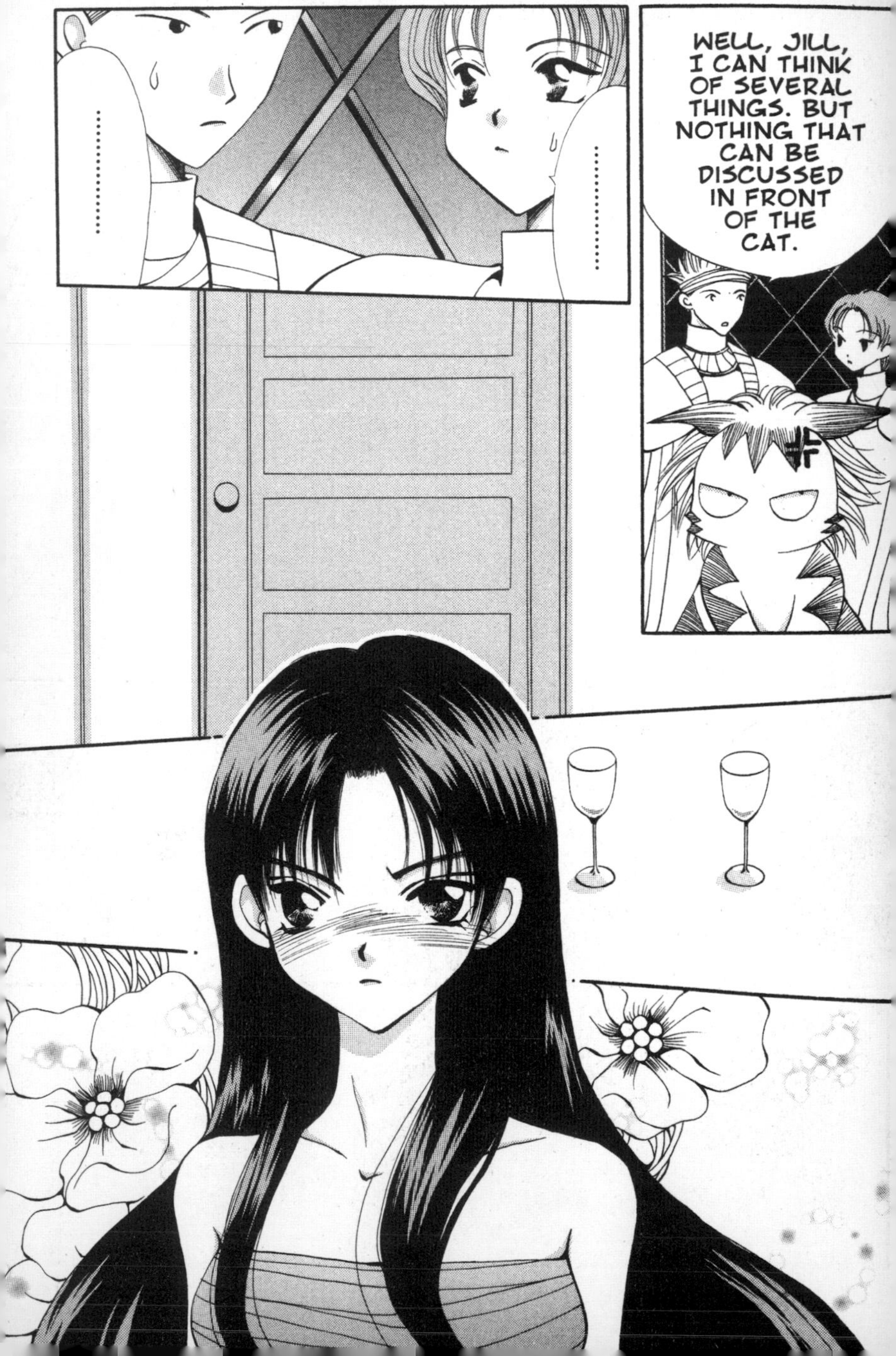
WELL, JILL, I CAN THINK OF SEVERAL THINGS. BUT NOTHING THAT CAN BE DISCUSSED IN FRONT OF THE CAT.

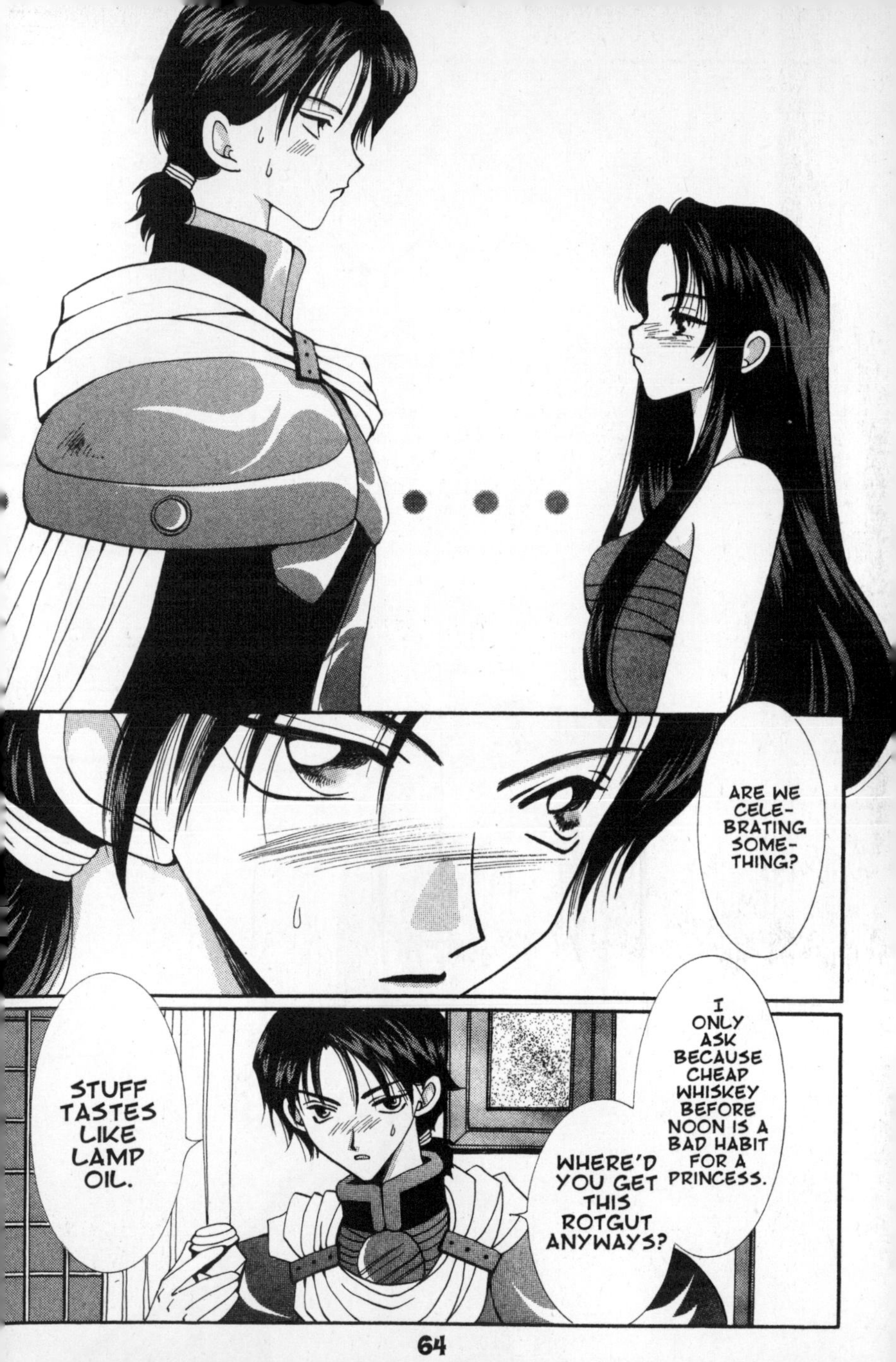
...
ARE WE CELE-BRATING SOME-THING?
I ONLY ASK BECAUSE CHEAP WHISKEY BEFORE NOON IS A BAD HABIT FOR A PRINCESS.
WHERE'D YOU GET THIS ROTGUT ANYWAYS?
STUFF TASTES LIKE LAMP OIL.

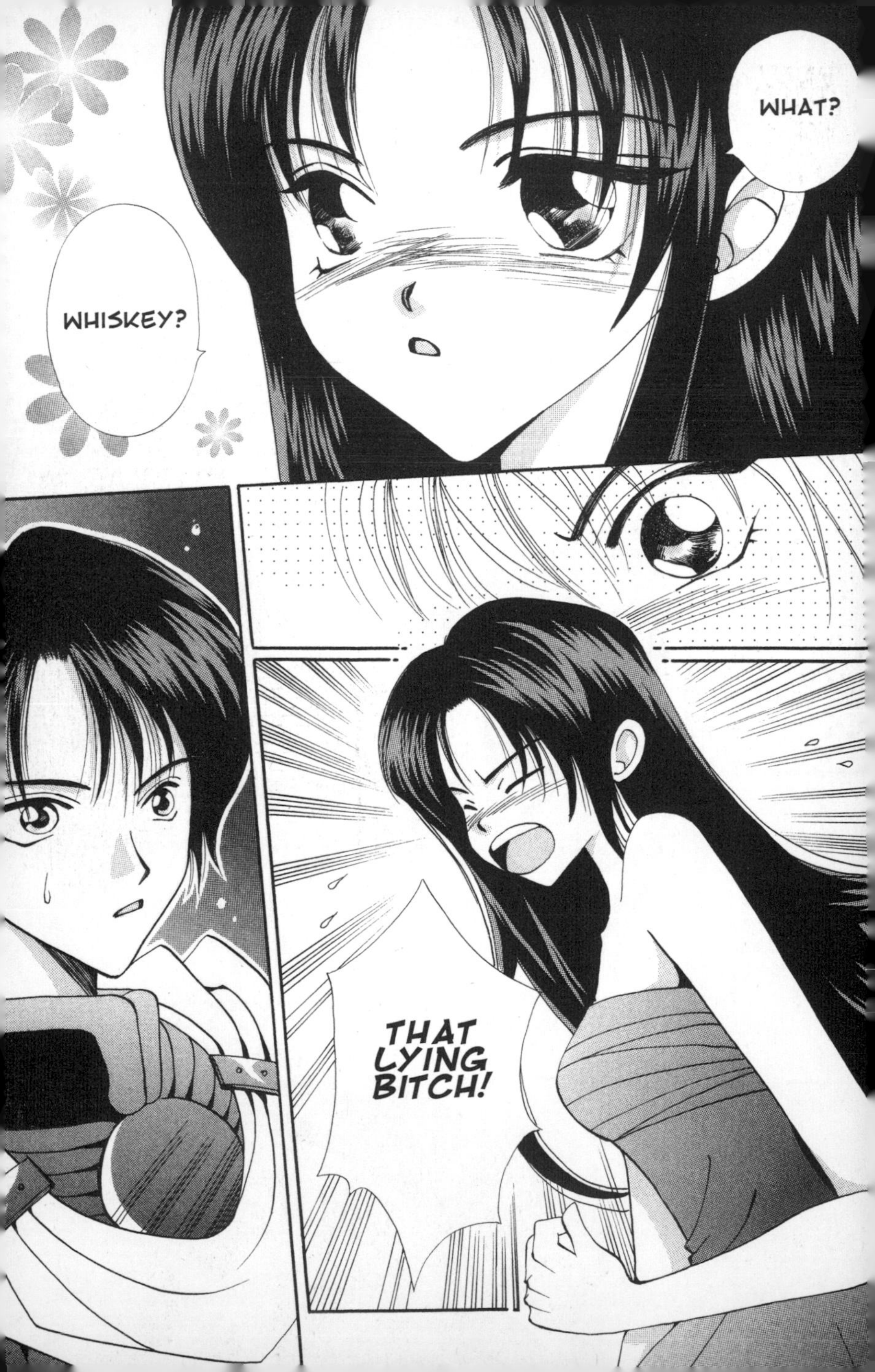
WHAT?
WHISKEY?
THAT LYING BITCH!

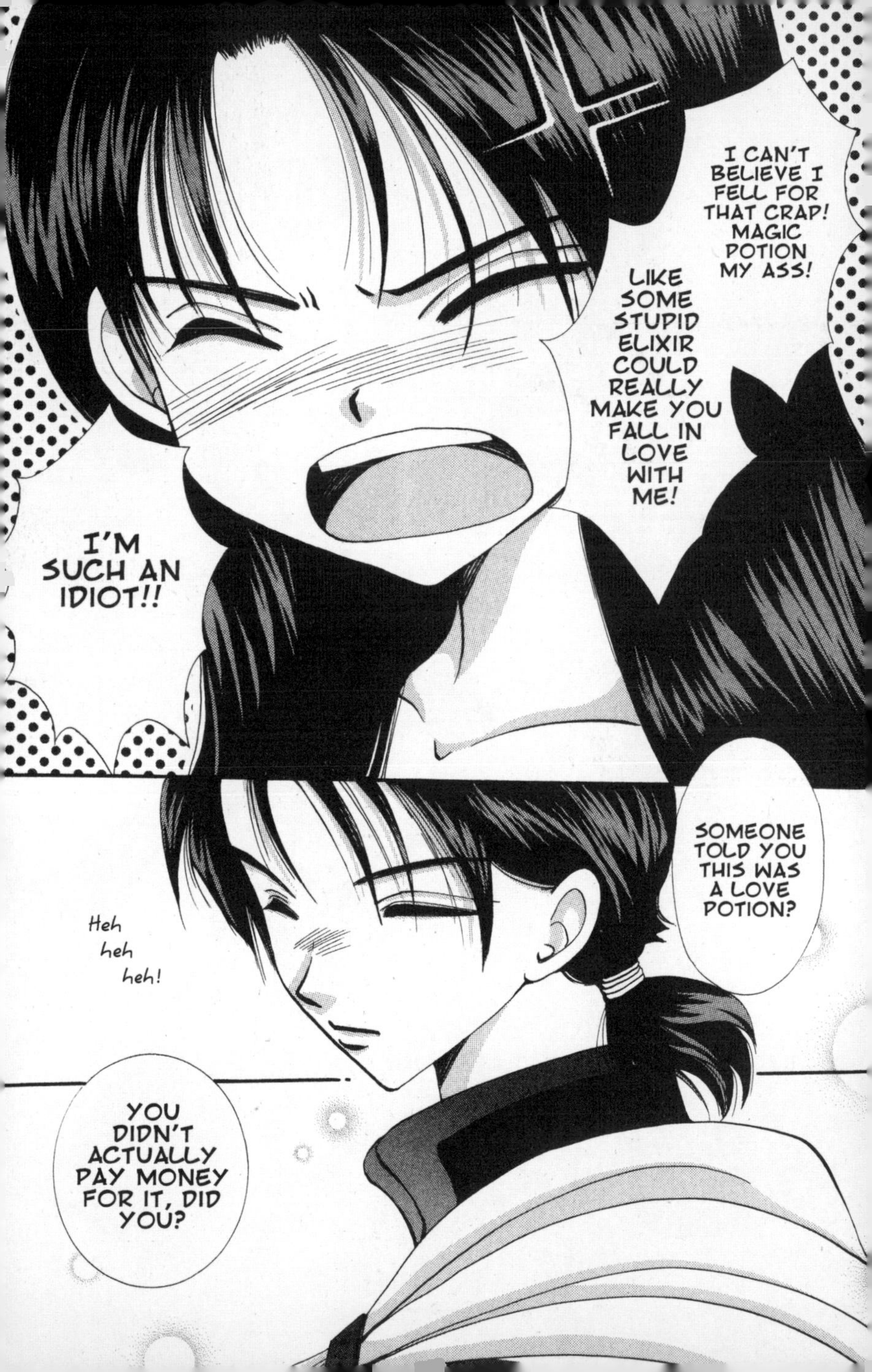
I CAN'T BELIEVE I FELL FOR THAT CRAP! MAGIC POTION MY ASS!
LIKE SOME STUPID ELIXIR COULD REALLY MAKE YOU FALL IN LOVE WITH ME!
I'M SUCH AN IDIOT!!
SOMEONE TOLD YOU THIS WAS A LOVE POTION?
Heh heh heh!
YOU DIDN'T ACTUALLY PAY MONEY FOR IT, DID YOU?

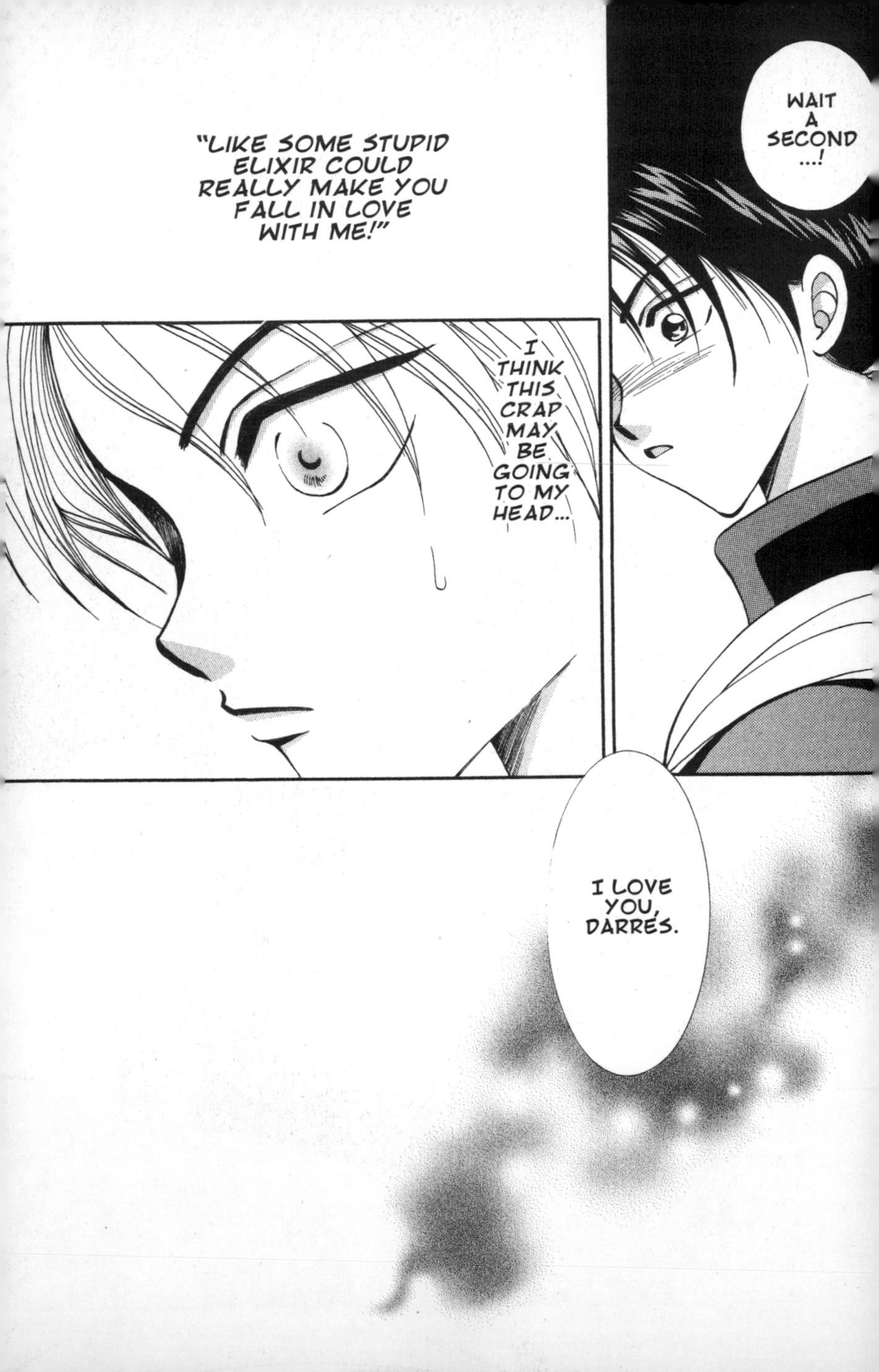
WAIT A SECOND ...!
"LIKE SOME STUPID ELIXIR COULD REALLY MAKE YOU FALL IN LOVE WITH ME!"
I THINK THIS CRAP MAY BE GOING TO MY HEAD...
I LOVE YOU, DARRES.

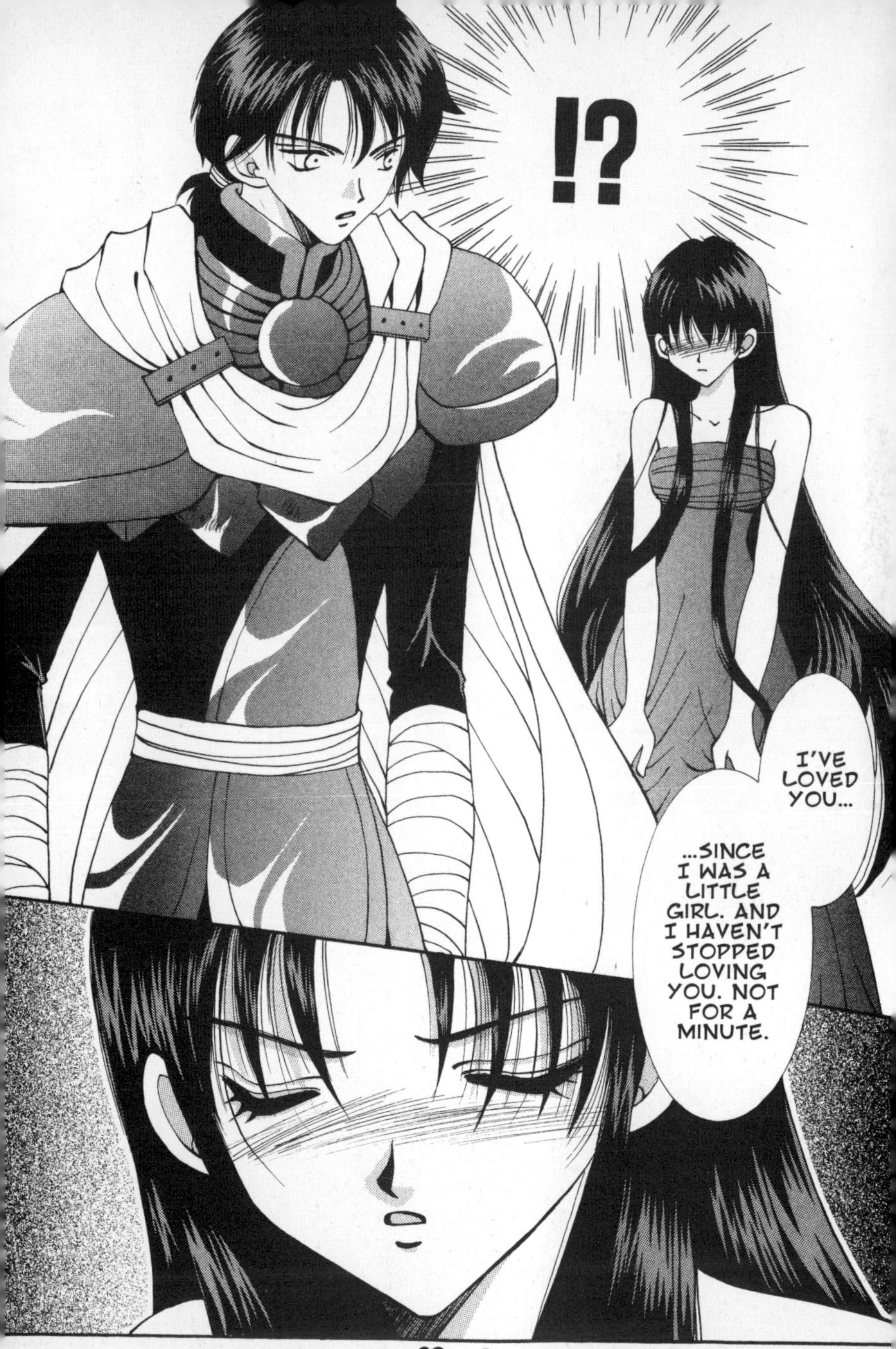
!?
I'VE LOVED YOU...
...SINCE I WAS A LITTLE GIRL. AND I HAVEN'T STOPPED LOVING YOU. NOT FOR A MINUTE.

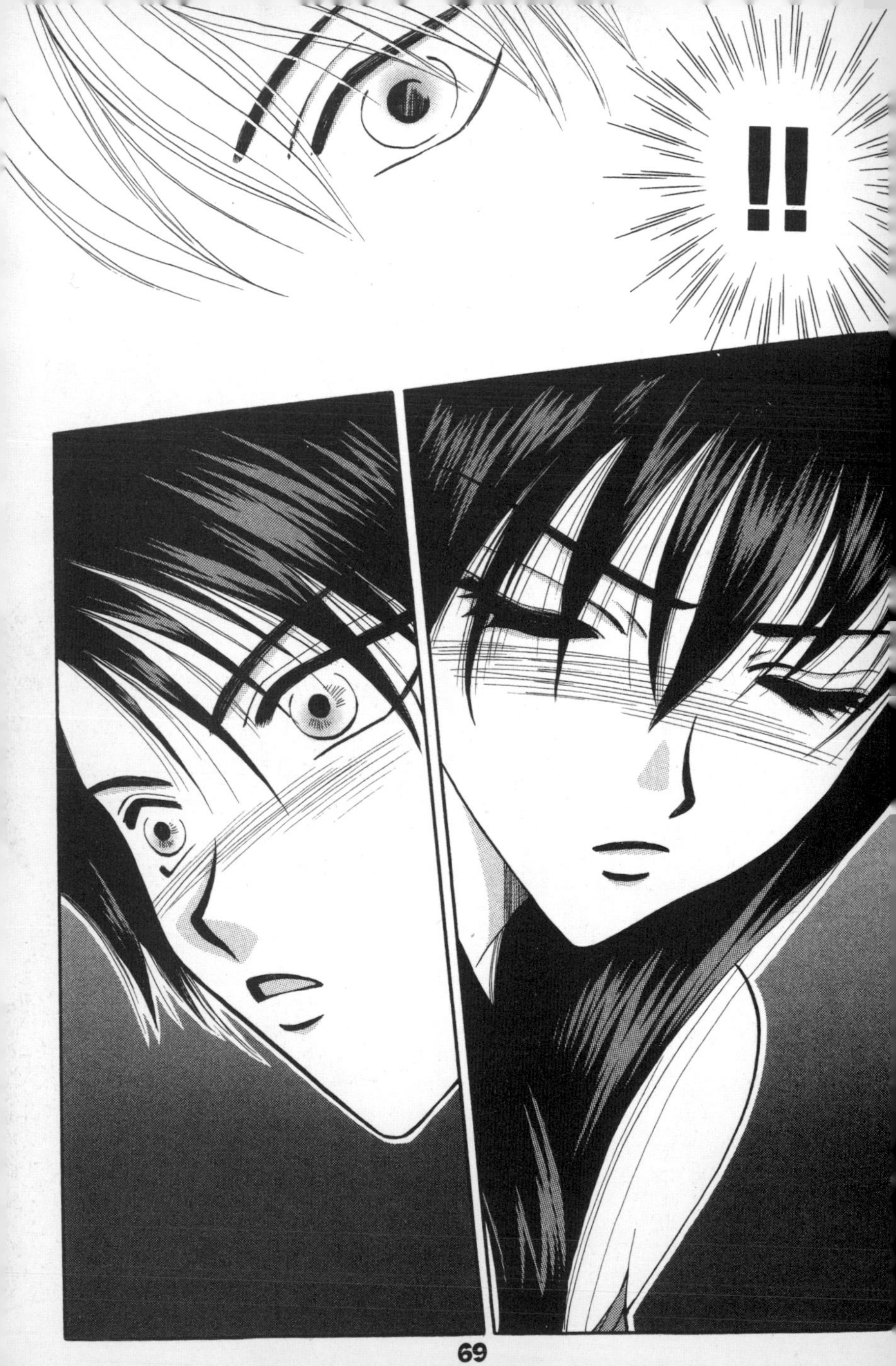
!!

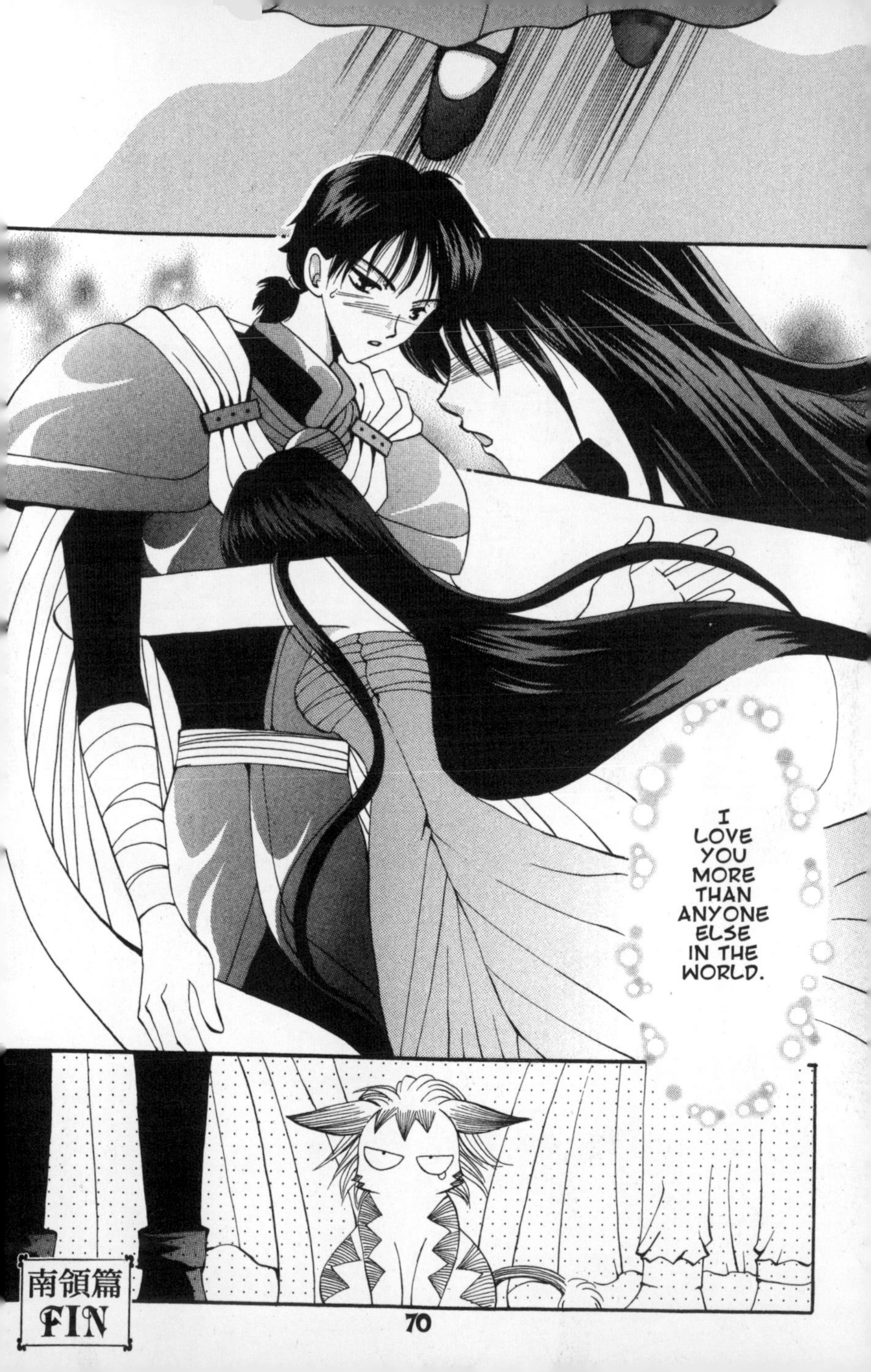
I LOVE YOU MORE THAN ANYONE ELSE IN THE WORLD.
南領篇
FIN

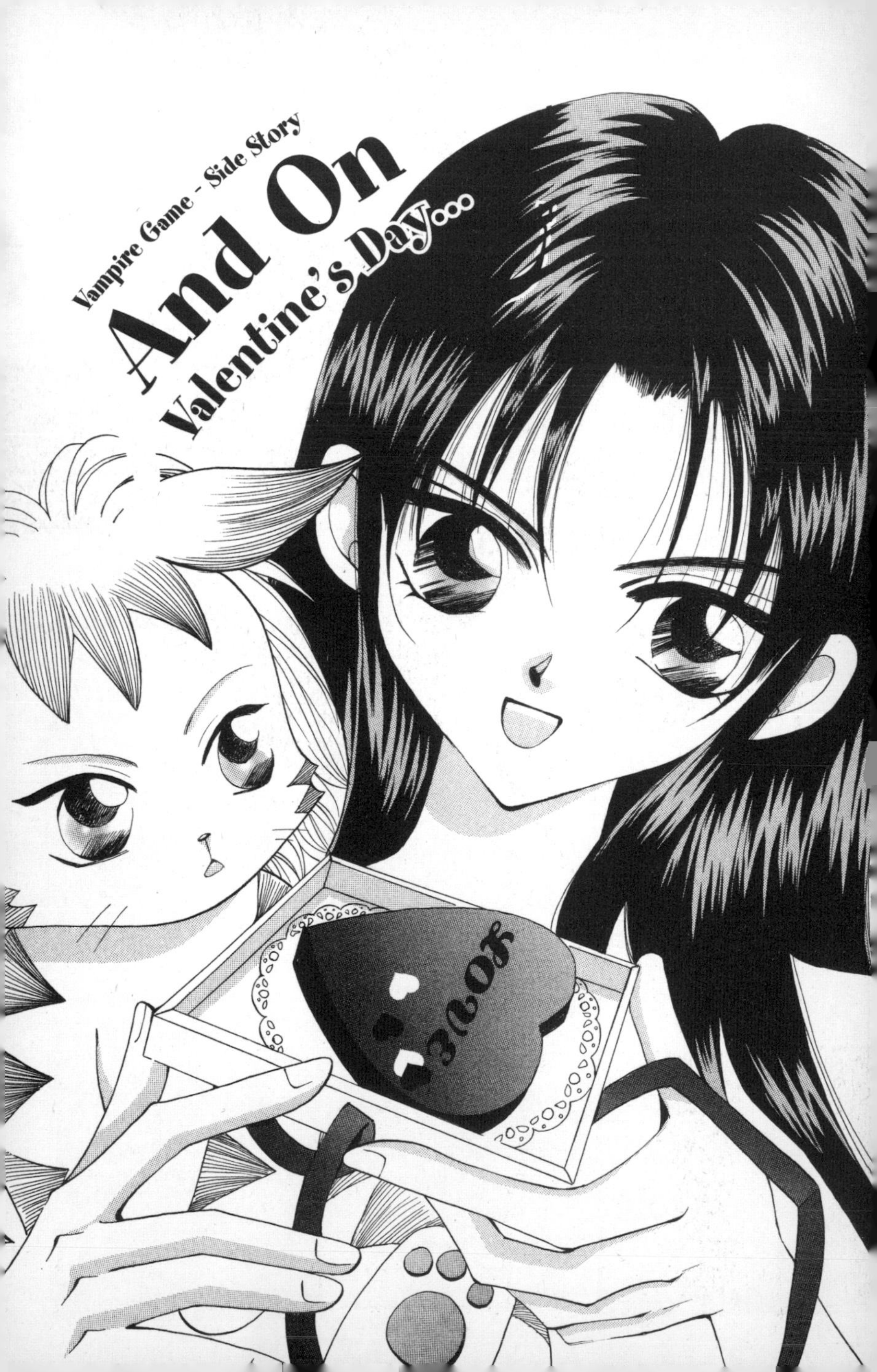
Vampire Game - Side Story
And On
Valentine's Day...

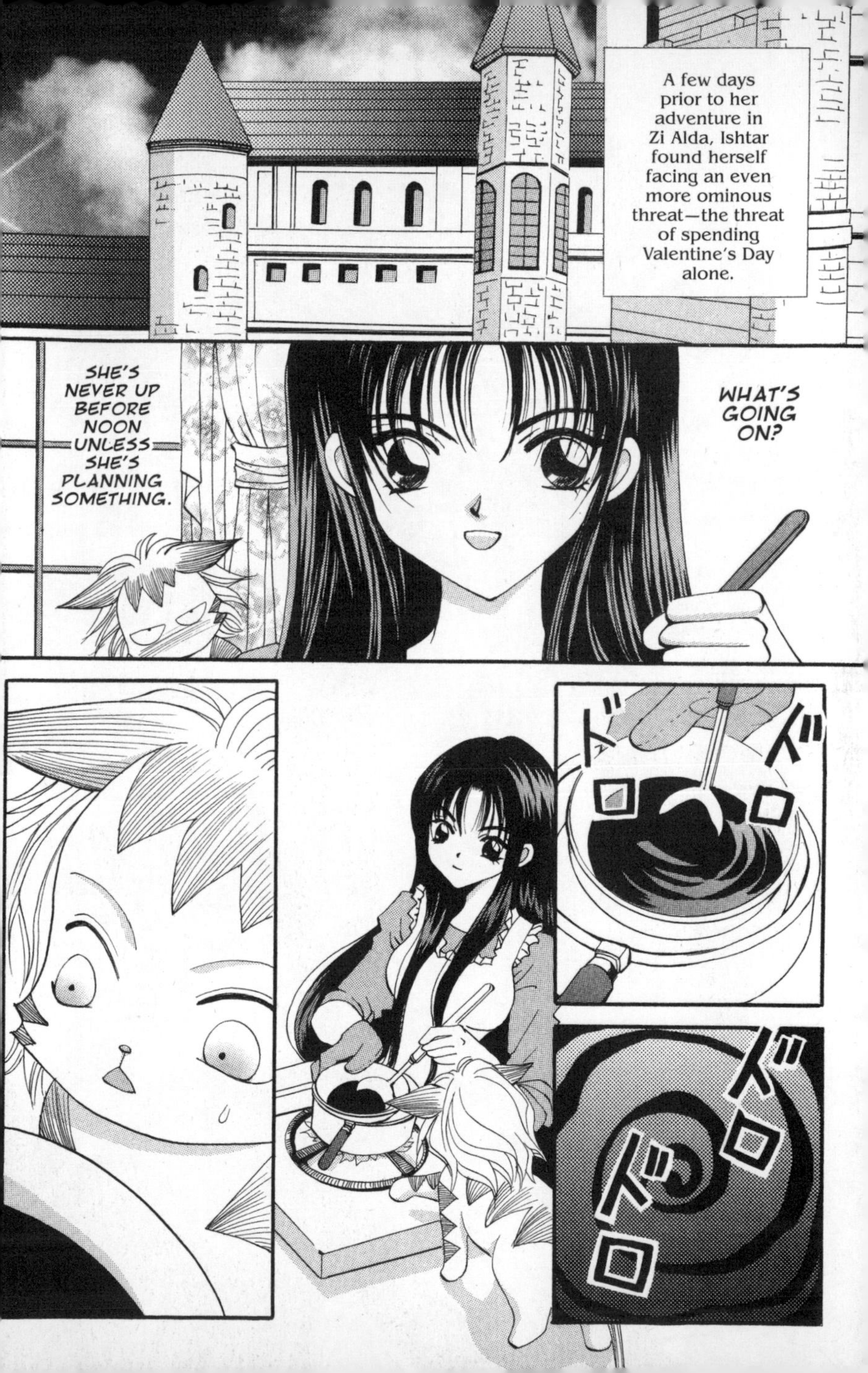
A few days prior to her adventure in Zi Alda, Ishtar found herself facing an even more ominous threat—the threat of spending Valentine's Day alone.
WHAT'S GOING ON?
SHE'S NEVER UP BEFORE NOON UNLESS SHE'S PLANNING SOMETHING.
ドロドロ

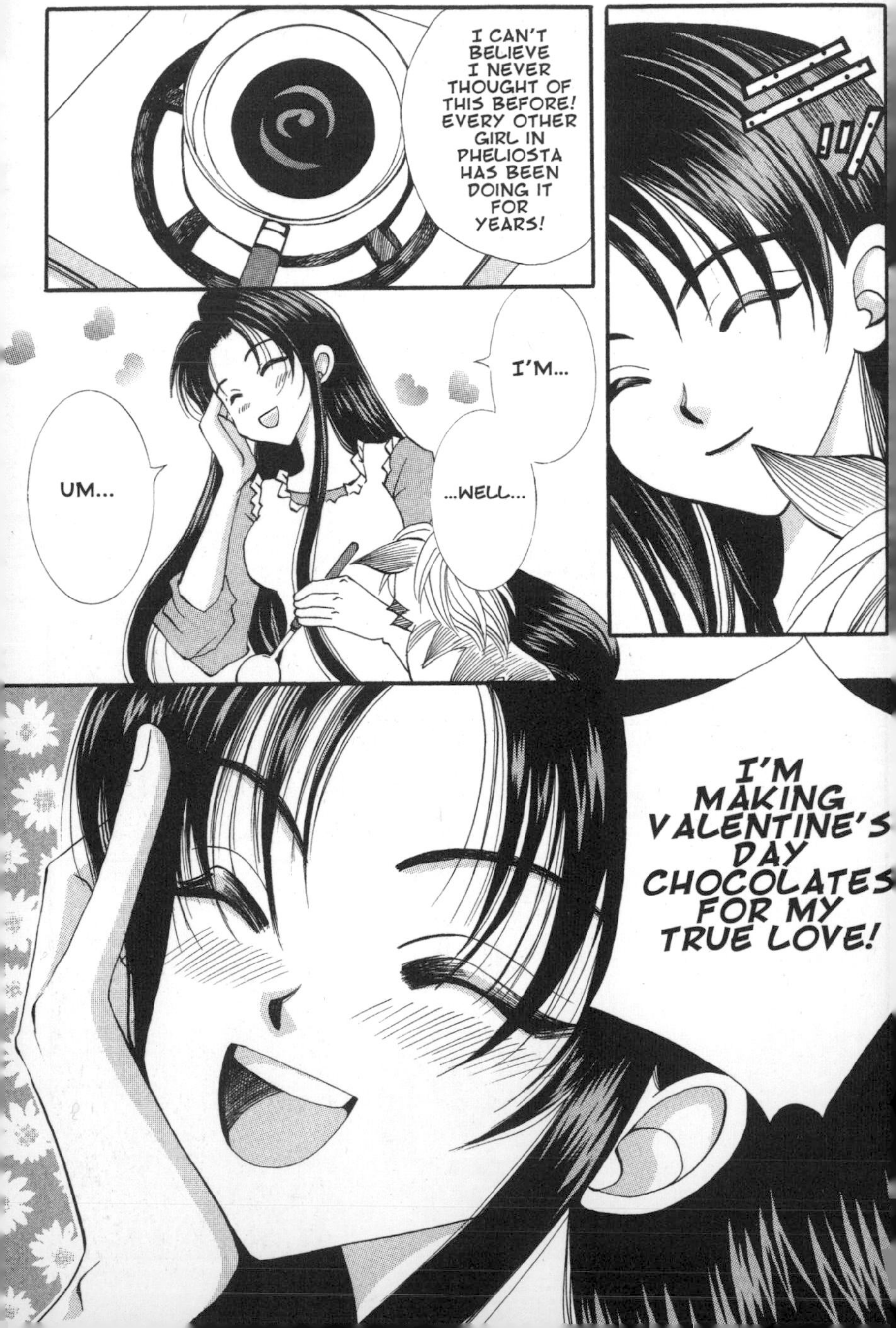
I CAN'T BELIEVE I NEVER THOUGHT OF THIS BEFORE! EVERY OTHER GIRL IN PHELIOSTA HAS BEEN DOING IT FOR YEARS!
I'M...
...WELL...
UM...
I'M MAKING VALENTINE'S DAY CHOCOLATES FOR MY TRUE LOVE!

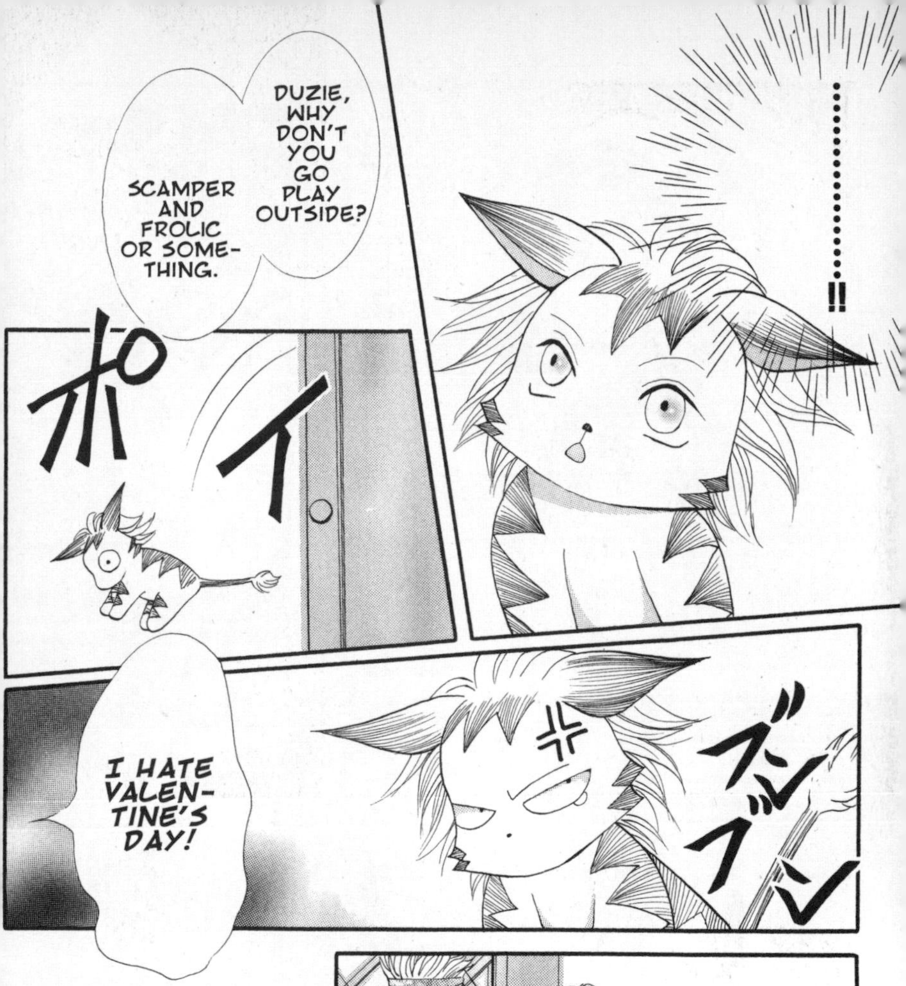
......!!
DUZIE, WHY DON'T YOU GO PLAY OUTSIDE?
SCAMPER AND FROLIC OR SOME-THING.
ポイ
I HATE VALEN-TINE'S DAY!
ブンブン

Jill's Valentine...

(Don't worry, it doesn't involve zombies...)

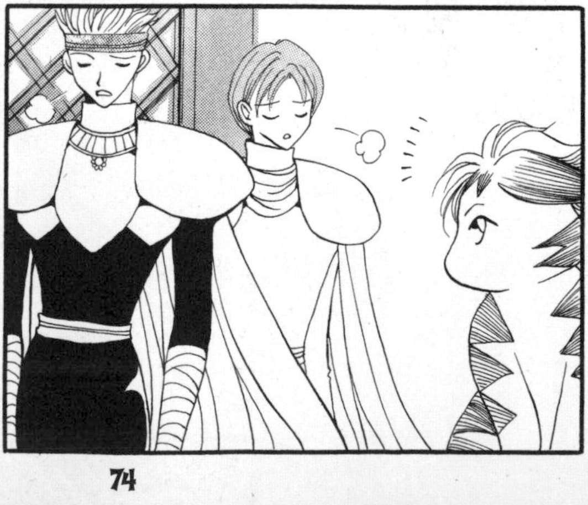

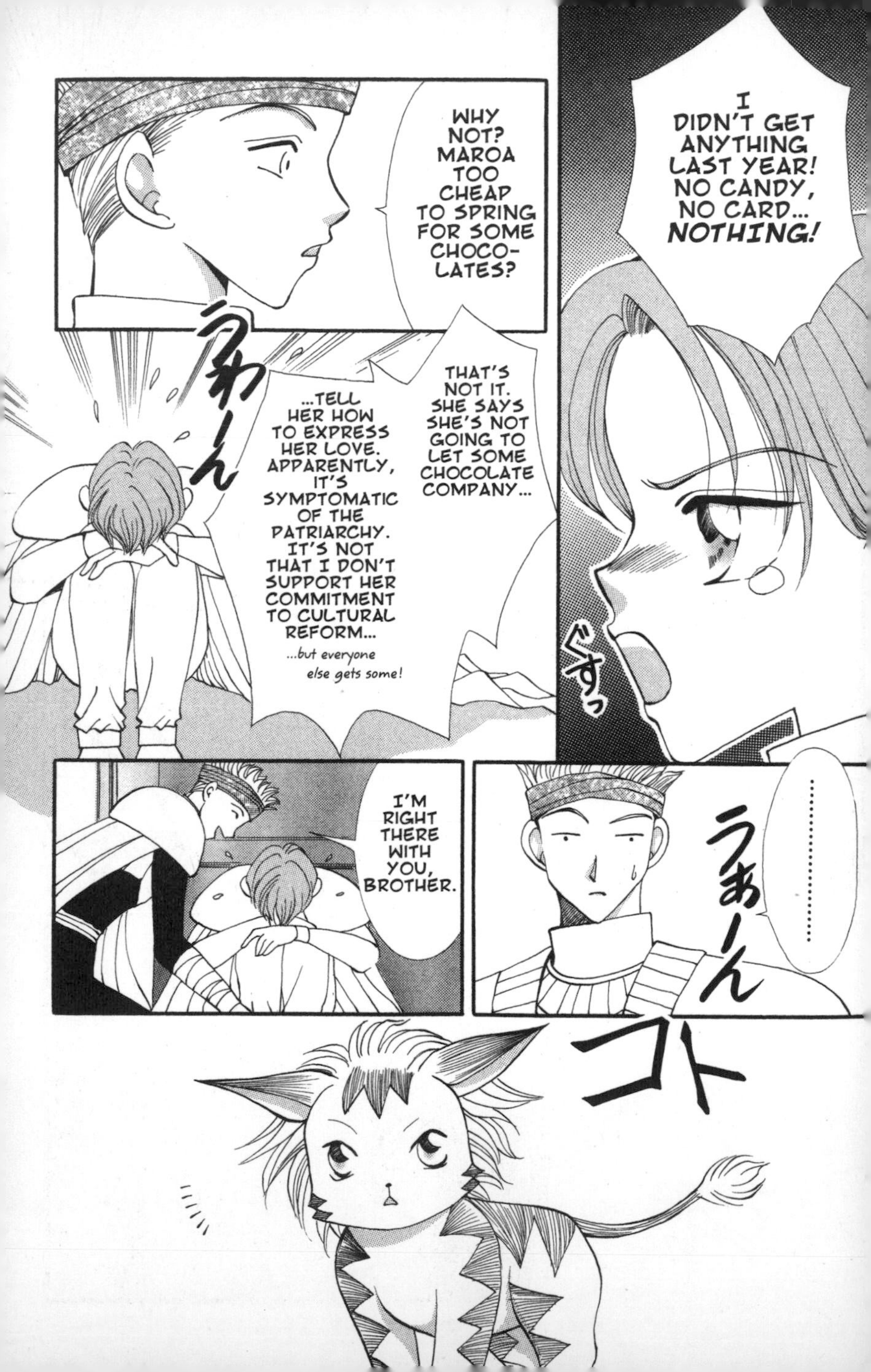
I DIDN'T GET ANYTHING LAST YEAR! NO CANDY, NO CARD... **NOTHING!**
ぐすっ
WHY NOT? MAROA TOO CHEAP TO SPRING FOR SOME CHOCO-LATES?
うわーん
THAT'S NOT IT. SHE SAYS SHE'S NOT GOING TO LET SOME CHOCOLATE COMPANY...
...TELL HER HOW TO EXPRESS HER LOVE. APPARENTLY, IT'S SYMPTOMATIC OF THE PATRIARCHY. IT'S NOT THAT I DON'T SUPPORT HER COMMITMENT TO CULTURAL REFORM...
...but everyone else gets some!
....
うぁーん
I'M RIGHT THERE WITH YOU, BROTHER.
コト

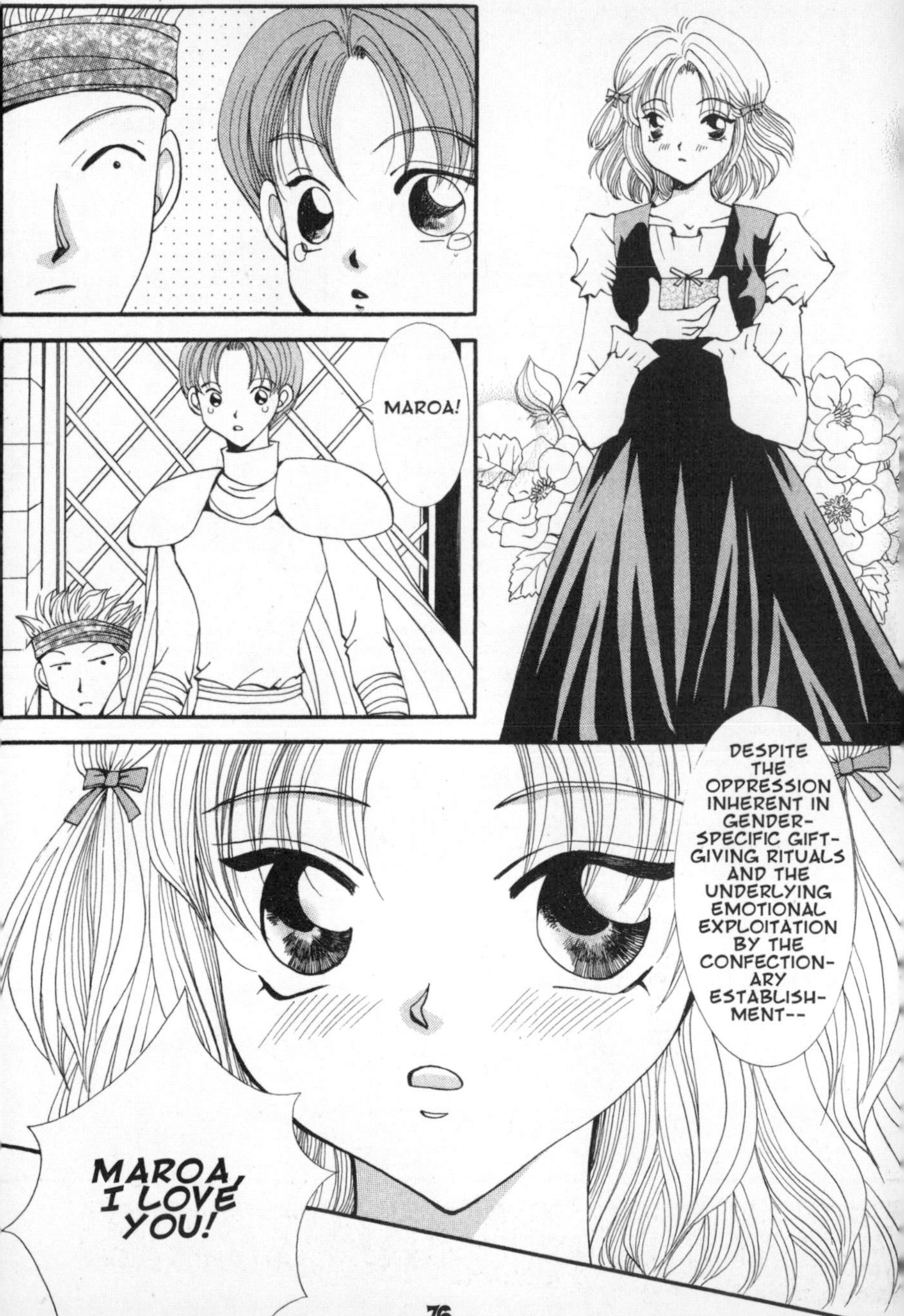
MAROA!
DESPITE THE OPPRESSION INHERENT IN GENDER-SPECIFIC GIFT-GIVING RITUALS AND THE UNDERLYING EMOTIONAL EXPLOITATION BY THE CONFECTIONARY ESTABLISHMENT--
MAROA, I LOVE YOU!

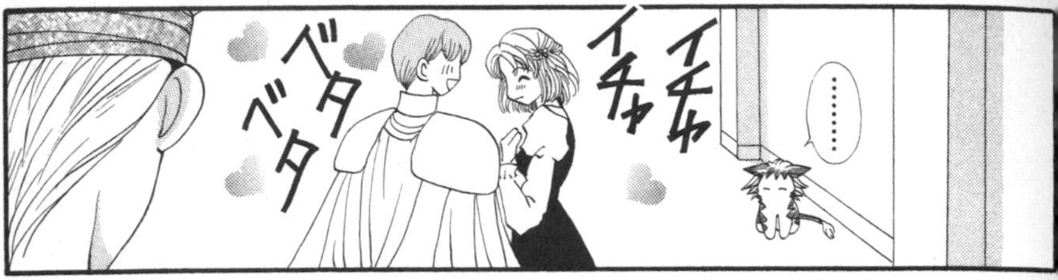
……
イチャイチャ
ベタベタ

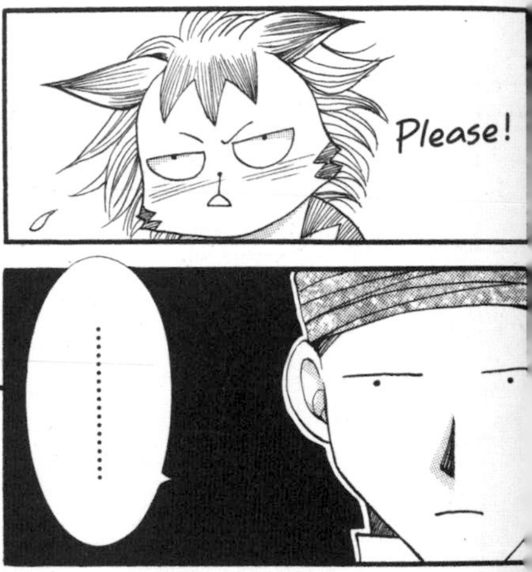
Please!
……

Krai's Valentine
(or lack thereof)...

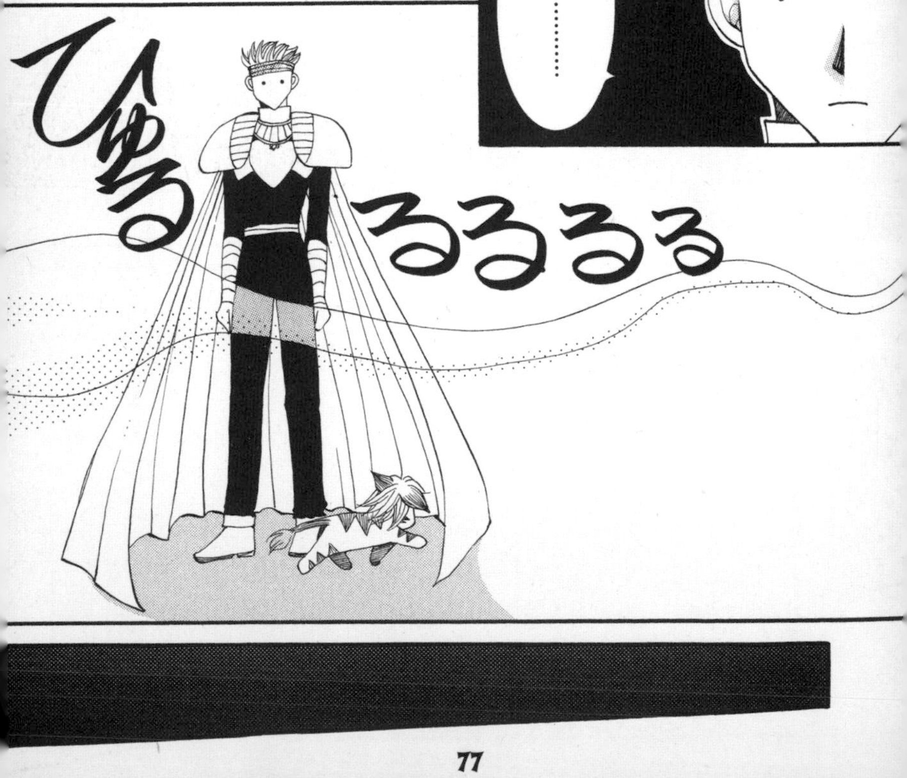
ひゅるるるるるる

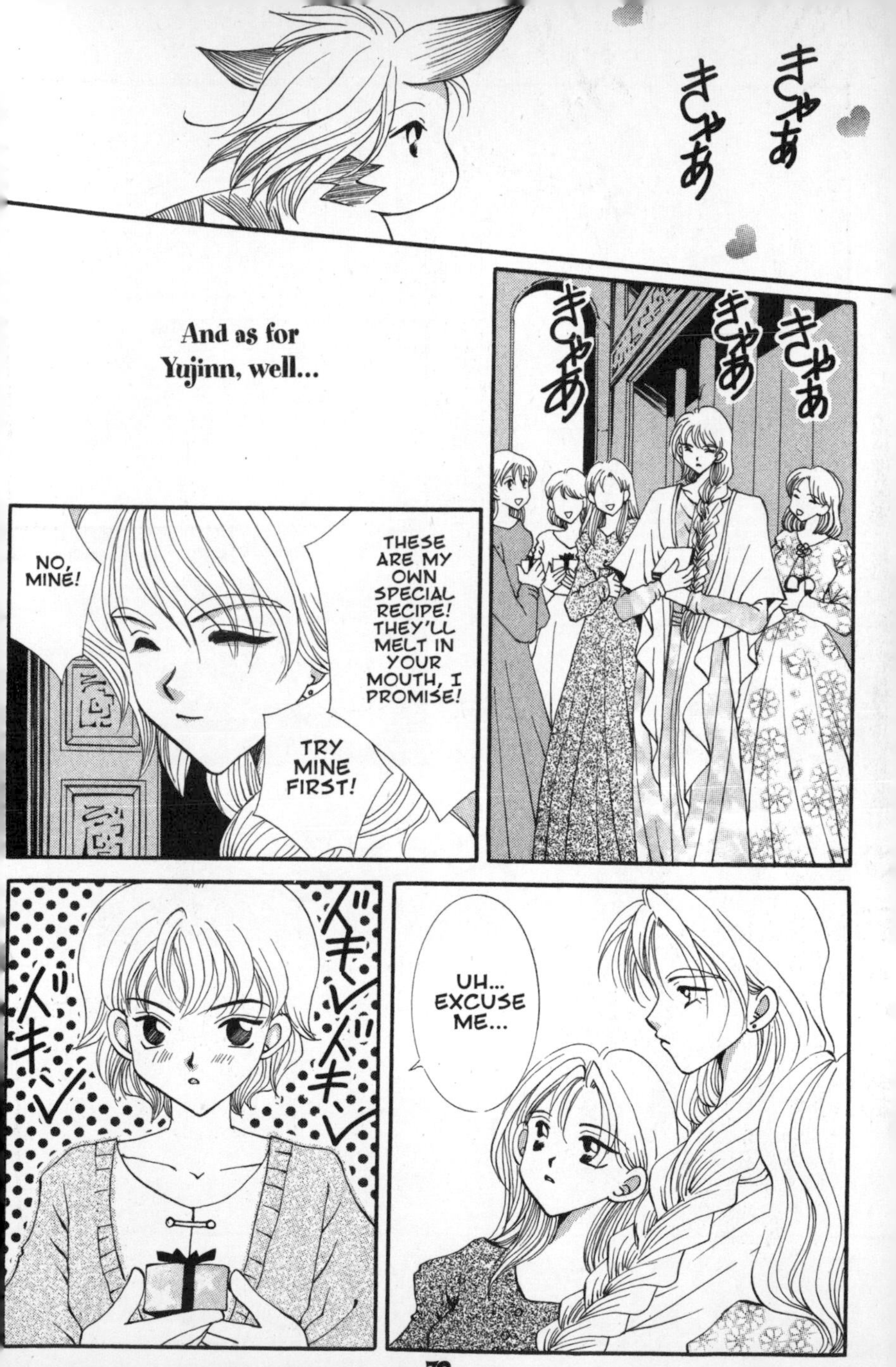
きゃあ きゃあ
きゃあ きゃあ きゃあ
And as for Yujinn, well...
THESE ARE MY OWN SPECIAL RECIPE! THEY'LL MELT IN YOUR MOUTH, I PROMISE!
TRY MINE FIRST!
NO, MINÉ!
UH... EXCUSE ME...
ドキン ドキン

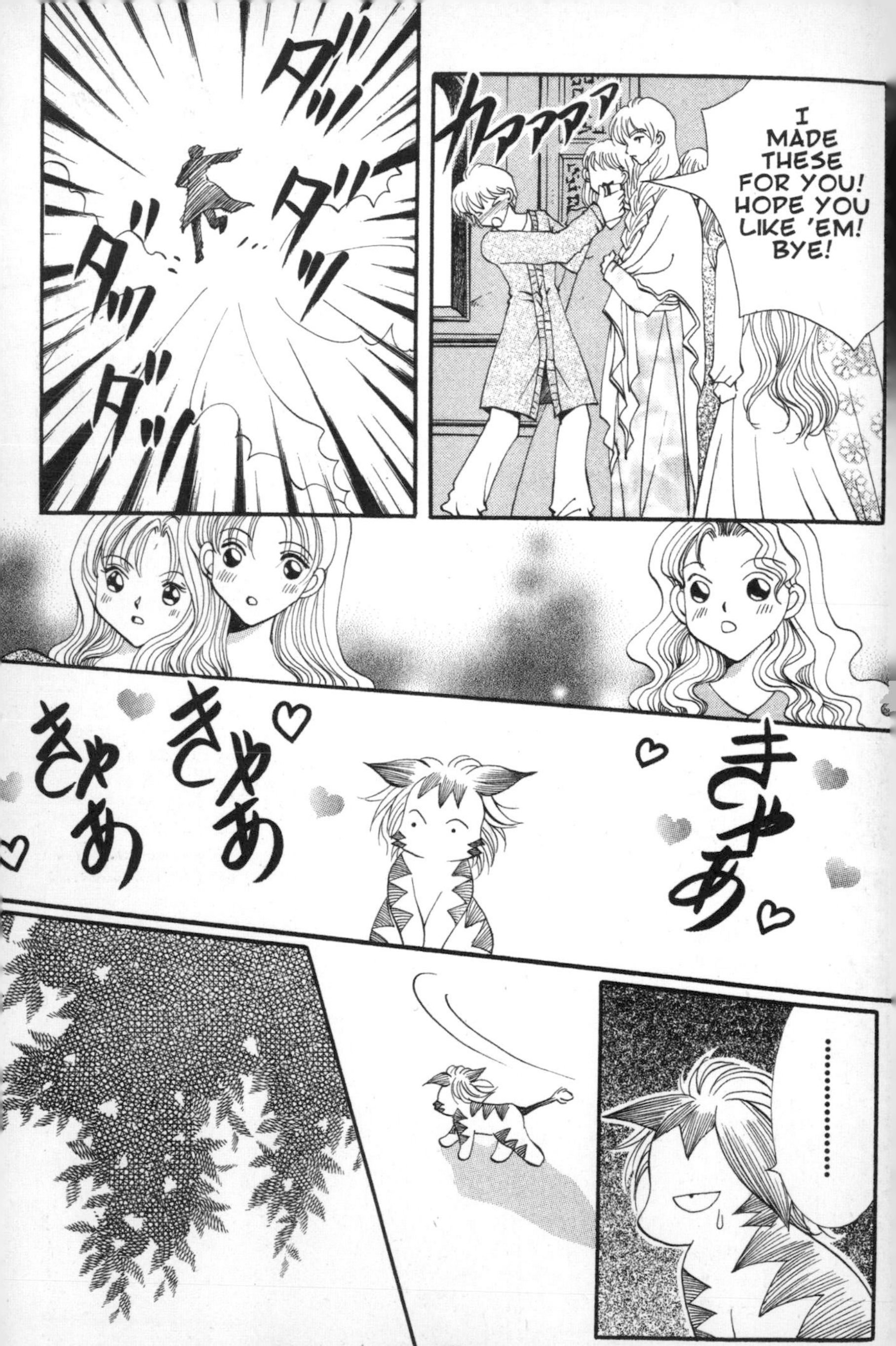

I MADE THESE FOR YOU! HOPE YOU LIKE 'EM! BYE!
カァァァァ
ダッ ダッ ダッ ダッ ダッ
きゃあ
きゃあ
....

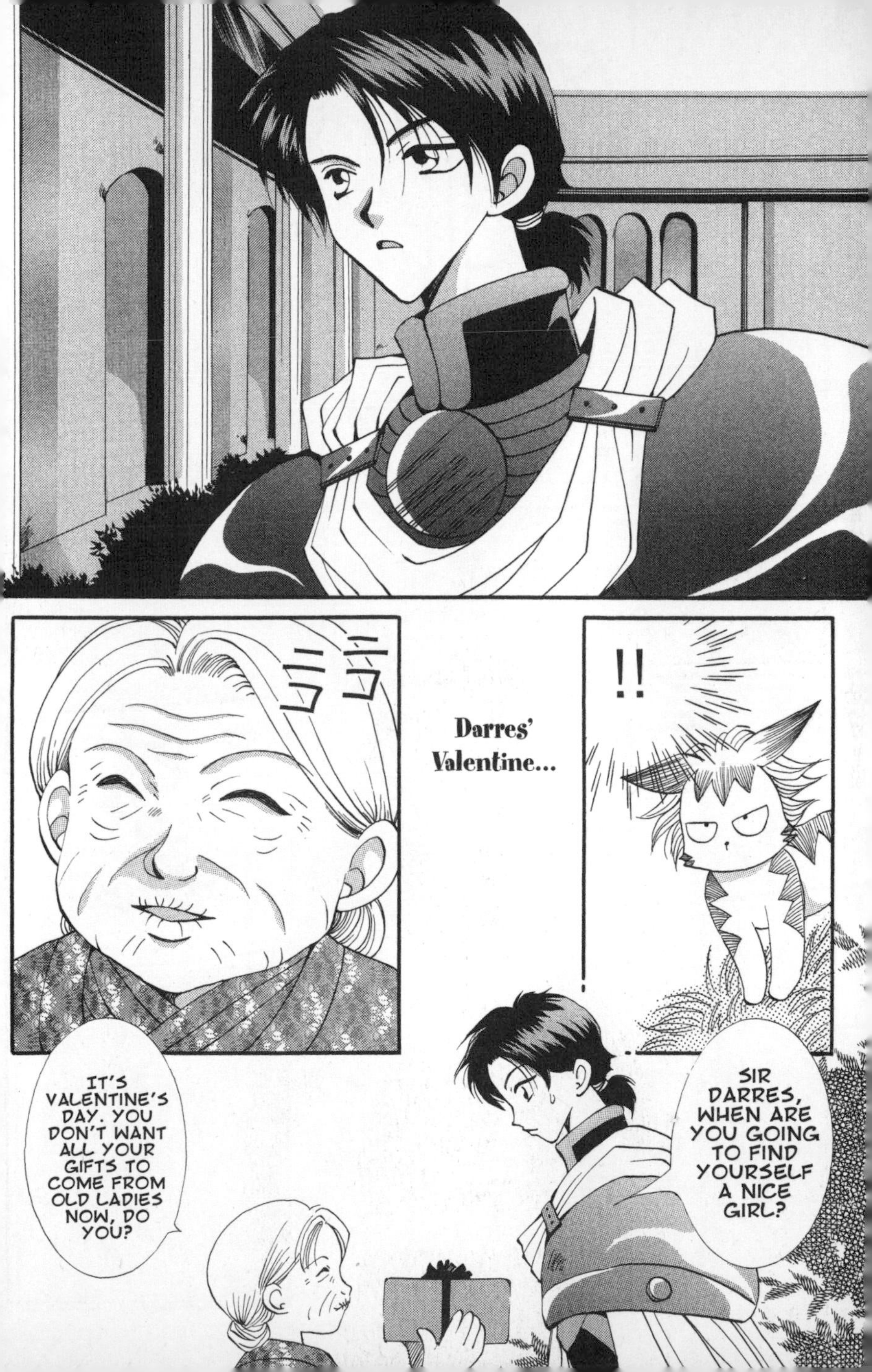
!!
Darres' Valentine...
SIR DARRES, WHEN ARE YOU GOING TO FIND YOURSELF A NICE GIRL?
IT'S VALENTINE'S DAY. YOU DON'T WANT ALL YOUR GIFTS TO COME FROM OLD LADIES NOW, DO YOU?

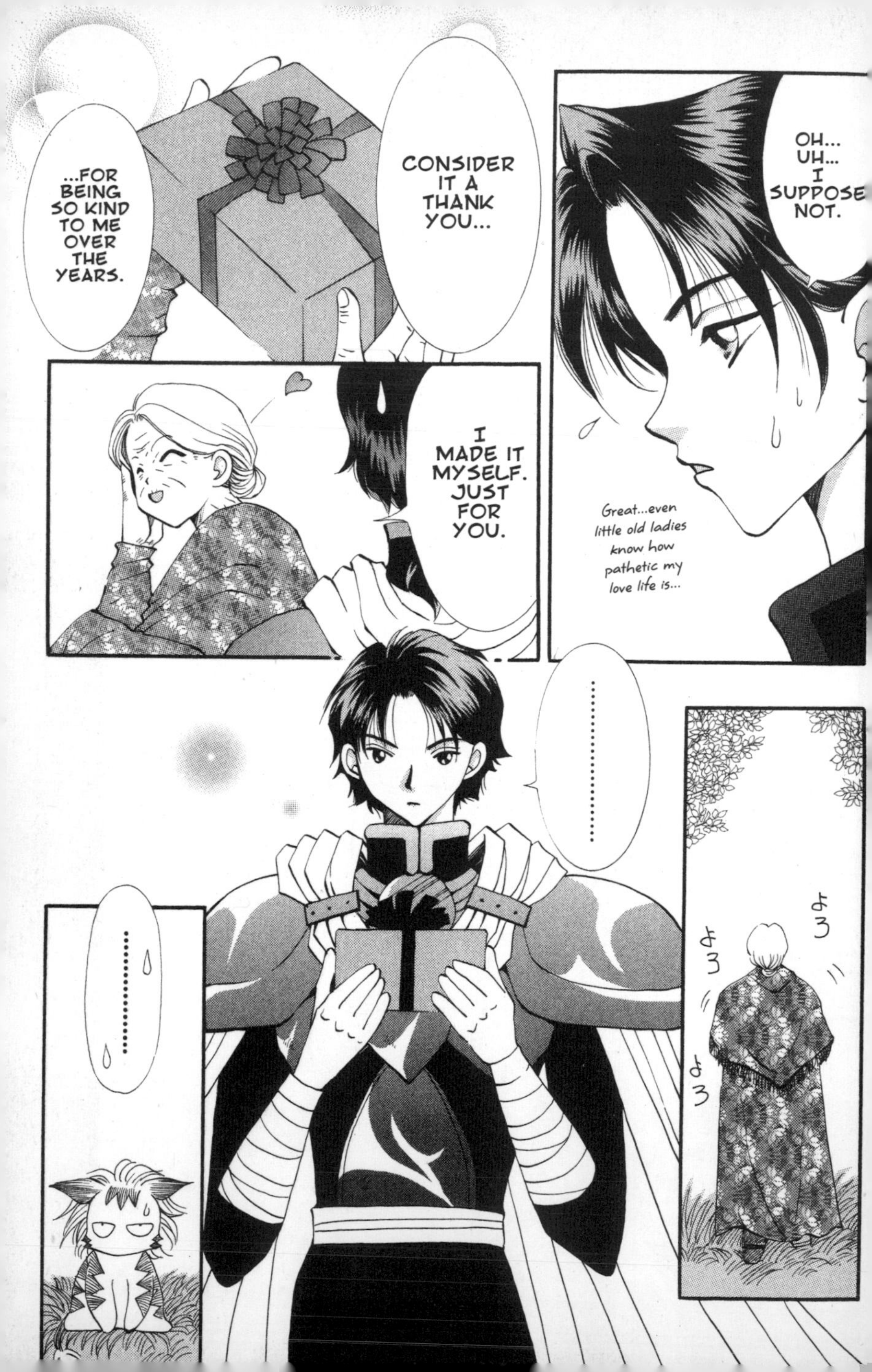
OH... UH... I SUPPOSE NOT.
Great...even little old ladies know how pathetic my love life is...
CONSIDER IT A THANK YOU...
...FOR BEING SO KIND TO ME OVER THE YEARS.
I MADE IT MYSELF. JUST FOR YOU.
よろ
よろ
よろ
......
......

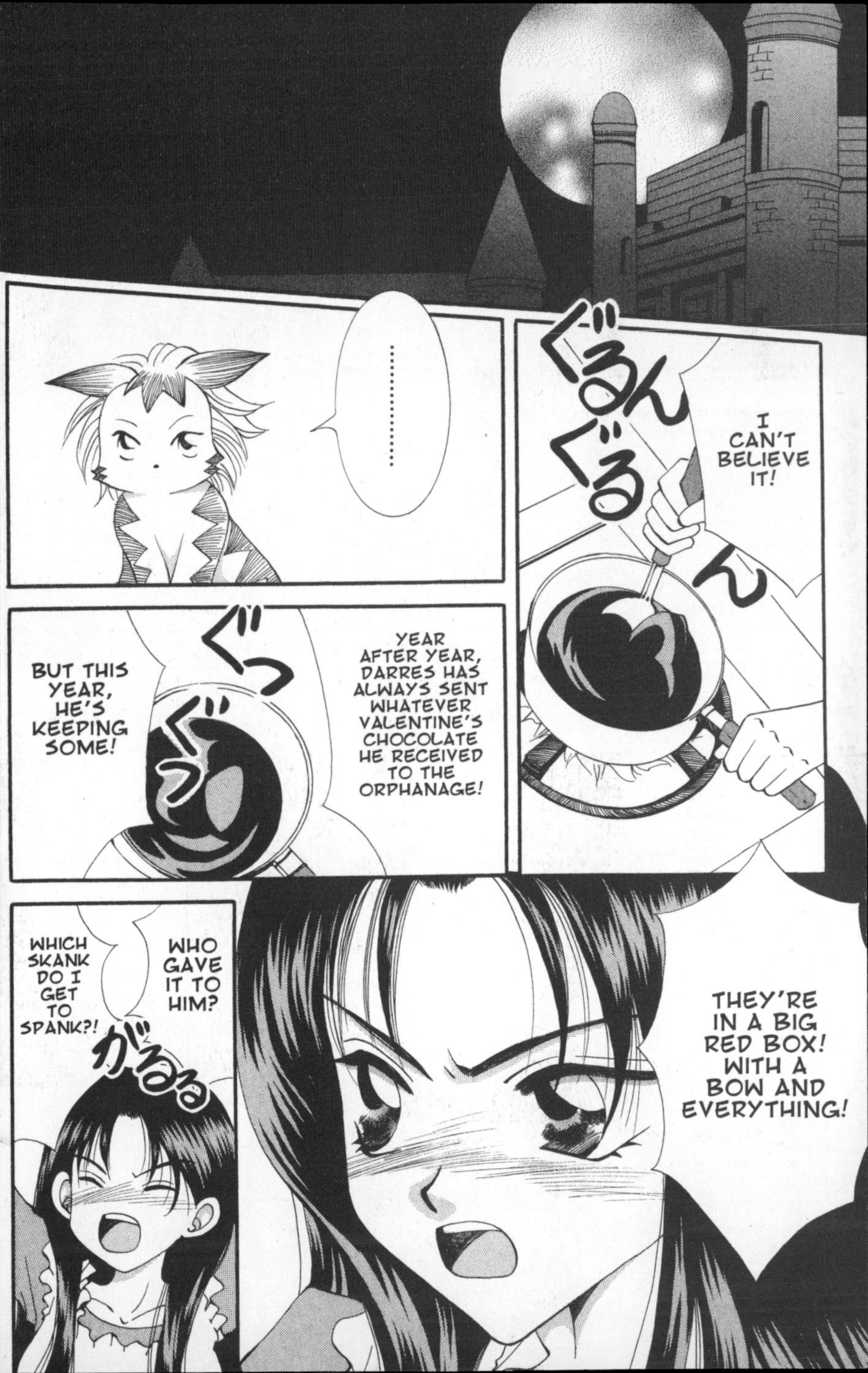
ぐるんぐるん
I CAN'T BELIEVE IT!
......
YEAR AFTER YEAR, DARRES HAS ALWAYS SENT WHATEVER VALENTINE'S CHOCOLATE HE RECEIVED TO THE ORPHANAGE!
ぐつぐつ
BUT THIS YEAR, HE'S KEEPING SOME!
THEY'RE IN A BIG RED BOX! WITH A BOW AND EVERYTHING!
WHO GAVE IT TO HIM?
WHICH SKANK DO I GET TO SPANK?!
がるる

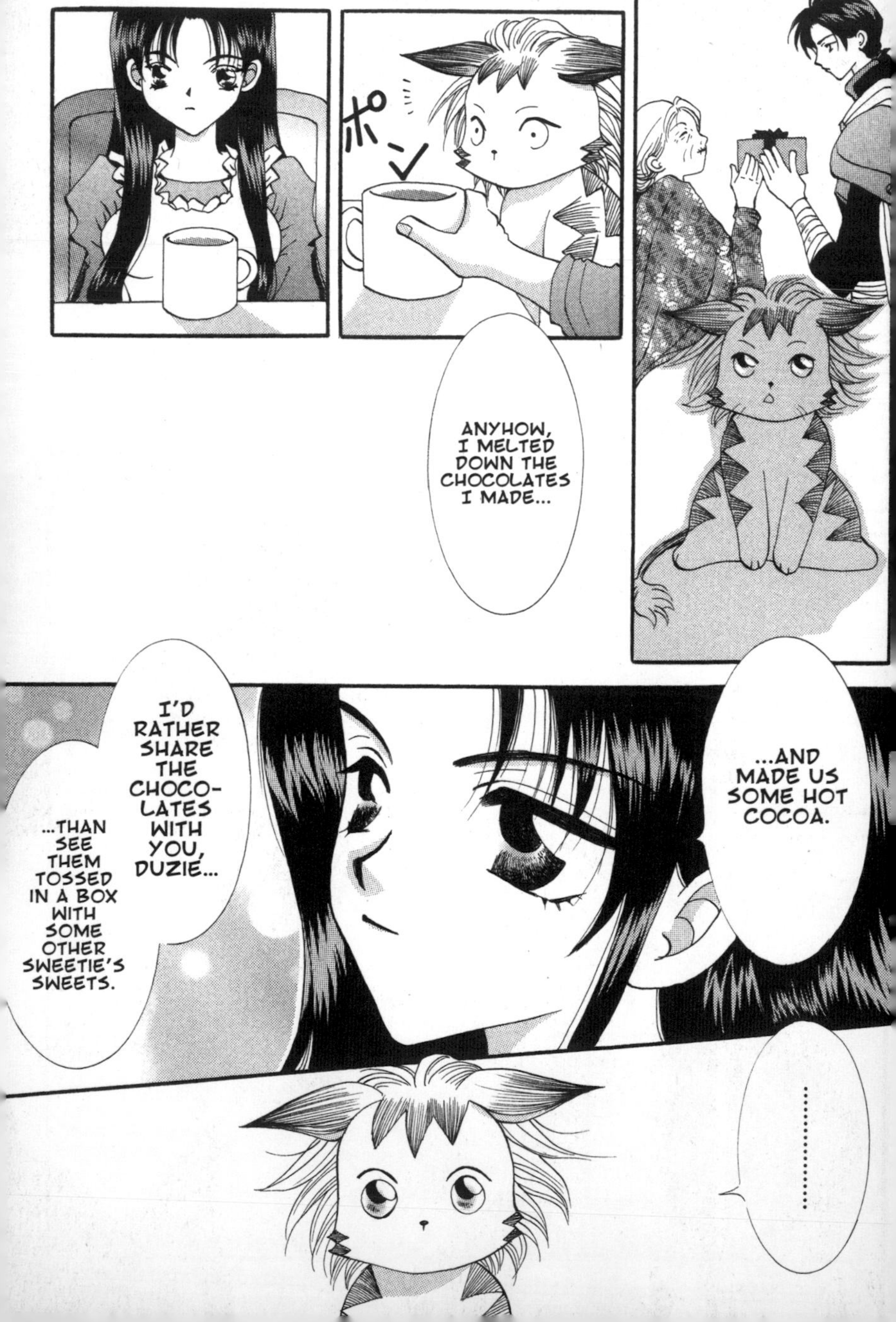
ポン
ANYHOW, I MELTED DOWN THE CHOCOLATES I MADE...
...AND MADE US SOME HOT COCOA.
I'D RATHER SHARE THE CHOCO-LATES WITH YOU, DUZIE...
...THAN SEE THEM TOSSED IN A BOX WITH SOME OTHER SWEETIE'S SWEETS.
......

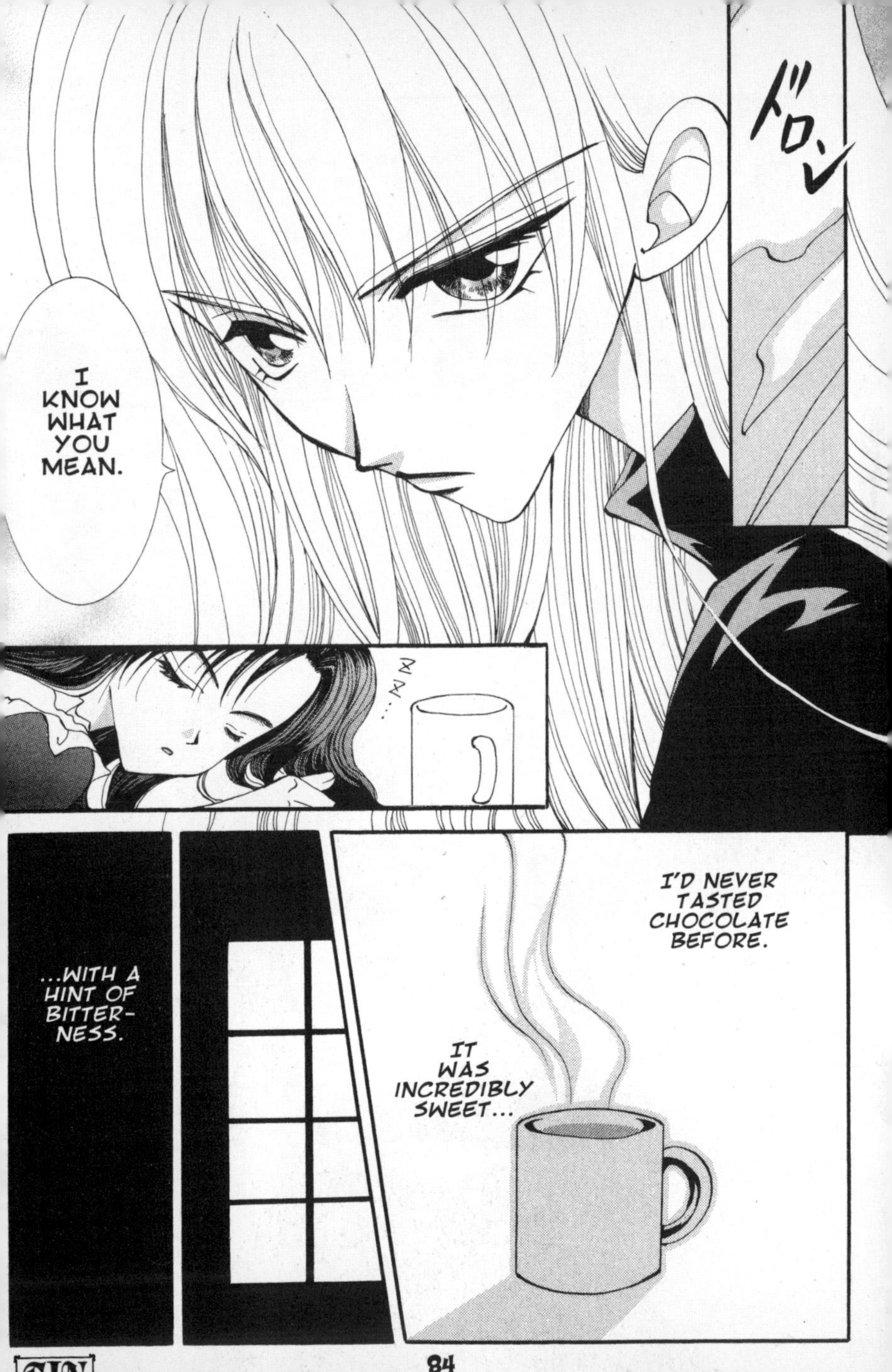
ドロン
I KNOW WHAT YOU MEAN.
I'D NEVER TASTED CHOCOLATE BEFORE.
IT WAS INCREDIBLY SWEET...
...WITH A HINT OF BITTER-NESS.

FIN

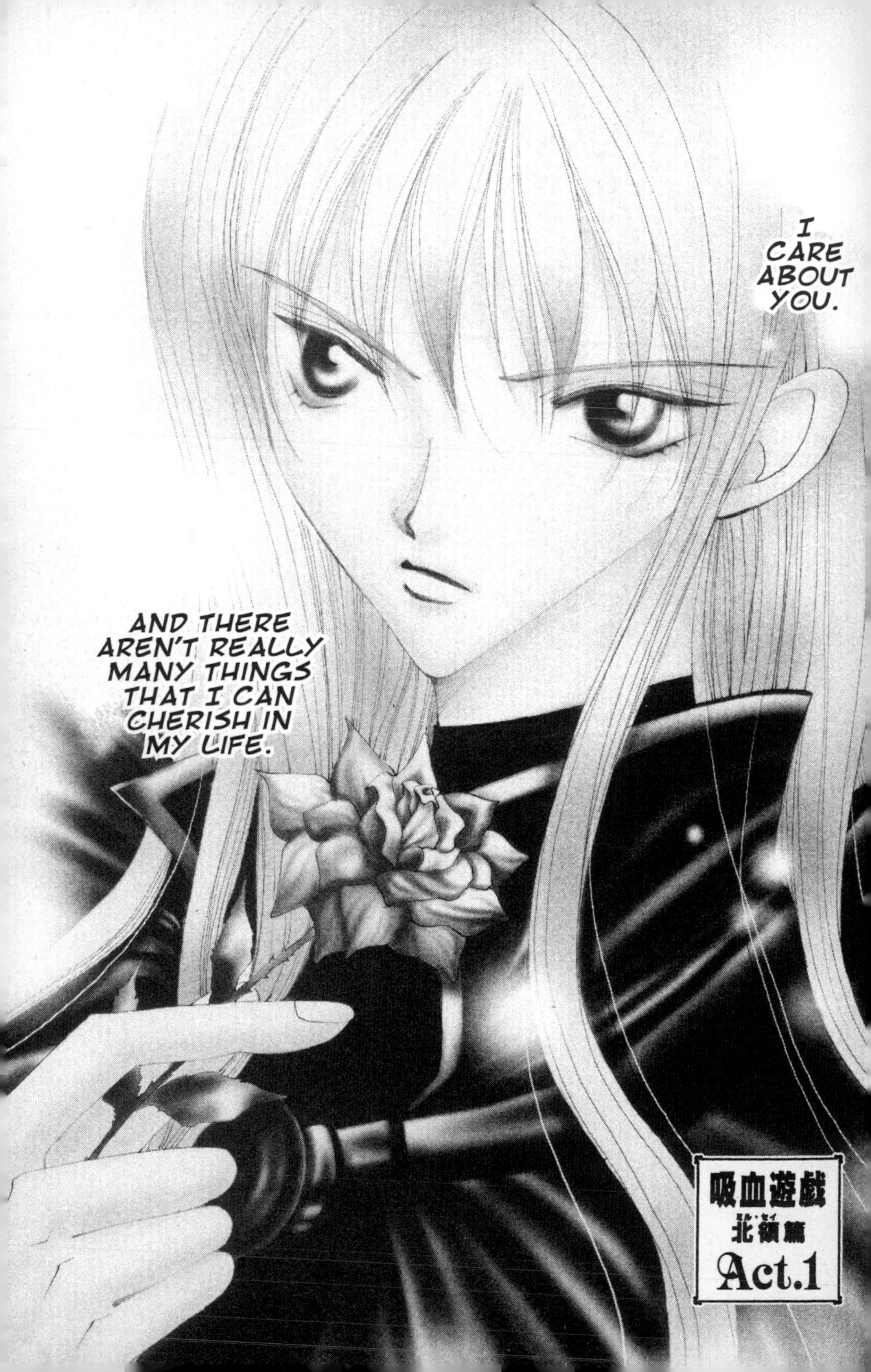
I CARE ABOUT YOU.
AND THERE AREN'T REALLY MANY THINGS THAT I CAN CHERISH IN MY LIFE.
吸血遊戯
北領篇
Act.1

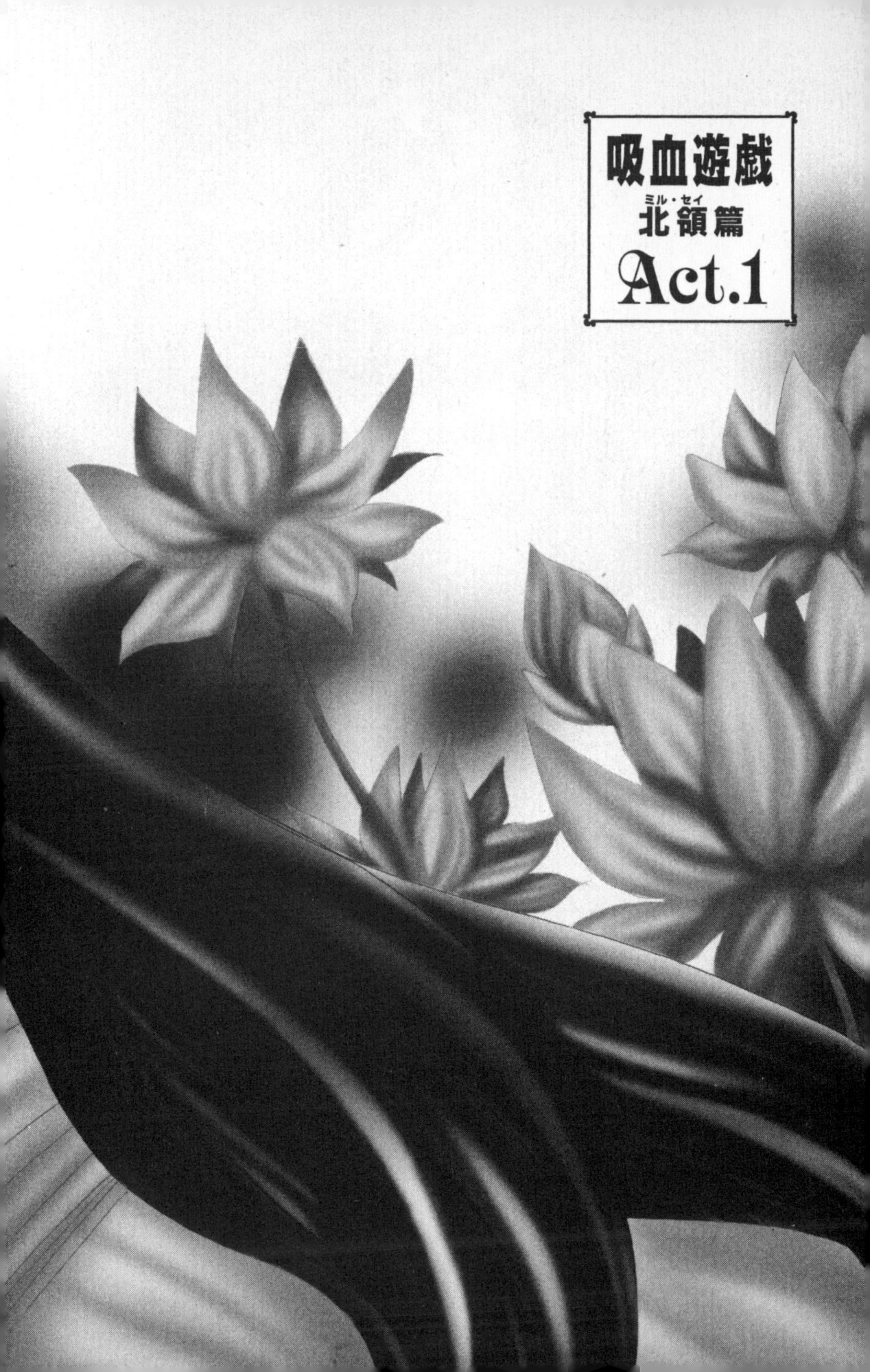
吸血遊戯
ミル・セイ
北領篇
Act.1

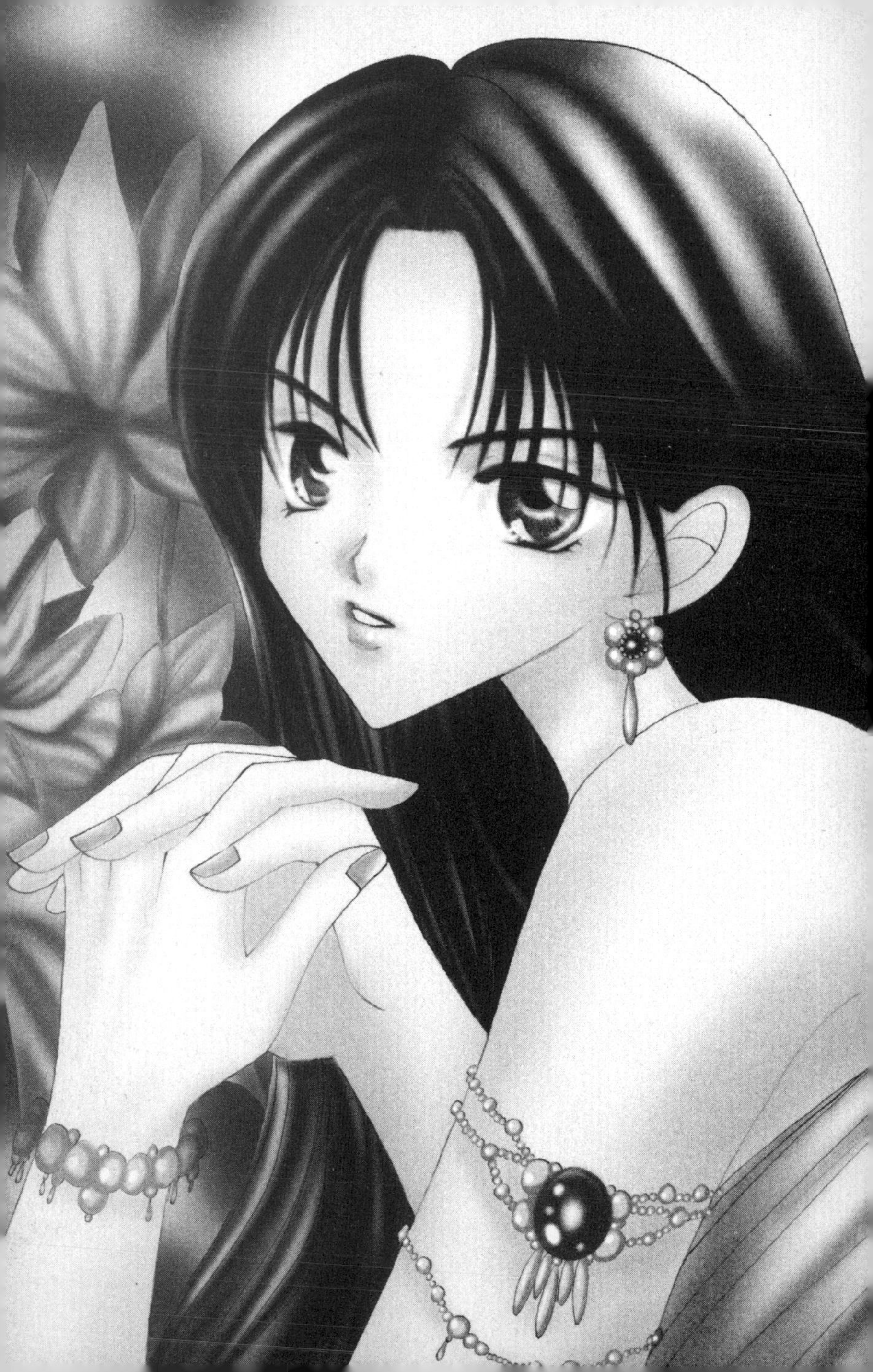

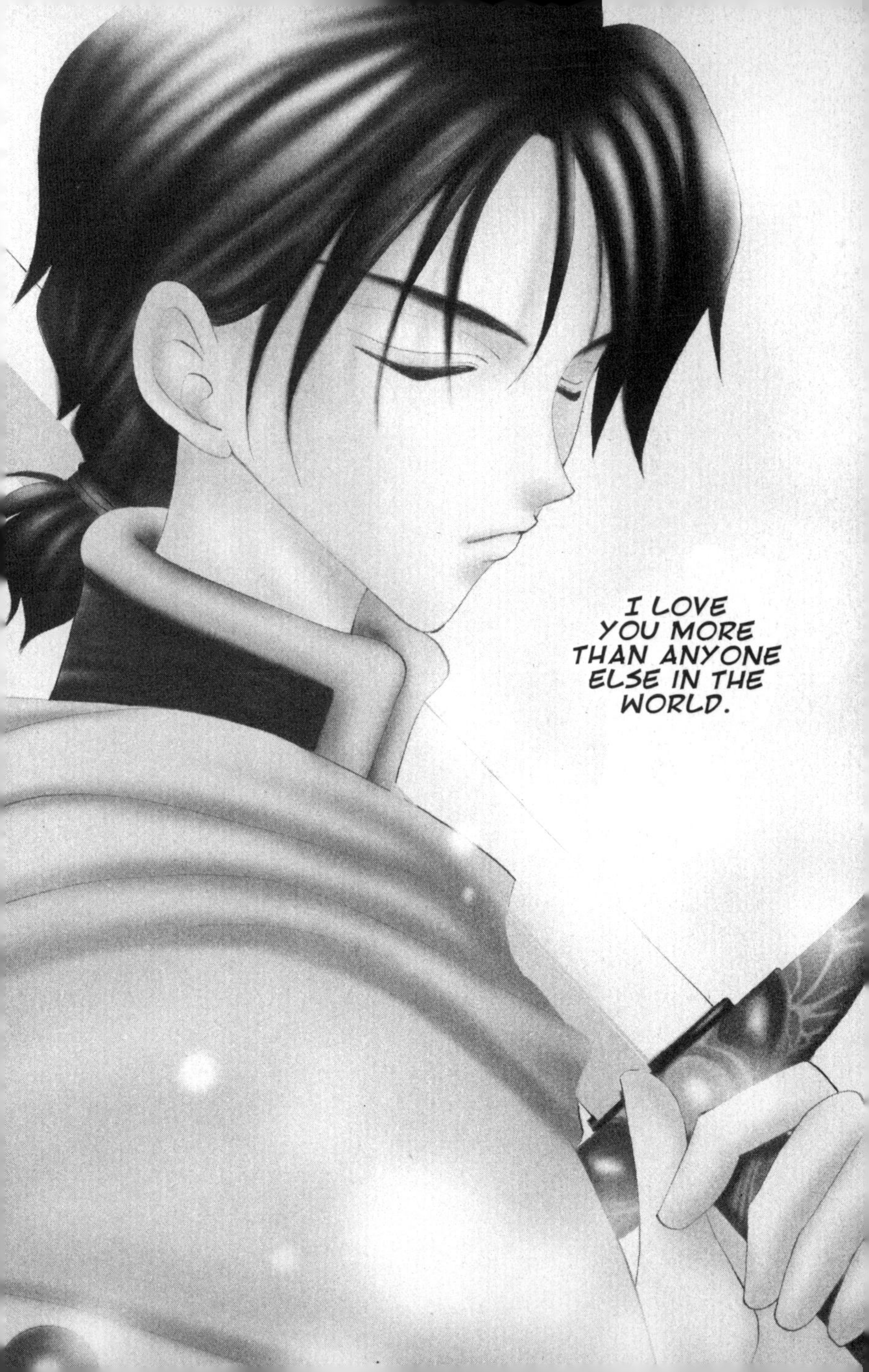
I LOVE YOU MORE THAN ANYONE ELSE IN THE WORLD.

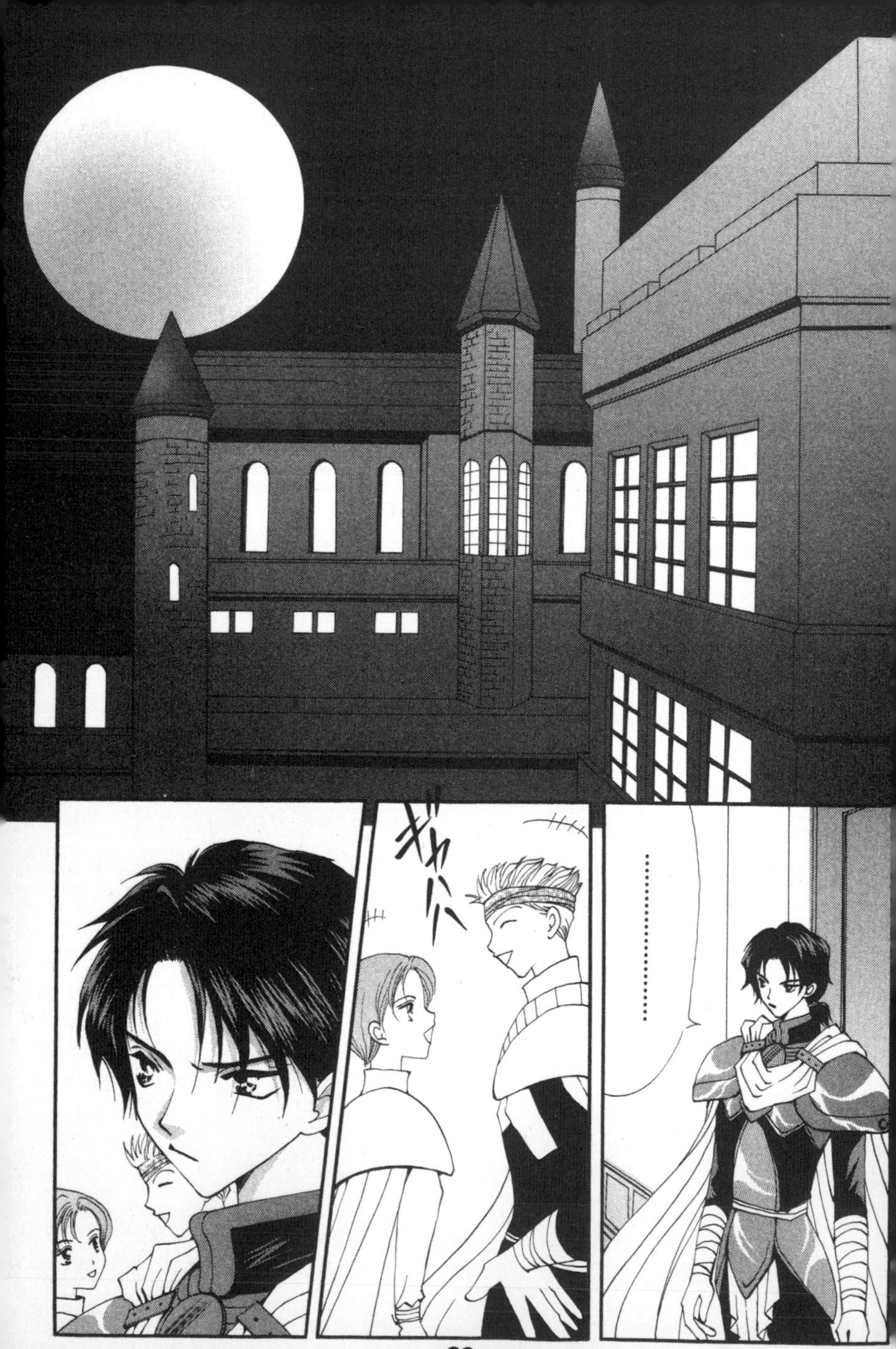
……
ギャハハ

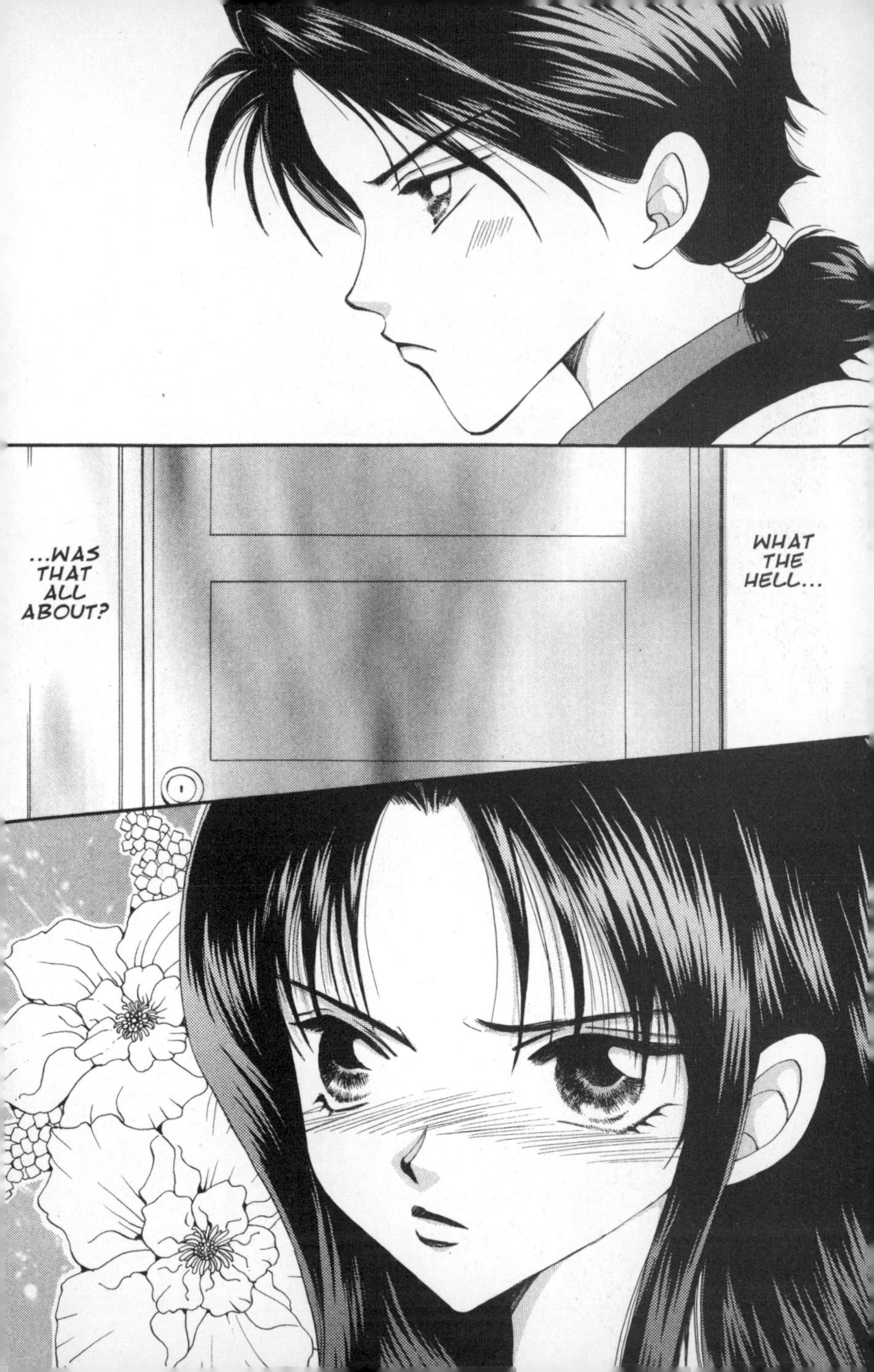
WHAT THE HELL...
...WAS THAT ALL ABOUT?

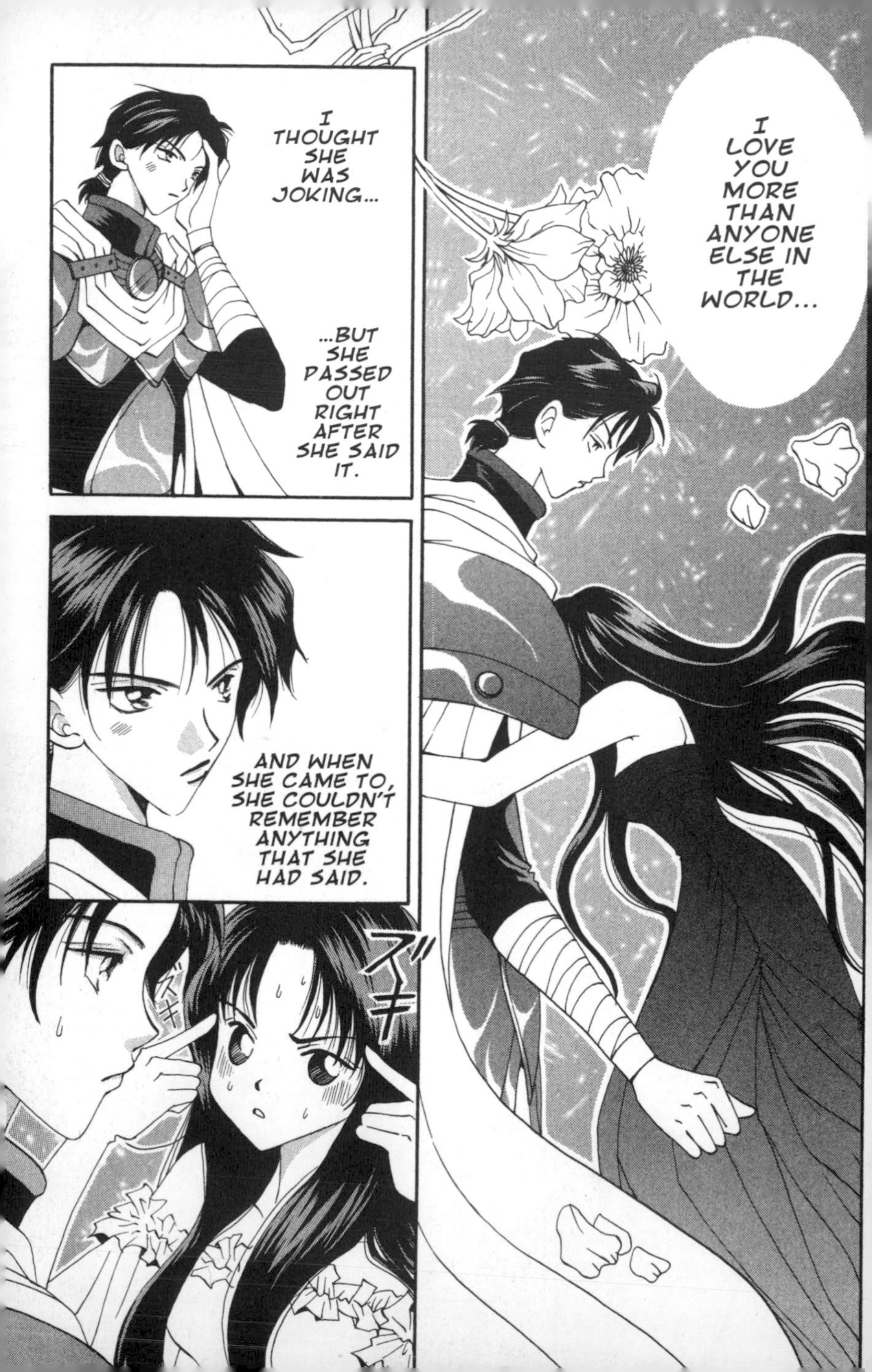
I LOVE YOU MORE THAN ANYONE ELSE IN THE WORLD...
I THOUGHT SHE WAS JOKING...
...BUT SHE PASSED OUT RIGHT AFTER SHE SAID IT.
AND WHEN SHE CAME TO, SHE COULDN'T REMEMBER ANYTHING THAT SHE HAD SAID.
ズキ
ズキ

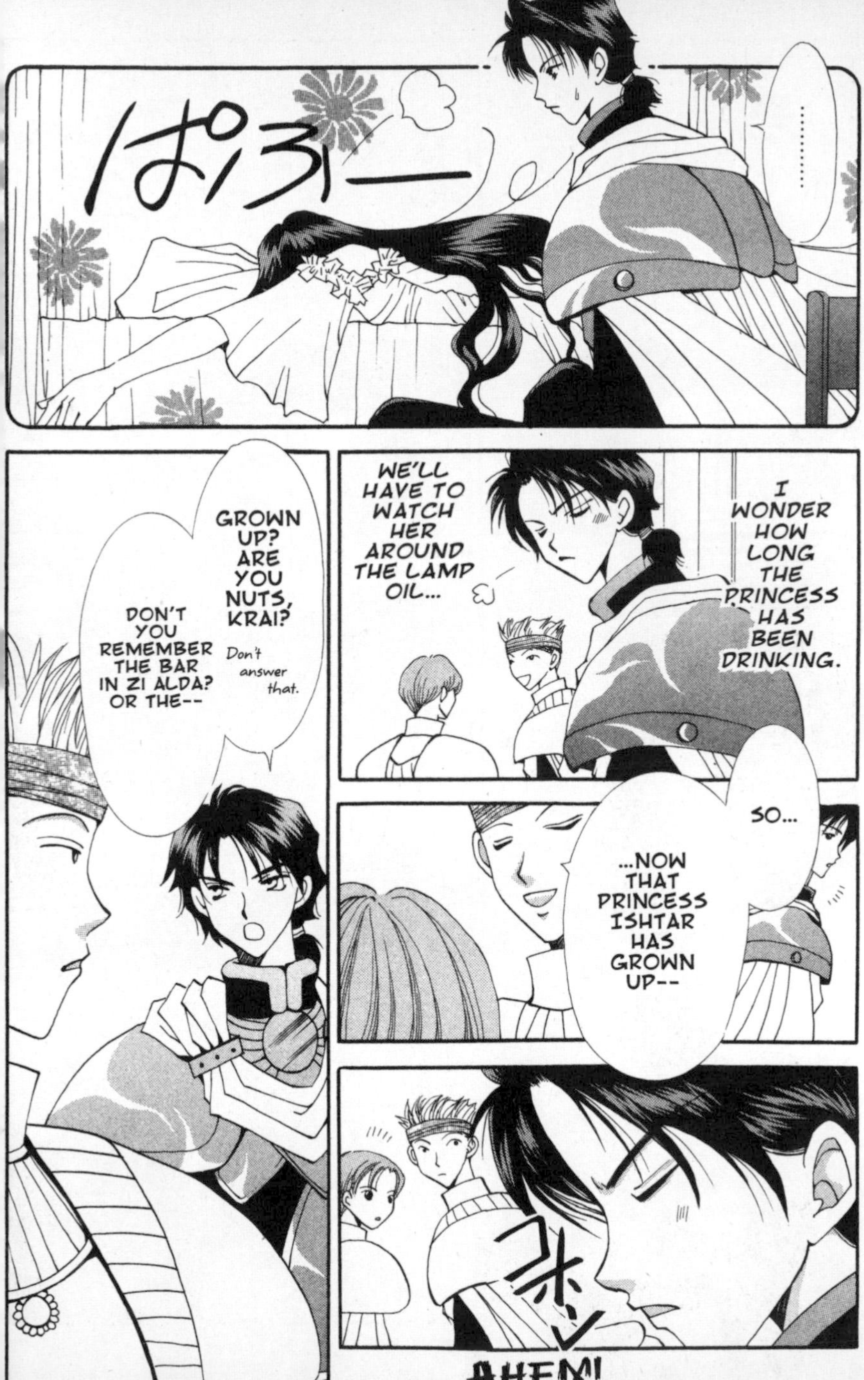
ぱふー
......
I WONDER HOW LONG THE PRINCESS HAS BEEN DRINKING.
WE'LL HAVE TO WATCH HER AROUND THE LAMP OIL...
SO...
...NOW THAT PRINCESS ISHTAR HAS GROWN UP--
コホン
AHEM!
GROWN UP? ARE YOU NUTS, KRAI?
DON'T YOU REMEMBER THE BAR IN ZI ALDA? OR THE--
Don't answer that.

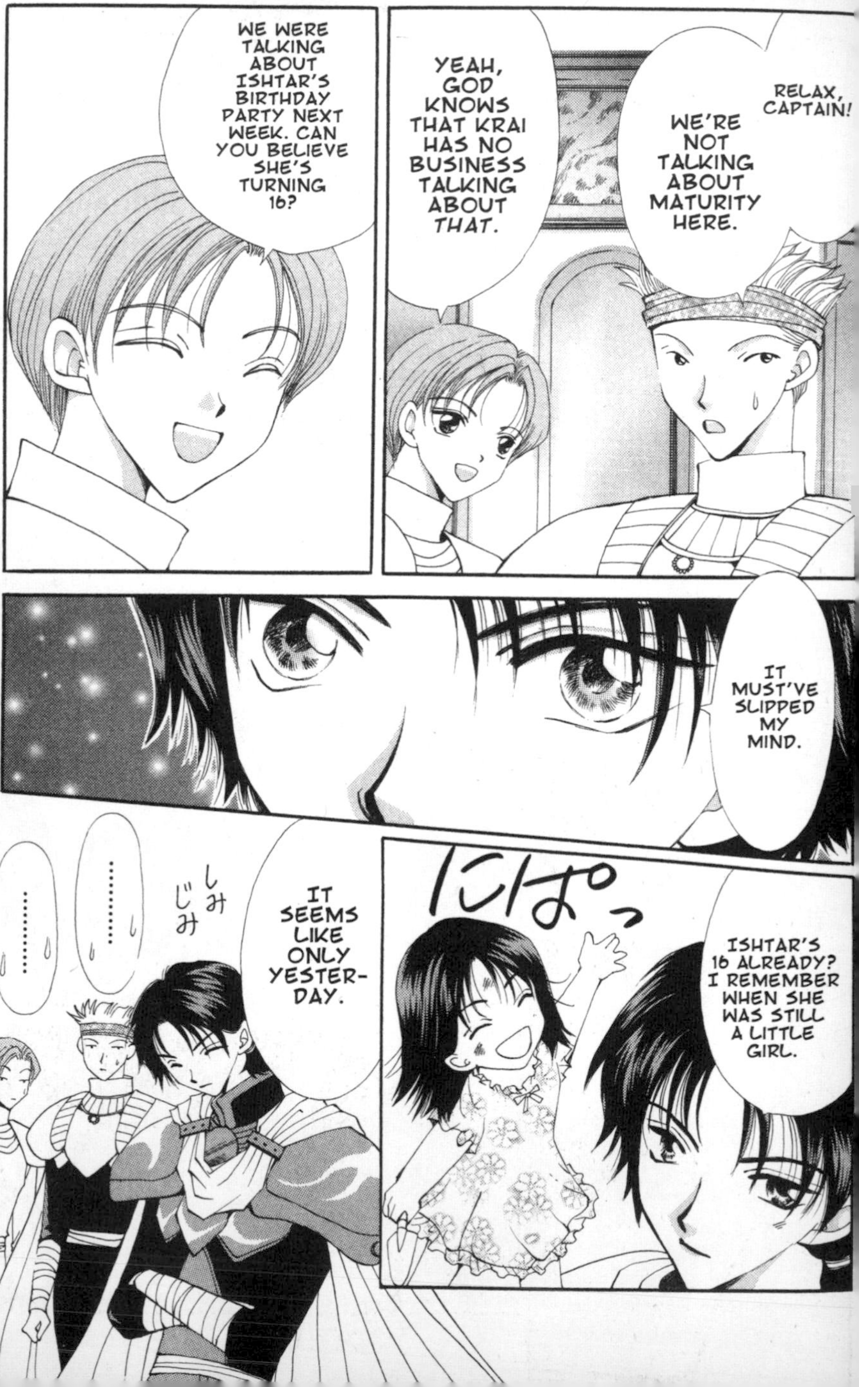
RELAX, CAPTAIN!
WE'RE NOT TALKING ABOUT MATURITY HERE.
YEAH, GOD KNOWS THAT KRAI HAS NO BUSINESS TALKING ABOUT *THAT*.
WE WERE TALKING ABOUT ISHTAR'S BIRTHDAY PARTY NEXT WEEK. CAN YOU BELIEVE SHE'S TURNING 16?
IT MUST'VE SLIPPED MY MIND.
にぱっ
ISHTAR'S 16 ALREADY? I REMEMBER WHEN SHE WAS STILL A LITTLE GIRL.
IT SEEMS LIKE ONLY YESTER-DAY.
しみじみ
......
......

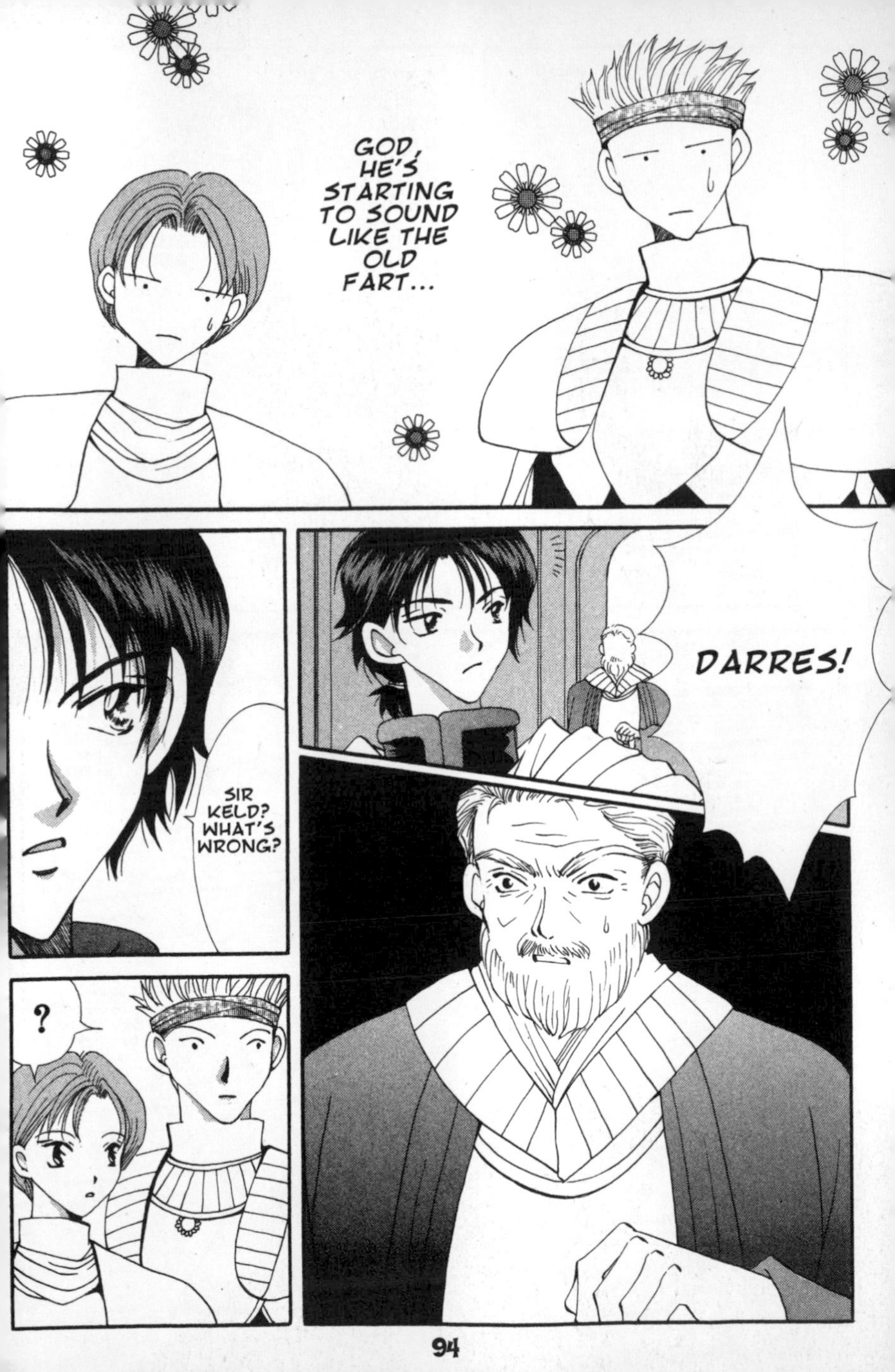
GOD, HE'S STARTING TO SOUND LIKE THE OLD FART...
DARRES!
SIR KELD? WHAT'S WRONG?
?

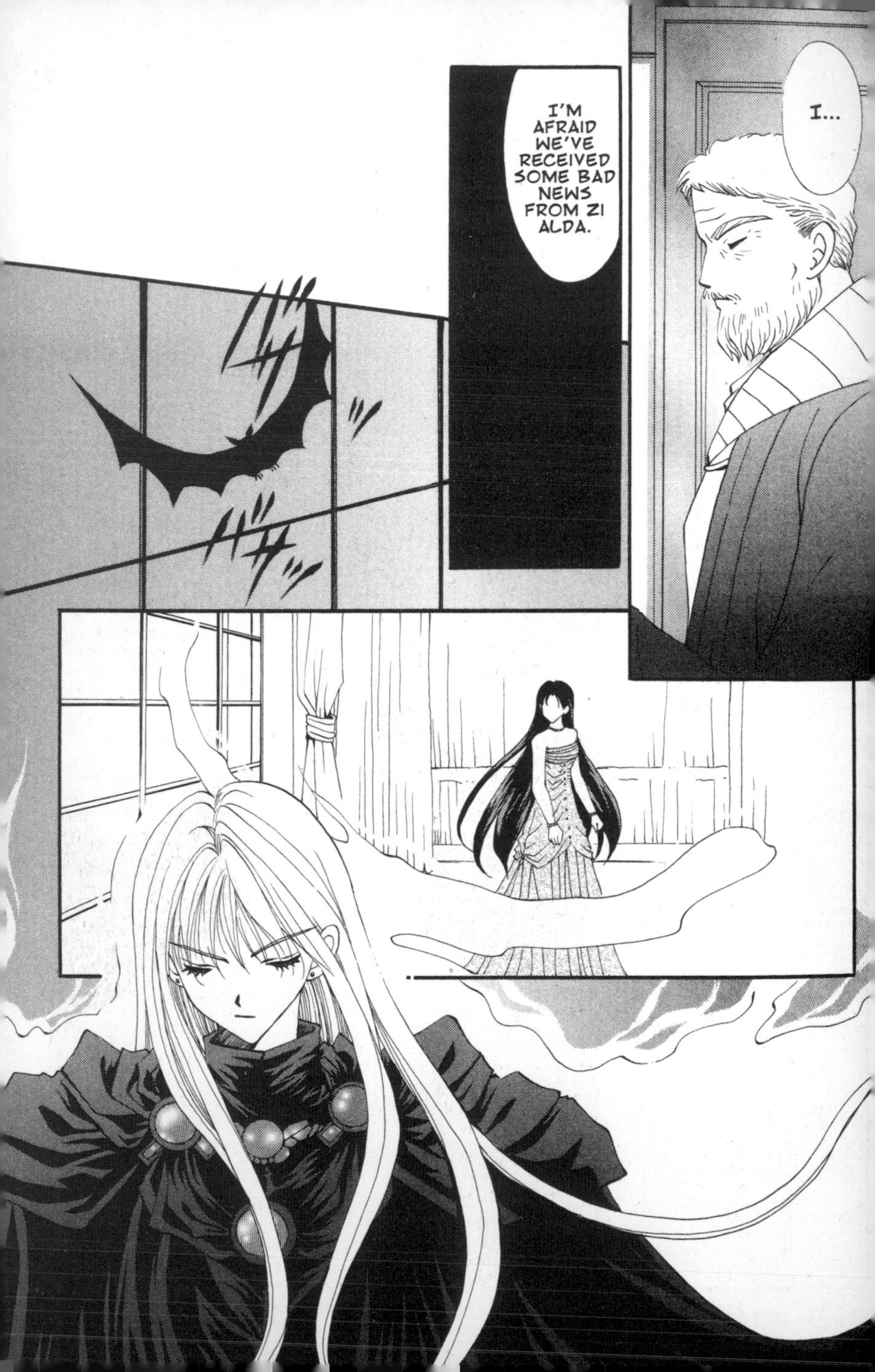

... I...
I'M AFRAID WE'VE RECEIVED SOME BAD NEWS FROM ZI ALDA.

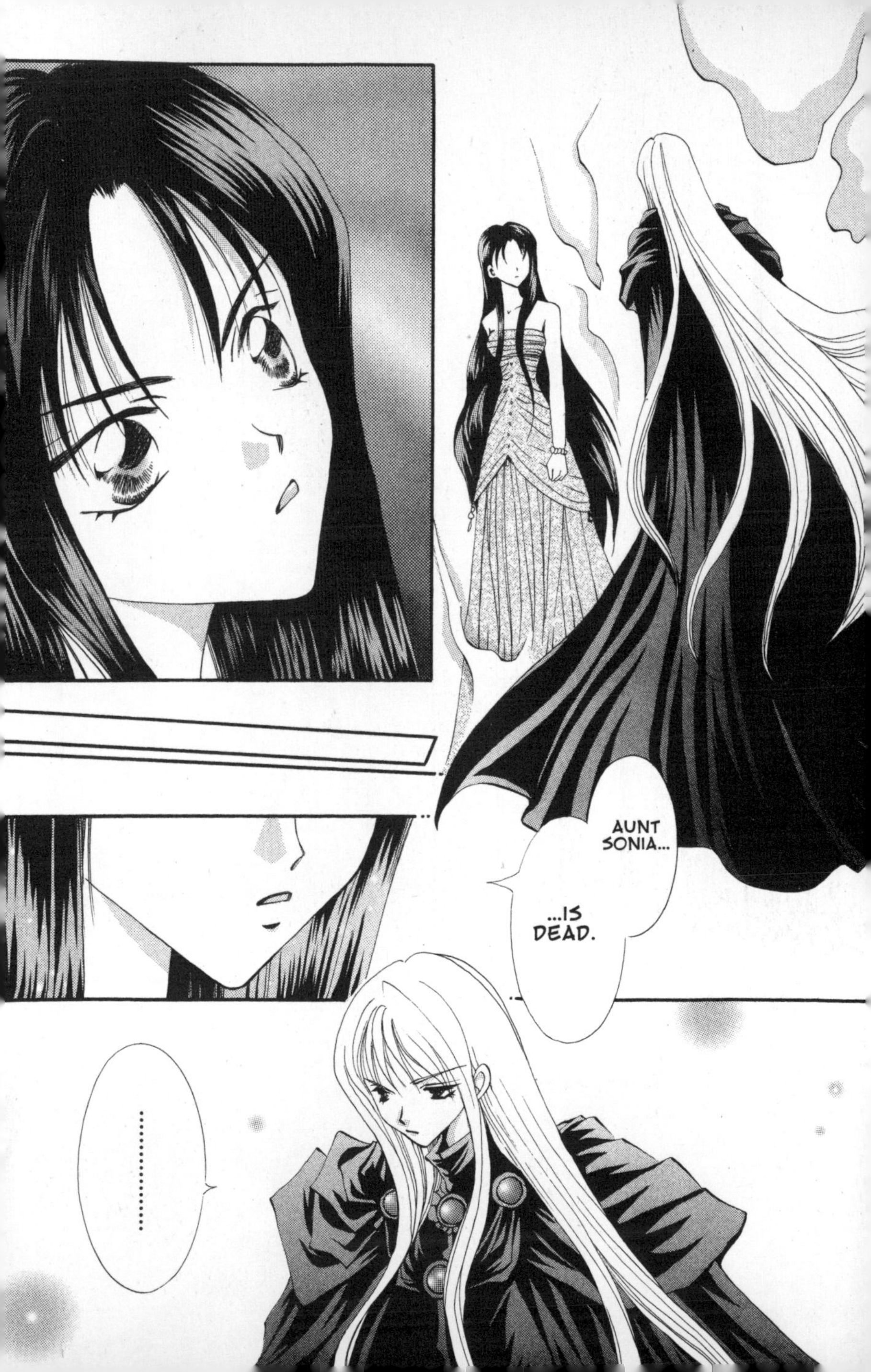
AUNT SONIA...
...IS DEAD.
....

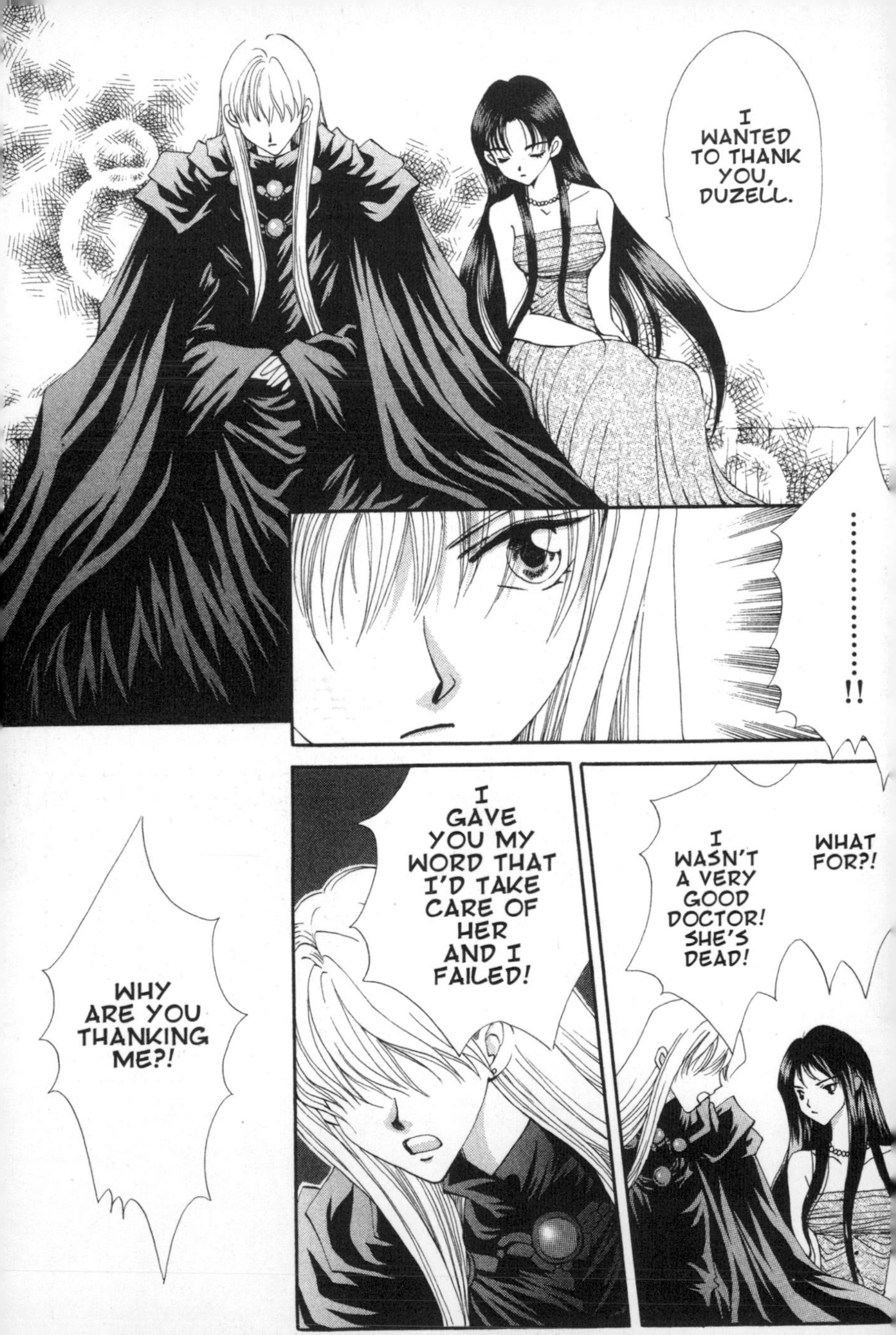
I WANTED TO THANK YOU, DUZELL.
......!!
WHAT FOR?!
I WASN'T A VERY GOOD DOCTOR! SHE'S DEAD!
I GAVE YOU MY WORD THAT I'D TAKE CARE OF HER AND I FAILED!
WHY ARE YOU THANKING ME?!

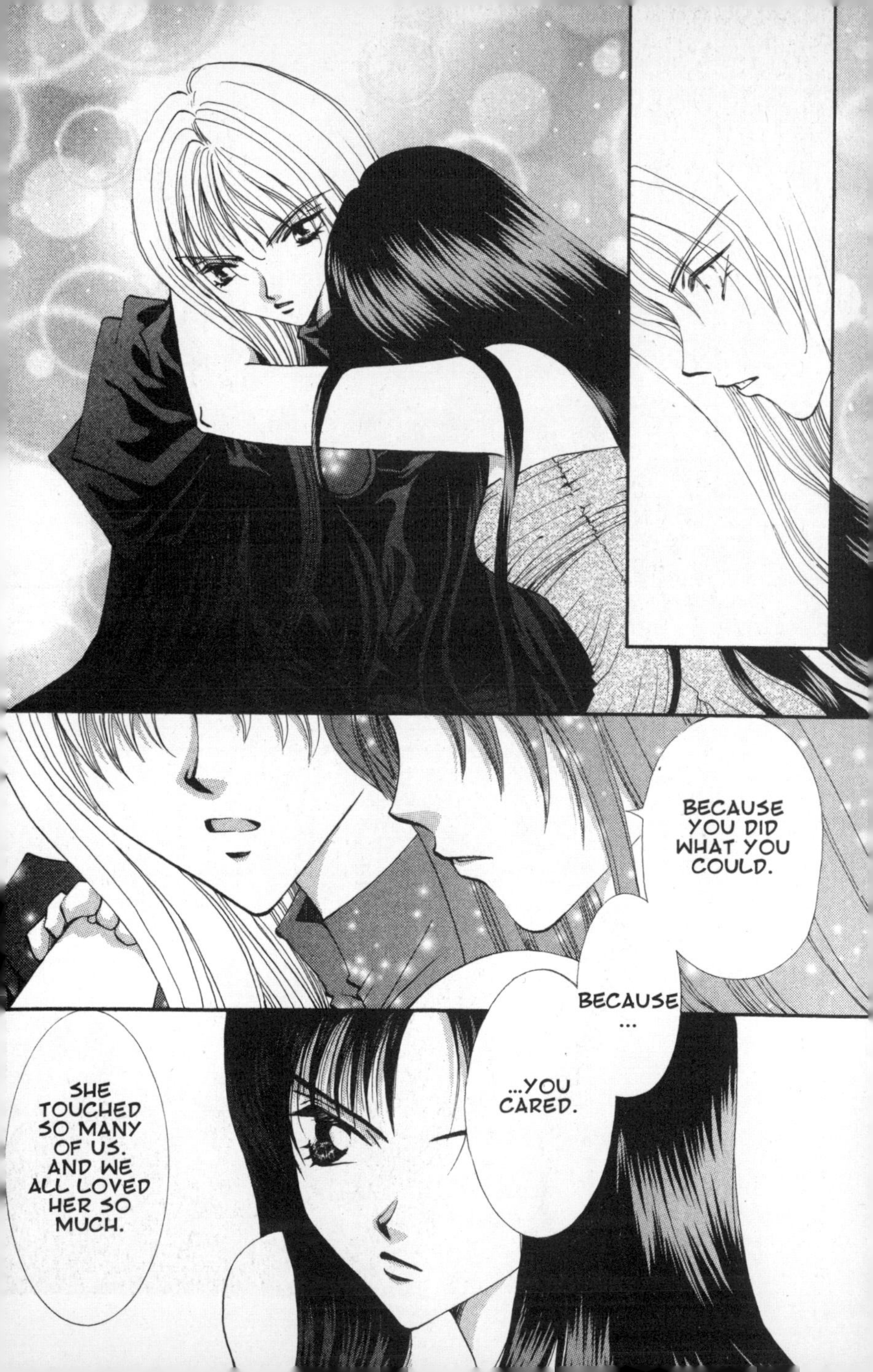
BECAUSE YOU DID WHAT YOU COULD.
BECAUSE ...
...YOU CARED.
SHE TOUCHED SO MANY OF US. AND WE ALL LOVED HER SO MUCH.

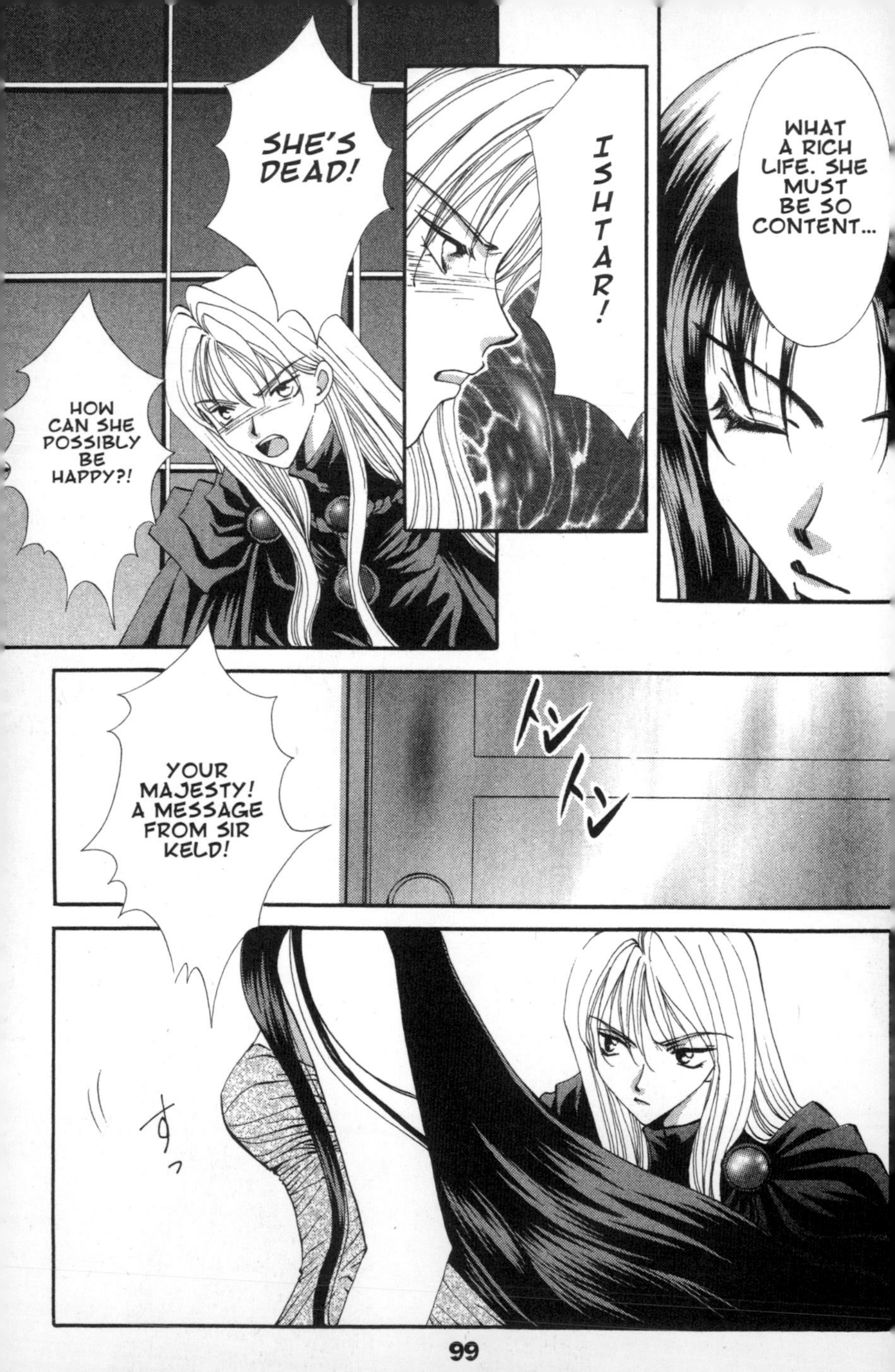
WHAT A RICH LIFE. SHE MUST BE SO CONTENT...
ISHTAR!
SHE'S DEAD!
HOW CAN SHE POSSIBLY BE HAPPY?!
トン トン
YOUR MAJESTY! A MESSAGE FROM SIR KELD!
すっ

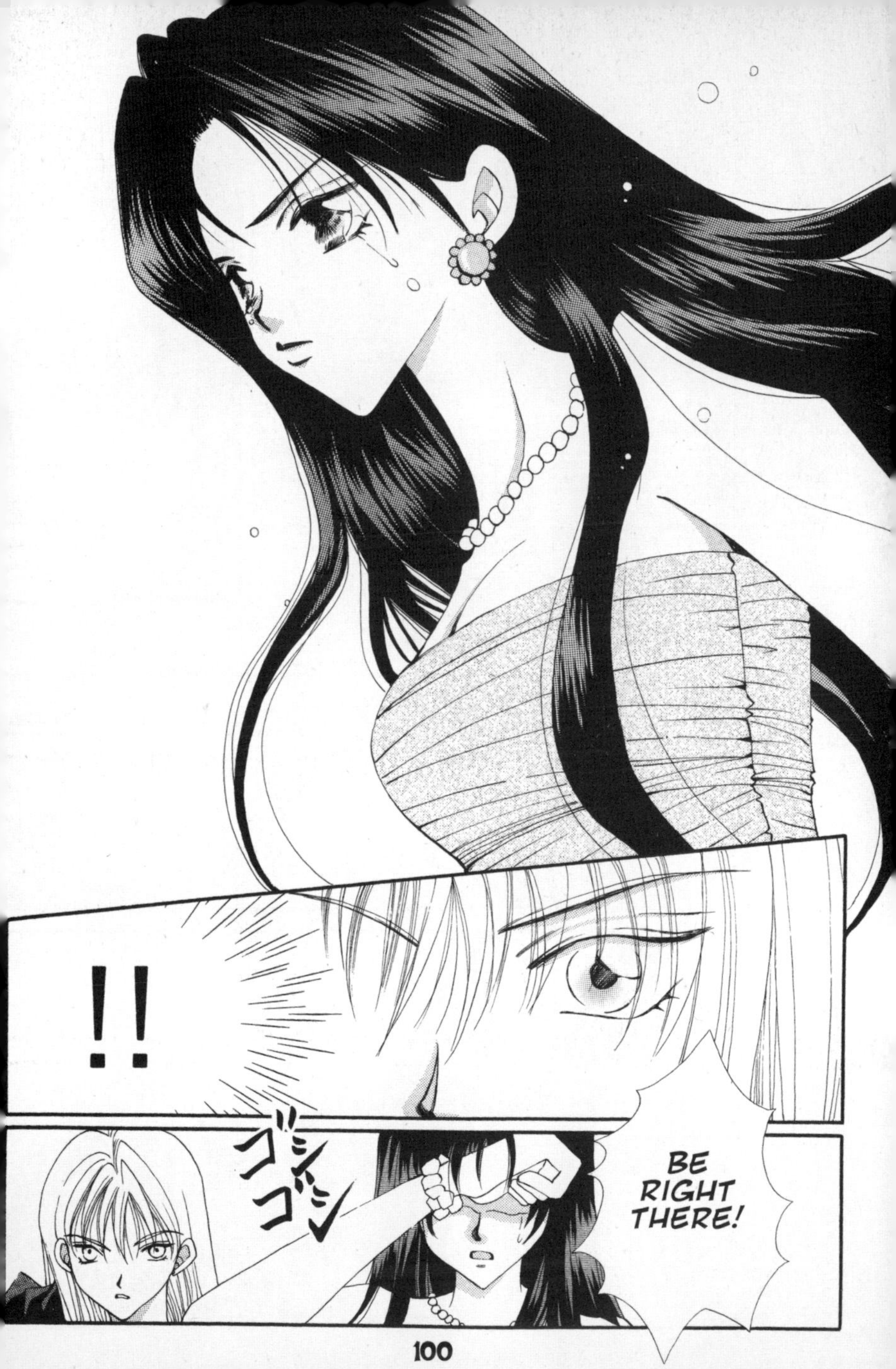
!!
BE RIGHT THERE!

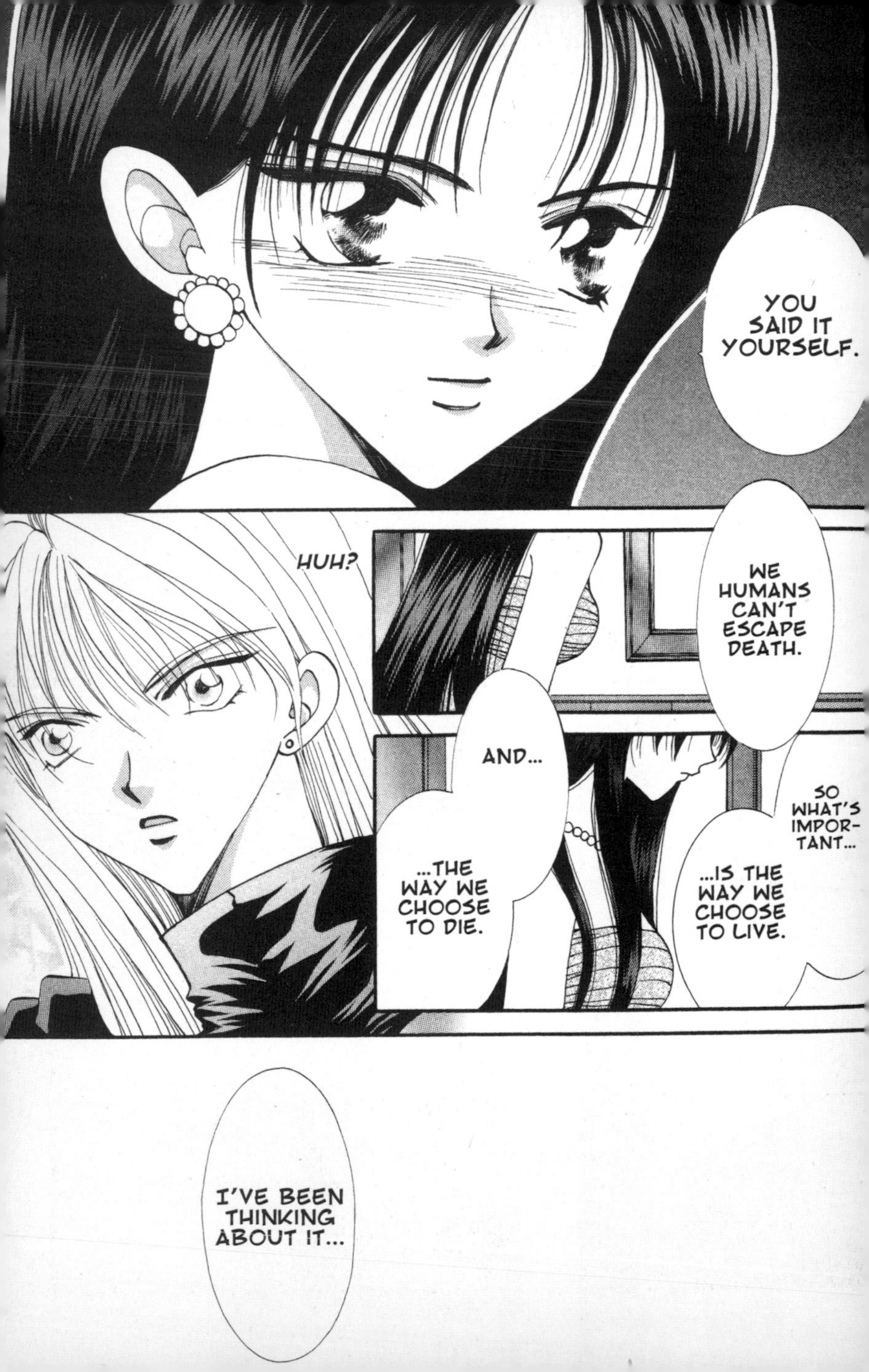
YOU SAID IT YOURSELF.
WE HUMANS CAN'T ESCAPE DEATH.
SO WHAT'S IMPOR-TANT...
...IS THE WAY WE CHOOSE TO LIVE.
AND...
...THE WAY WE CHOOSE TO DIE.
HUH?
I'VE BEEN THINKING ABOUT IT...

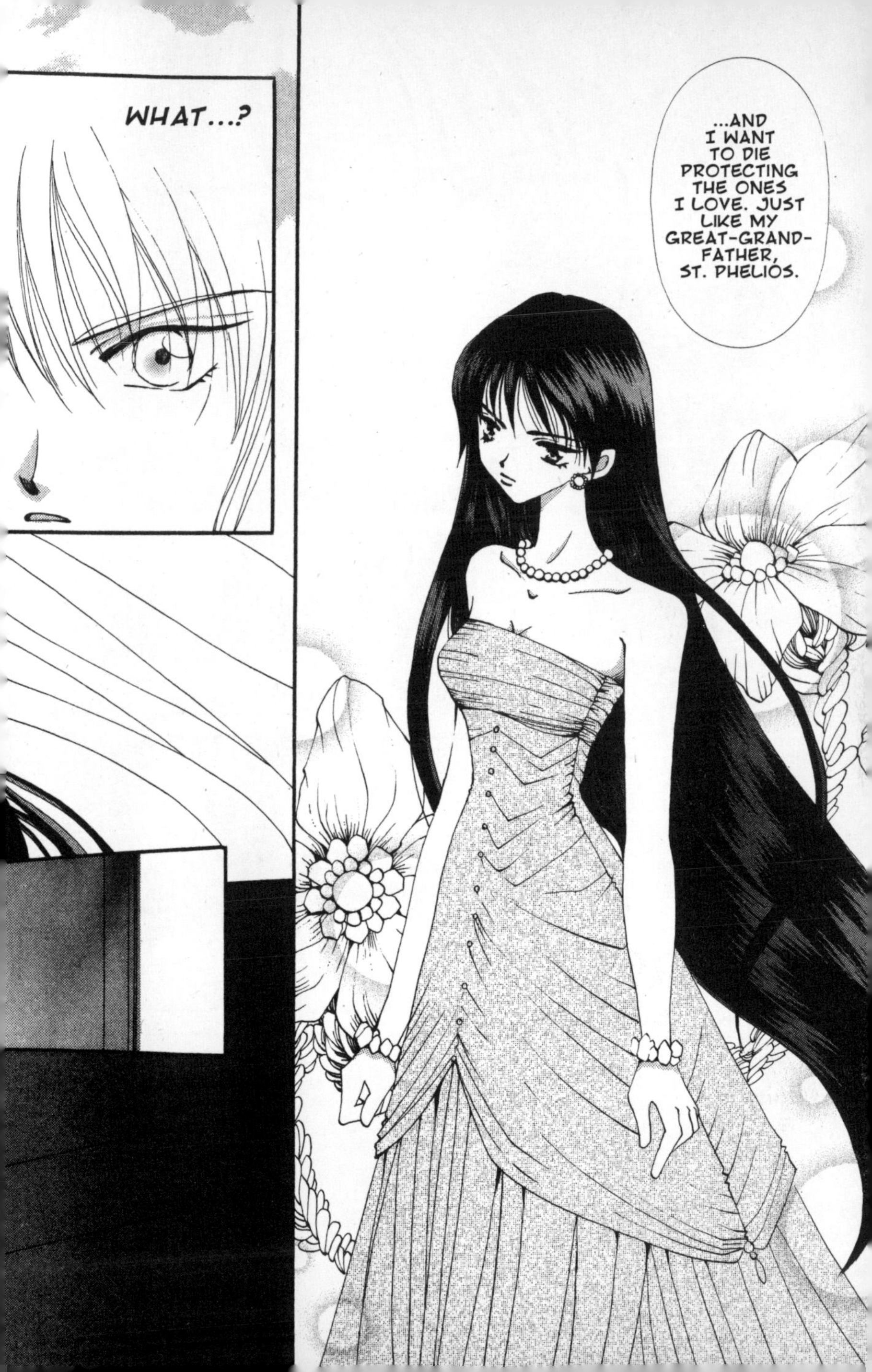
...AND I WANT TO DIE PROTECTING THE ONES I LOVE. JUST LIKE MY GREAT-GRAND-FATHER, ST. PHELIOS.
WHAT...?

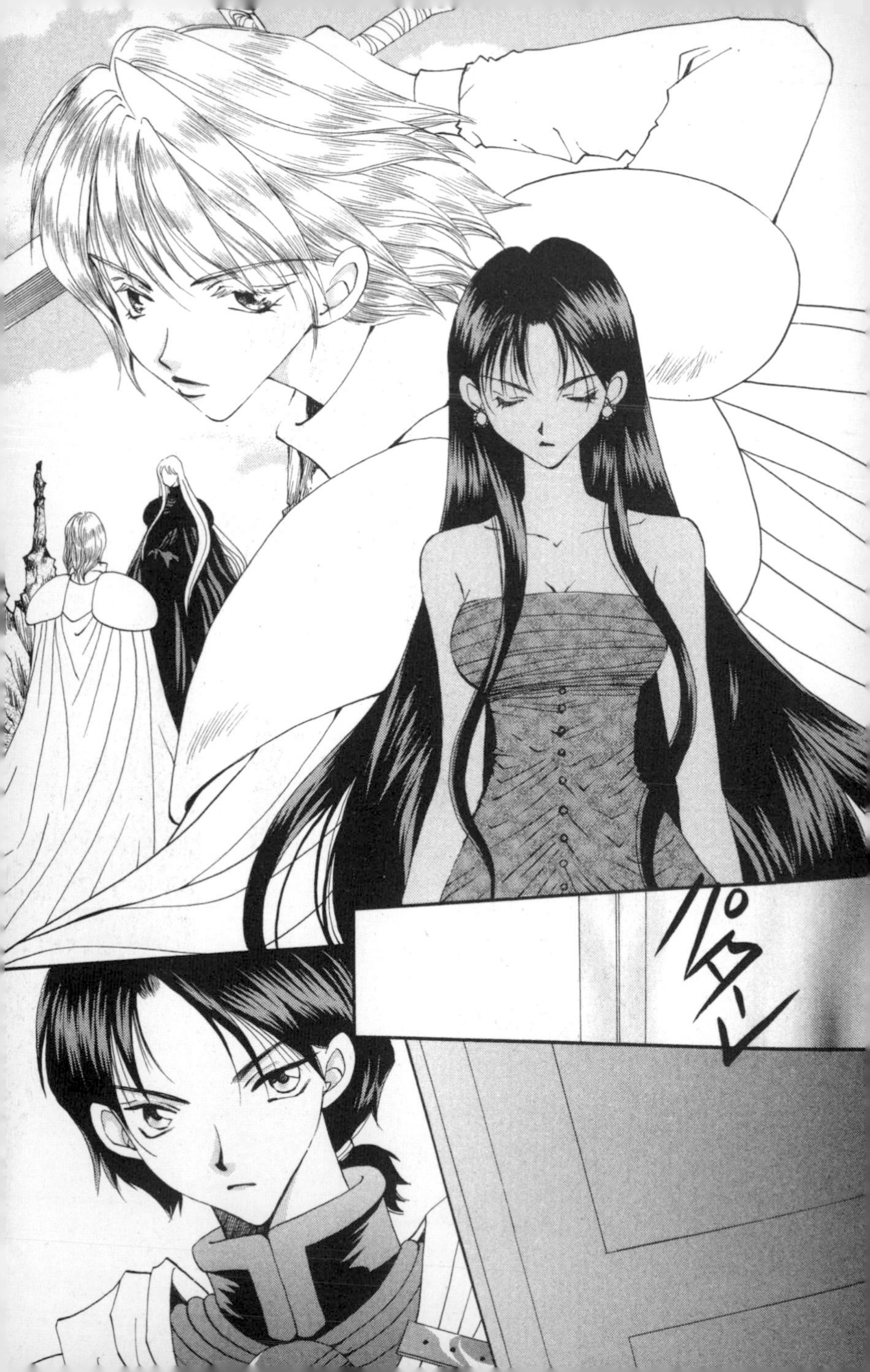
パタン

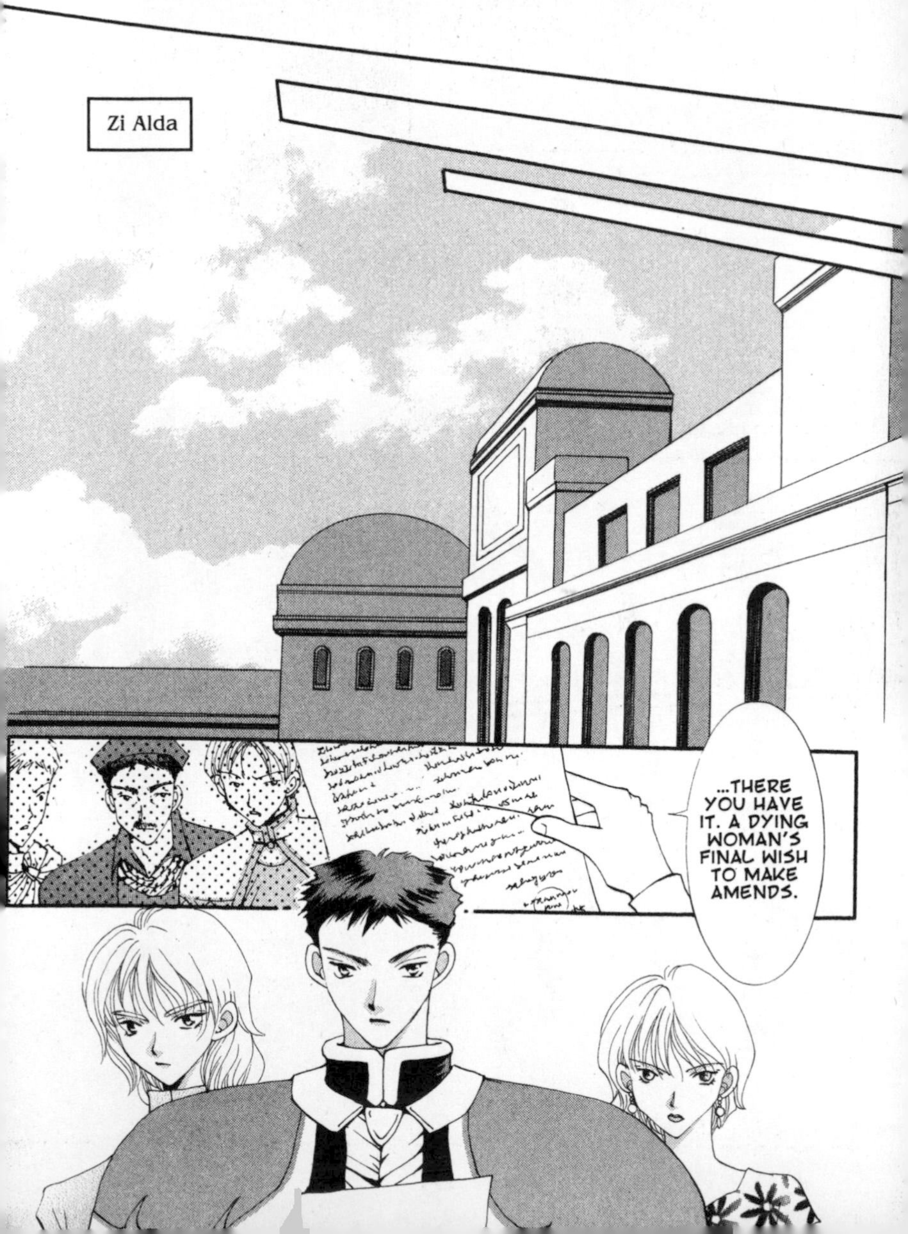
Zi Alda
...THERE YOU HAVE IT. A DYING WOMAN'S FINAL WISH TO MAKE AMENDS.

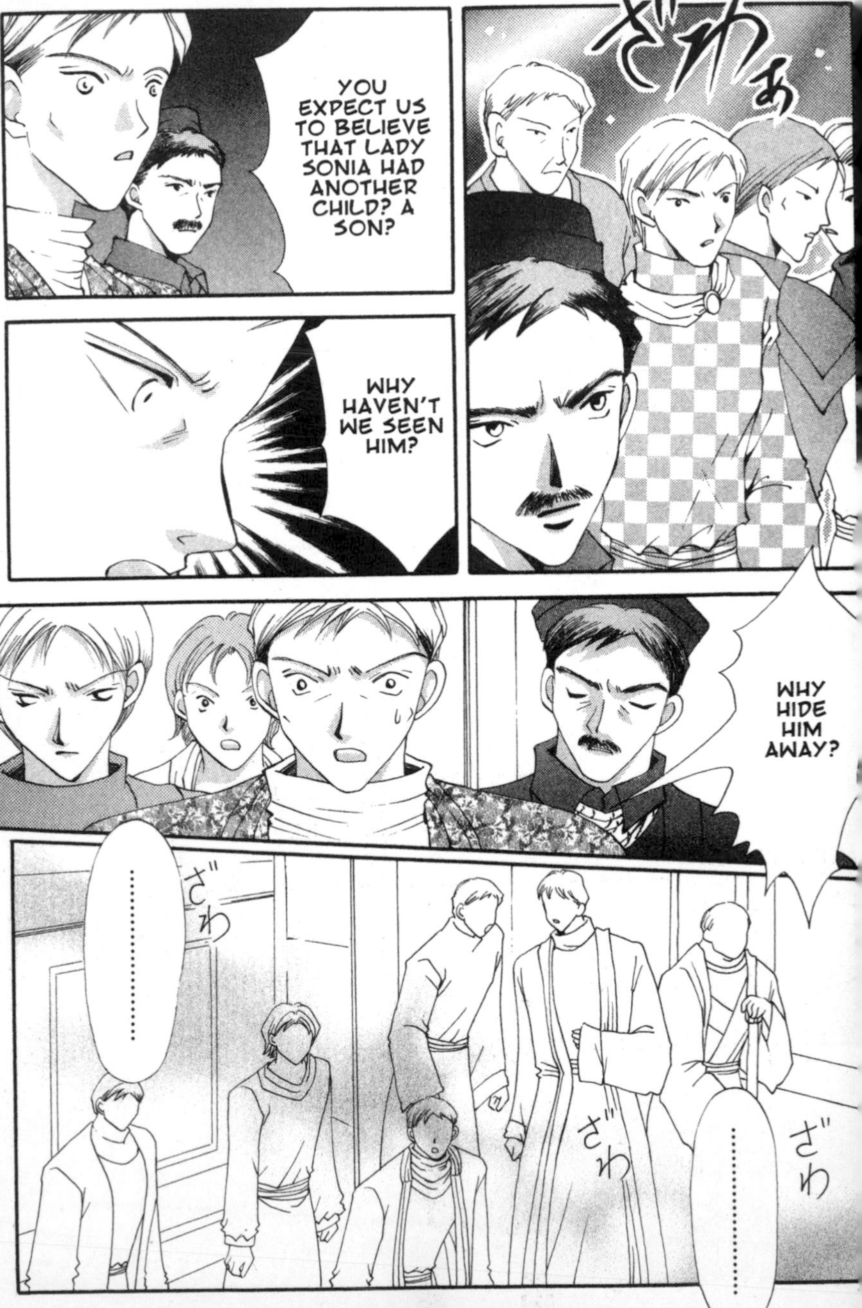
ざわぁ
YOU EXPECT US TO BELIEVE THAT LADY SONIA HAD ANOTHER CHILD? A SON?
WHY HAVEN'T WE SEEN HIM?
WHY HIDE HIM AWAY?
ざわ
......
ざわ
ざわ
......

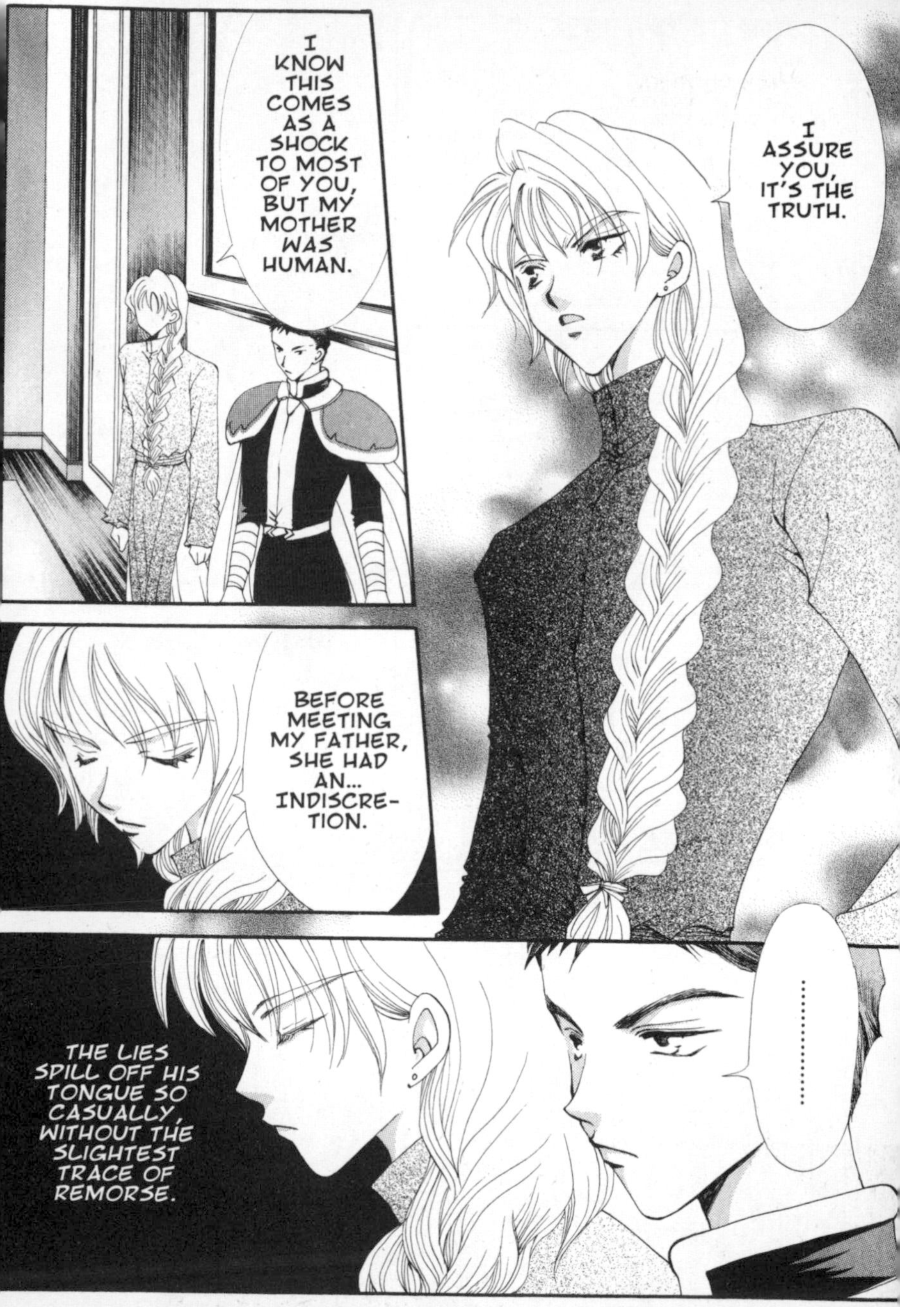
I ASSURE YOU, IT'S THE TRUTH.
I KNOW THIS COMES AS A SHOCK TO MOST OF YOU, BUT MY MOTHER WAS HUMAN.
BEFORE MEETING MY FATHER, SHE HAD AN... INDISCRE-TION.
....
THE LIES SPILL OFF HIS TONGUE SO CASUALLY, WITHOUT THE SLIGHTEST TRACE OF REMORSE.

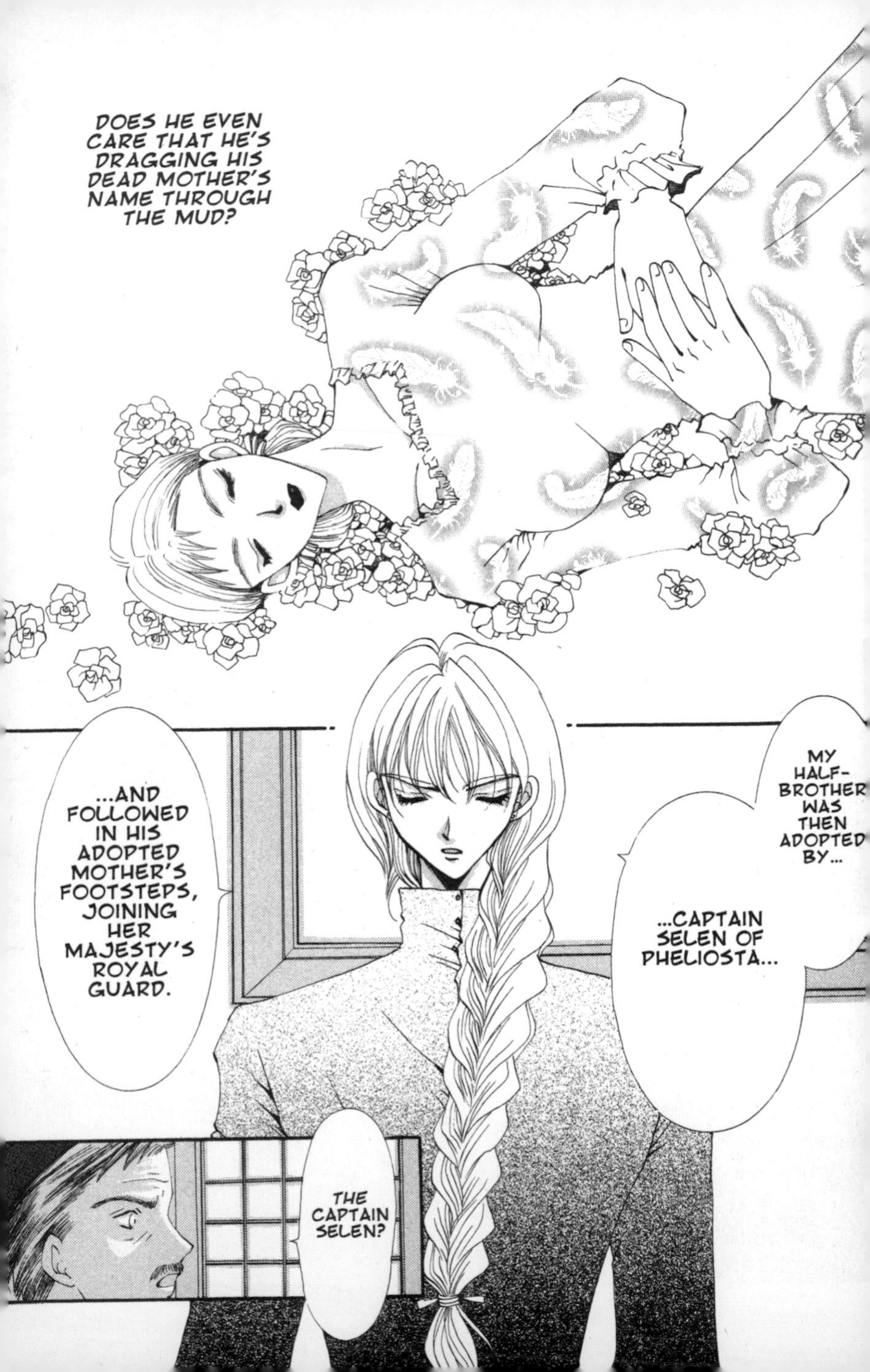
DOES HE EVEN CARE THAT HE'S DRAGGING HIS DEAD MOTHER'S NAME THROUGH THE MUD?
MY HALF-BROTHER WAS THEN ADOPTED BY...
...CAPTAIN SELEN OF PHELIOSTA...
...AND FOLLOWED IN HIS ADOPTED MOTHER'S FOOTSTEPS, JOINING HER MAJESTY'S ROYAL GUARD.
THE CAPTAIN SELEN?

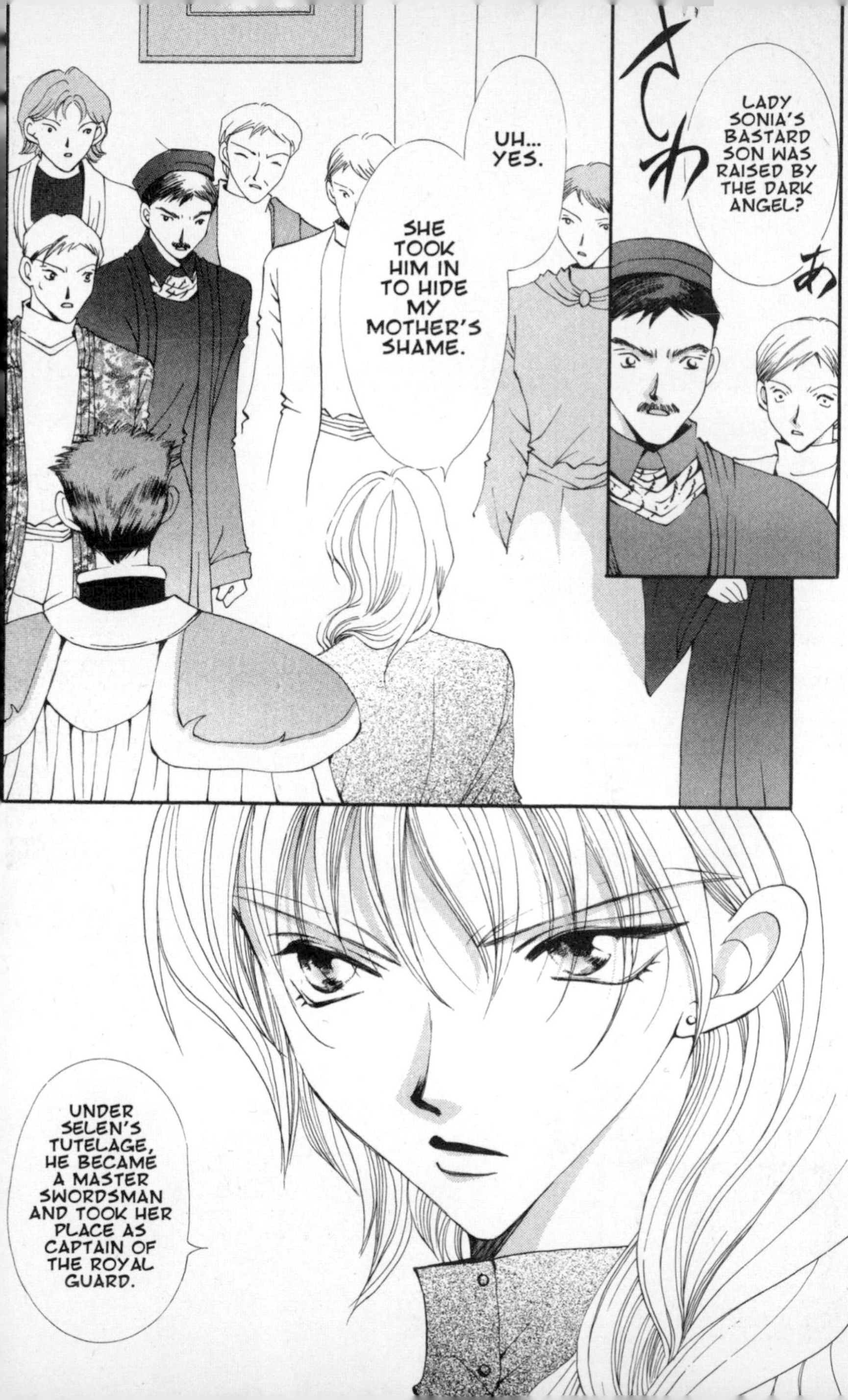
さわ
LADY SONIA'S BASTARD SON WAS RAISED BY THE DARK ANGEL?
あ
UH... YES.
SHE TOOK HIM IN TO HIDE MY MOTHER'S SHAME.
UNDER SELEN'S TUTELAGE, HE BECAME A MASTER SWORDSMAN AND TOOK HER PLACE AS CAPTAIN OF THE ROYAL GUARD.

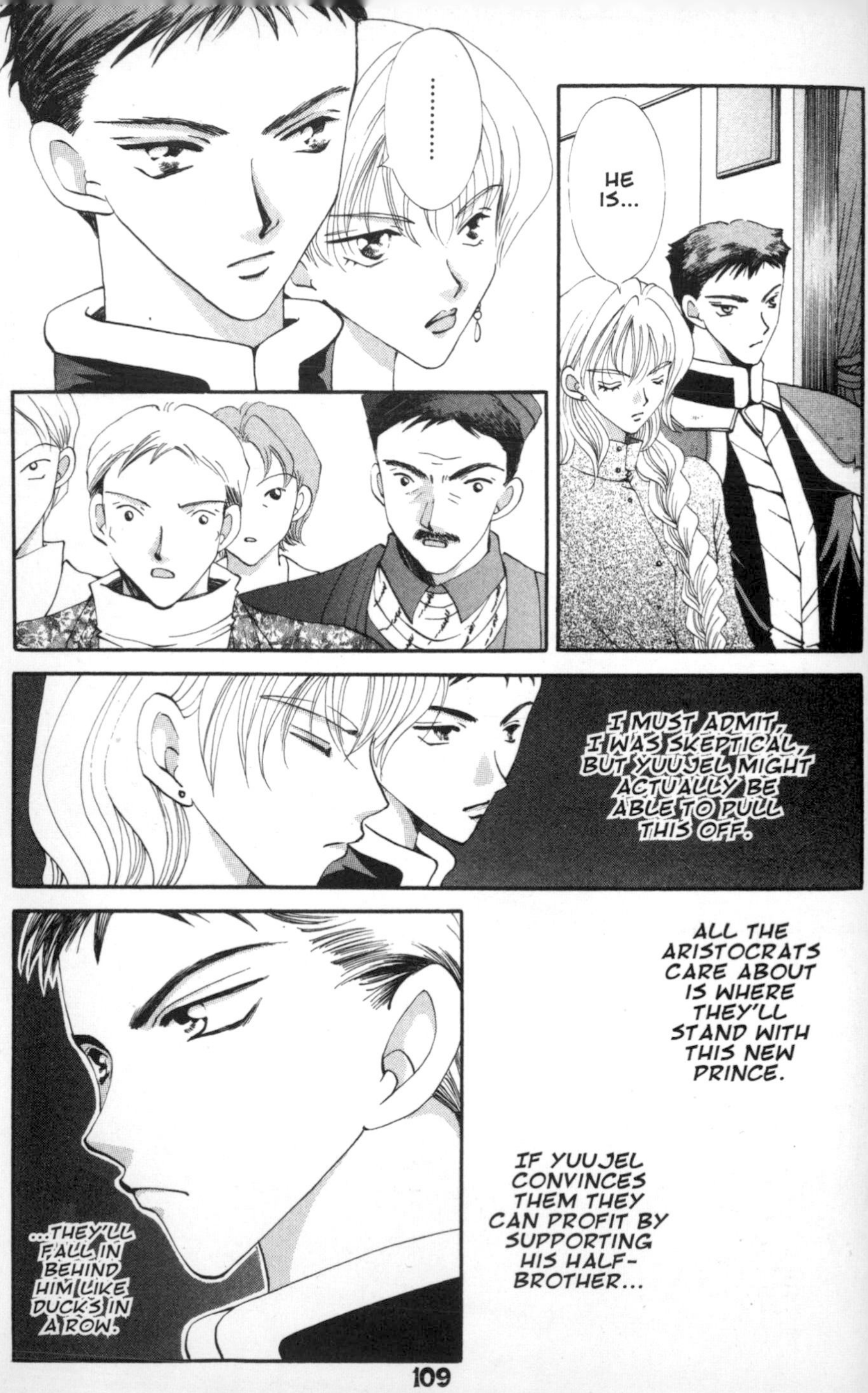
HE IS...
....
I MUST ADMIT, I WAS SKEPTICAL, BUT YUUJEL MIGHT ACTUALLY BE ABLE TO PULL THIS OFF.
ALL THE ARISTOCRATS CARE ABOUT IS WHERE THEY'LL STAND WITH THIS NEW PRINCE.
IF YUUJEL CONVINCES THEM THEY CAN PROFIT BY SUPPORTING HIS HALF-BROTHER...
...THEY'LL FALL IN BEHIND HIM LIKE DUCKS IN A ROW.

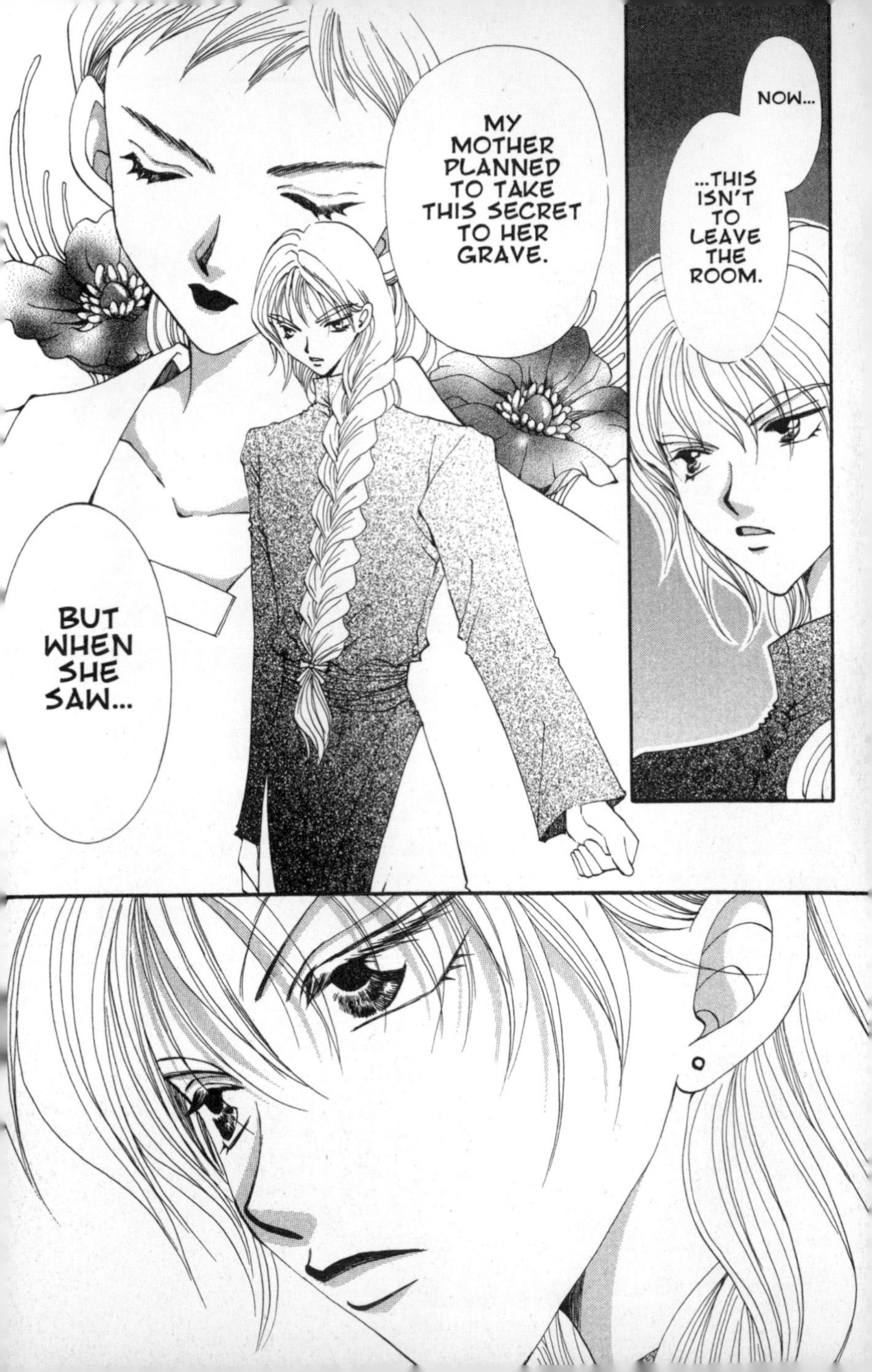
NOW...
...THIS ISN'T TO LEAVE THE ROOM.
MY MOTHER PLANNED TO TAKE THIS SECRET TO HER GRAVE.
BUT WHEN SHE SAW...

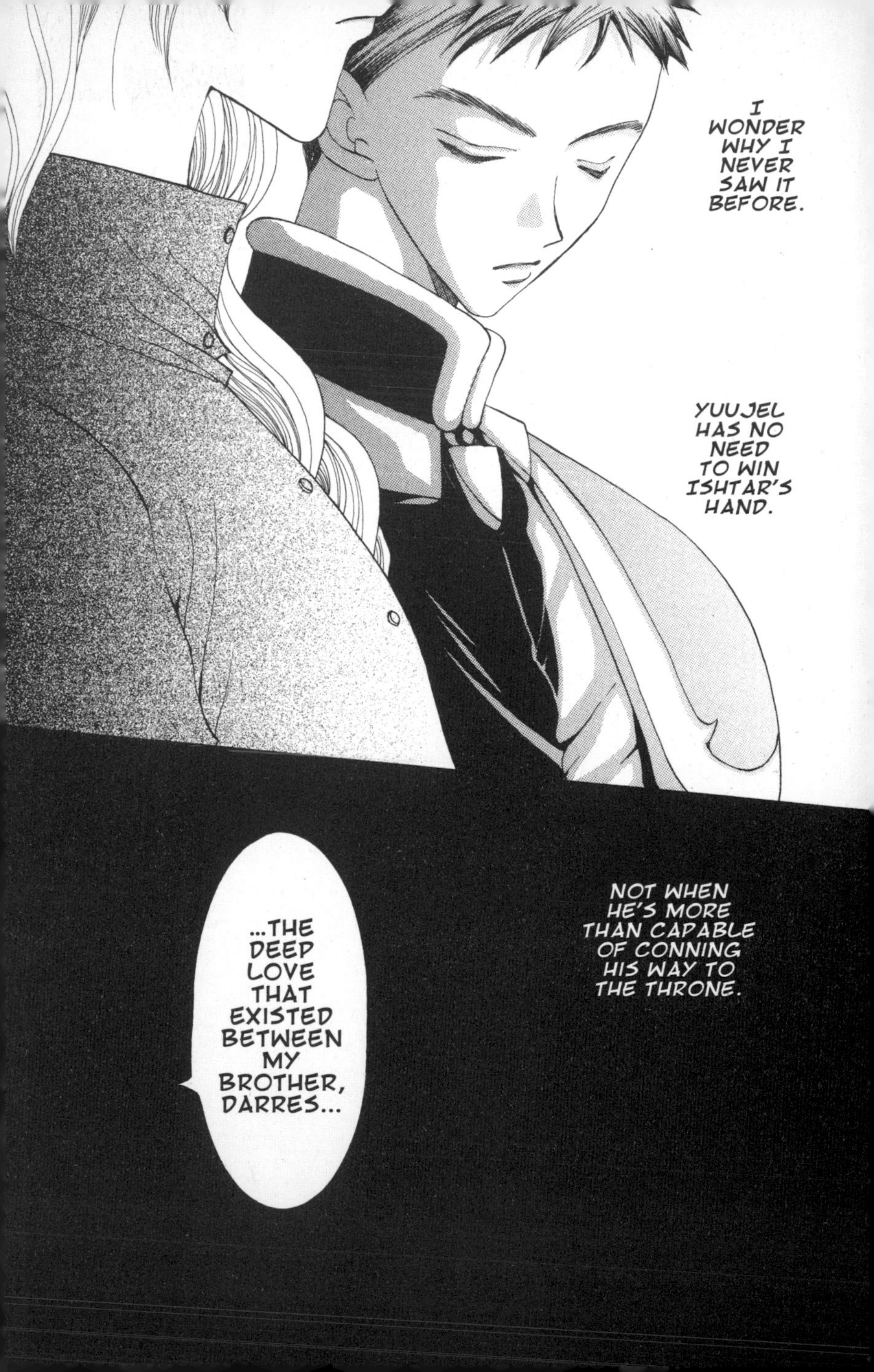
I WONDER WHY I NEVER SAW IT BEFORE.
YUUJEL HAS NO NEED TO WIN ISHTAR'S HAND.
NOT WHEN HE'S MORE THAN CAPABLE OF CONNING HIS WAY TO THE THRONE.
...THE DEEP LOVE THAT EXISTED BETWEEN MY BROTHER, DARRES...

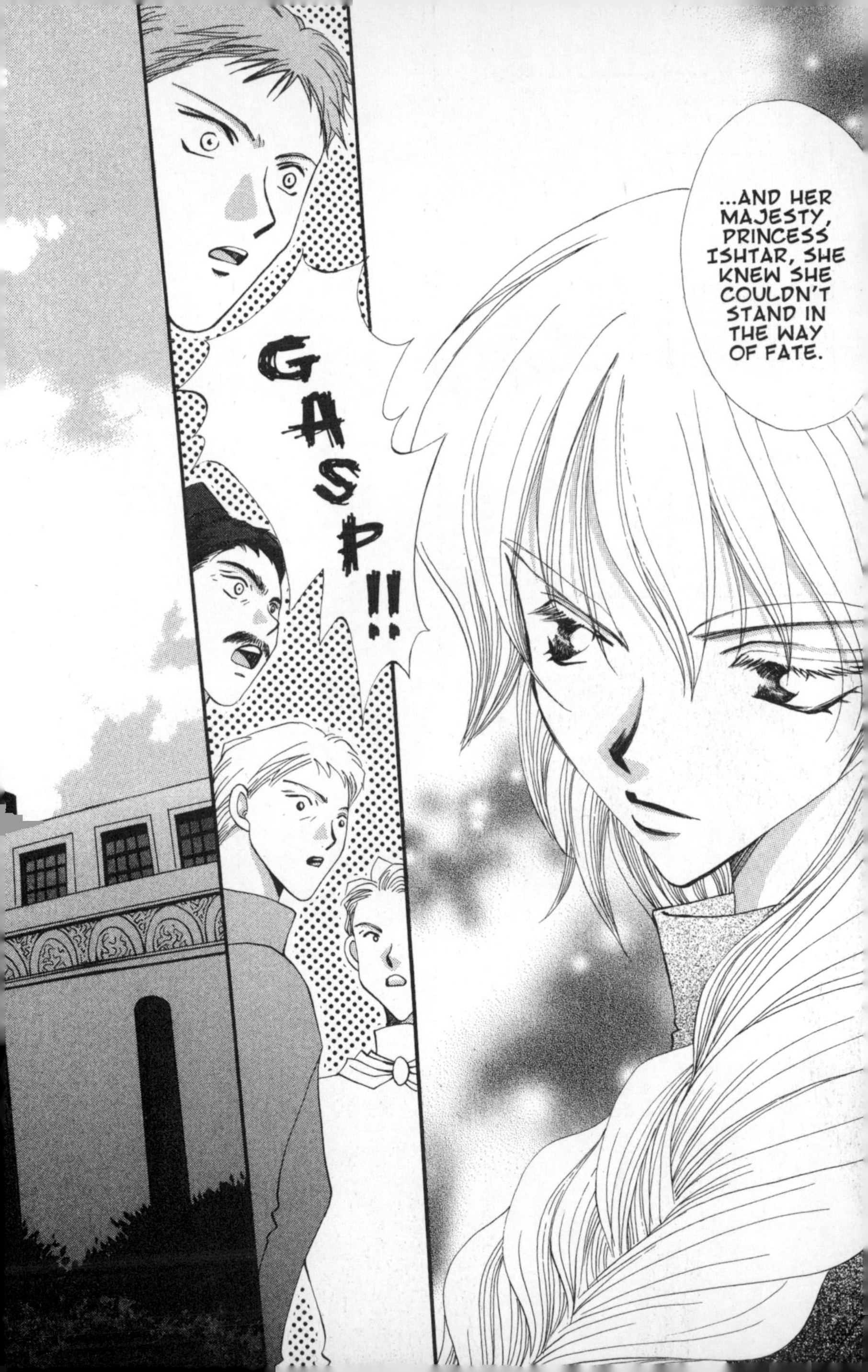
...AND HER MAJESTY, PRINCESS ISHTAR, SHE KNEW SHE COULDN'T STAND IN THE WAY OF FATE.
GASP!!

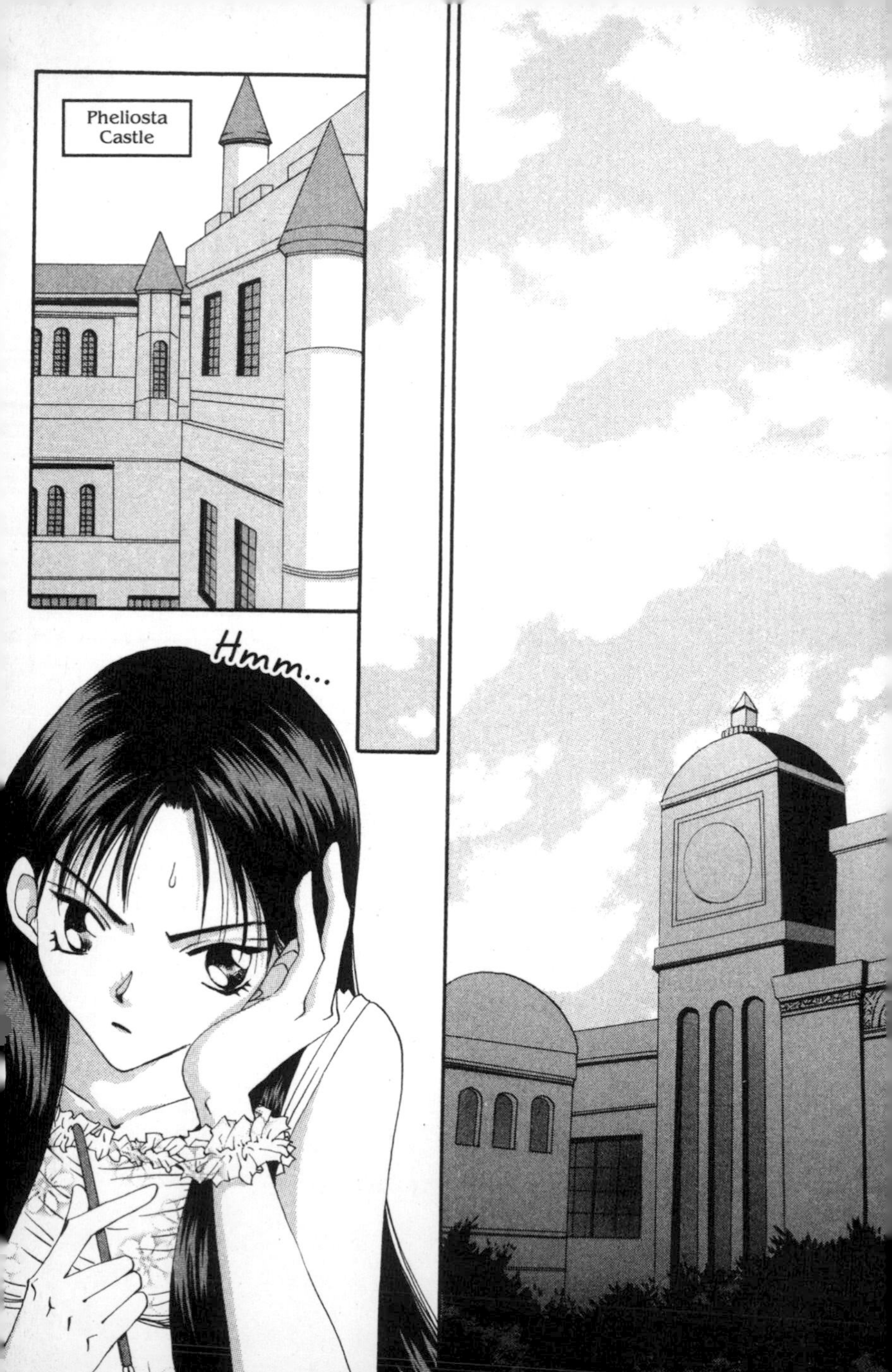
Pheliosta Castle
Hmm...

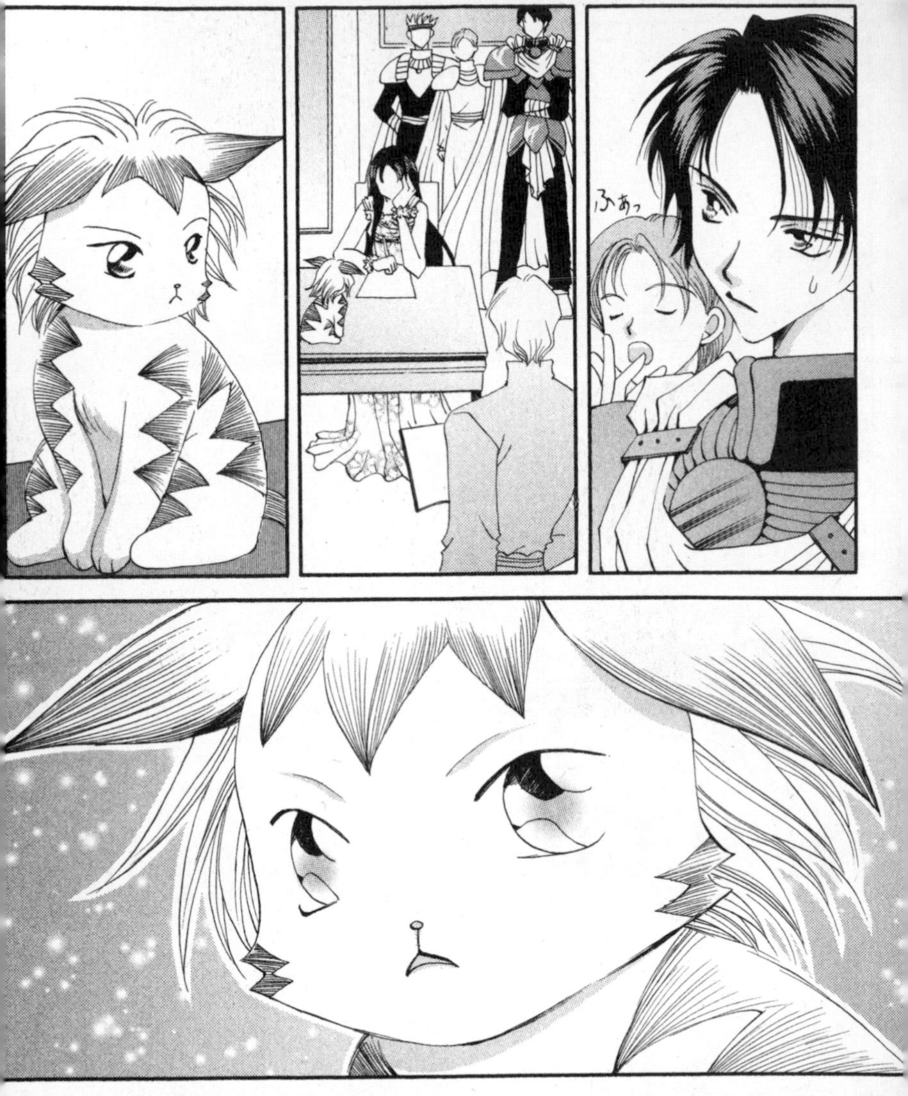
ふあっ
I COULDN'T SAY WHY...

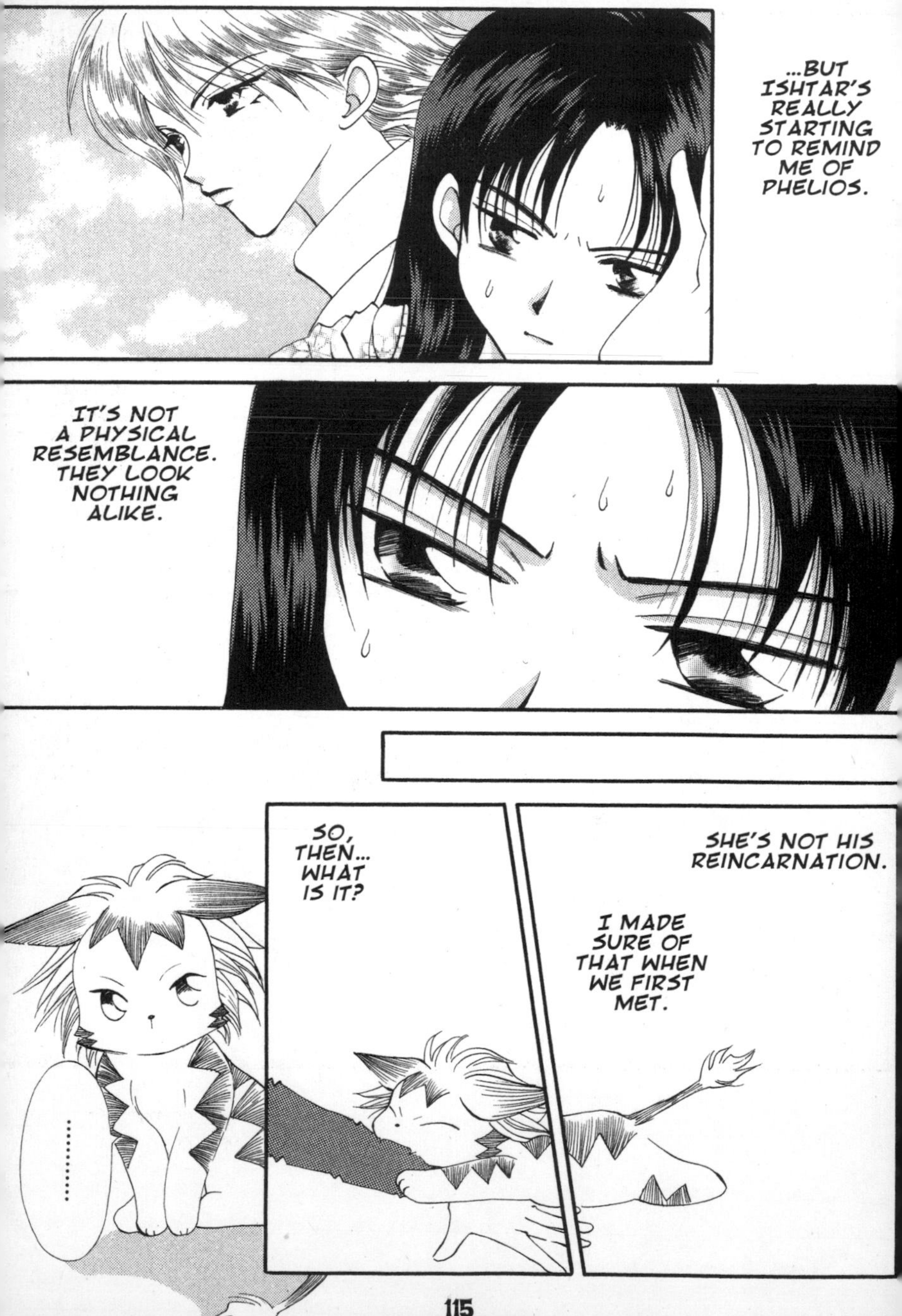
...BUT ISHTAR'S REALLY STARTING TO REMIND ME OF PHELIOS.
IT'S NOT A PHYSICAL RESEMBLANCE. THEY LOOK NOTHING ALIKE.
SHE'S NOT HIS REINCARNATION.
I MADE SURE OF THAT WHEN WE FIRST MET.
SO, THEN... WHAT IS IT?
....

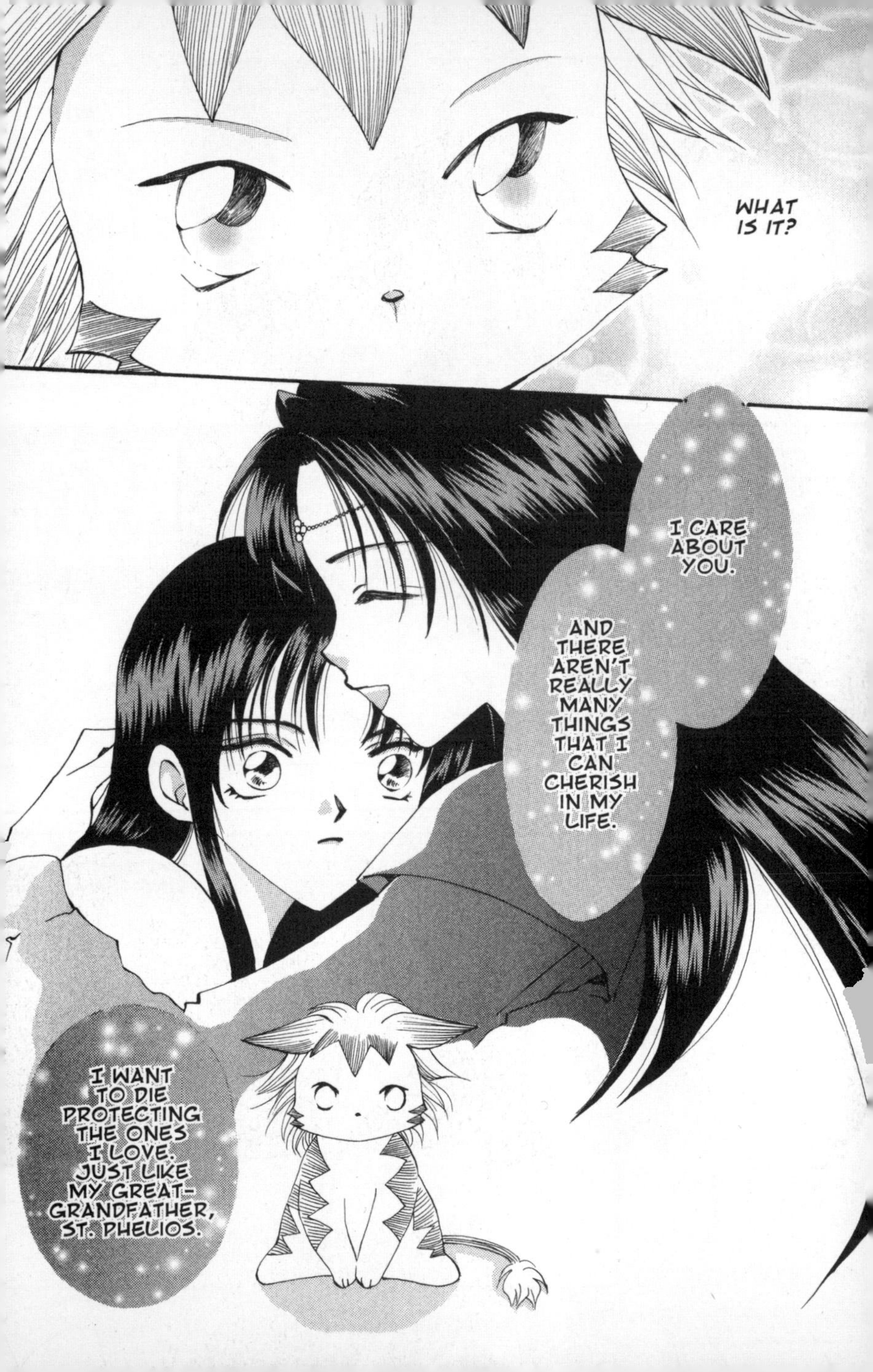
WHAT IS IT?
I CARE ABOUT YOU.
AND THERE AREN'T REALLY MANY THINGS THAT I CAN CHERISH IN MY LIFE.
I WANT TO DIE PROTECTING THE ONES I LOVE. JUST LIKE MY GREAT-GRANDFATHER, ST. PHELIOS.

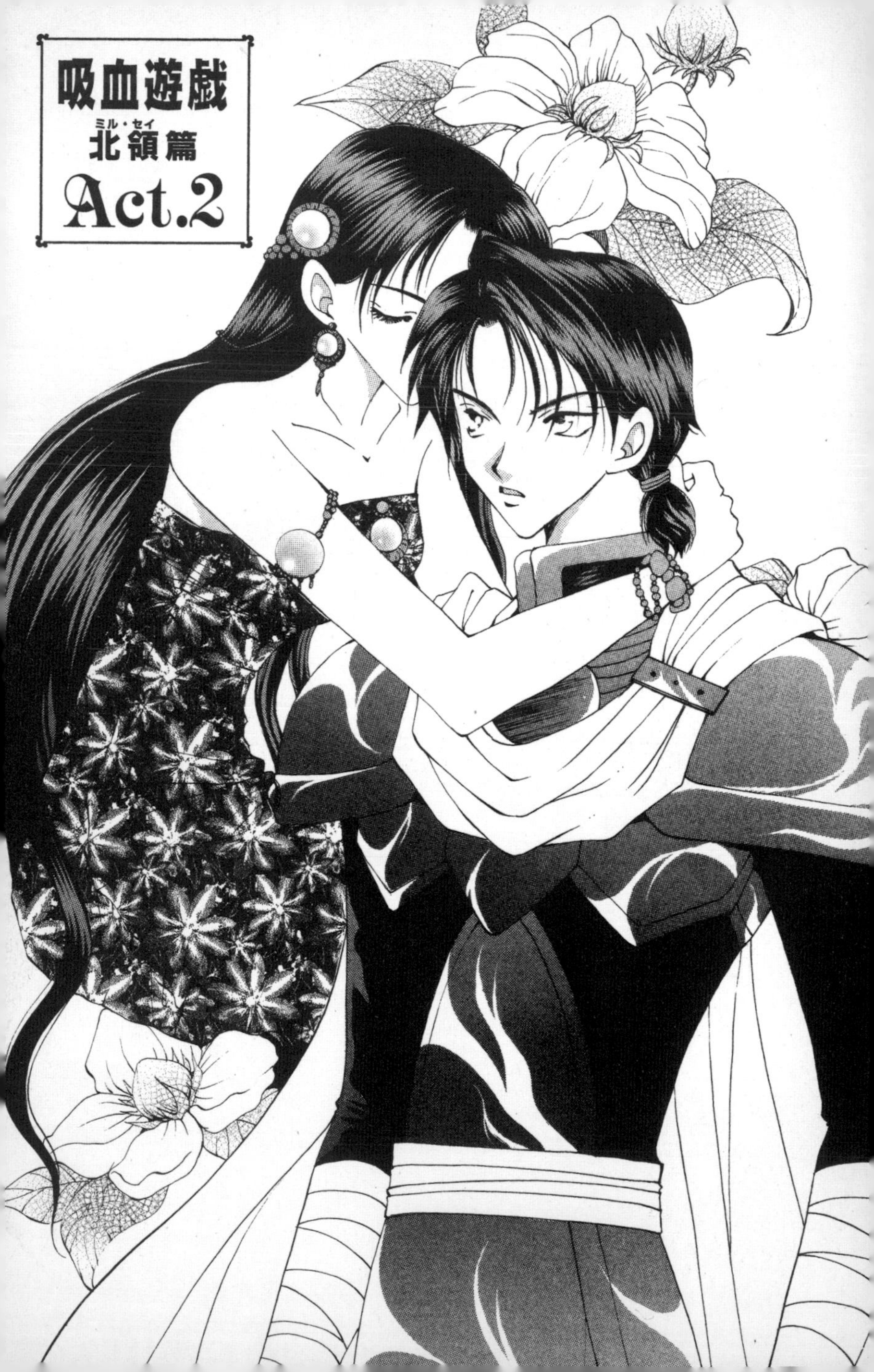
吸血遊戯
ミル・セイ
北領篇
Act.2

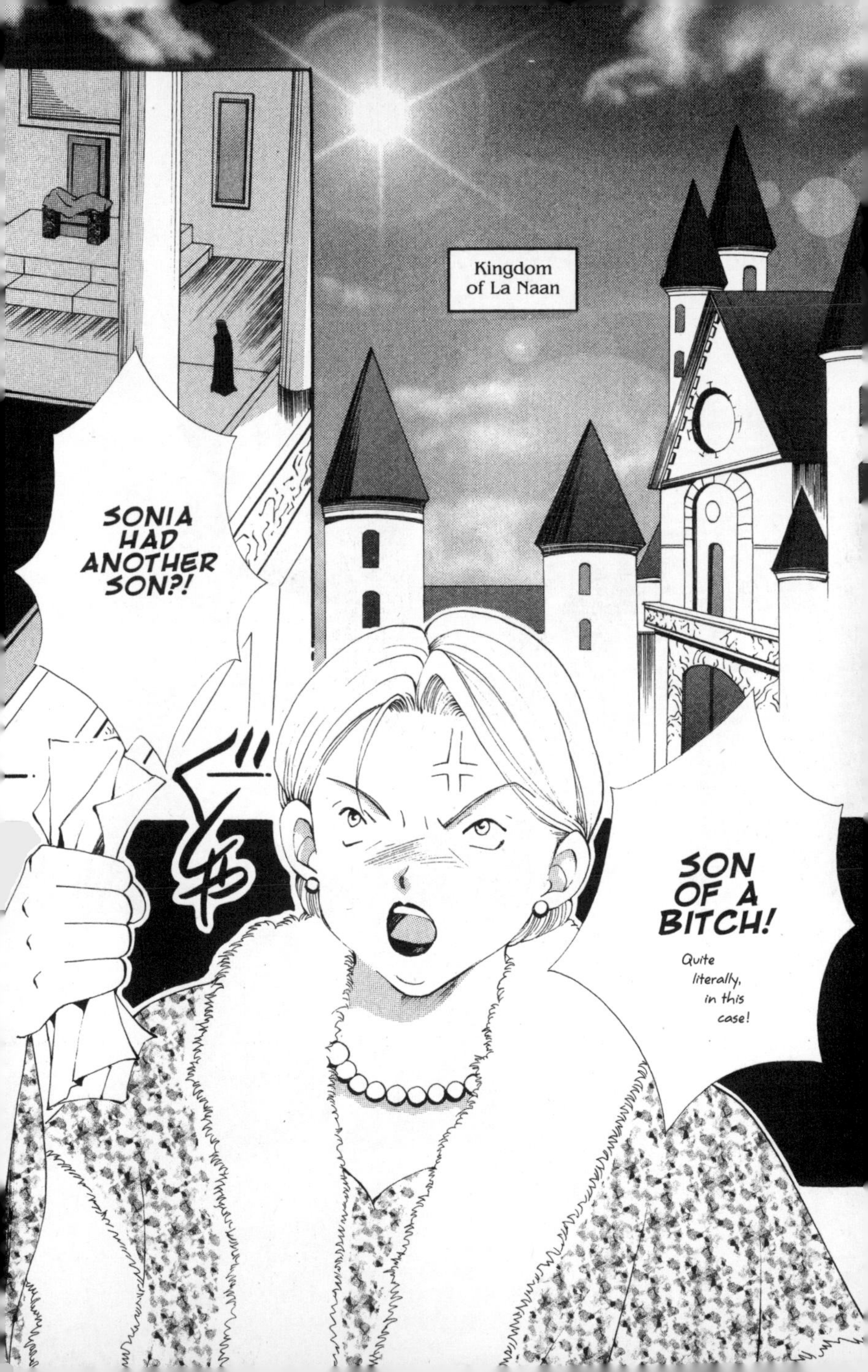
Kingdom of La Naan
SONIA HAD ANOTHER SON?!
SON OF A BITCH!
Quite literally, in this case!

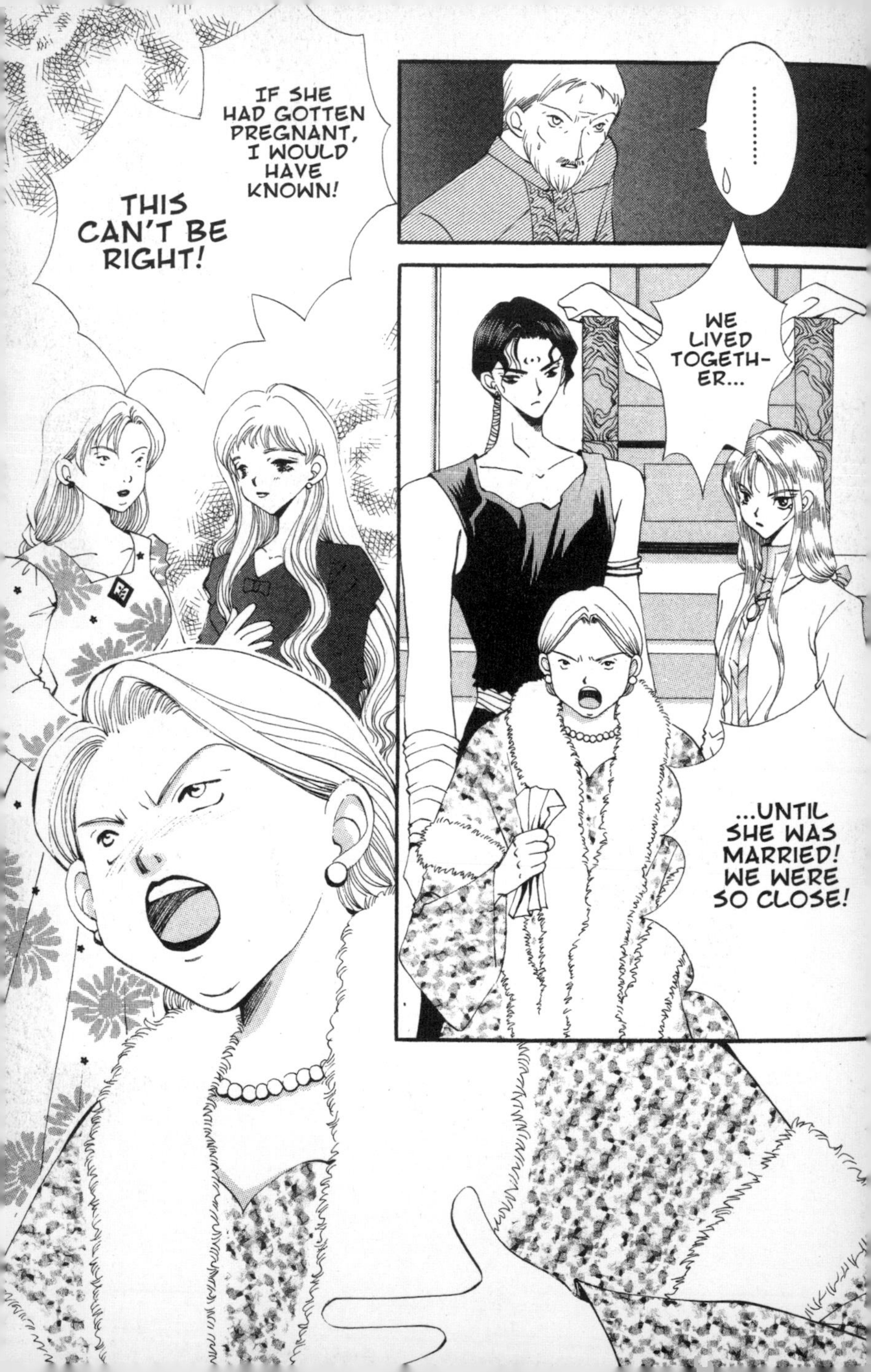
......
WE LIVED TOGETH-ER...
...UNTIL SHE WAS MARRIED! WE WERE SO CLOSE!
IF SHE HAD GOTTEN PREGNANT, I WOULD HAVE KNOWN!
THIS CAN'T BE RIGHT!

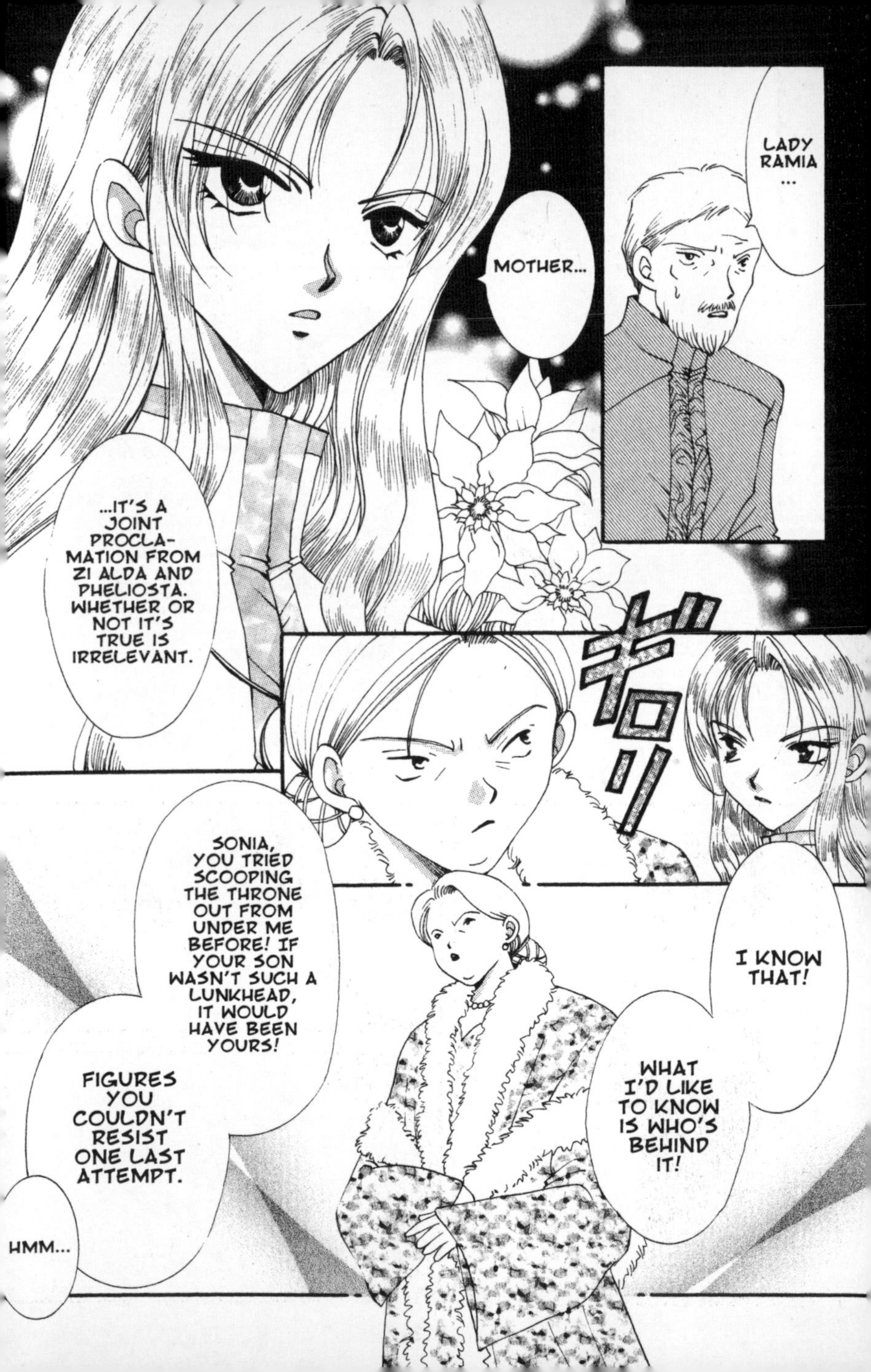
LADY RAMIA ...
MOTHER...
...IT'S A JOINT PROCLAMATION FROM ZI ALDA AND PHELIOSTA. WHETHER OR NOT IT'S TRUE IS IRRELEVANT.
ギロリ
I KNOW THAT!
WHAT I'D LIKE TO KNOW IS WHO'S BEHIND IT!
SONIA, YOU TRIED SCOOPING THE THRONE OUT FROM UNDER ME BEFORE! IF YOUR SON WASN'T SUCH A LUNKHEAD, IT WOULD HAVE BEEN YOURS!
FIGURES YOU COULDN'T RESIST ONE LAST ATTEMPT.
HMM...

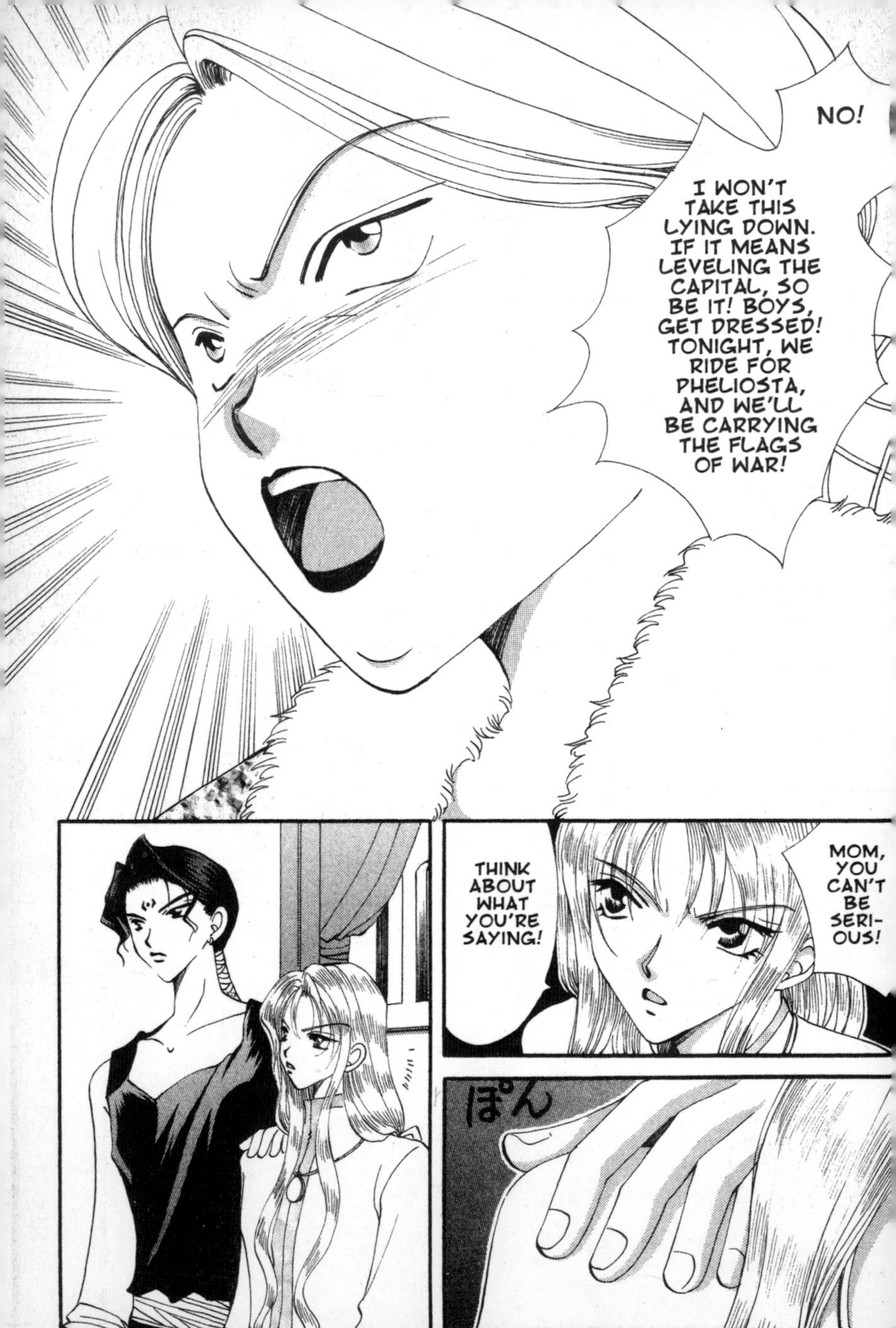
NO!
I WON'T TAKE THIS LYING DOWN. IF IT MEANS LEVELING THE CAPITAL, SO BE IT! BOYS, GET DRESSED! TONIGHT, WE RIDE FOR PHELIOSTA, AND WE'LL BE CARRYING THE FLAGS OF WAR!
MOM, YOU CAN'T BE SERI-OUS!
THINK ABOUT WHAT YOU'RE SAYING!
ぽん

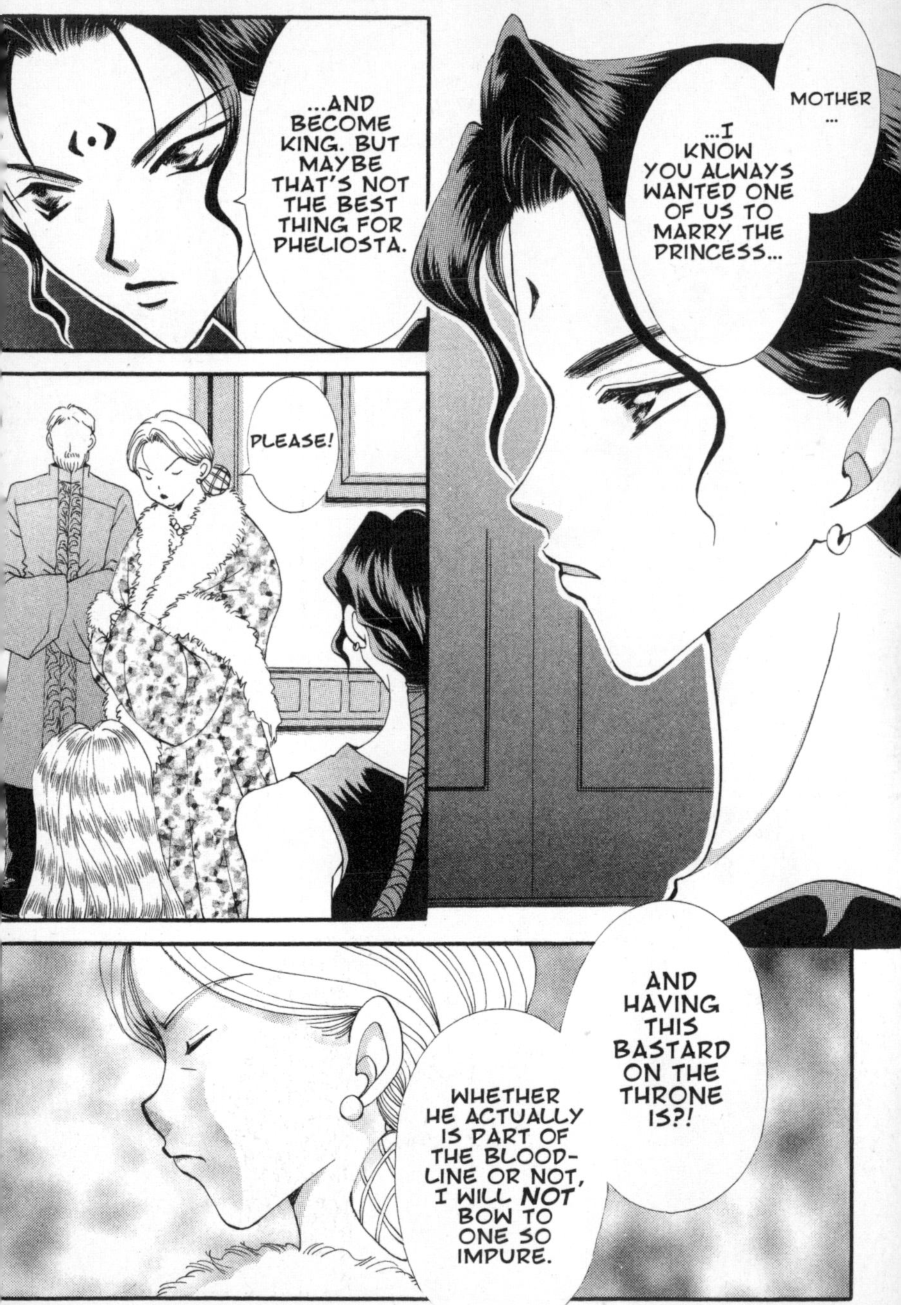
MOTHER ...
...I KNOW YOU ALWAYS WANTED ONE OF US TO MARRY THE PRINCESS...
...AND BECOME KING. BUT MAYBE THAT'S NOT THE BEST THING FOR PHELIOSTA.
PLEASE!
AND HAVING THIS BASTARD ON THE THRONE IS?!
WHETHER HE ACTUALLY IS PART OF THE BLOOD-LINE OR NOT, I WILL *NOT* BOW TO ONE SO IMPURE.

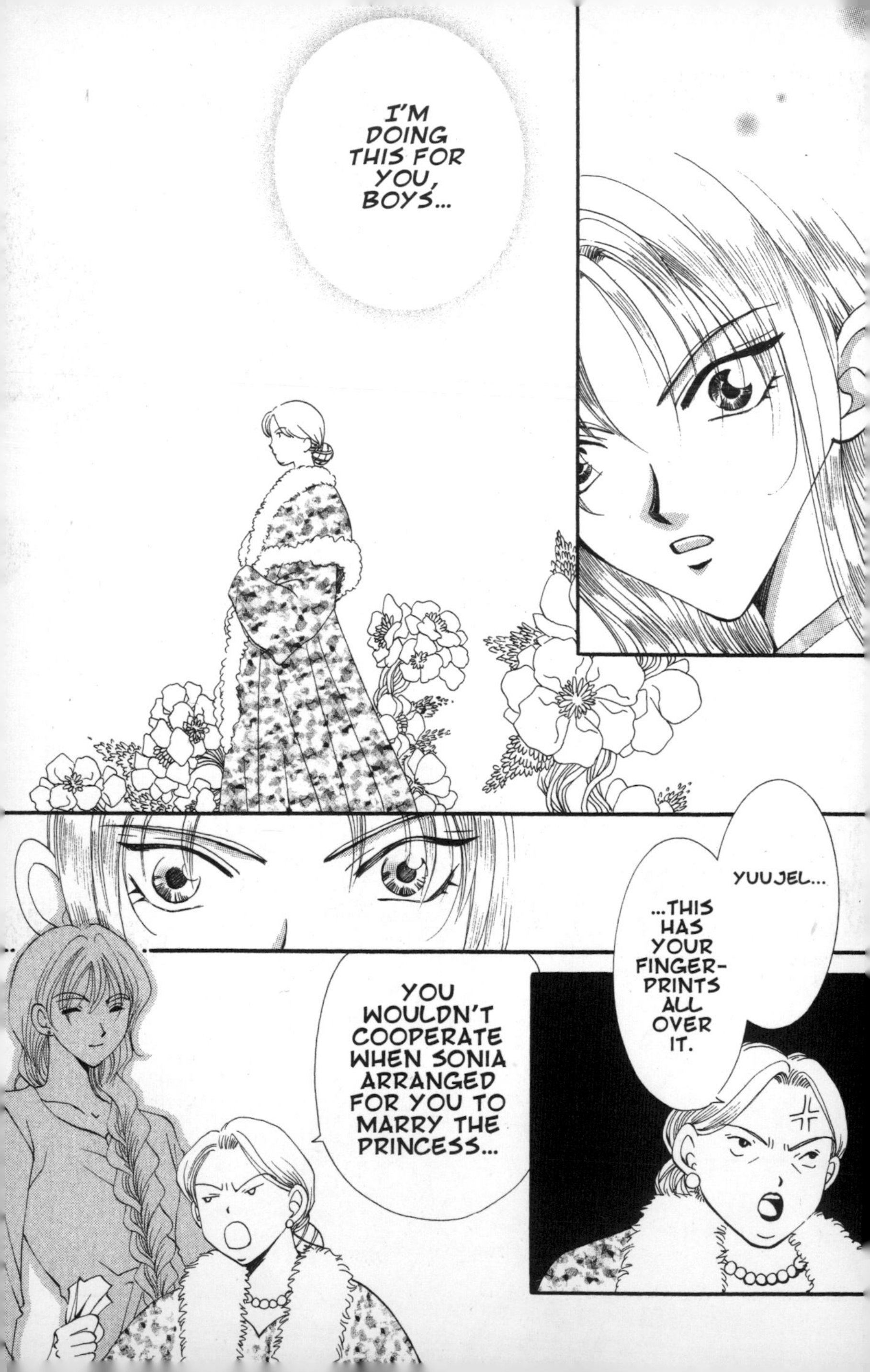
I'M DOING THIS FOR YOU, BOYS...
YUUJEL...
...THIS HAS YOUR FINGER-PRINTS ALL OVER IT.
YOU WOULDN'T COOPERATE WHEN SONIA ARRANGED FOR YOU TO MARRY THE PRINCESS...

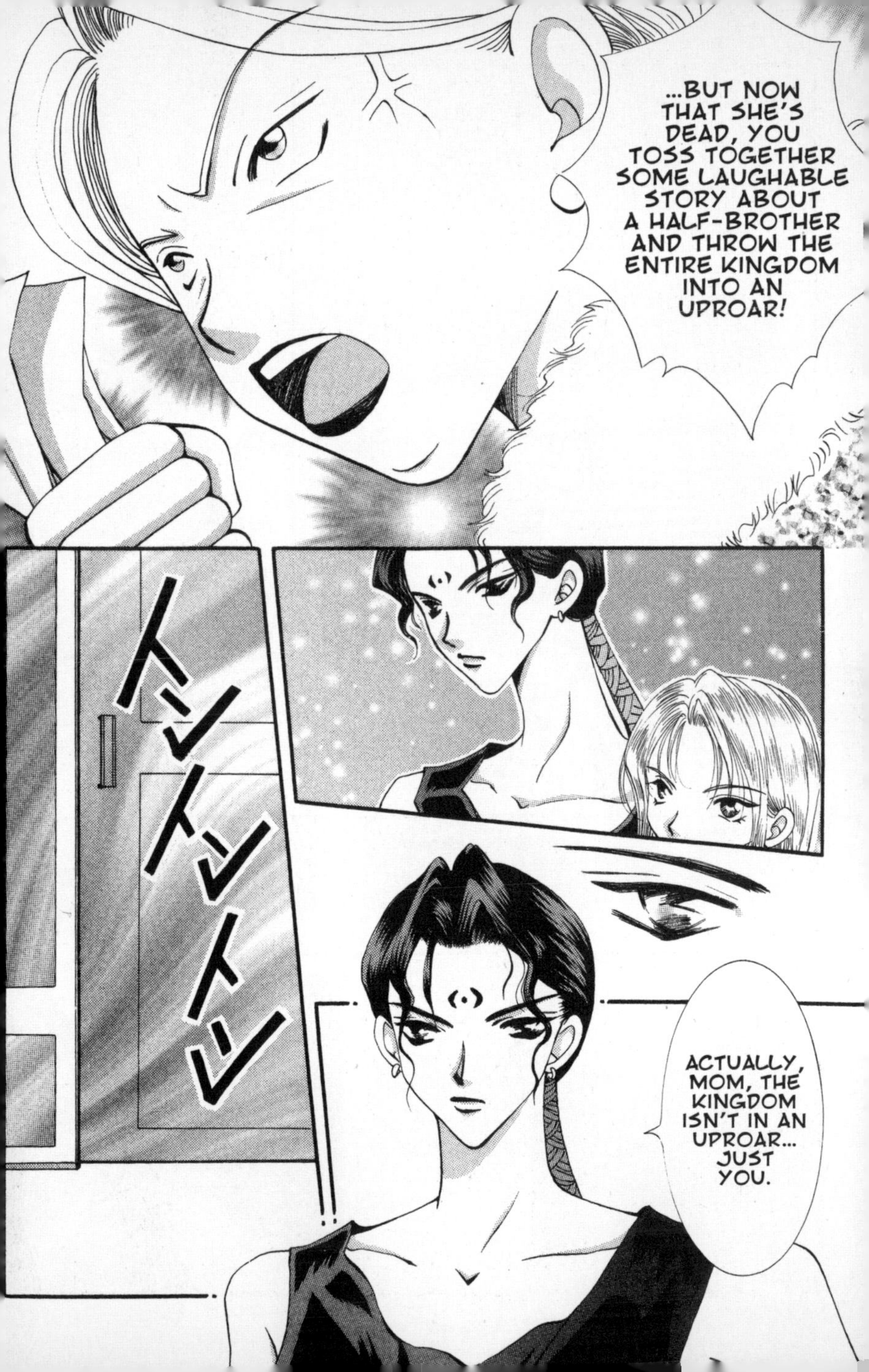
...BUT NOW THAT SHE'S DEAD, YOU TOSS TOGETHER SOME LAUGHABLE STORY ABOUT A HALF-BROTHER AND THROW THE ENTIRE KINGDOM INTO AN UPROAR!
ACTUALLY, MOM, THE KINGDOM ISN'T IN AN UPROAR... JUST YOU.
トントントン

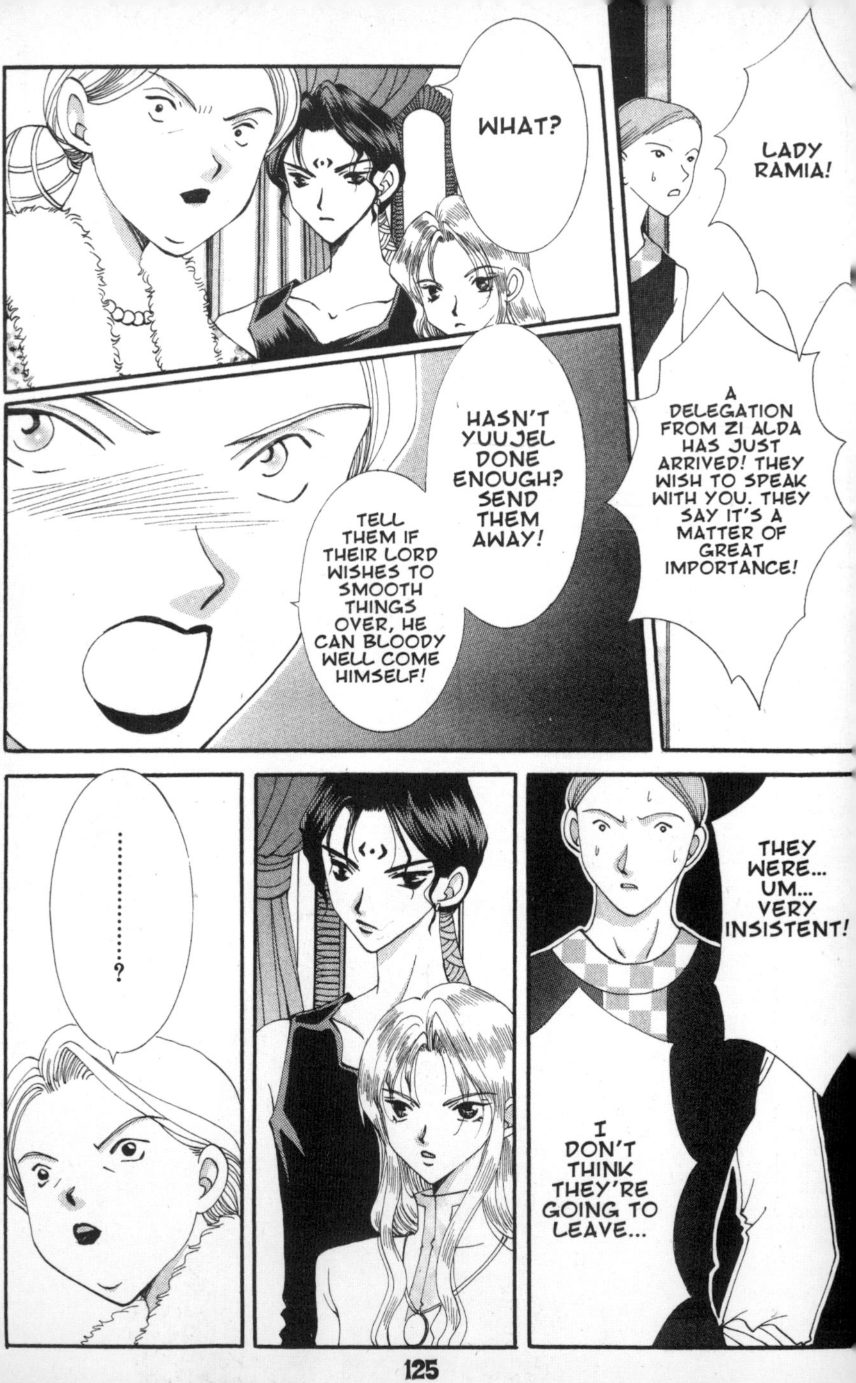
LADY RAMIA!
A DELEGATION FROM ZI ALDA HAS JUST ARRIVED! THEY WISH TO SPEAK WITH YOU. THEY SAY IT'S A MATTER OF GREAT IMPORTANCE!
WHAT?
HASN'T YUUJEL DONE ENOUGH? SEND THEM AWAY!
TELL THEM IF THEIR LORD WISHES TO SMOOTH THINGS OVER, HE CAN BLOODY WELL COME HIMSELF!
THEY WERE... UM... VERY INSISTENT!
I DON'T THINK THEY'RE GOING TO LEAVE...
..........?

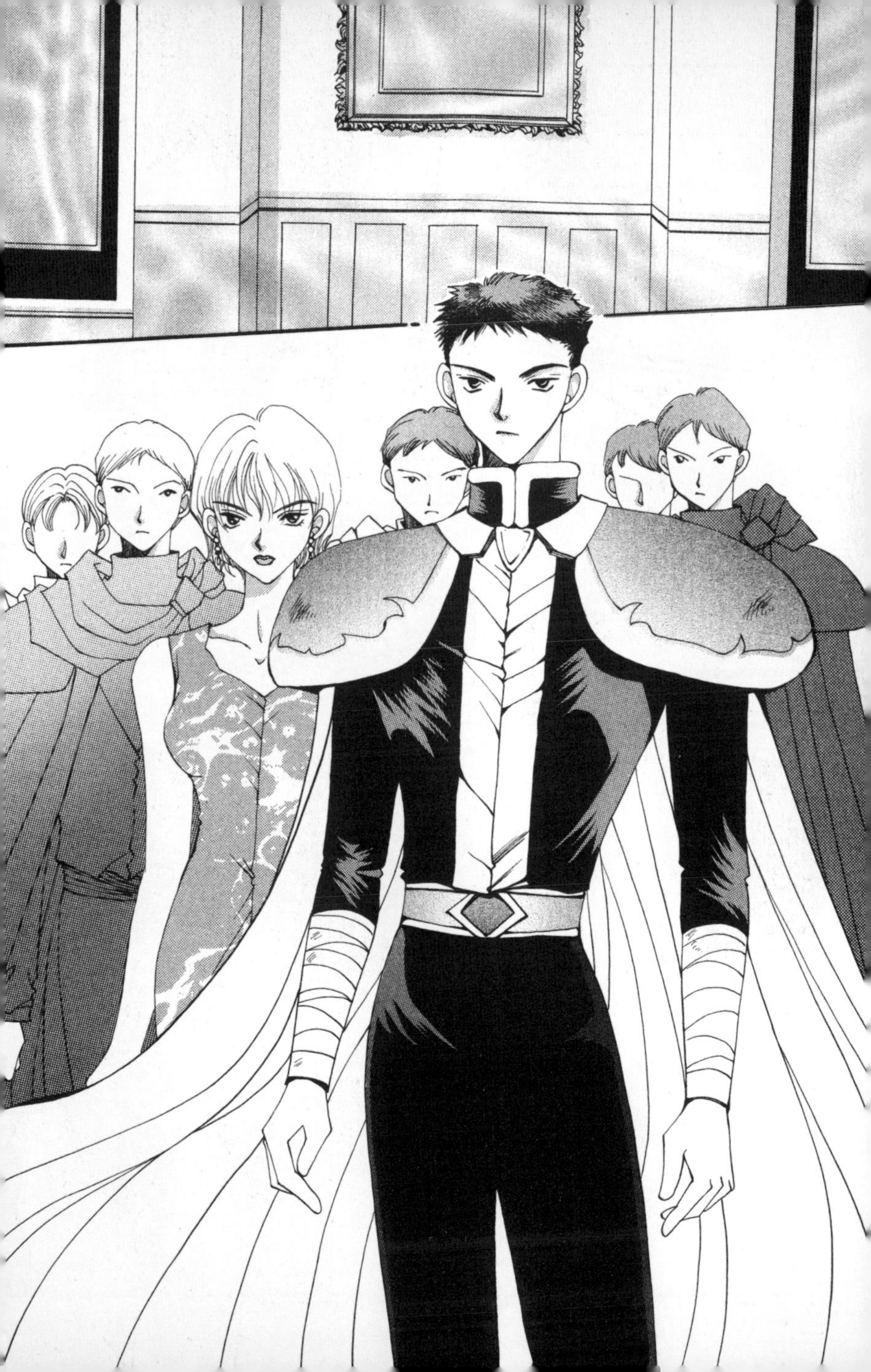

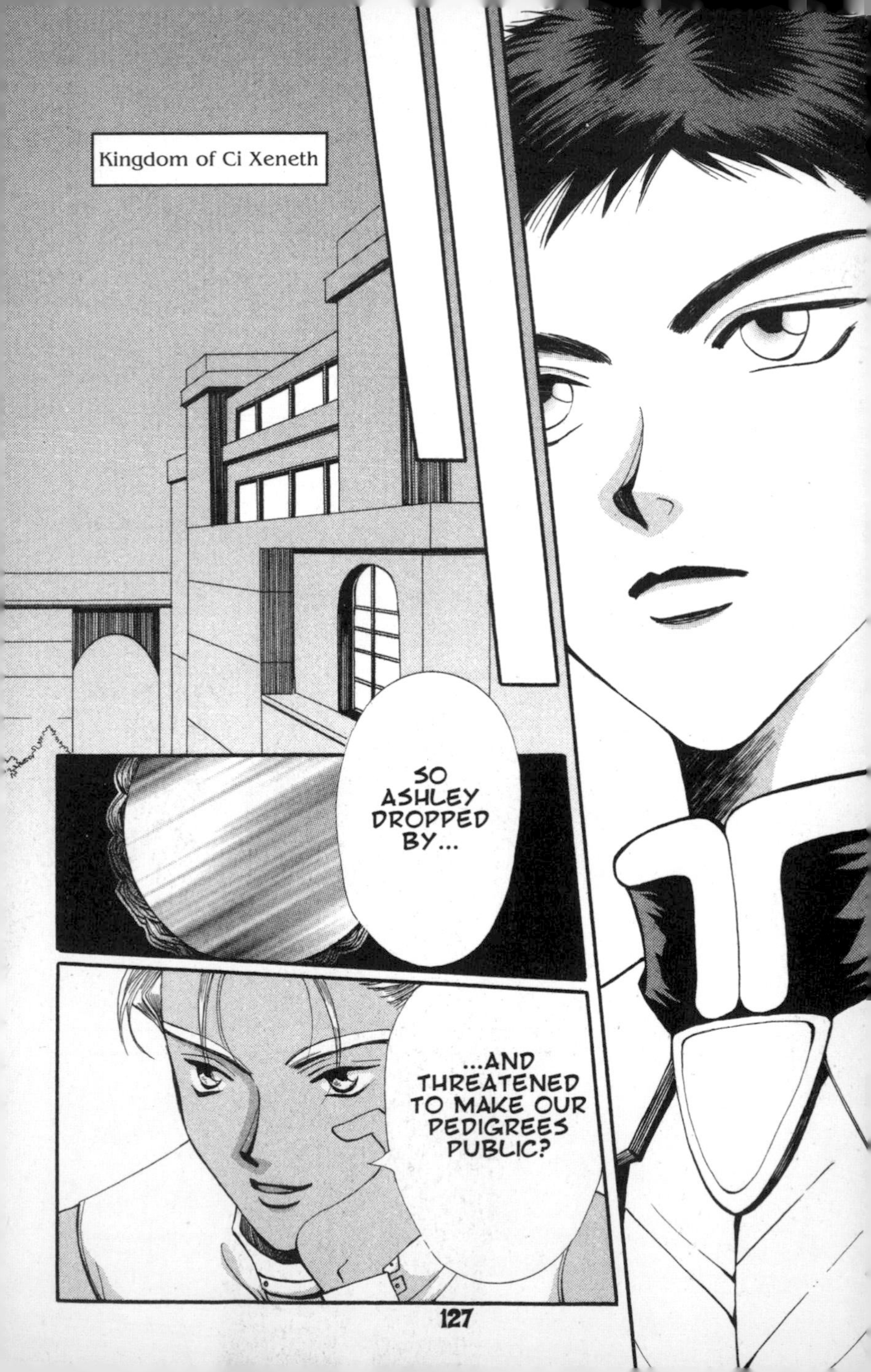
Kingdom of Ci Xeneth
SO ASHLEY DROPPED BY...
...AND THREATENED TO MAKE OUR PEDIGREES PUBLIC?

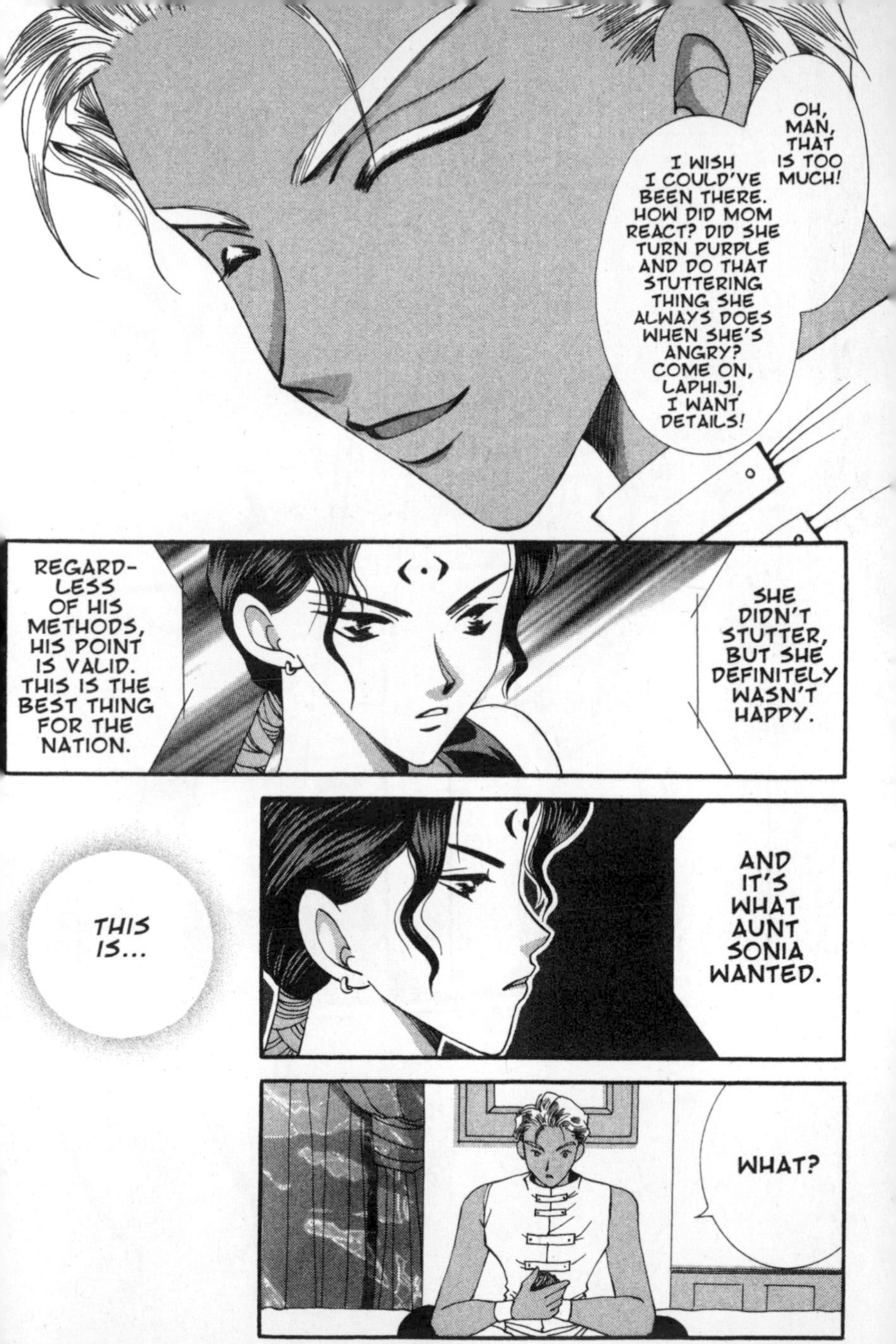
OH, MAN, THAT IS TOO MUCH!
I WISH I COULD'VE BEEN THERE. HOW DID MOM REACT? DID SHE TURN PURPLE AND DO THAT STUTTERING THING SHE ALWAYS DOES WHEN SHE'S ANGRY? COME ON, LAPHIJI, I WANT DETAILS!
SHE DIDN'T STUTTER, BUT SHE DEFINITELY WASN'T HAPPY.
REGARD-LESS OF HIS METHODS, HIS POINT IS VALID. THIS IS THE BEST THING FOR THE NATION.
AND IT'S WHAT AUNT SONIA WANTED.
THIS IS...
WHAT?

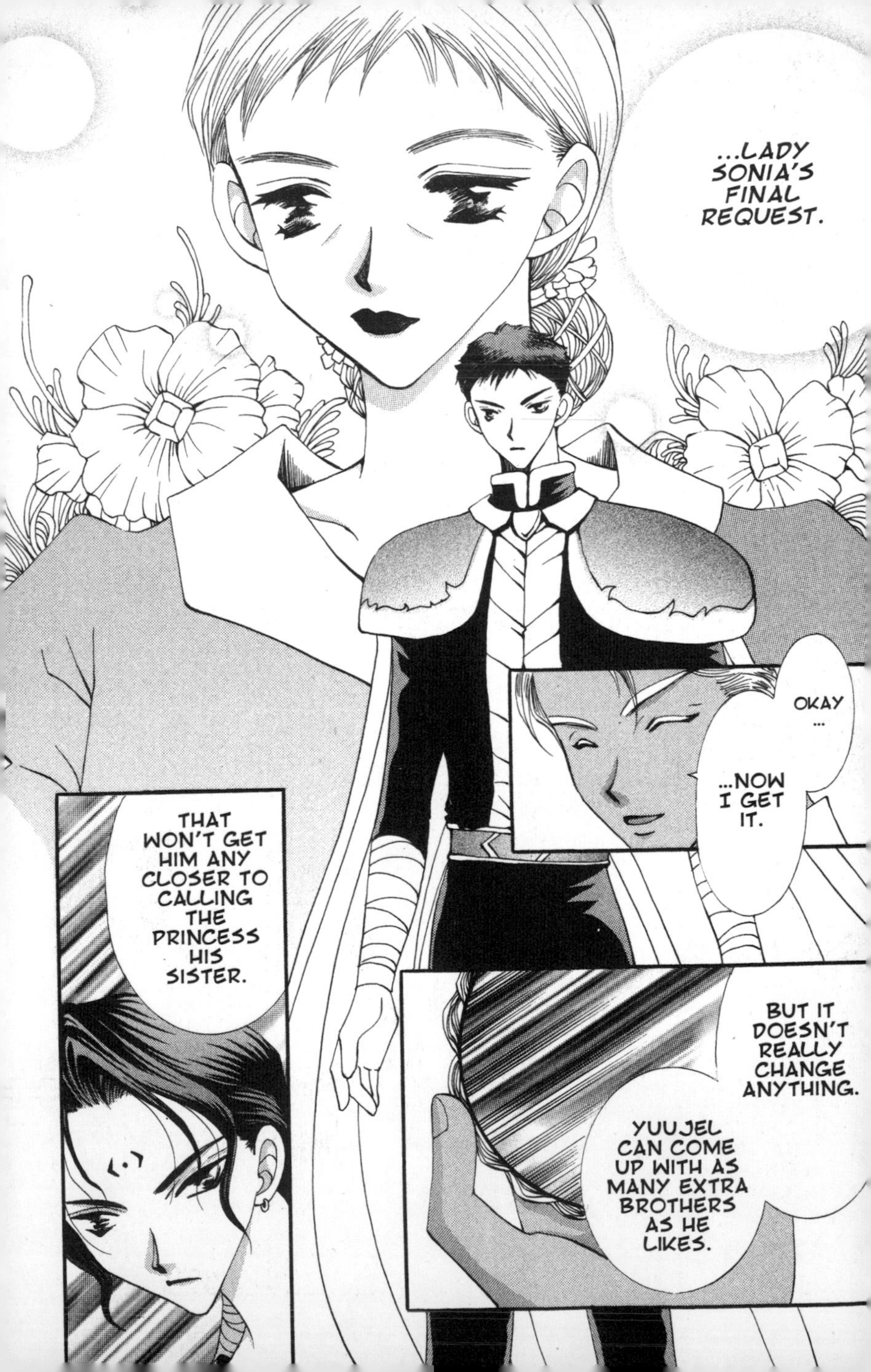
...LADY SONIA'S FINAL REQUEST.
OKAY...
...NOW I GET IT.
BUT IT DOESN'T REALLY CHANGE ANYTHING.
YUUJEL CAN COME UP WITH AS MANY EXTRA BROTHERS AS HE LIKES.
THAT WON'T GET HIM ANY CLOSER TO CALLING THE PRINCESS HIS SISTER.

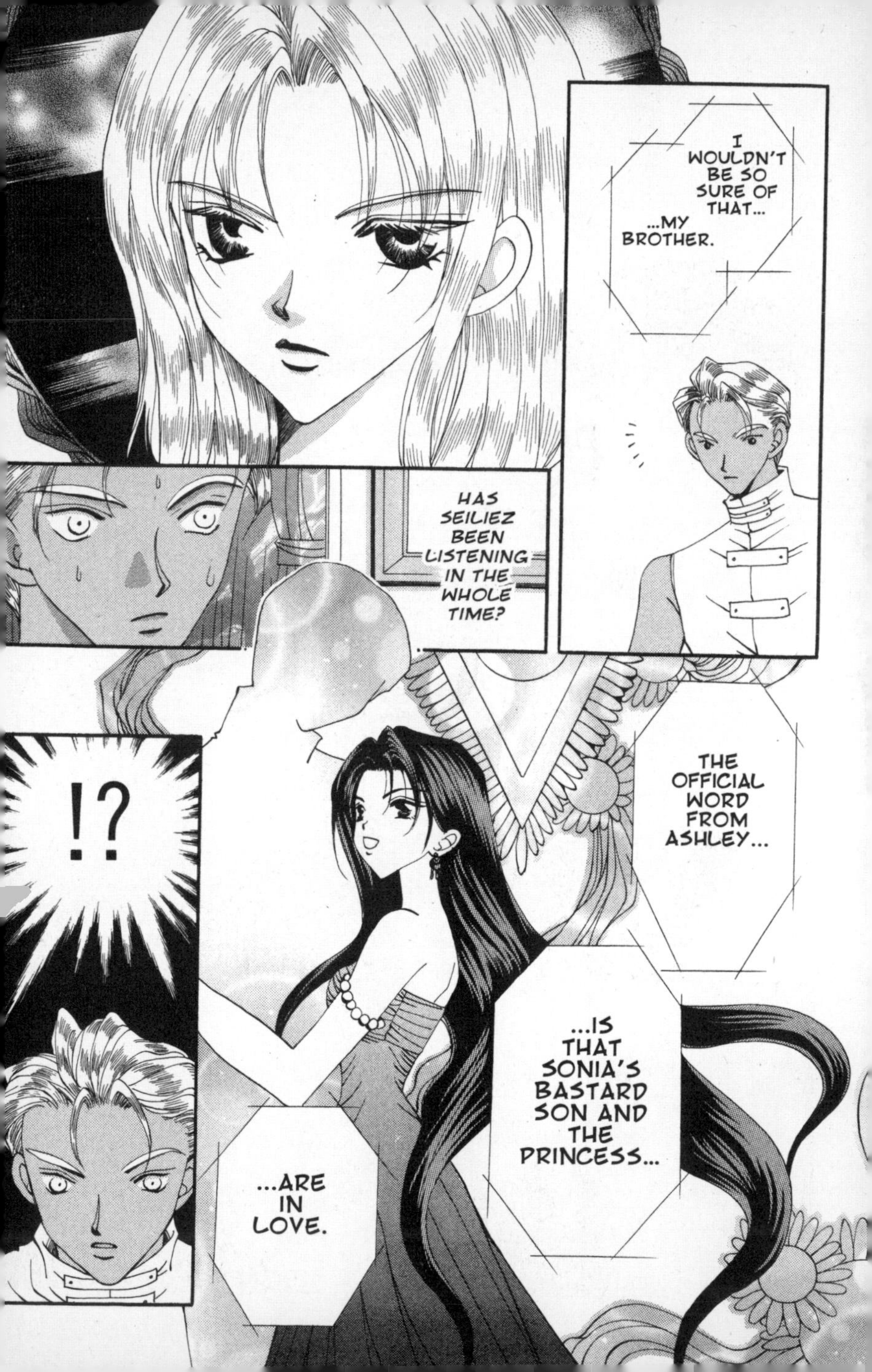
I WOULDN'T BE SO SURE OF THAT...
...MY BROTHER.
HAS SEILIEZ BEEN LISTENING IN THE WHOLE TIME?
THE OFFICIAL WORD FROM ASHLEY...
...IS THAT SONIA'S BASTARD SON AND THE PRINCESS...
...ARE IN LOVE.
!?

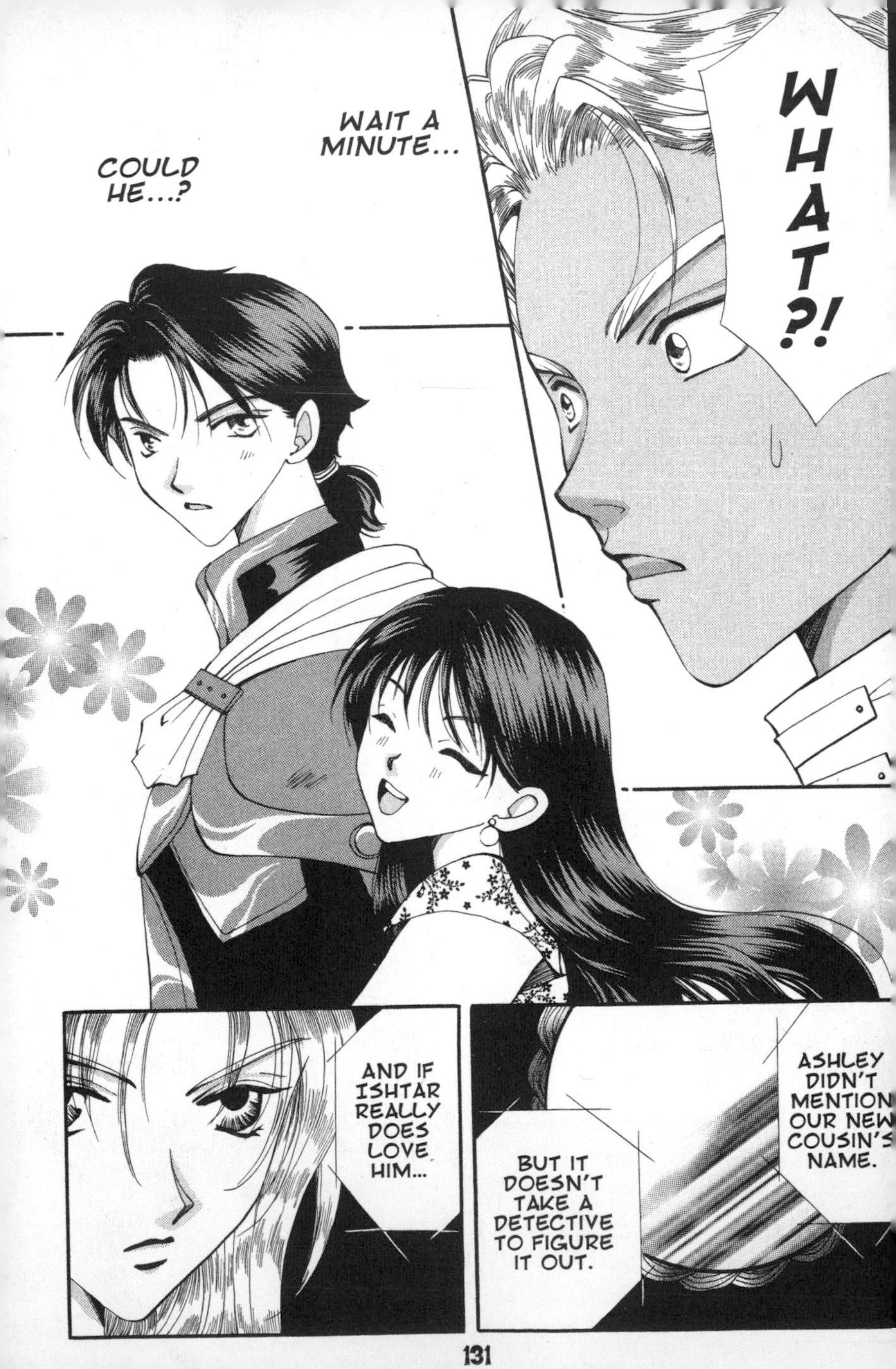
WHAT?!
WAIT A MINUTE...
COULD HE...?
ASHLEY DIDN'T MENTION OUR NEW COUSIN'S NAME.
BUT IT DOESN'T TAKE A DETECTIVE TO FIGURE IT OUT.
AND IF ISHTAR REALLY DOES LOVE HIM...

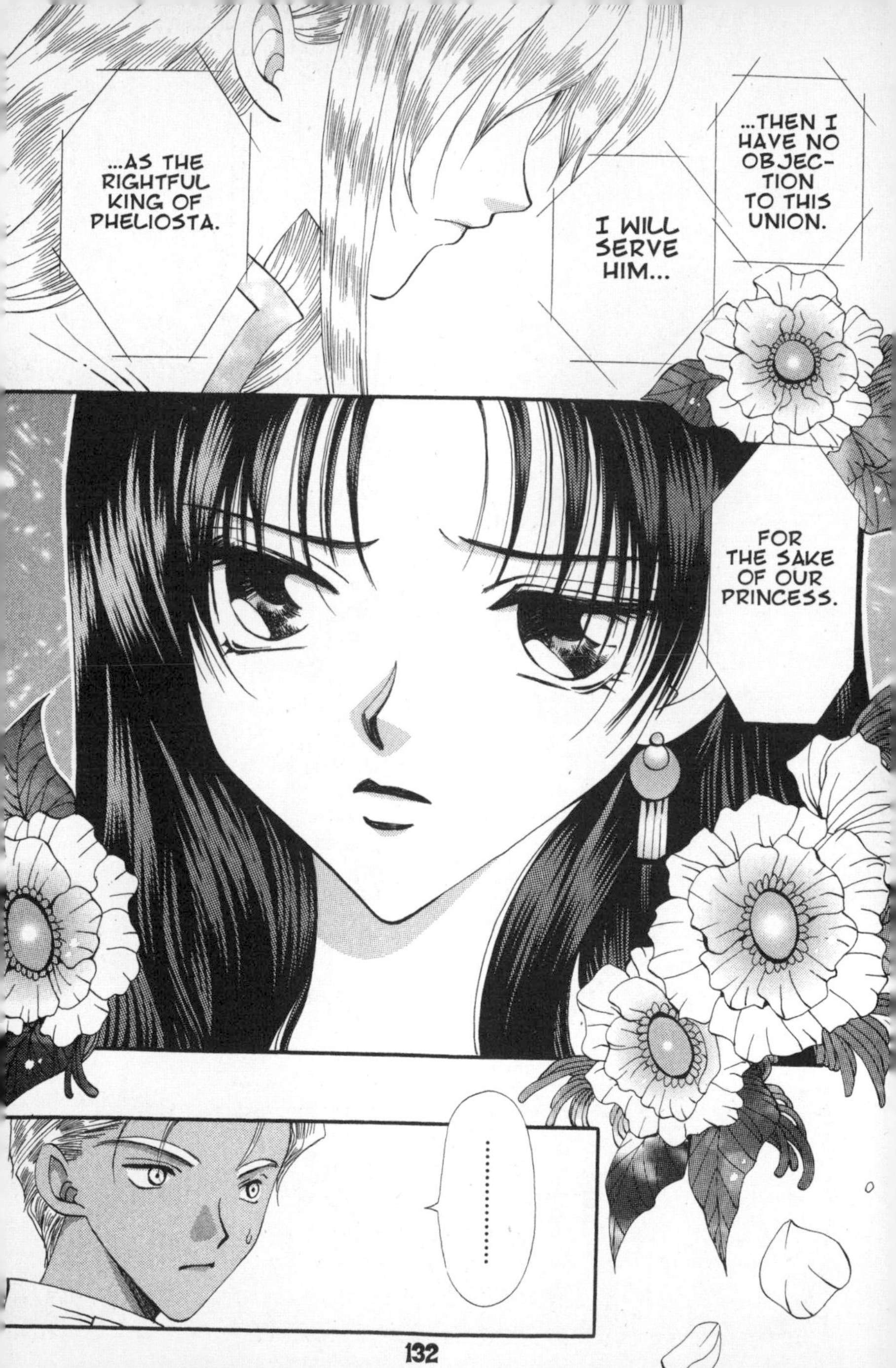
...THEN I HAVE NO OBJECTION TO THIS UNION.
I WILL SERVE HIM...
...AS THE RIGHTFUL KING OF PHELIOSTA.
FOR THE SAKE OF OUR PRINCESS.
....

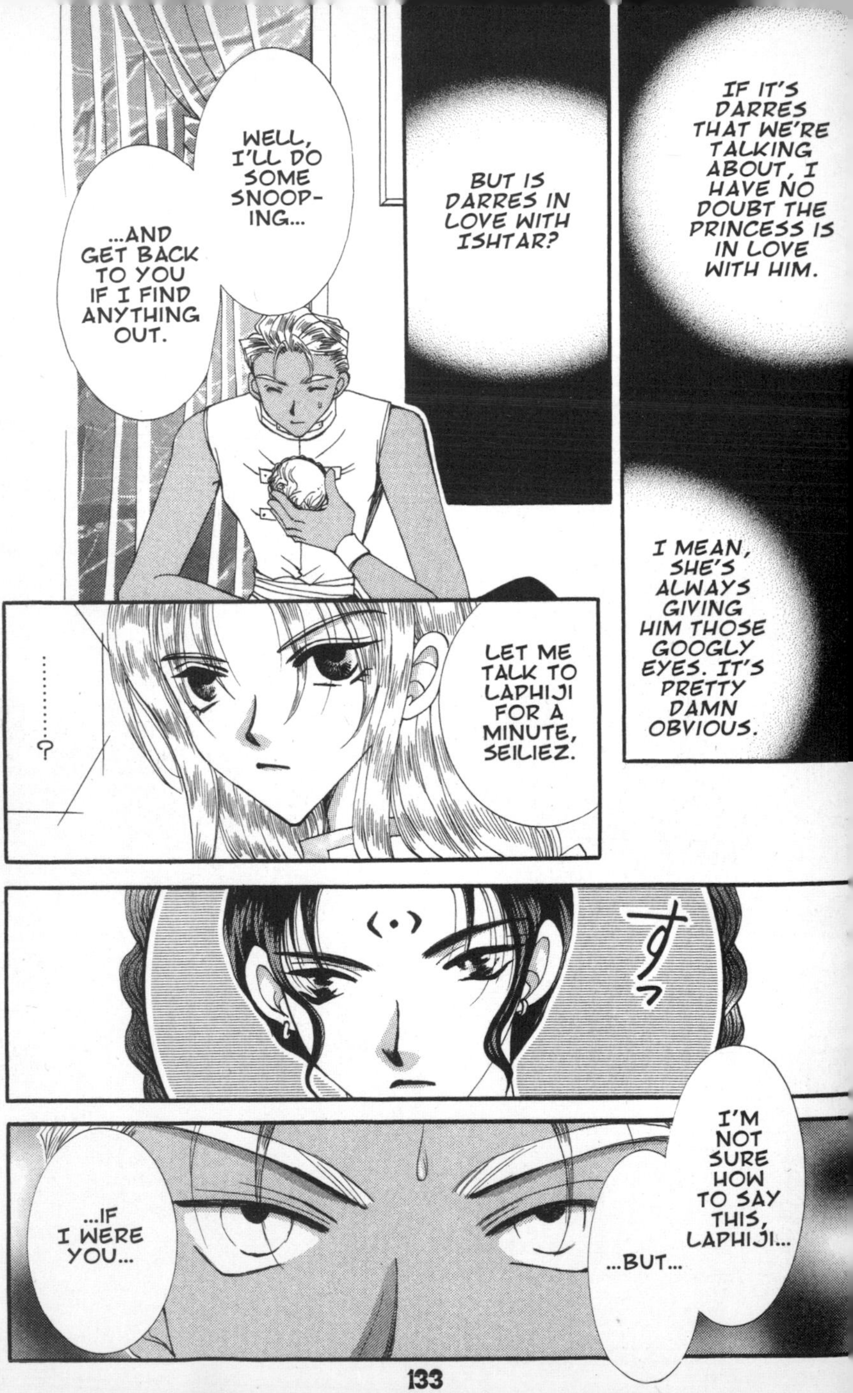
IF IT'S DARRES THAT WE'RE TALKING ABOUT, I HAVE NO DOUBT THE PRINCESS IS IN LOVE WITH HIM.
I MEAN, SHE'S ALWAYS GIVING HIM THOSE GOOGLY EYES. IT'S PRETTY DAMN OBVIOUS.
BUT IS DARRES IN LOVE WITH ISHTAR?
WELL, I'LL DO SOME SNOOP-ING...
...AND GET BACK TO YOU IF I FIND ANYTHING OUT.
LET ME TALK TO LAPHIJI FOR A MINUTE, SEILIEZ.
.........?
すっ
I'M NOT SURE HOW TO SAY THIS, LAPHIJI...
...BUT...
...IF I WERE YOU...

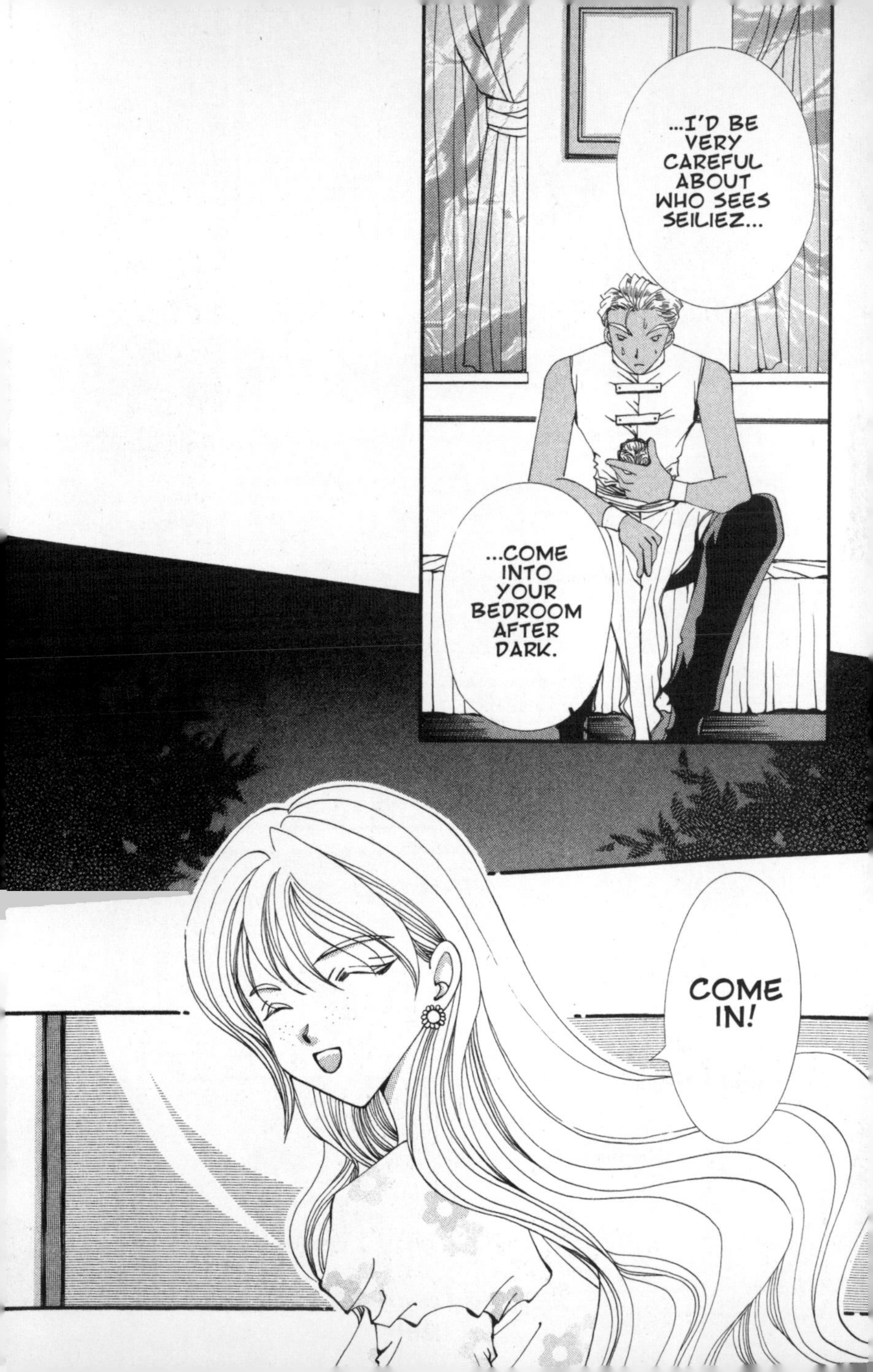
...I'D BE VERY CAREFUL ABOUT WHO SEES SEILIEZ...
...COME INTO YOUR BEDROOM AFTER DARK.
COME IN!

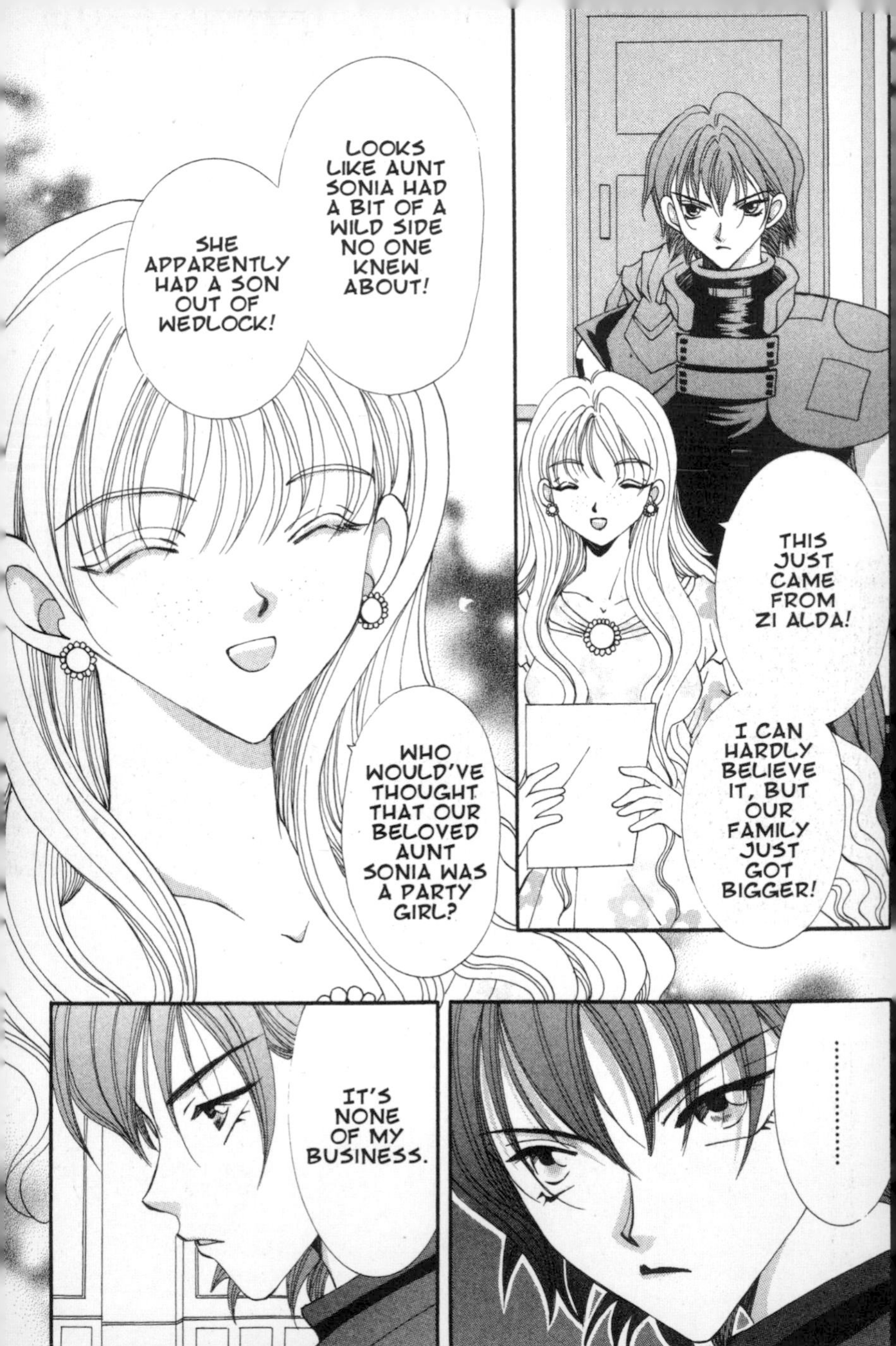
THIS JUST CAME FROM ZI ALDA!
I CAN HARDLY BELIEVE IT, BUT OUR FAMILY JUST GOT BIGGER!
LOOKS LIKE AUNT SONIA HAD A BIT OF A WILD SIDE NO ONE KNEW ABOUT!
SHE APPARENTLY HAD A SON OUT OF WEDLOCK!
WHO WOULD'VE THOUGHT THAT OUR BELOVED AUNT SONIA WAS A PARTY GIRL?
....
IT'S NONE OF MY BUSINESS.

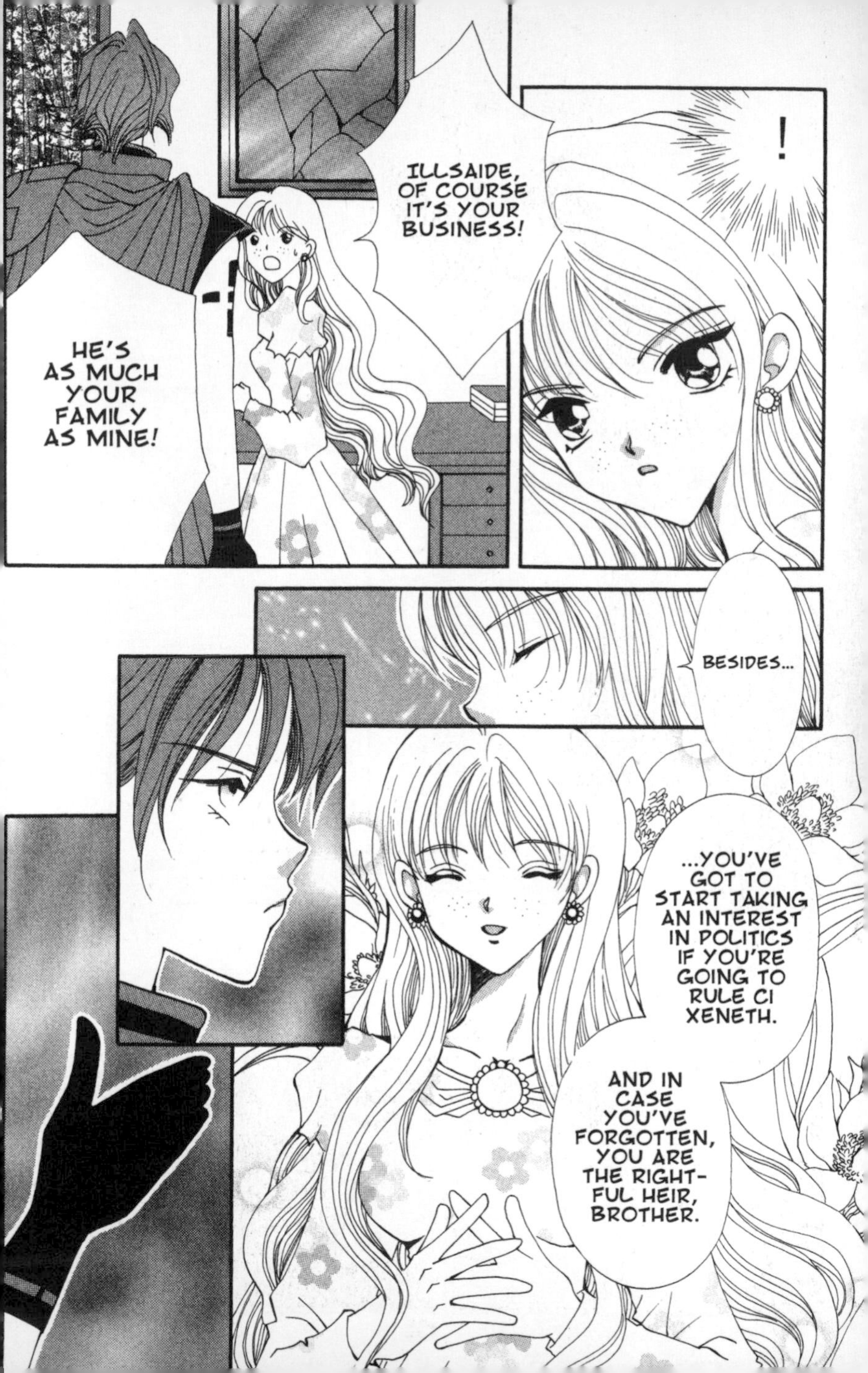
!
ILLSAIDE, OF COURSE IT'S YOUR BUSINESS!
HE'S AS MUCH YOUR FAMILY AS MINE!
BESIDES...
...YOU'VE GOT TO START TAKING AN INTEREST IN POLITICS IF YOU'RE GOING TO RULE CI XENETH.
AND IN CASE YOU'VE FORGOTTEN, YOU ARE THE RIGHT-FUL HEIR, BROTHER.

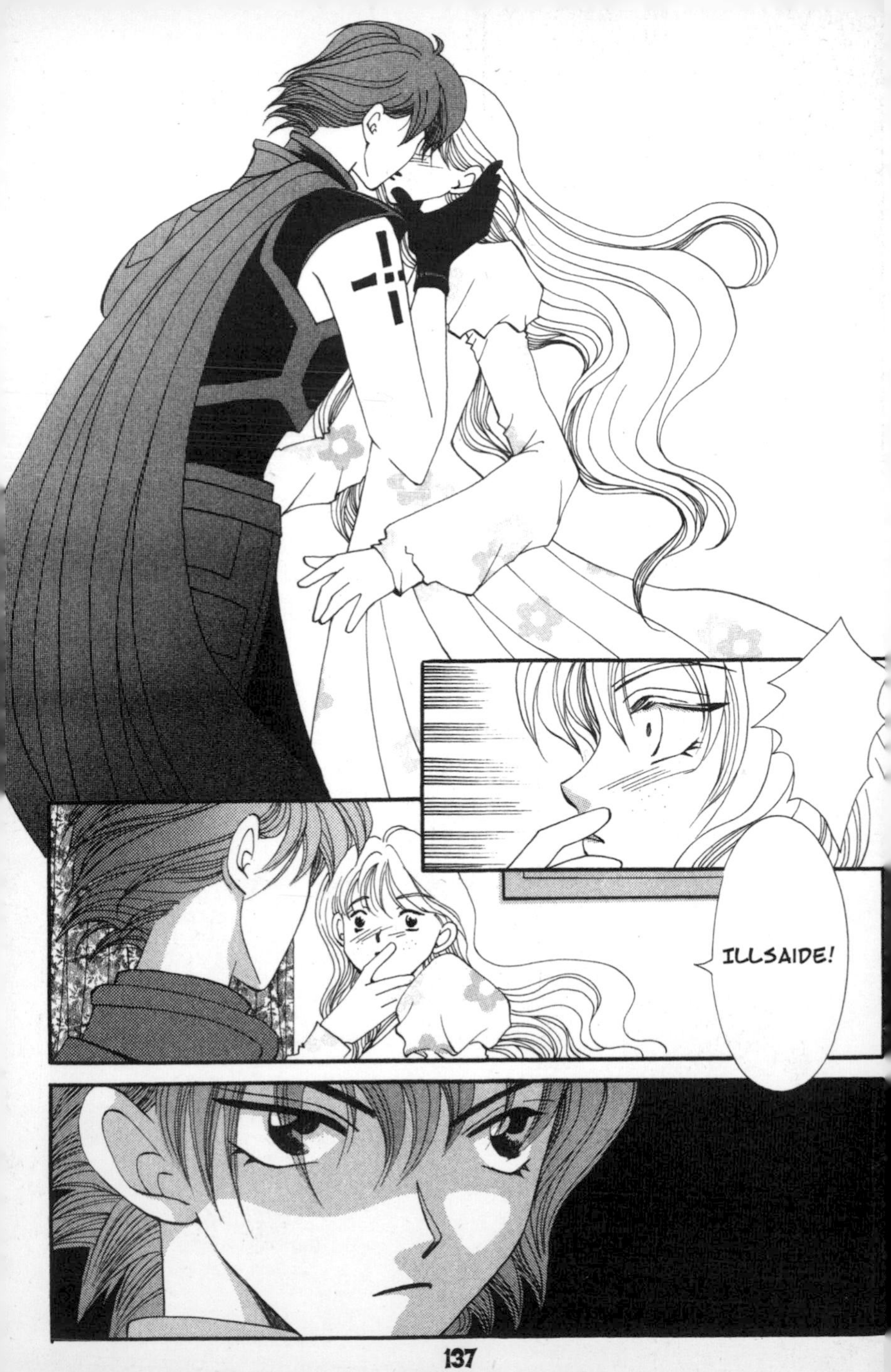
ILLSAIDE!

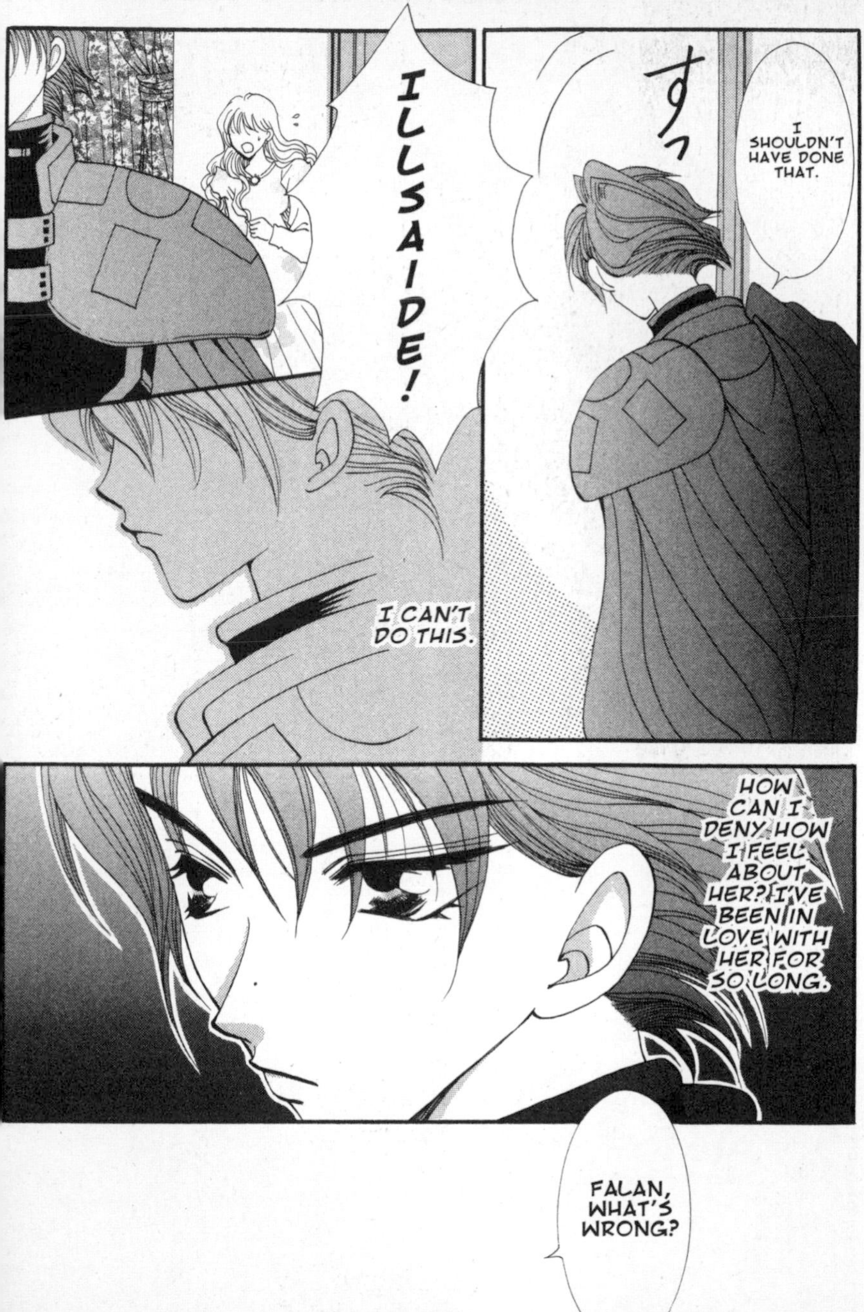
すっ
I SHOULDN'T HAVE DONE THAT.
ILLSAIDE!
I CAN'T DO THIS.
HOW CAN I DENY HOW I FEEL ABOUT HER? I'VE BEEN IN LOVE WITH HER FOR SO LONG.
FALAN, WHAT'S WRONG?

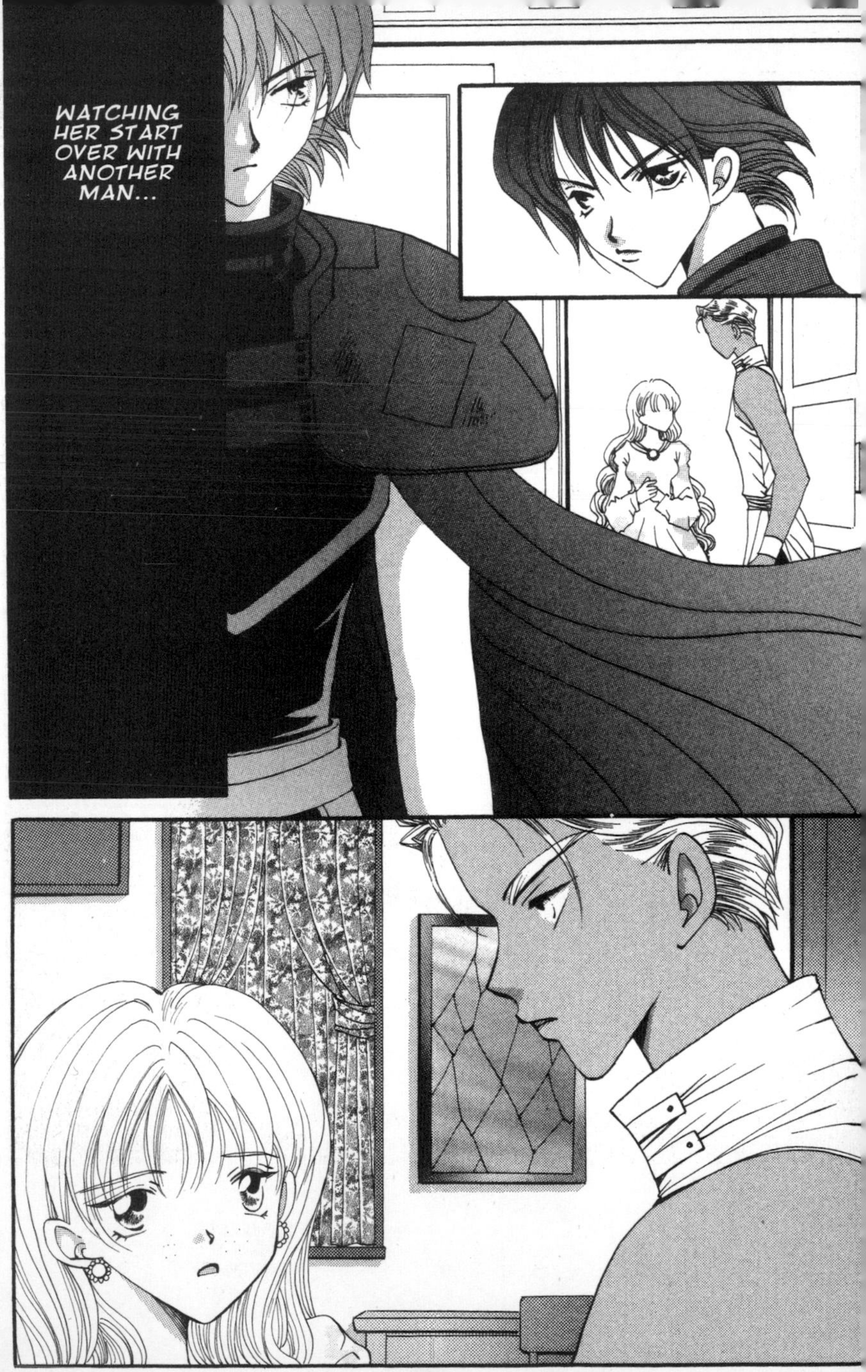
WATCHING HER START OVER WITH ANOTHER MAN...

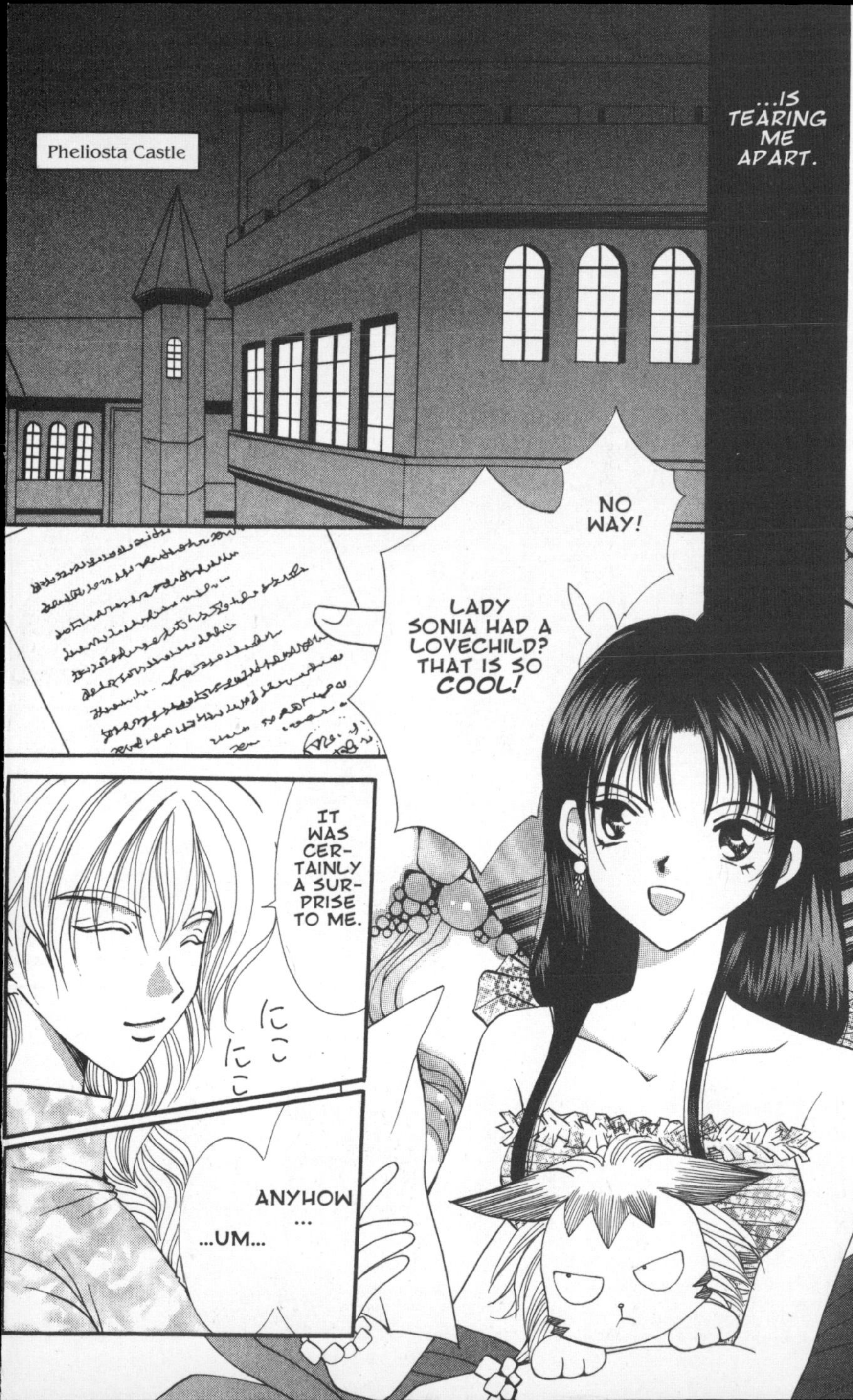
...IS TEARING ME APART.
Pheliosta Castle
NO WAY!
LADY SONIA HAD A LOVECHILD? THAT IS SO COOL!
IT WAS CER-TAINLY A SUR-PRISE TO ME.
にこにこ
ANYHOW ...
...UM...

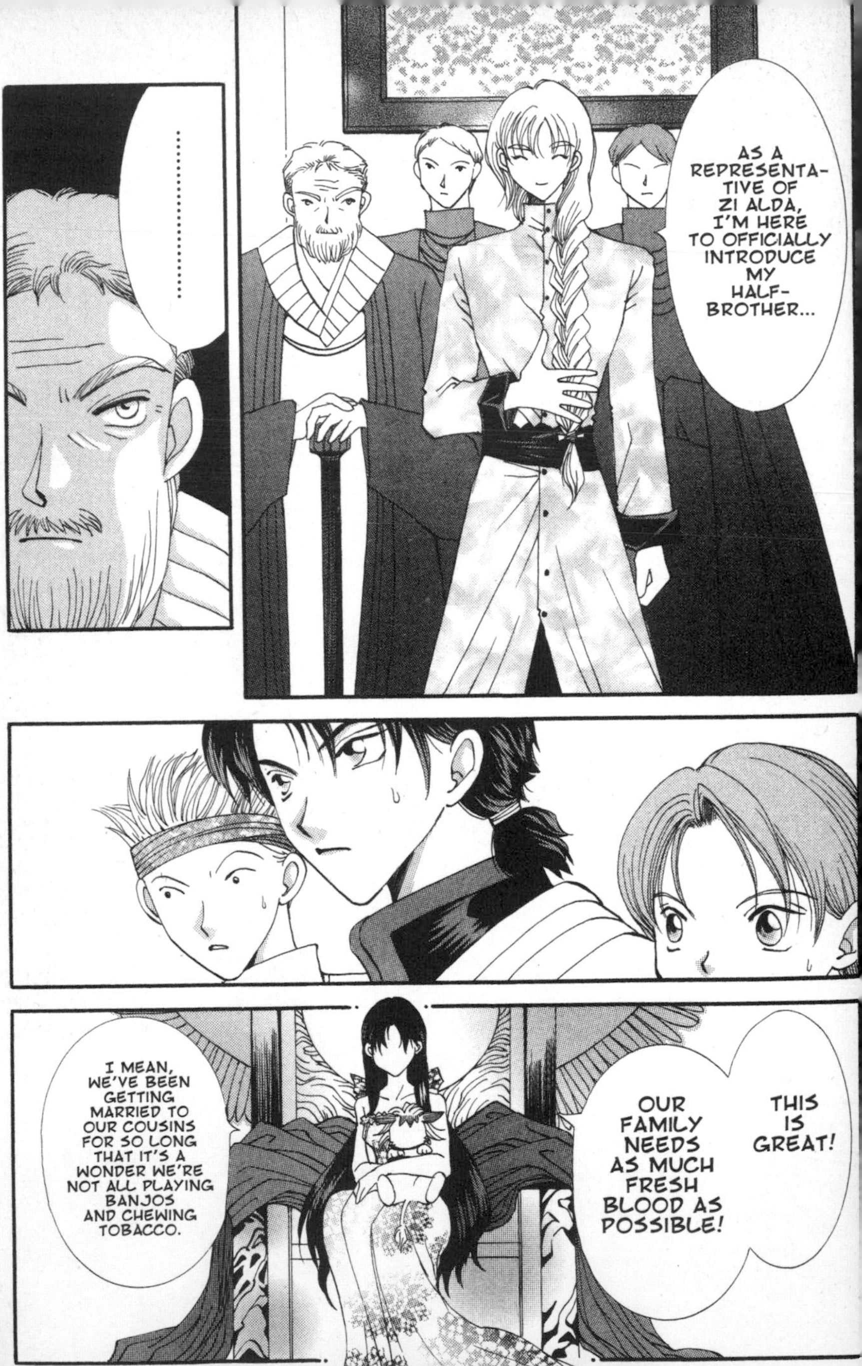
AS A REPRESENTATIVE OF ZI ALDA, I'M HERE TO OFFICIALLY INTRODUCE MY HALF-BROTHER...
......
THIS IS GREAT!
OUR FAMILY NEEDS AS MUCH FRESH BLOOD AS POSSIBLE!
I MEAN, WE'VE BEEN GETTING MARRIED TO OUR COUSINS FOR SO LONG THAT IT'S A WONDER WE'RE NOT ALL PLAYING BANJOS AND CHEWING TOBACCO.

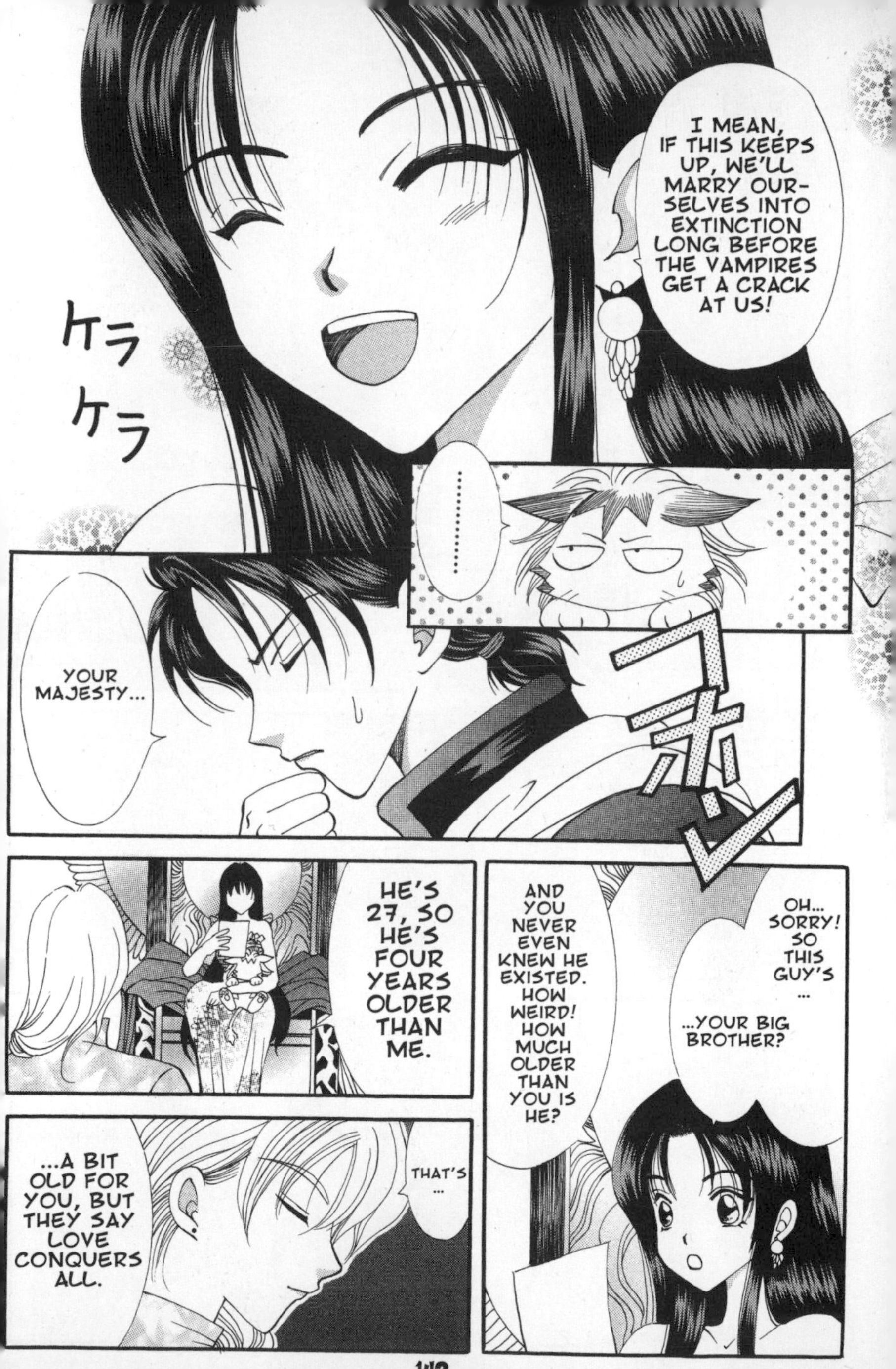
I MEAN, IF THIS KEEPS UP, WE'LL MARRY OUR-SELVES INTO EXTINCTION LONG BEFORE THE VAMPIRES GET A CRACK AT US!
ケラ ケラ
......
YOUR MAJESTY...
OH... SORRY! SO THIS GUY'S ...
...YOUR BIG BROTHER?
AND YOU NEVER EVEN KNEW HE EXISTED. HOW WEIRD! HOW MUCH OLDER THAN YOU IS HE?
HE'S 27, SO HE'S FOUR YEARS OLDER THAN ME.
THAT'S ...
...A BIT OLD FOR YOU, BUT THEY SAY LOVE CONQUERS ALL.

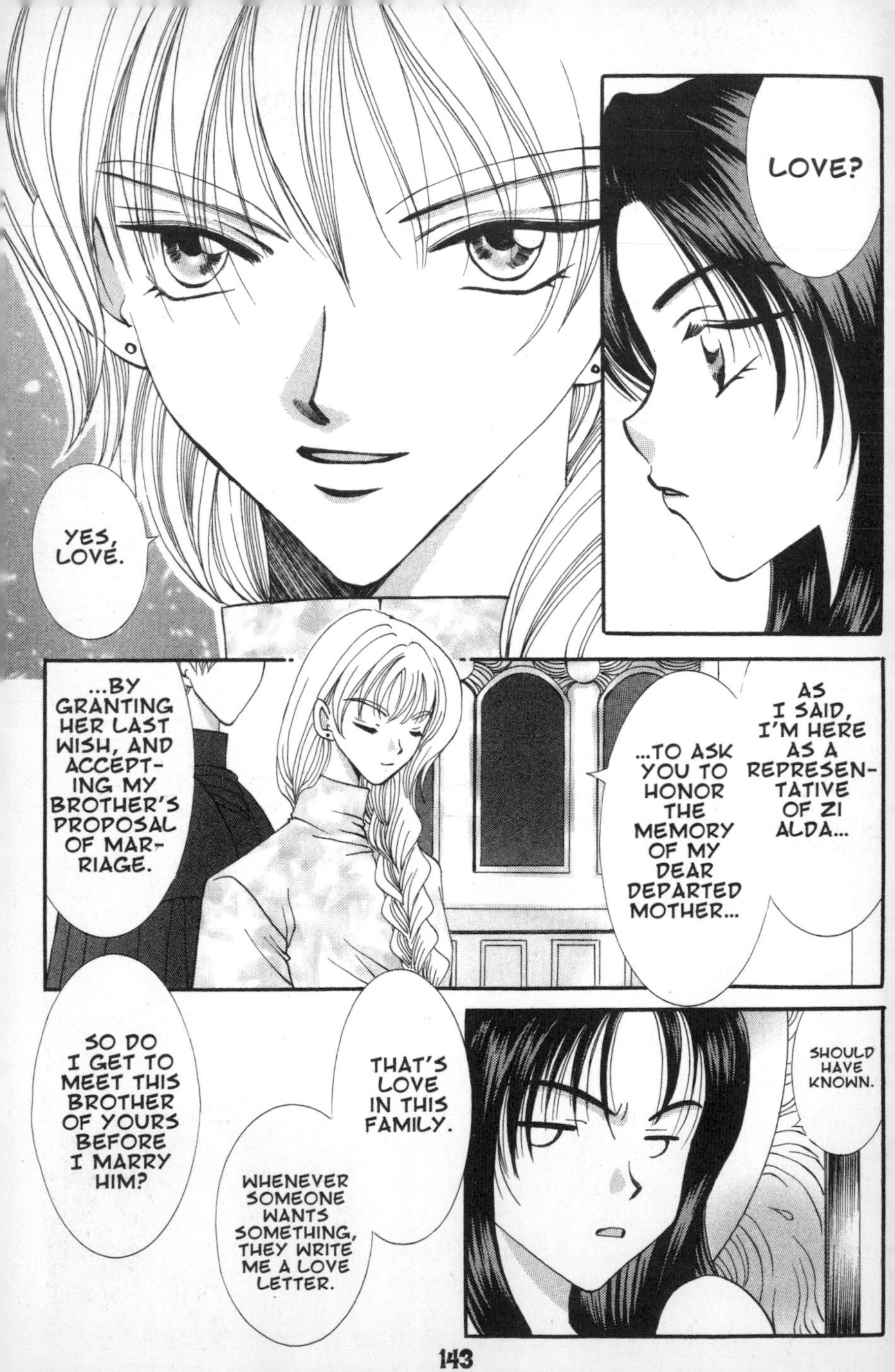
LOVE?
YES, LOVE.
AS I SAID, I'M HERE AS A REPRESEN-TATIVE OF ZI ALDA...
...TO ASK YOU TO HONOR THE MEMORY OF MY DEAR DEPARTED MOTHER...
...BY GRANTING HER LAST WISH, AND ACCEPT-ING MY BROTHER'S PROPOSAL OF MAR-RIAGE.
SHOULD HAVE KNOWN.
THAT'S LOVE IN THIS FAMILY.
WHENEVER SOMEONE WANTS SOMETHING, THEY WRITE ME A LOVE LETTER.
SO DO I GET TO MEET THIS BROTHER OF YOURS BEFORE I MARRY HIM?

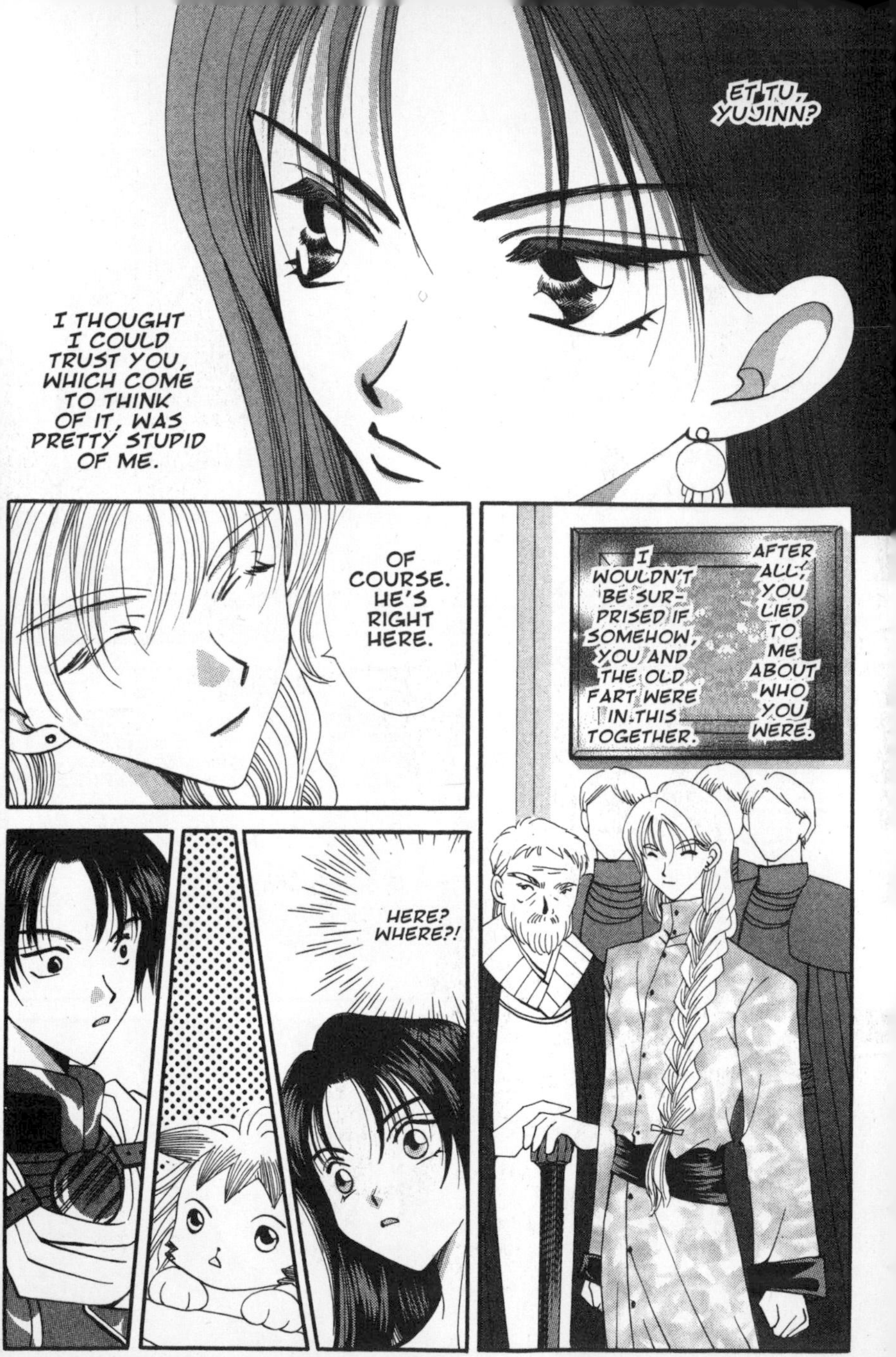
ET TU, YUJINN?
I THOUGHT I COULD TRUST YOU, WHICH COME TO THINK OF IT, WAS PRETTY STUPID OF ME.
AFTER ALL, YOU LIED TO ME ABOUT WHO YOU WERE.
I WOULDN'T BE SUR-PRISED IF SOMEHOW, YOU AND THE OLD FART WERE IN THIS TOGETHER.
OF COURSE. HE'S RIGHT HERE.
HERE? WHERE?!

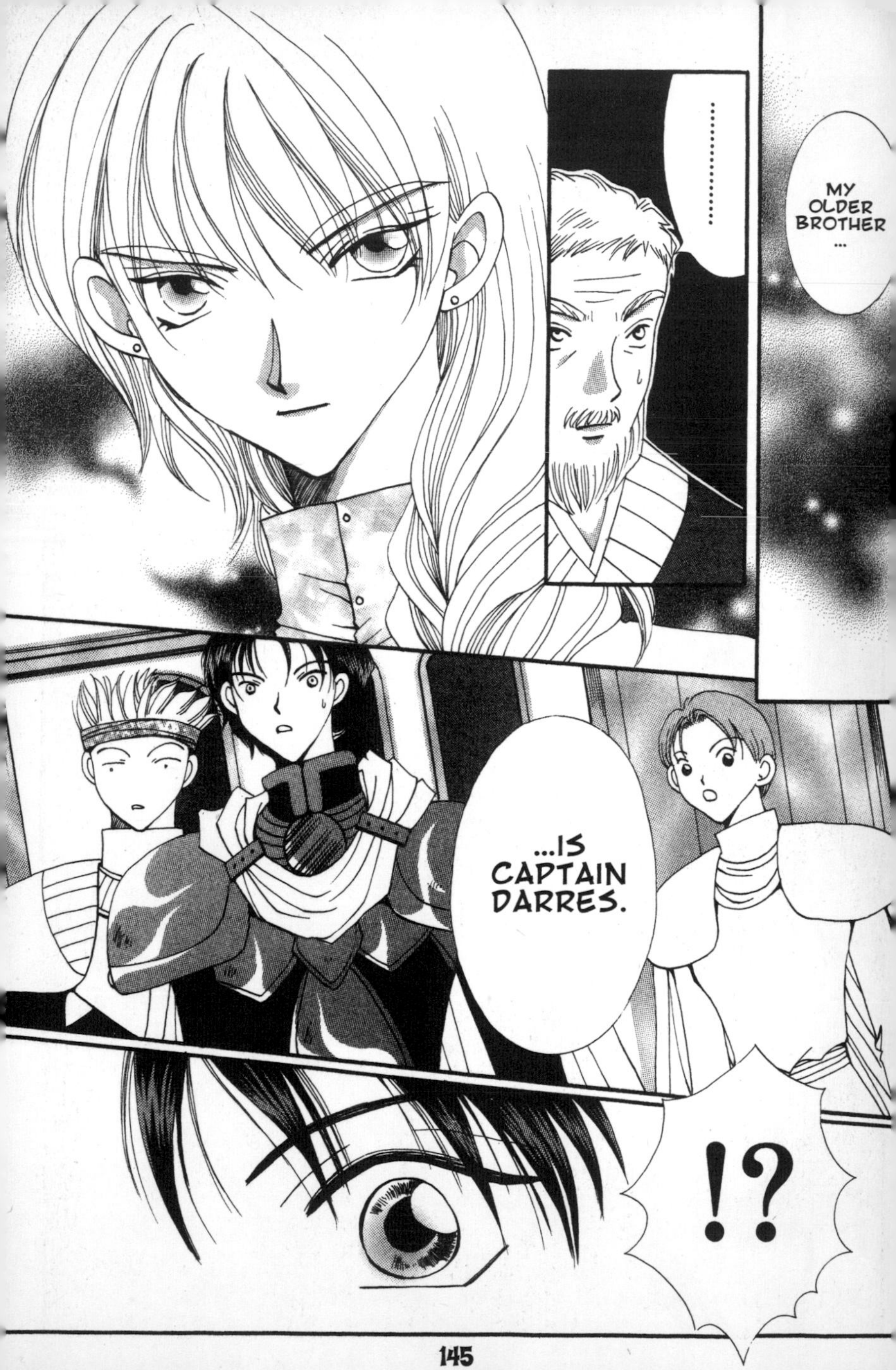
MY OLDER BROTHER ...
......
...IS CAPTAIN DARRES.
!?

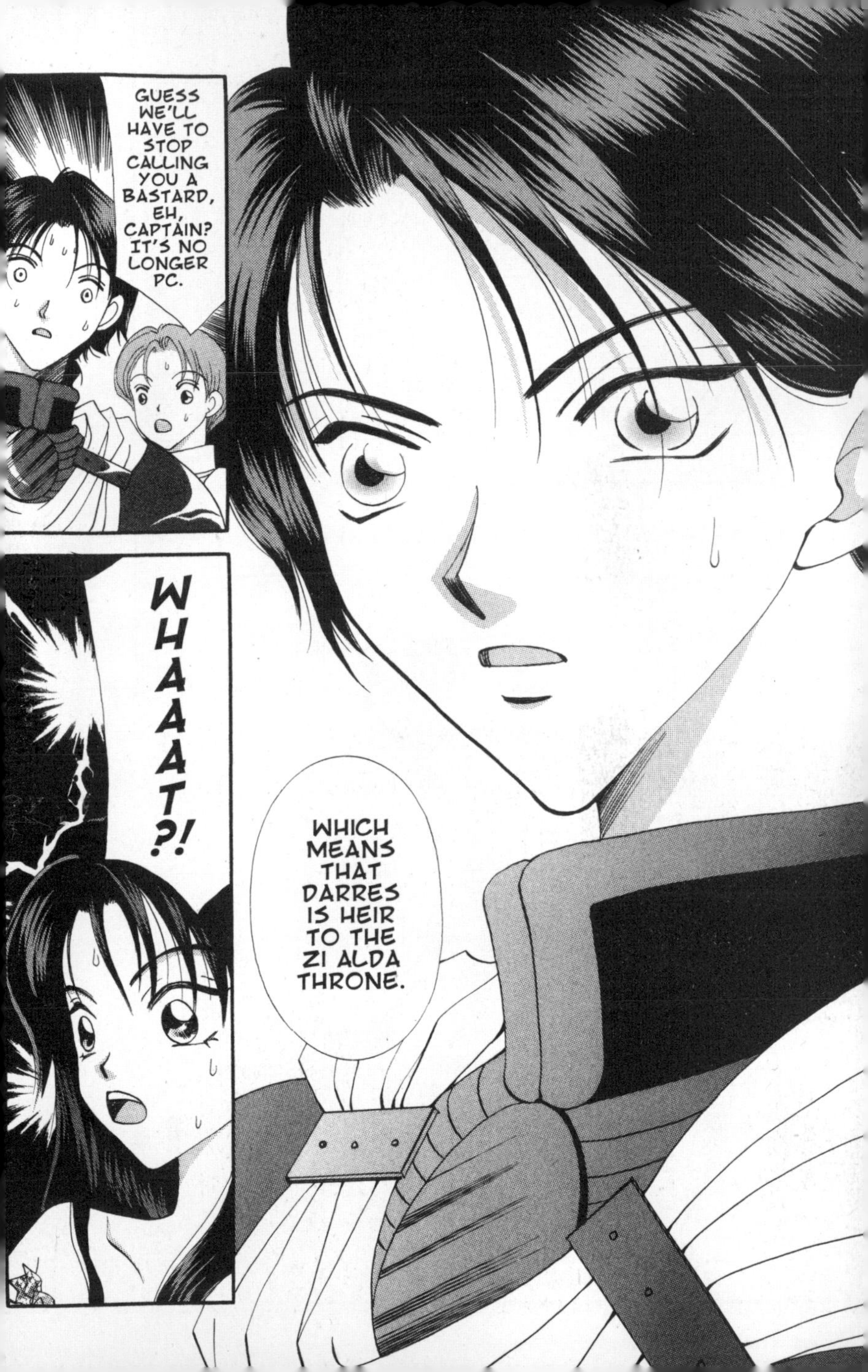
WHICH MEANS THAT DARRES IS HEIR TO THE ZI ALDA THRONE.
GUESS WE'LL HAVE TO STOP CALLING YOU A BASTARD, EH, CAPTAIN? IT'S NO LONGER PC.
WHAAAAT?!

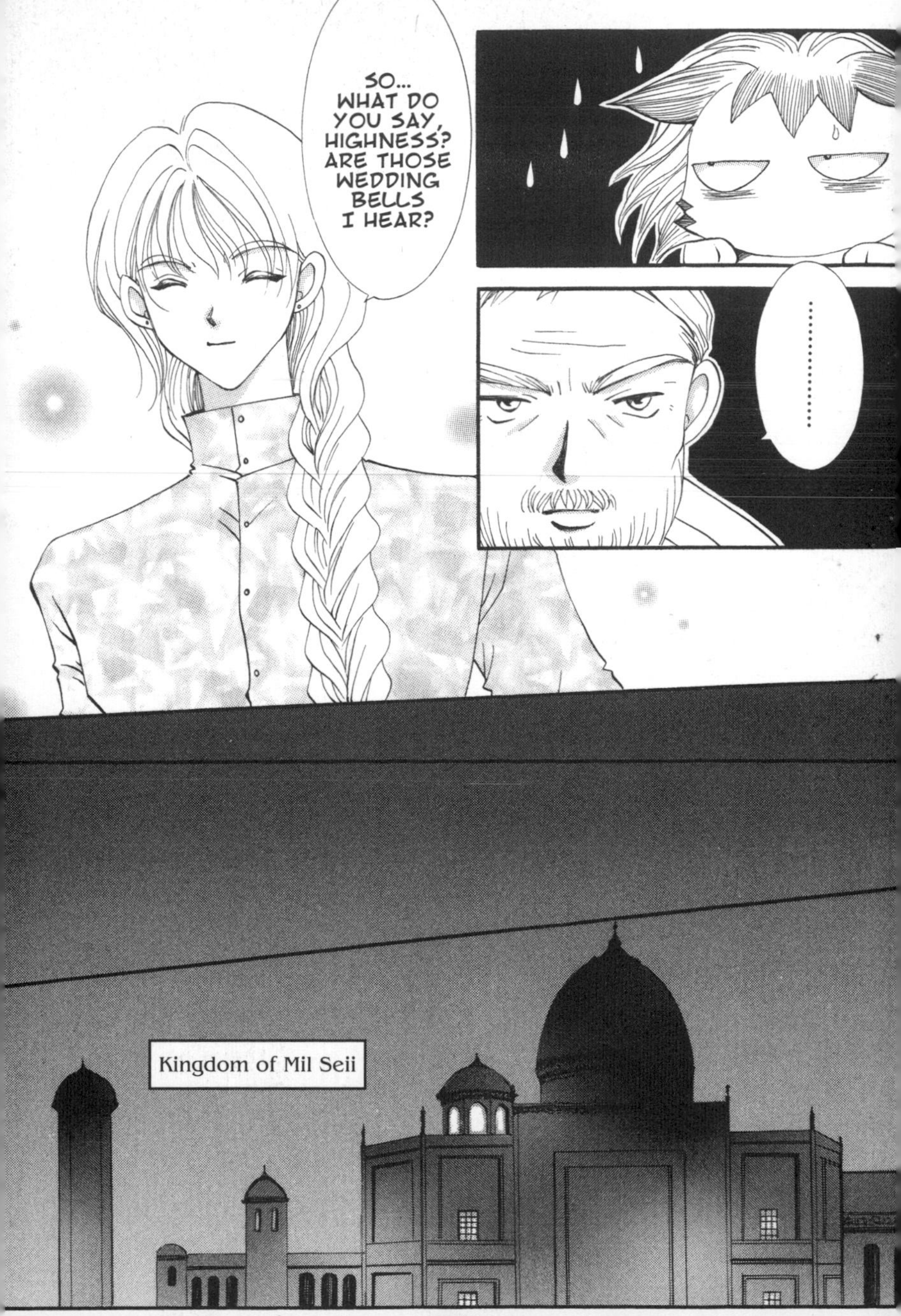
......
SO... WHAT DO YOU SAY, HIGHNESS? ARE THOSE WEDDING BELLS I HEAR?
Kingdom of Mil Seii

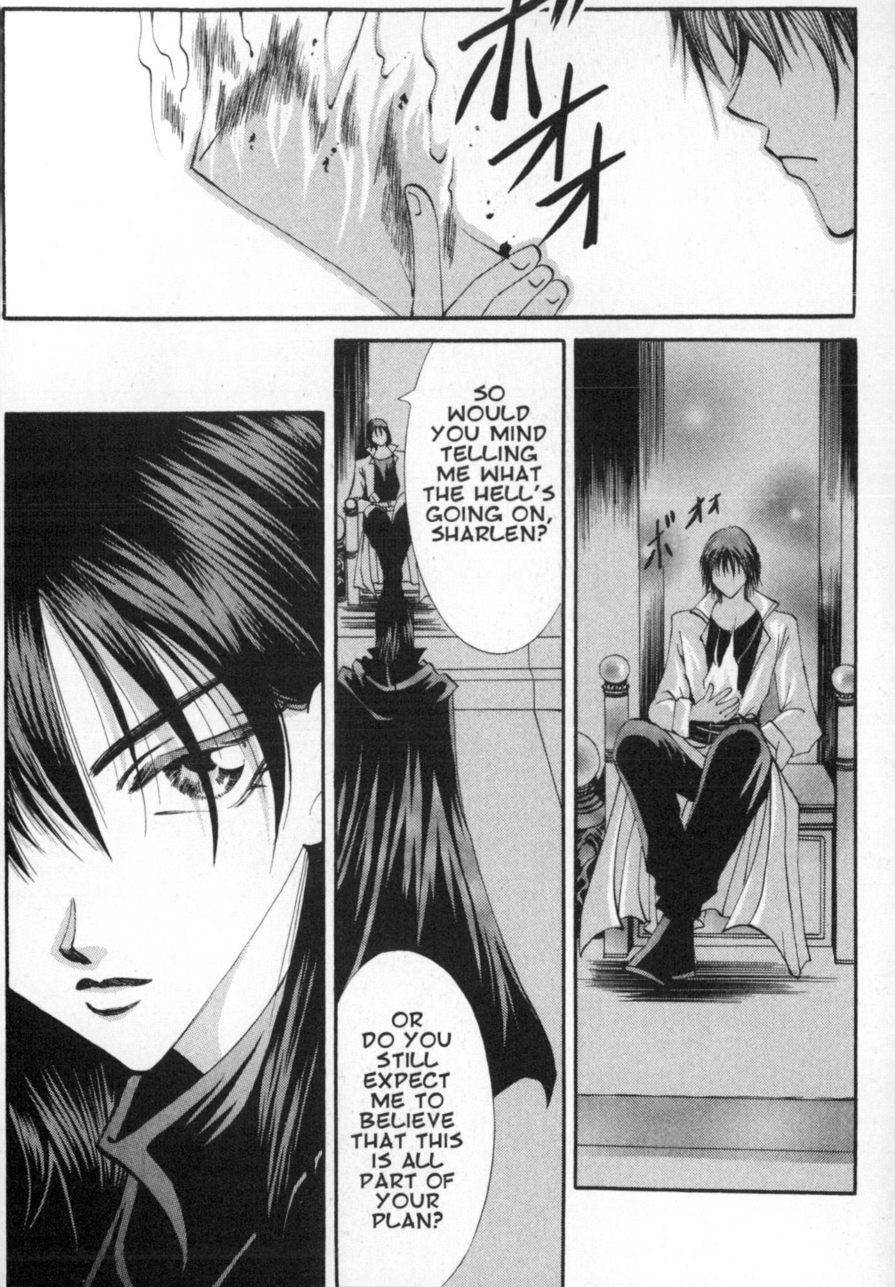
ボオオ
ボオオ
SO WOULD YOU MIND TELLING ME WHAT THE HELL'S GOING ON, SHARLEN?
OR DO YOU STILL EXPECT ME TO BELIEVE THAT THIS IS ALL PART OF YOUR PLAN?

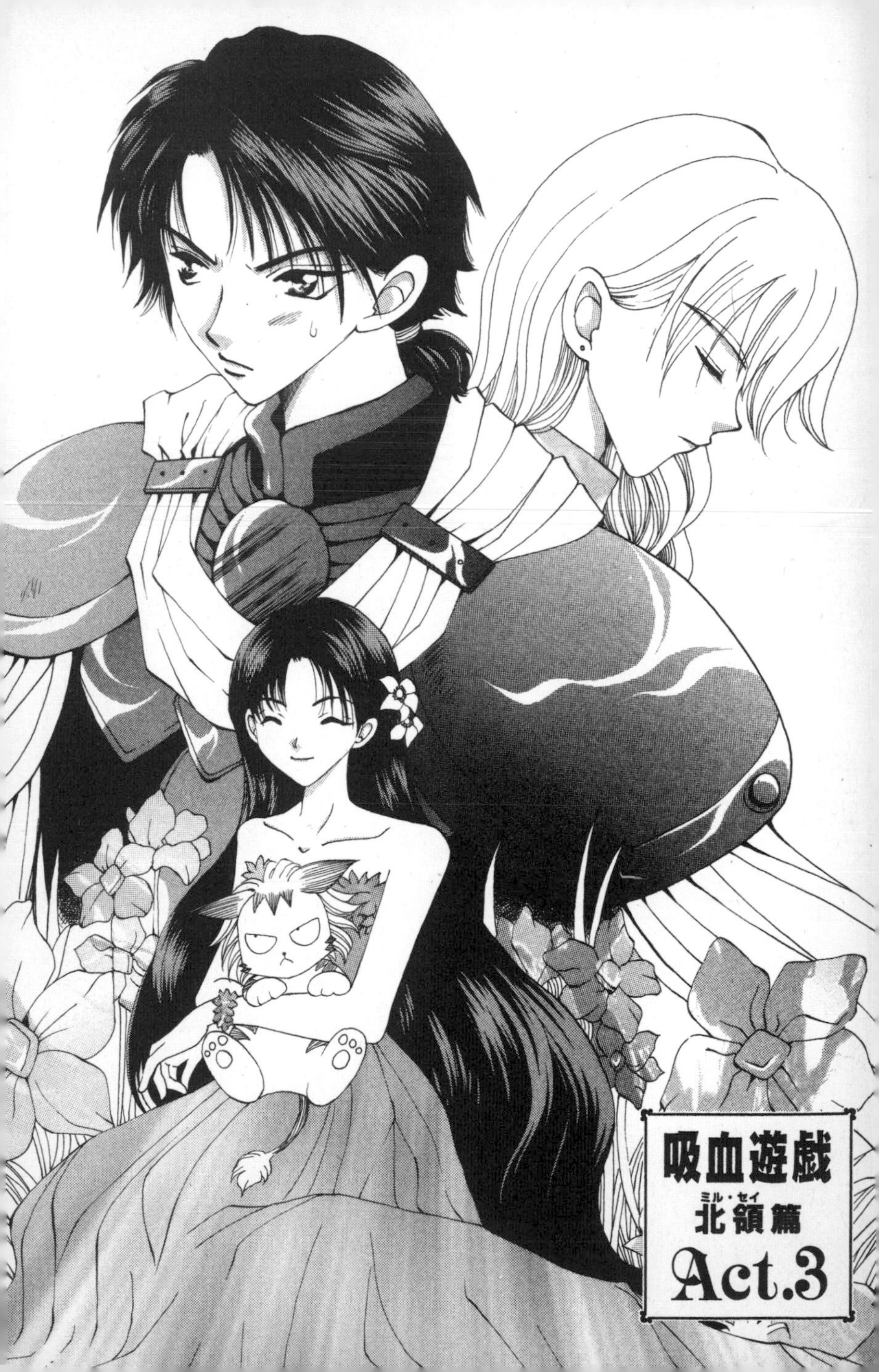
吸血遊戯
ミル・セイ
北領篇
Act.3

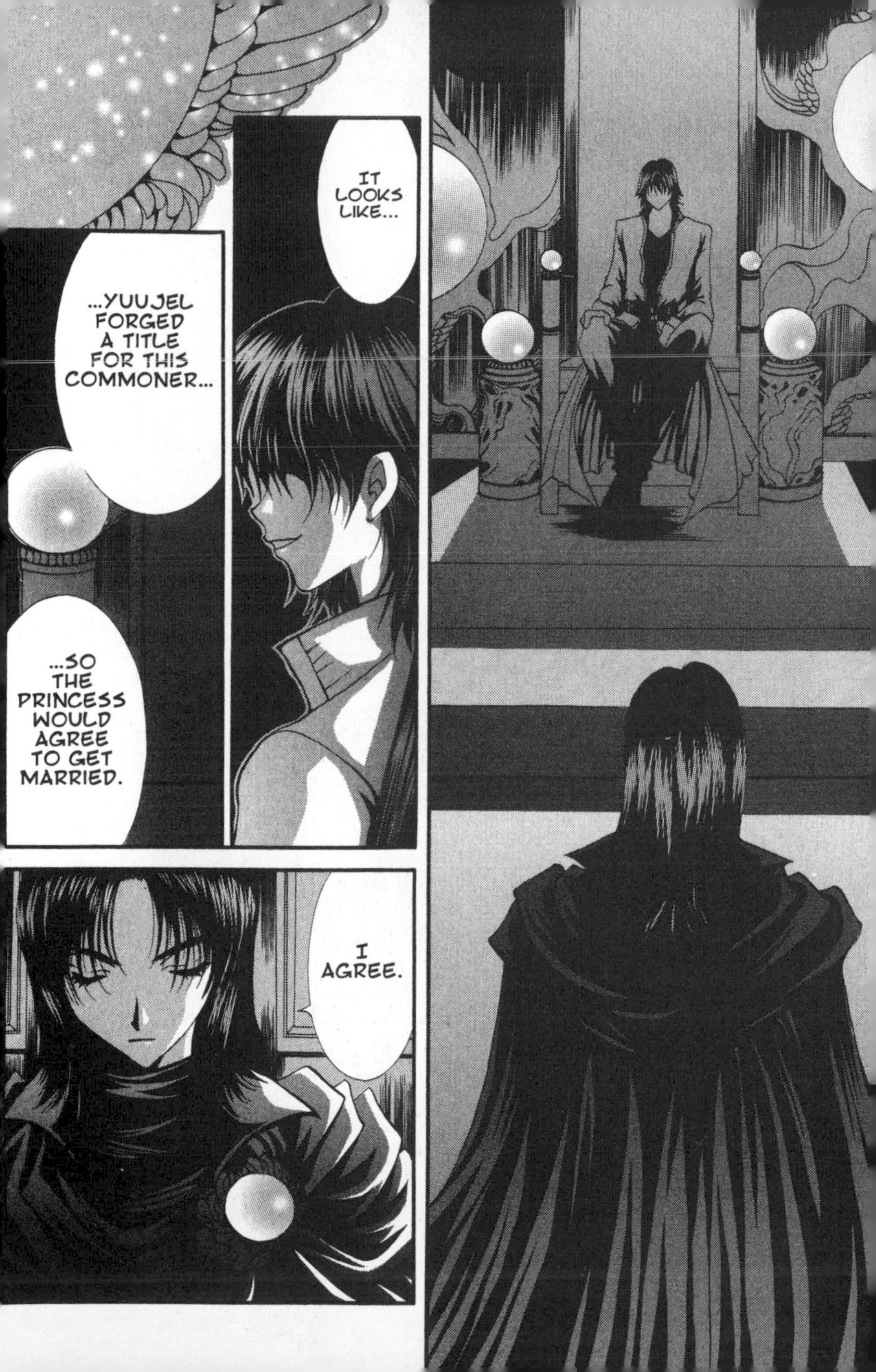
IT LOOKS LIKE...
...YUUJEL FORGED A TITLE FOR THIS COMMONER...
...SO THE PRINCESS WOULD AGREE TO GET MARRIED.
I AGREE.

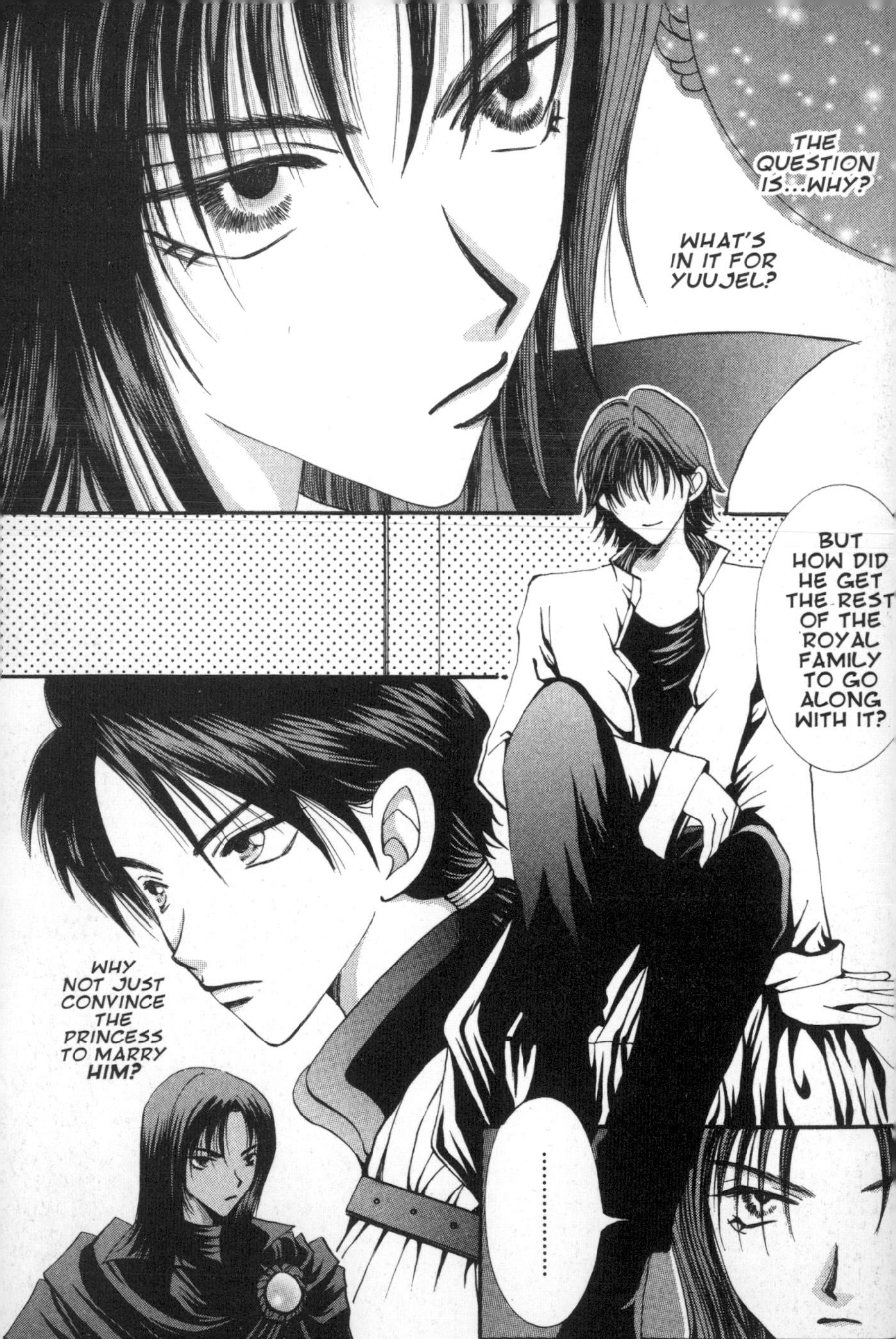
THE QUESTION IS...WHY?
WHAT'S IN IT FOR YUUJEL?
BUT HOW DID HE GET THE REST OF THE ROYAL FAMILY TO GO ALONG WITH IT?
WHY NOT JUST CONVINCE THE PRINCESS TO MARRY HIM?
......

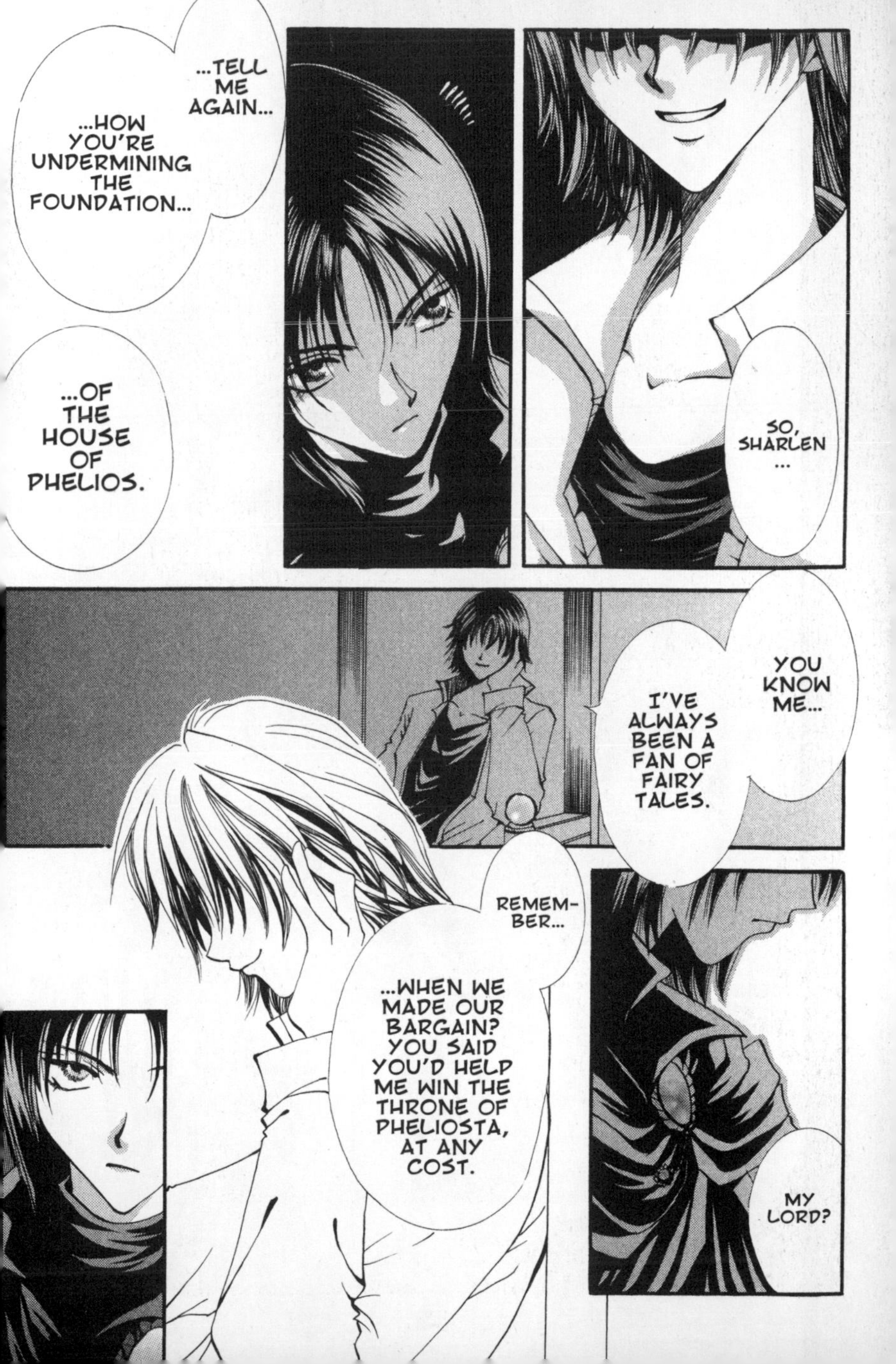
SO, SHARLEN ...
...TELL ME AGAIN...
...HOW YOU'RE UNDERMINING THE FOUNDATION...
...OF THE HOUSE OF PHELIOS.
YOU KNOW ME...
I'VE ALWAYS BEEN A FAN OF FAIRY TALES.
MY LORD?
REMEMBER...
...WHEN WE MADE OUR BARGAIN? YOU SAID YOU'D HELP ME WIN THE THRONE OF PHELIOSTA, AT ANY COST.

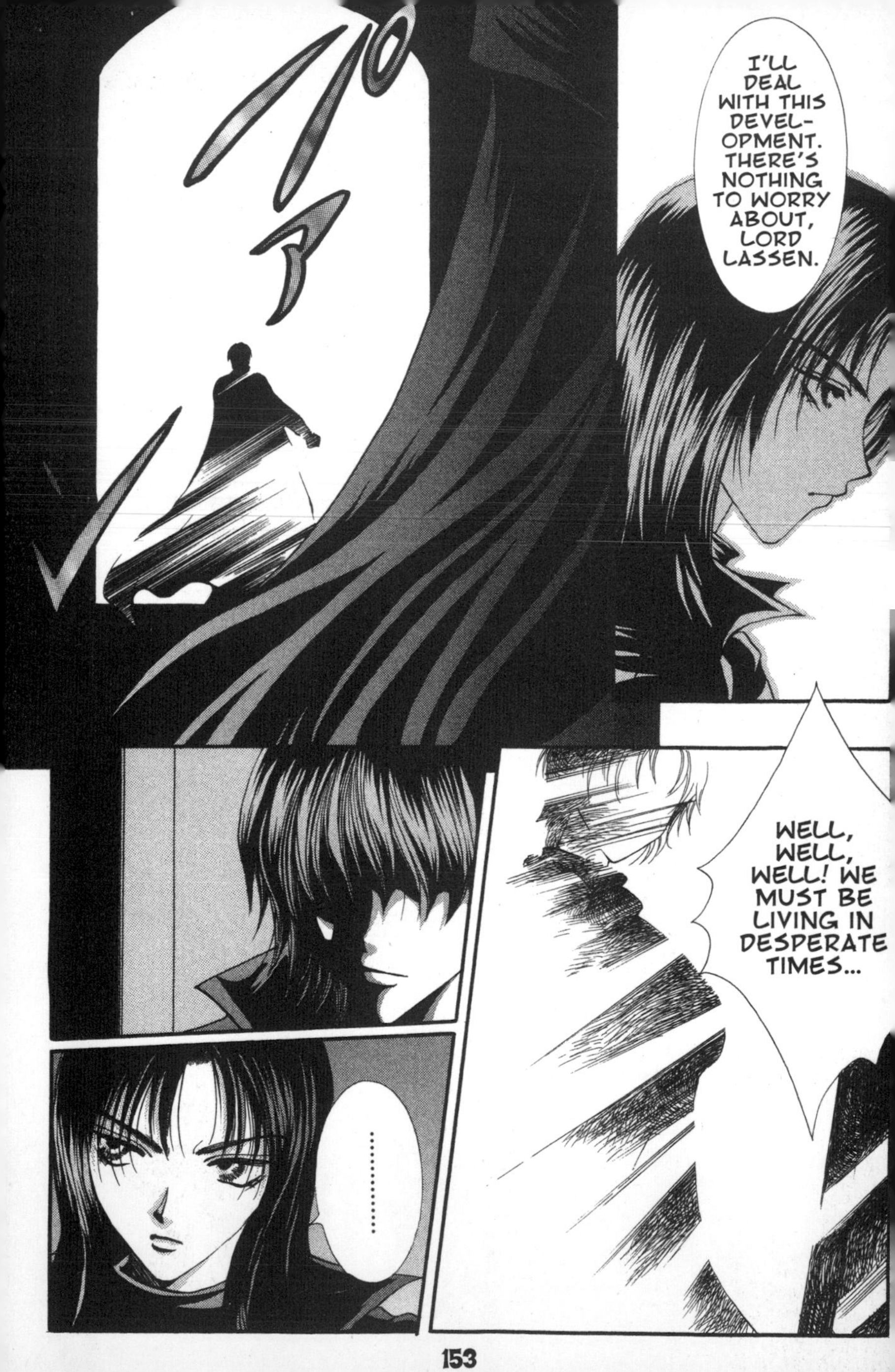
I'LL DEAL WITH THIS DEVEL-OPMENT. THERE'S NOTHING TO WORRY ABOUT, LORD LASSEN.
WELL, WELL, WELL! WE MUST BE LIVING IN DESPERATE TIMES...
....

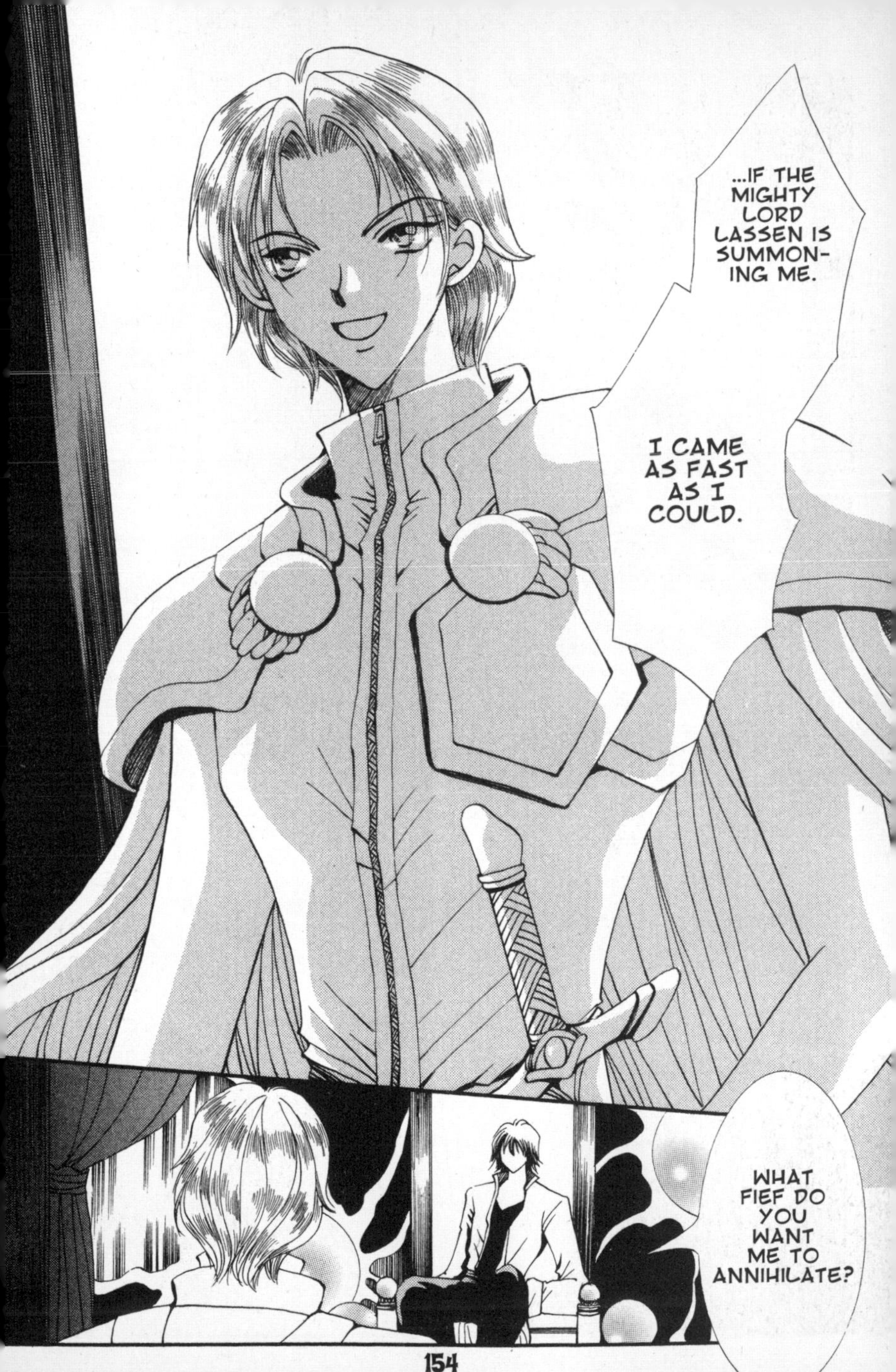
...IF THE MIGHTY LORD LASSEN IS SUMMONING ME.
I CAME AS FAST AS I COULD.
WHAT FIEF DO YOU WANT ME TO ANNIHILATE?

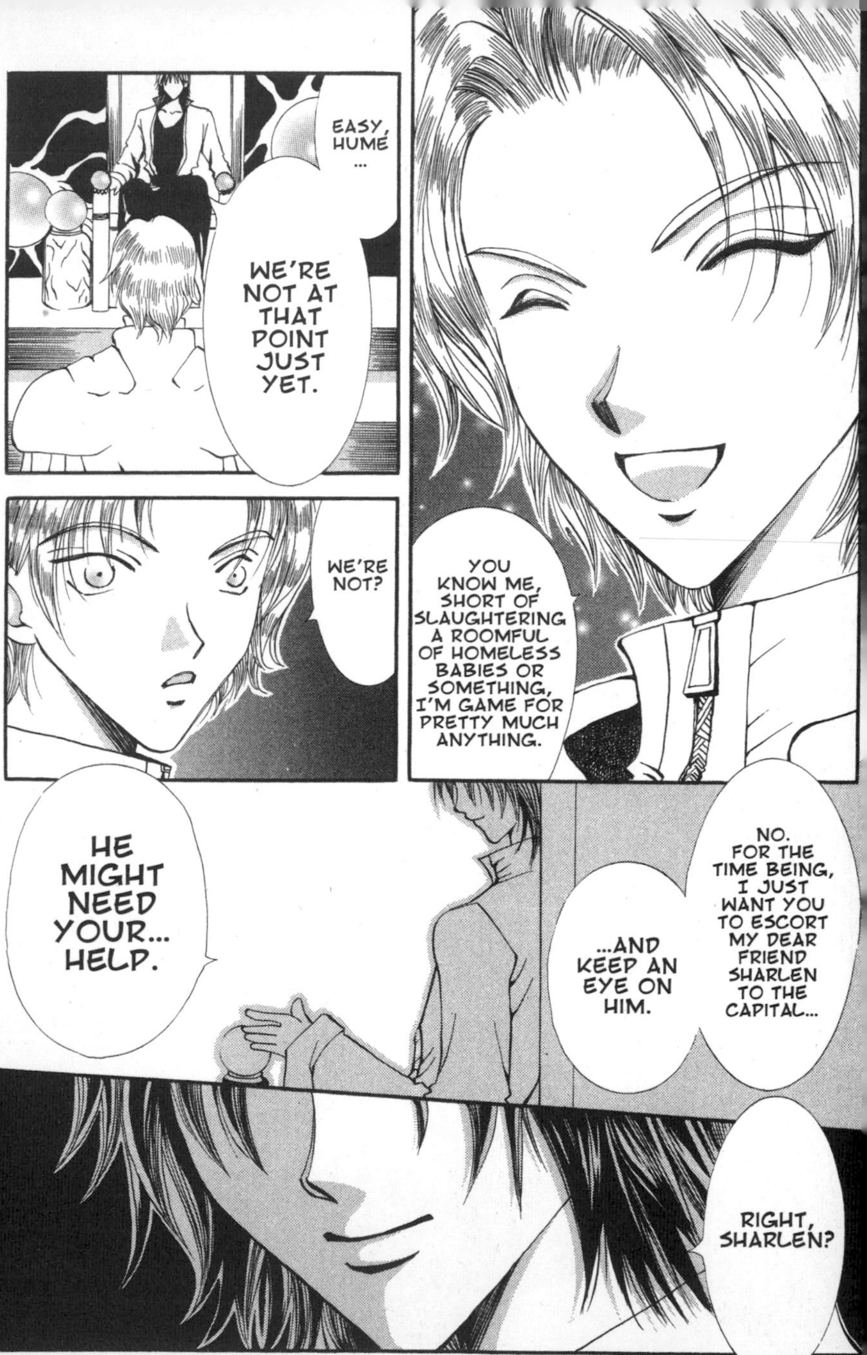
YOU KNOW ME, SHORT OF SLAUGHTERING A ROOMFUL OF HOMELESS BABIES OR SOMETHING, I'M GAME FOR PRETTY MUCH ANYTHING.
EASY, HUME...
WE'RE NOT AT THAT POINT JUST YET.
WE'RE NOT?
NO. FOR THE TIME BEING, I JUST WANT YOU TO ESCORT MY DEAR FRIEND SHARLEN TO THE CAPITAL...
...AND KEEP AN EYE ON HIM.
HE MIGHT NEED YOUR... HELP.
RIGHT, SHARLEN?

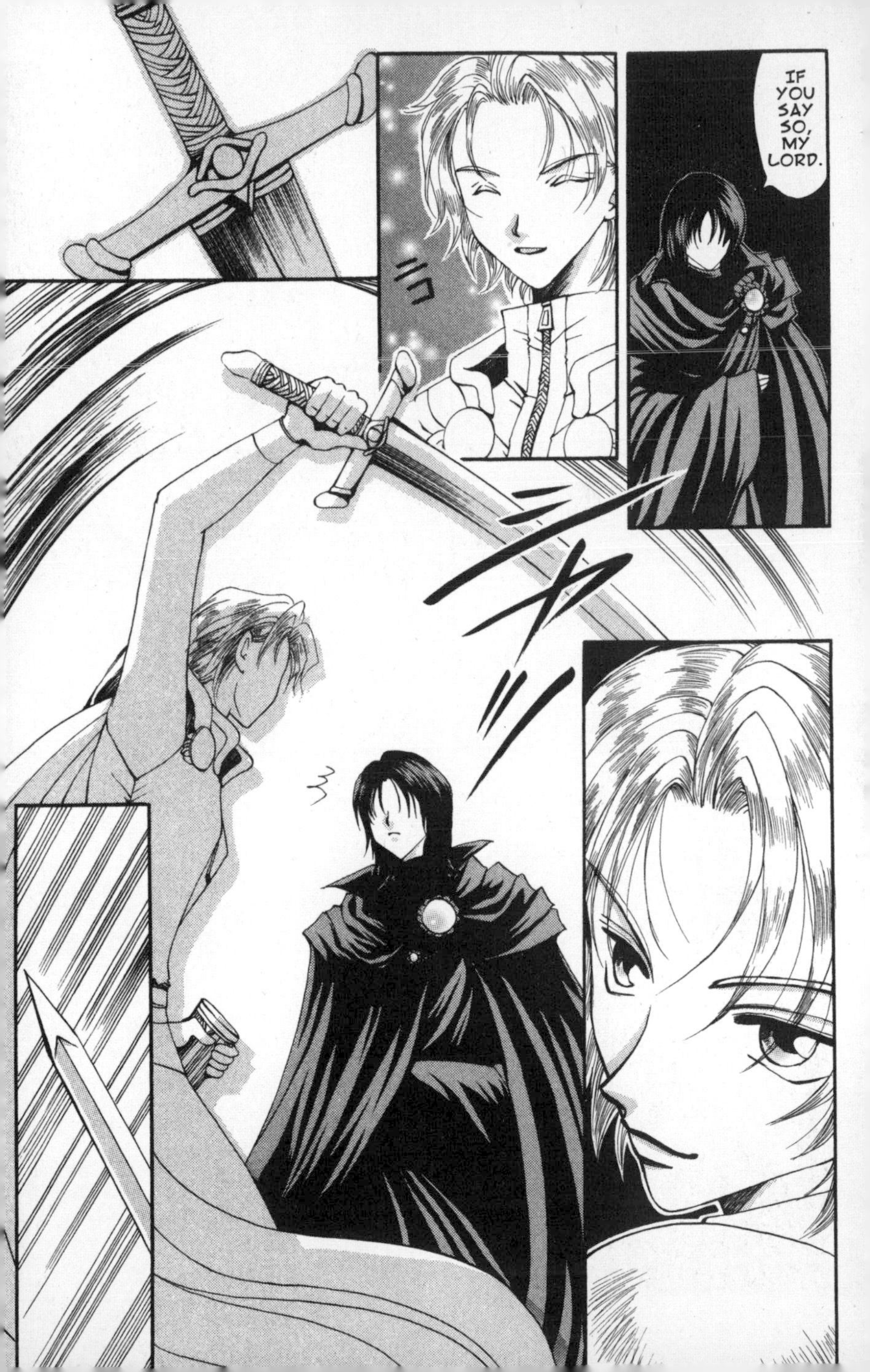
IF YOU SAY SO, MY LORD.

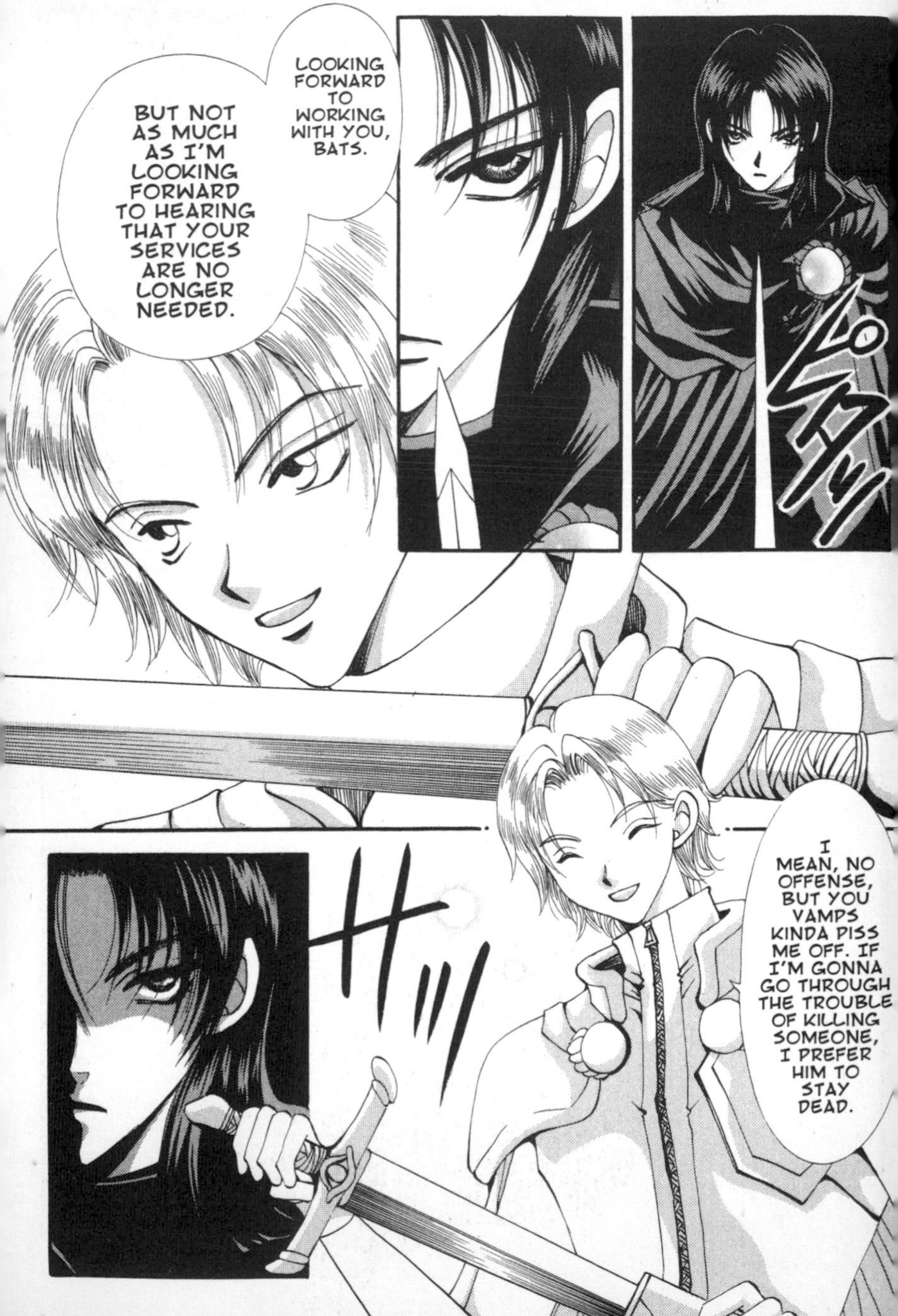
LOOKING FORWARD TO WORKING WITH YOU, BATS.
BUT NOT AS MUCH AS I'M LOOKING FORWARD TO HEARING THAT YOUR SERVICES ARE NO LONGER NEEDED.
I MEAN, NO OFFENSE, BUT YOU VAMPS KINDA PISS ME OFF. IF I'M GONNA GO THROUGH THE TROUBLE OF KILLING SOMEONE, I PREFER HIM TO STAY DEAD.

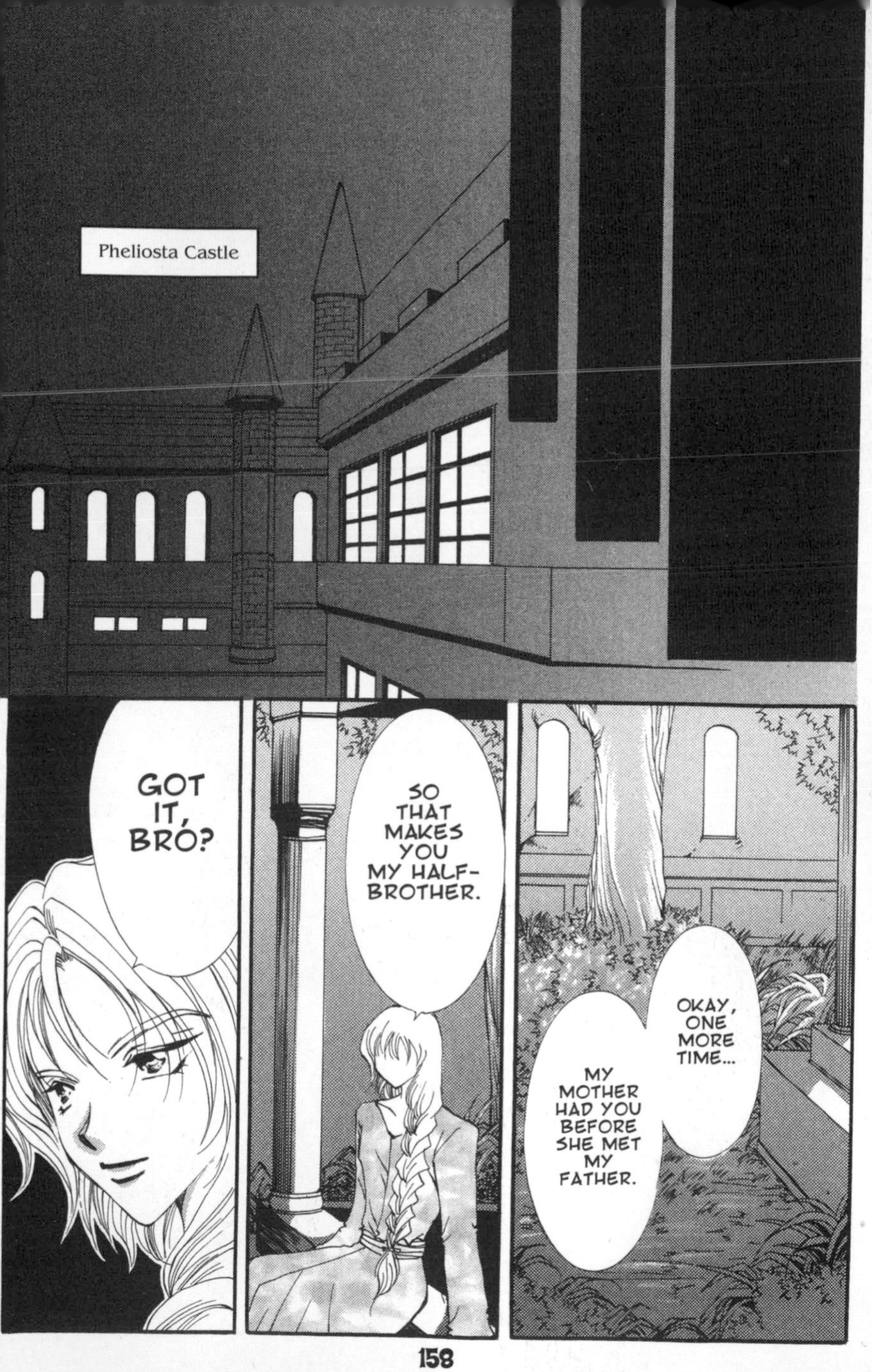
Pheliosta Castle
OKAY, ONE MORE TIME...
MY MOTHER HAD YOU BEFORE SHE MET MY FATHER.
SO THAT MAKES YOU MY HALF-BROTHER.
GOT IT, BRO?

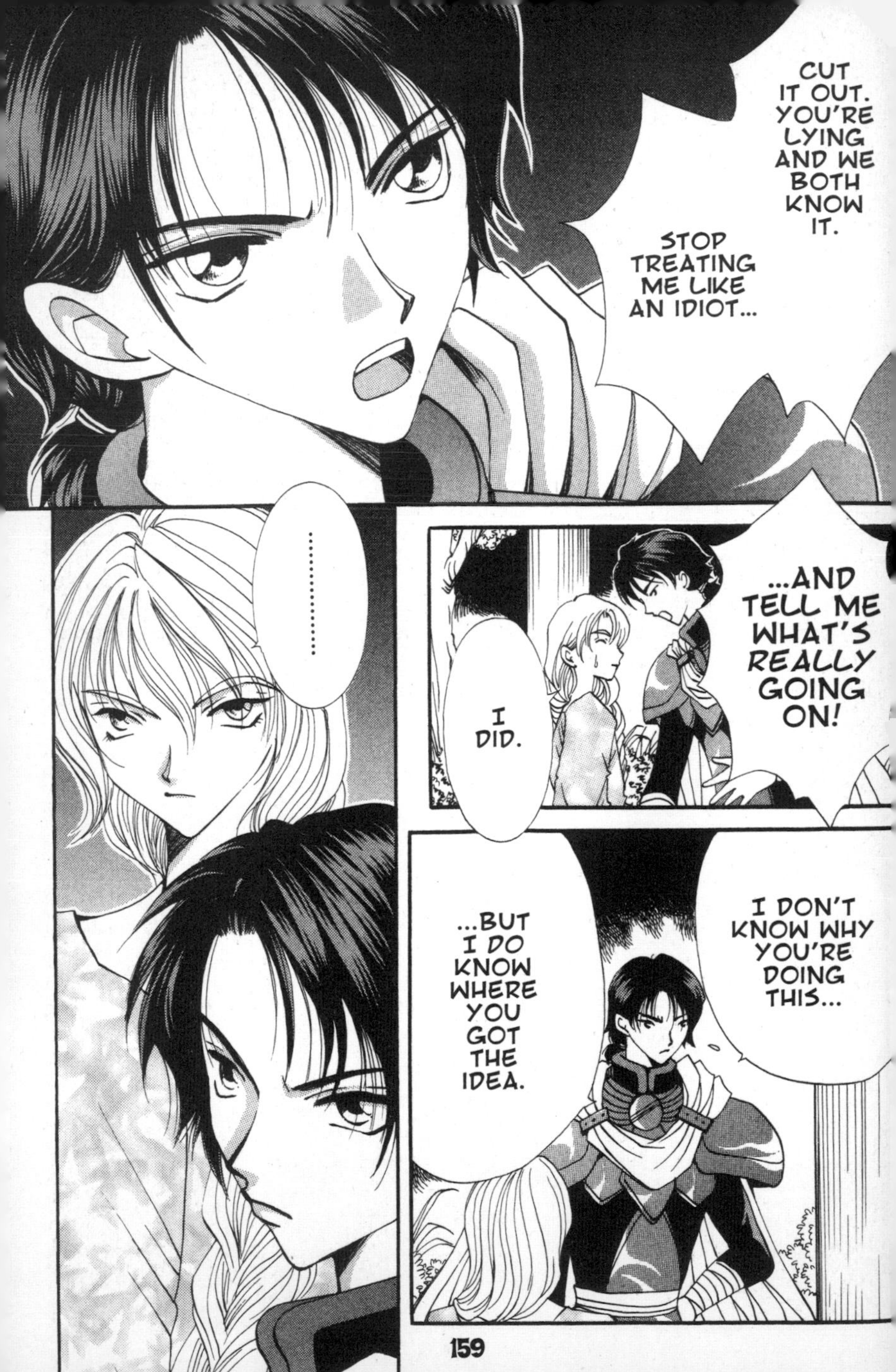
CUT IT OUT. YOU'RE LYING AND WE BOTH KNOW IT.
STOP TREATING ME LIKE AN IDIOT...
...AND TELL ME WHAT'S REALLY GOING ON!
I DID.
I DON'T KNOW WHY YOU'RE DOING THIS...
...BUT I DO KNOW WHERE YOU GOT THE IDEA.
....

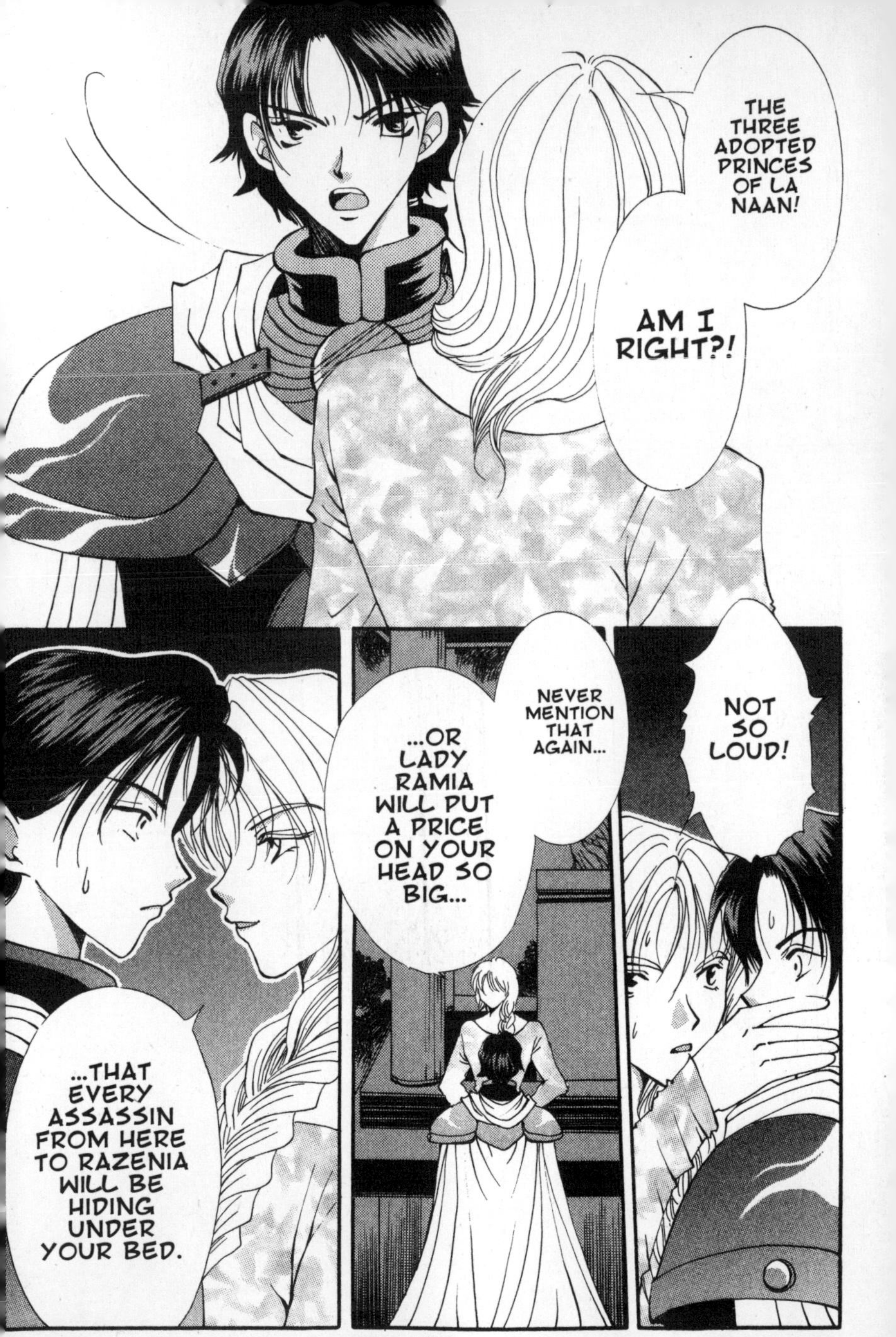
THE THREE ADOPTED PRINCES OF LA NAAN!
AM I RIGHT?!
NOT SO LOUD!
NEVER MENTION THAT AGAIN...
...OR LADY RAMIA WILL PUT A PRICE ON YOUR HEAD SO BIG...
...THAT EVERY ASSASSIN FROM HERE TO RAZENIA WILL BE HIDING UNDER YOUR BED.

キョロ
I STILL DON'T GET IT.
WHY ME?
I'M JUST THE ROYAL BABYSITTER.
I DON'T KNOW ANYTHING ABOUT POLITICS.
I DON'T WANT TO BE YOUR BROTHER, AND I SURE AS HELL DON'T WANT TO BE YOUR PAWN!
DARRES, YOU DON'T UNDER-STAND.
THIS ISN'T ABOUT ME OR YOU. IT'S ABOUT PHELIOSTA. AND IT'S ABOUT ISHTAR.

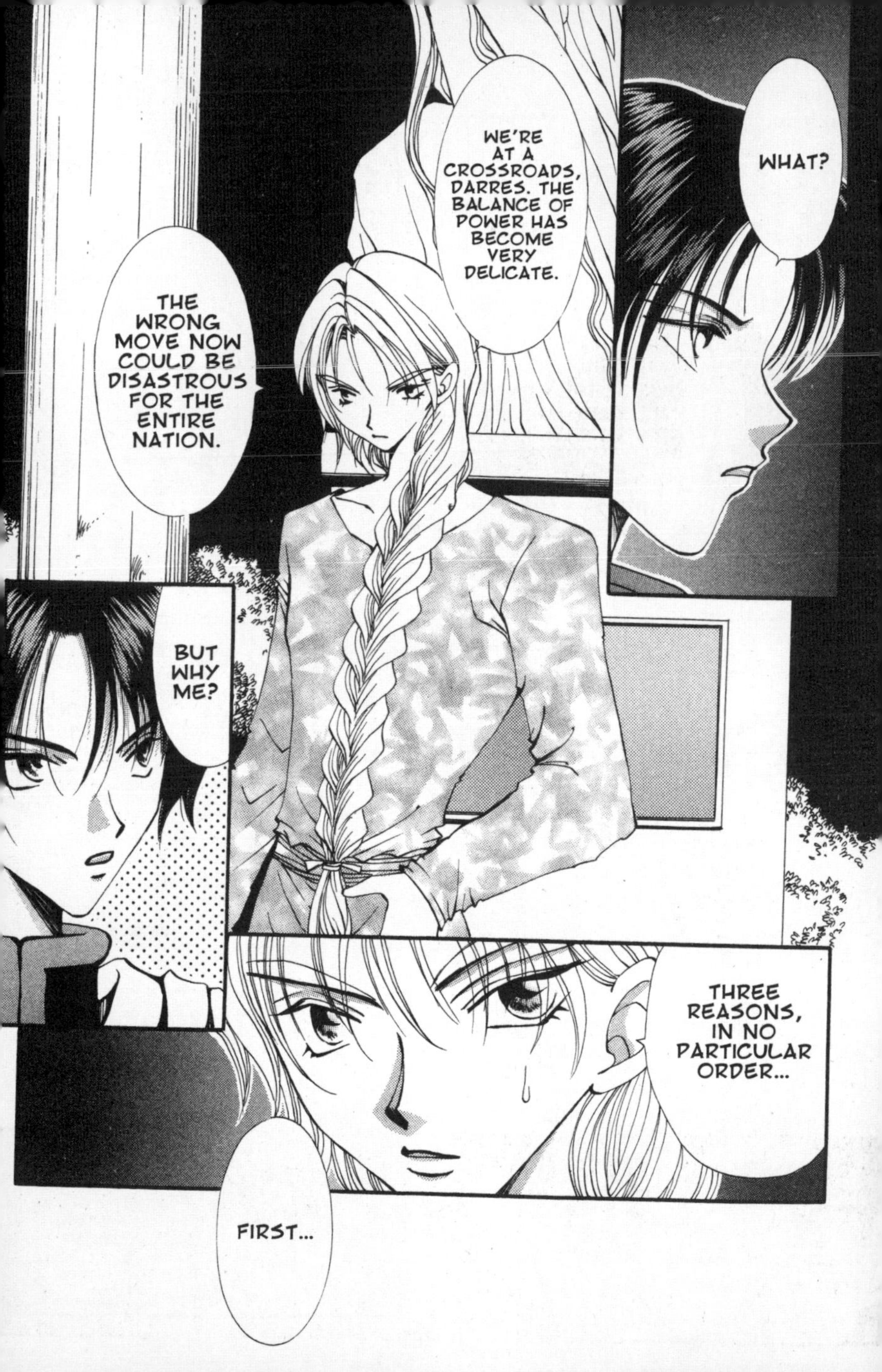
WHAT?
WE'RE AT A CROSSROADS, DARRES. THE BALANCE OF POWER HAS BECOME VERY DELICATE.
THE WRONG MOVE NOW COULD BE DISASTROUS FOR THE ENTIRE NATION.
BUT WHY ME?
THREE REASONS, IN NO PARTICULAR ORDER...
FIRST...

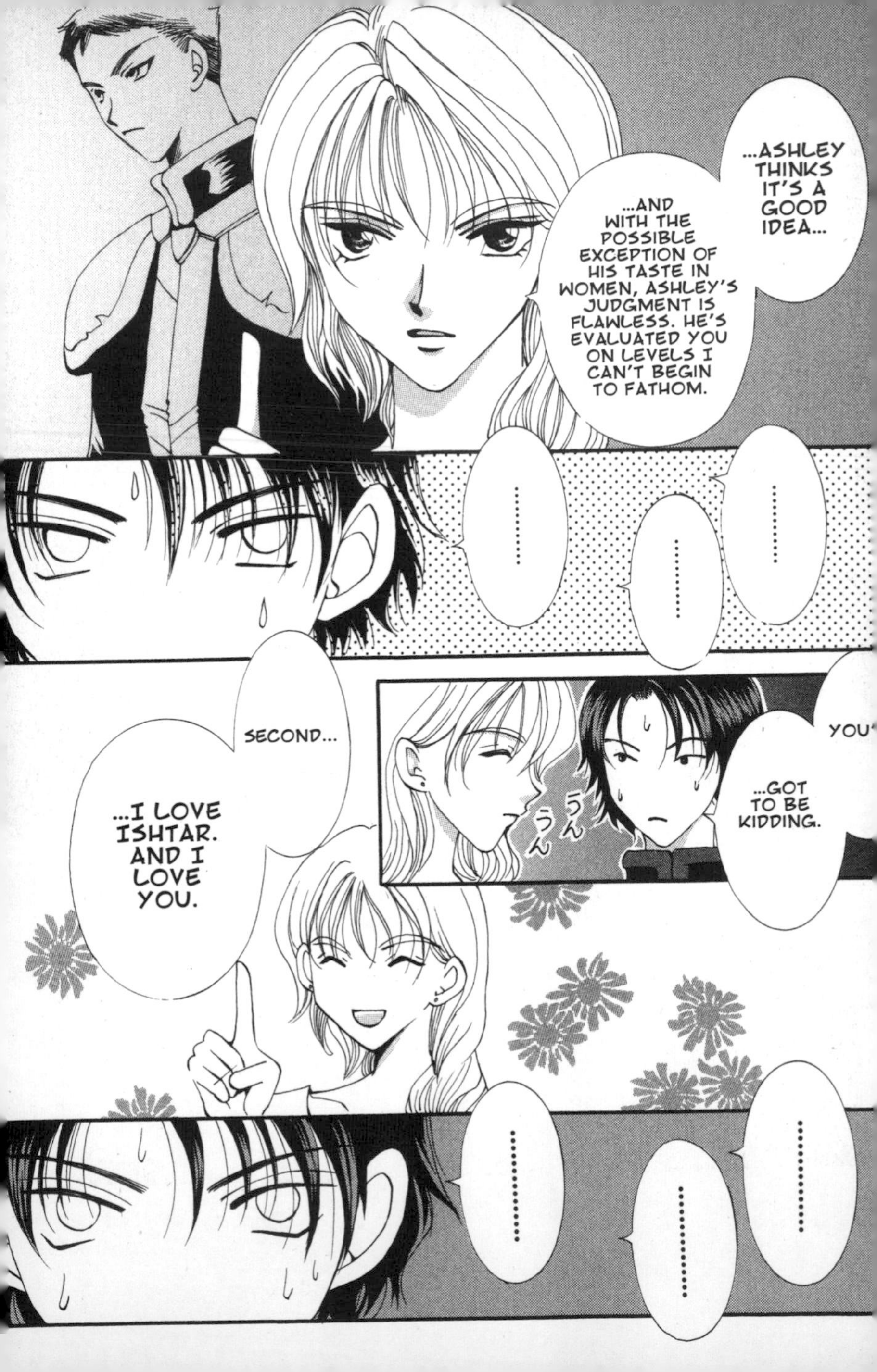
...ASHLEY THINKS IT'S A GOOD IDEA...
...AND WITH THE POSSIBLE EXCEPTION OF HIS TASTE IN WOMEN, ASHLEY'S JUDGMENT IS FLAWLESS. HE'S EVALUATED YOU ON LEVELS I CAN'T BEGIN TO FATHOM.
......
......
......
YOU'
...GOT TO BE KIDDING.
うん うん
SECOND...
...I LOVE ISHTAR. AND I LOVE YOU.
......
......
......

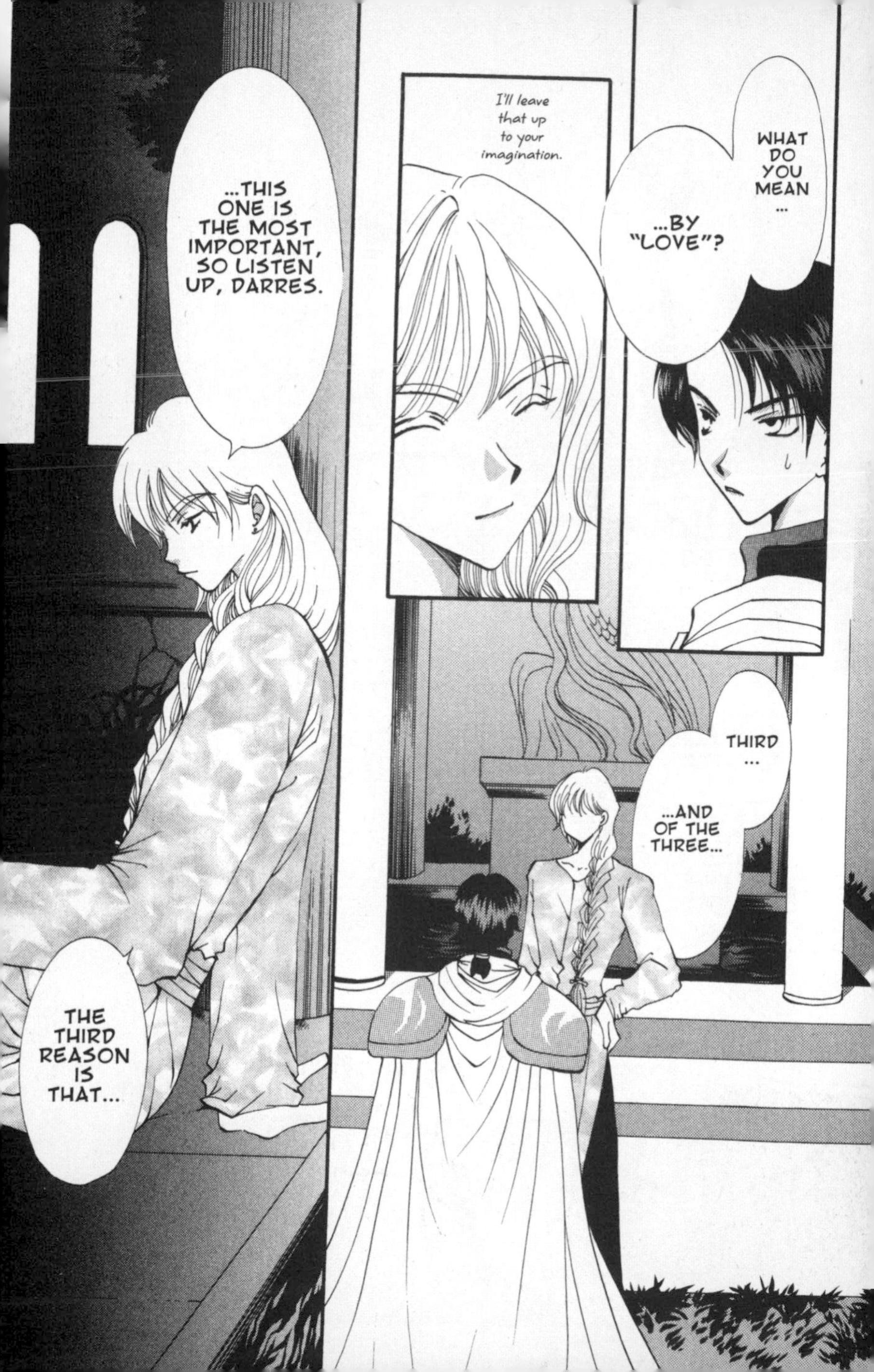
WHAT DO YOU MEAN...
...BY "LOVE"?
I'll leave that up to your imagination.
THIRD...
...AND OF THE THREE...
...THIS ONE IS THE MOST IMPORTANT, SO LISTEN UP, DARRES.
THE THIRD REASON IS THAT...

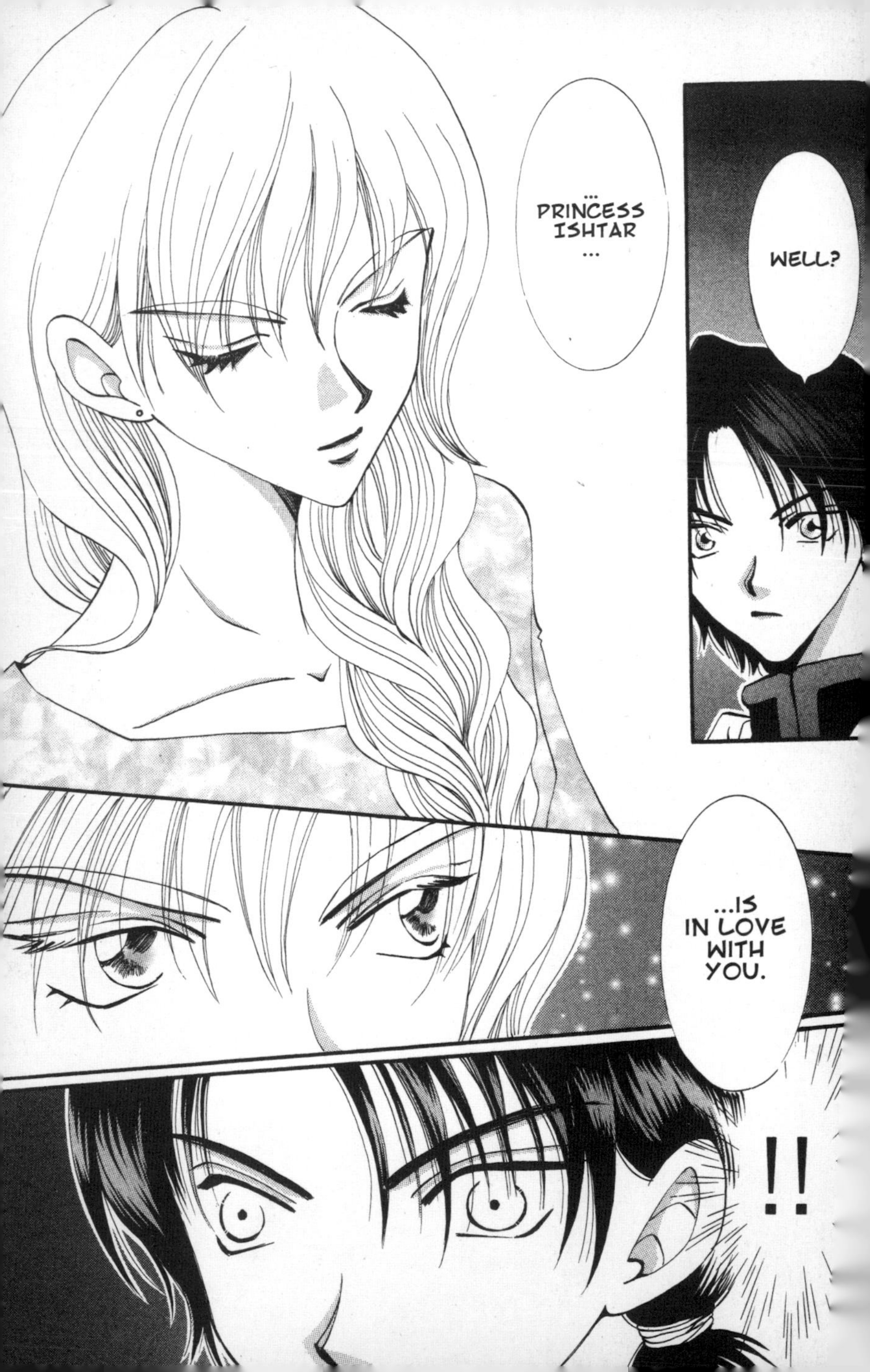
WELL?
...PRINCESS ISHTAR...
...IS IN LOVE WITH YOU.
!!

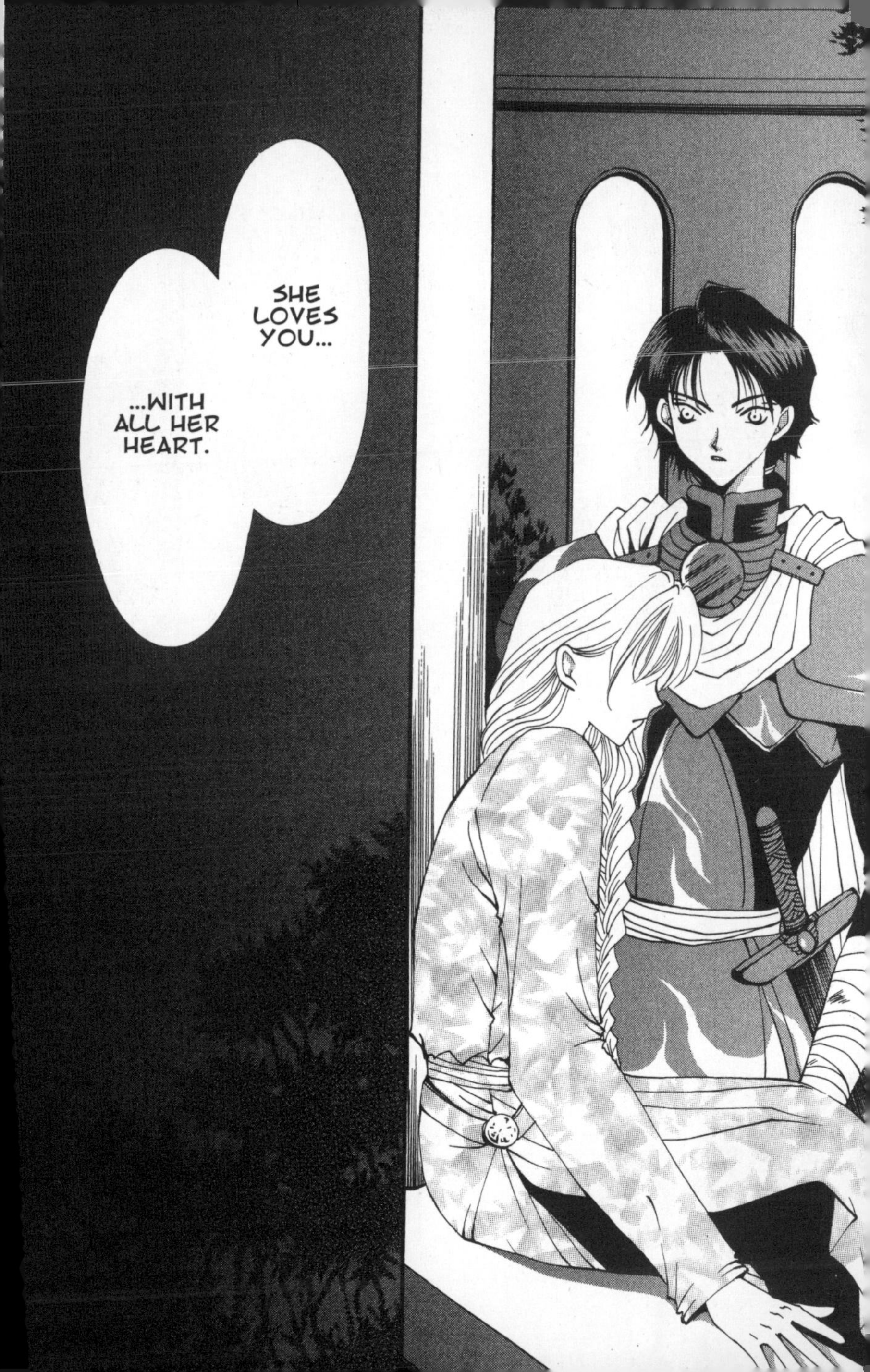
SHE LOVES YOU...
...WITH ALL HER HEART.

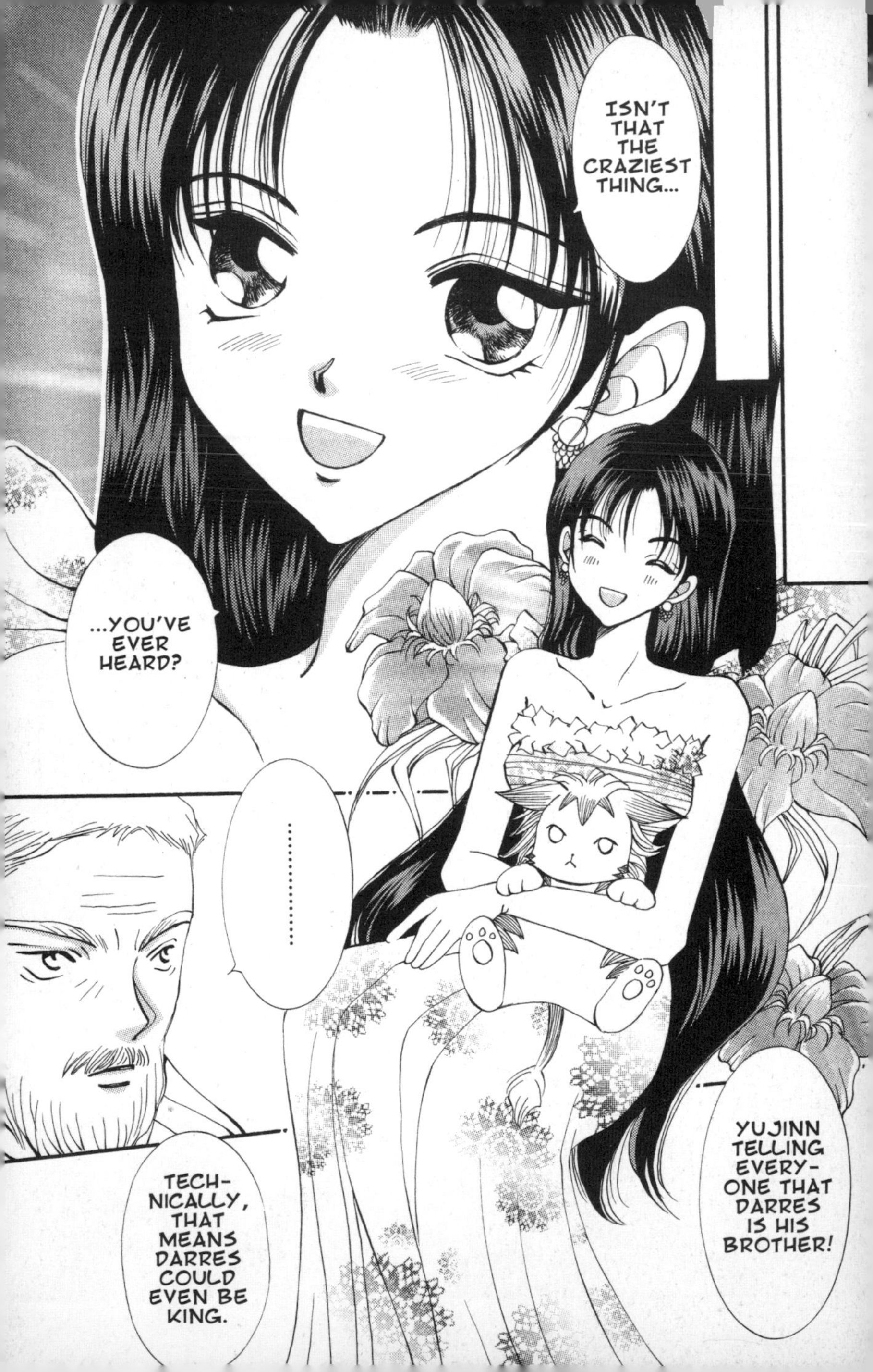
ISN'T THAT THE CRAZIEST THING...
...YOU'VE EVER HEARD?
YUJINN TELLING EVERY-ONE THAT DARRES IS HIS BROTHER!
......
TECH-NICALLY, THAT MEANS DARRES COULD EVEN BE KING.

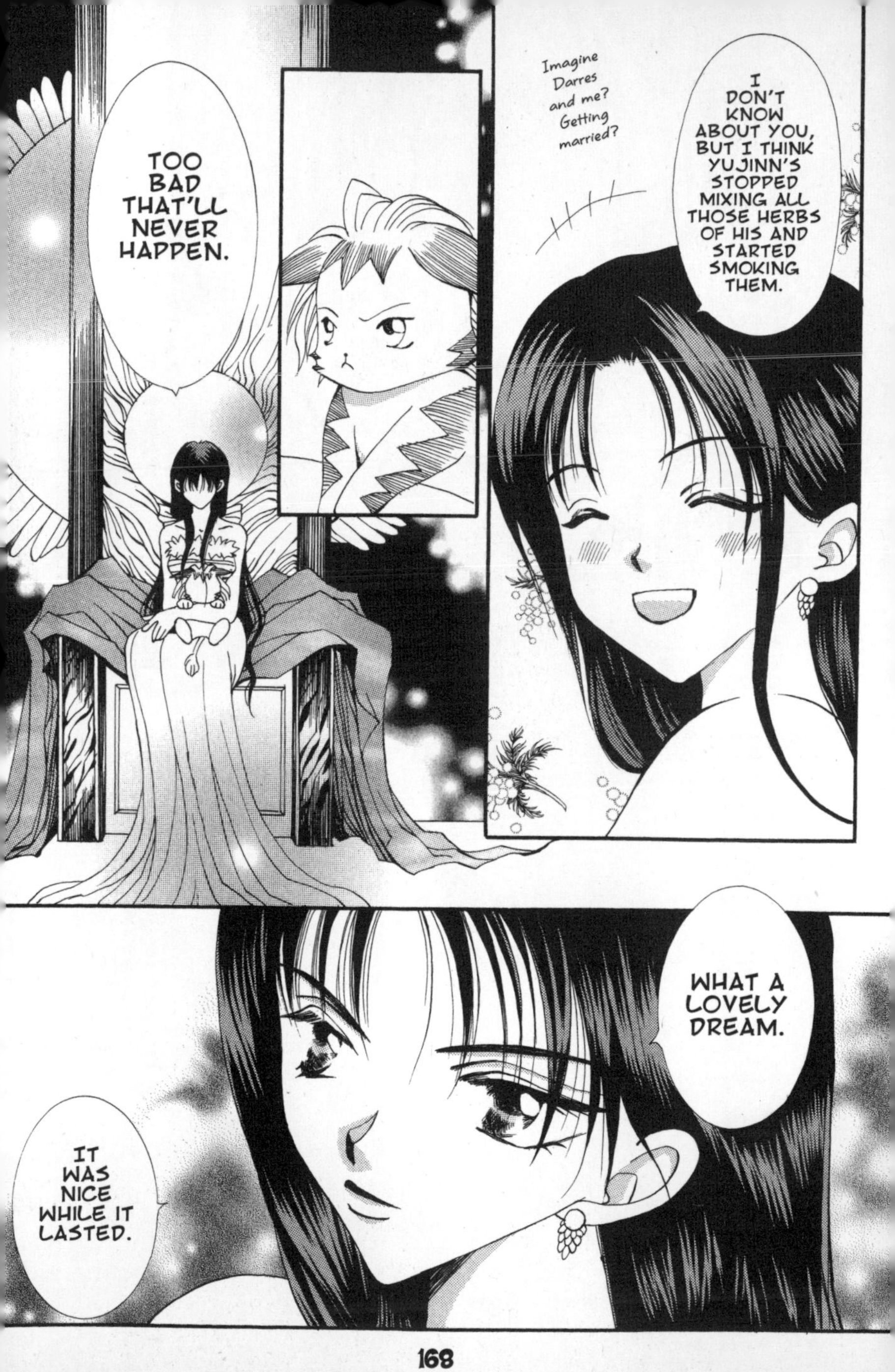
I DON'T KNOW ABOUT YOU, BUT I THINK YUJINN'S STOPPED MIXING ALL THOSE HERBS OF HIS AND STARTED SMOKING THEM.
Imagine Darres and me? Getting married?
TOO BAD THAT'LL NEVER HAPPEN.
WHAT A LOVELY DREAM.
IT WAS NICE WHILE IT LASTED.

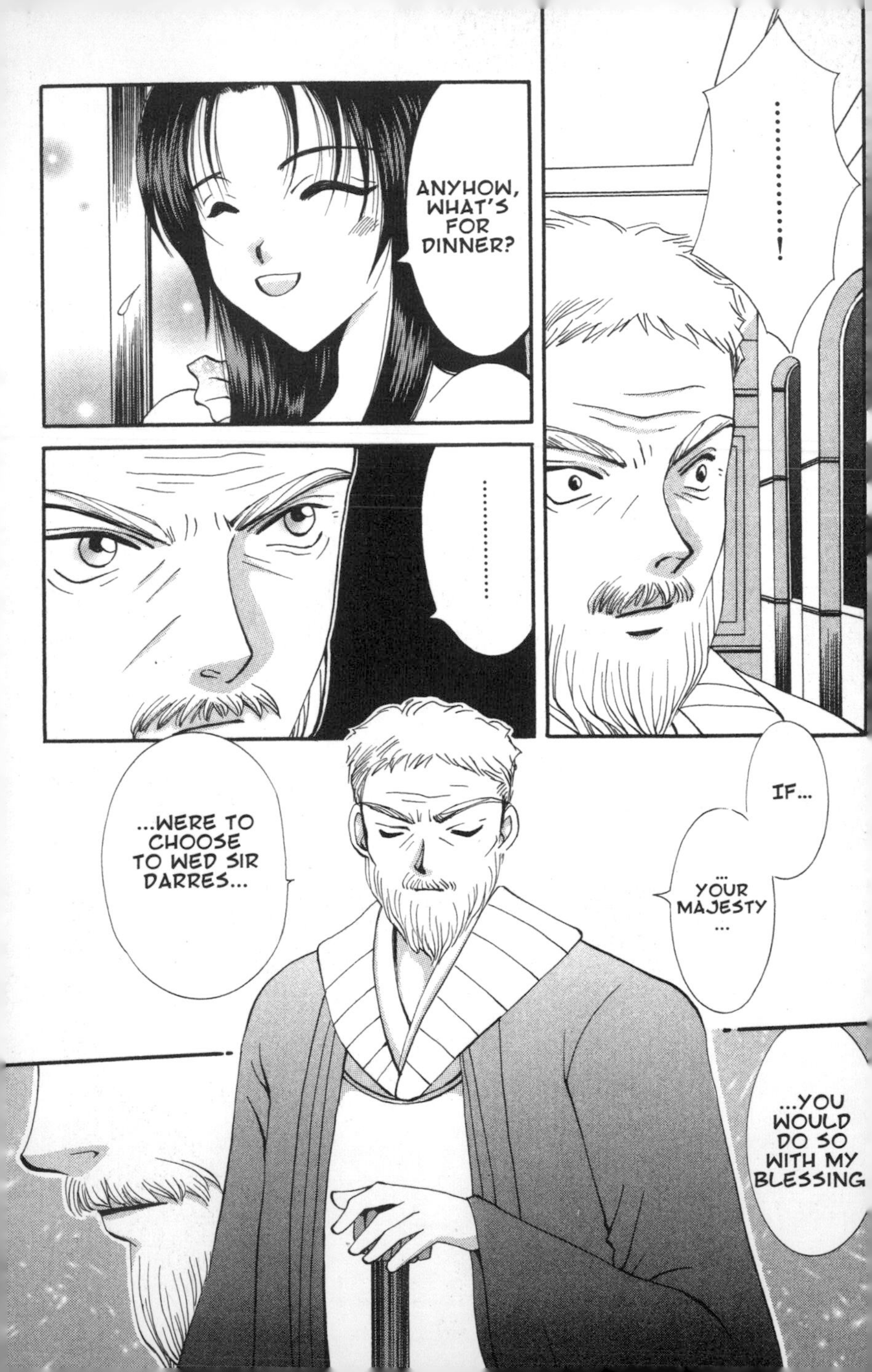
......!
ANYHOW, WHAT'S FOR DINNER?
......
IF...
...YOUR MAJESTY...
...WERE TO CHOOSE TO WED SIR DARRES...
...YOU WOULD DO SO WITH MY BLESSING

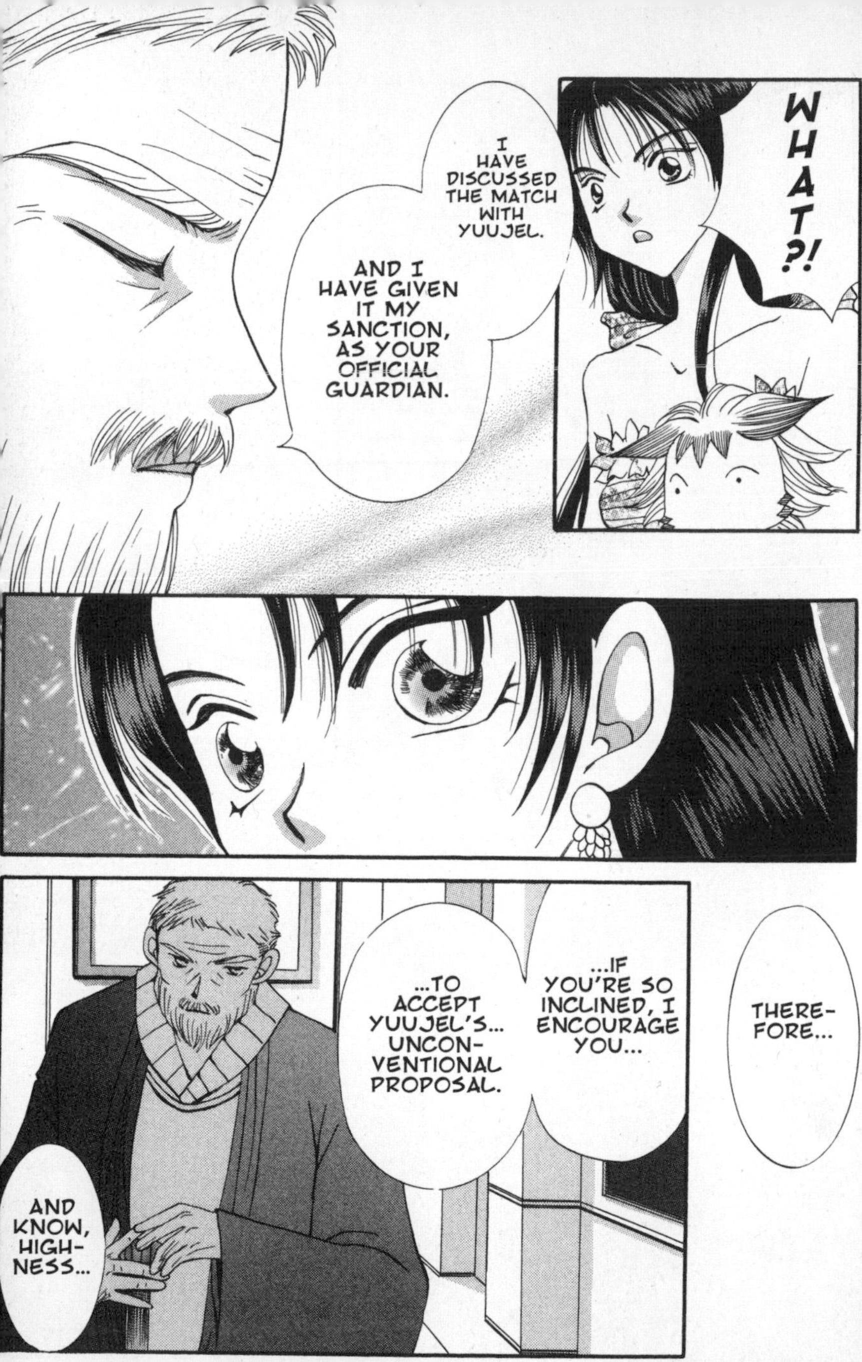
WHAT?!
I HAVE DISCUSSED THE MATCH WITH YUUJEL.
AND I HAVE GIVEN IT MY SANCTION, AS YOUR OFFICIAL GUARDIAN.
THERE-FORE...
...IF YOU'RE SO INCLINED, I ENCOURAGE YOU...
...TO ACCEPT YUUJEL'S... UNCON-VENTIONAL PROPOSAL.
AND KNOW, HIGH-NESS...

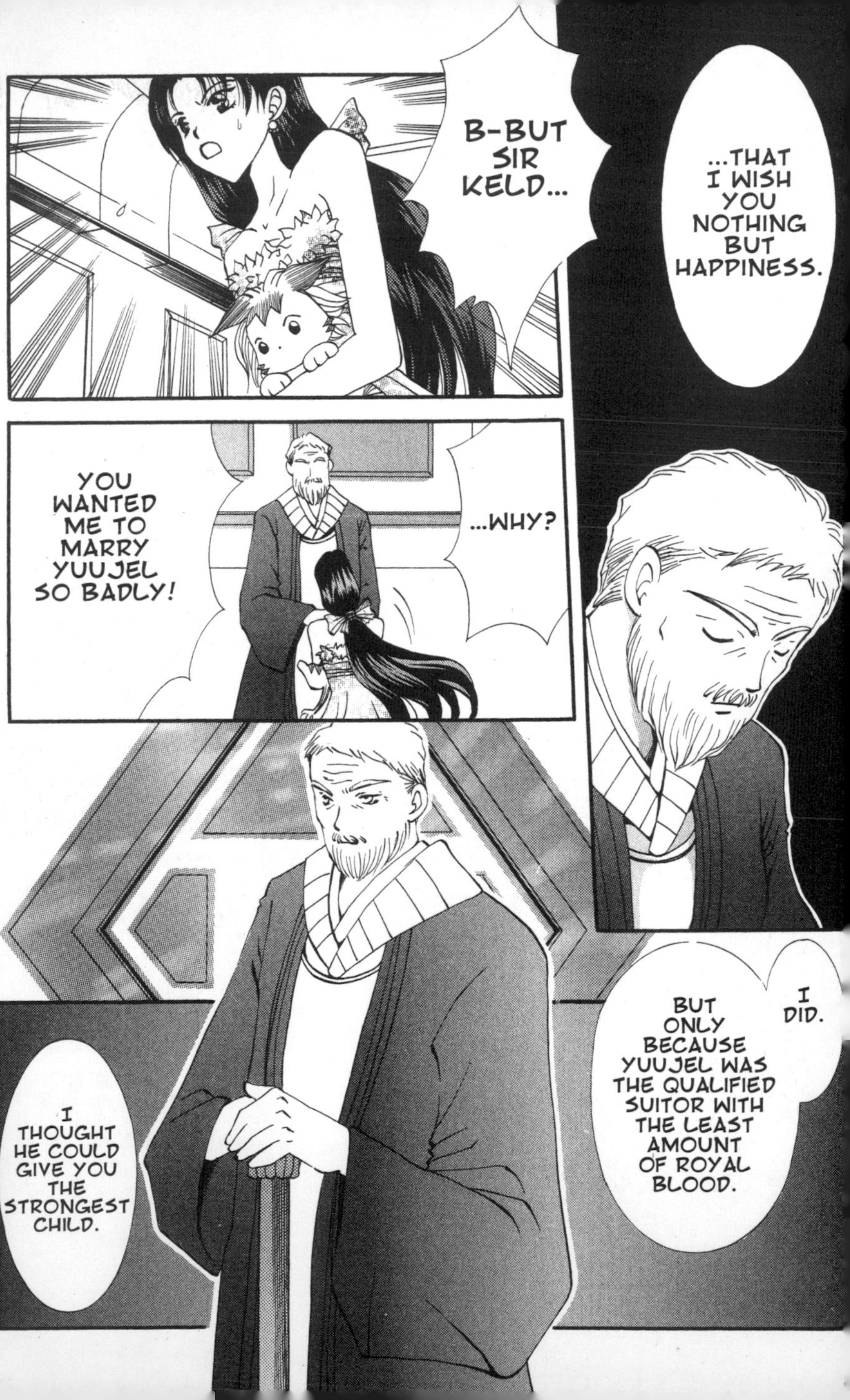
...THAT I WISH YOU NOTHING BUT HAPPINESS.
B-BUT SIR KELD...
...WHY?
YOU WANTED ME TO MARRY YUUJEL SO BADLY!
I DID.
BUT ONLY BECAUSE YUUJEL WAS THE QUALIFIED SUITOR WITH THE LEAST AMOUNT OF ROYAL BLOOD.
I THOUGHT HE COULD GIVE YOU THE STRONGEST CHILD.

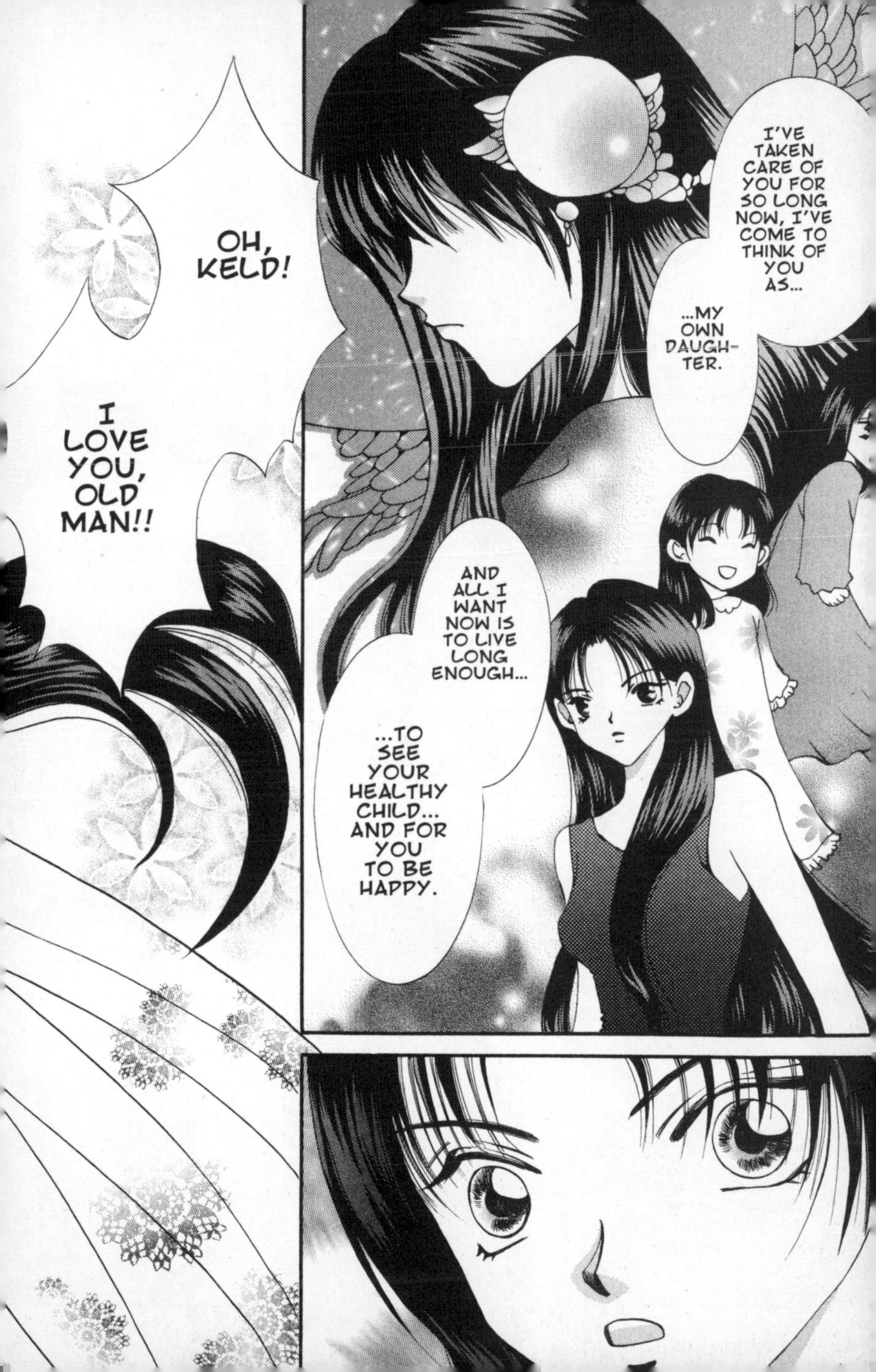
I'VE TAKEN CARE OF YOU FOR SO LONG NOW, I'VE COME TO THINK OF YOU AS...
...MY OWN DAUGHTER.
AND ALL I WANT NOW IS TO LIVE LONG ENOUGH...
...TO SEE YOUR HEALTHY CHILD... AND FOR YOU TO BE HAPPY.
OH, KELD!
I LOVE YOU, OLD MAN!!

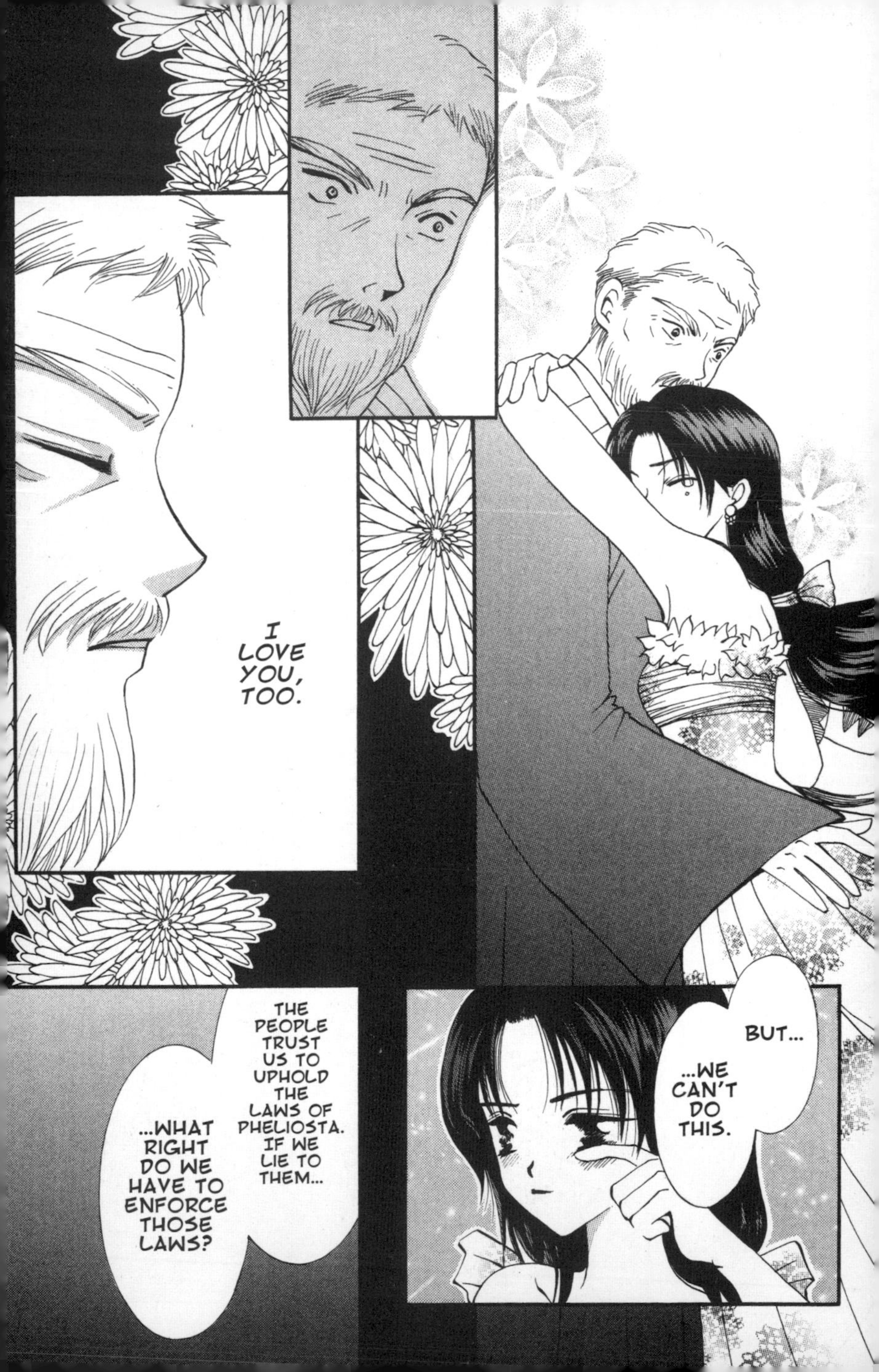
I LOVE YOU, TOO.
BUT...
...WE CAN'T DO THIS.
THE PEOPLE TRUST US TO UPHOLD THE LAWS OF PHELIOSTA. IF WE LIE TO THEM...
...WHAT RIGHT DO WE HAVE TO ENFORCE THOSE LAWS?

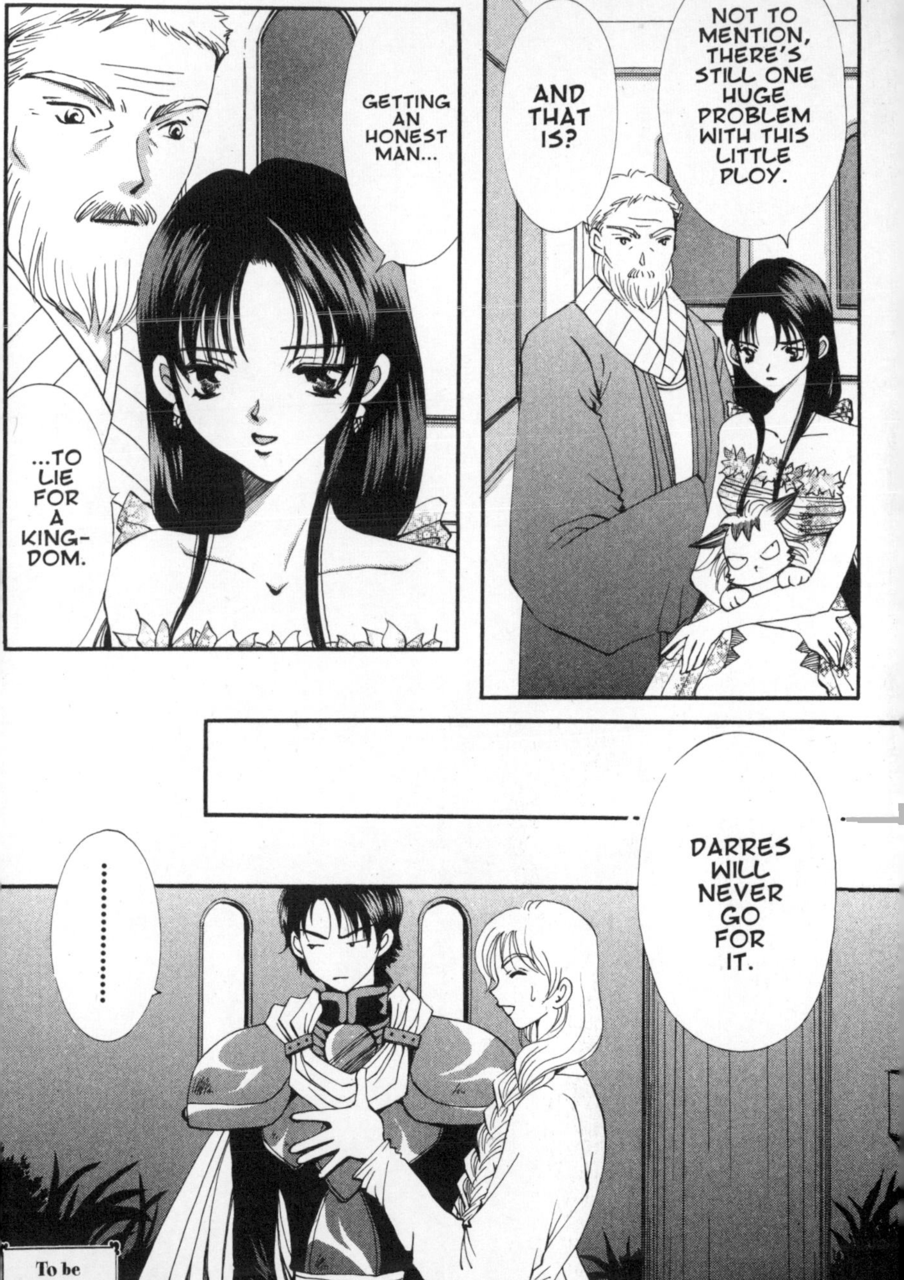
NOT TO MENTION, THERE'S STILL ONE HUGE PROBLEM WITH THIS LITTLE PLOY.
AND THAT IS?
GETTING AN HONEST MAN...
...TO LIE FOR A KING-DOM.
DARRES WILL NEVER GO FOR IT.
....

To be continued in Volume 11

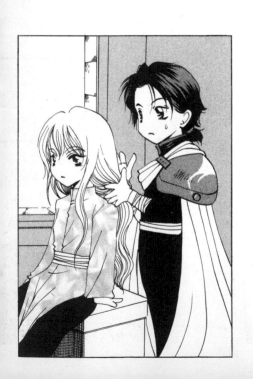

Post-modern-script

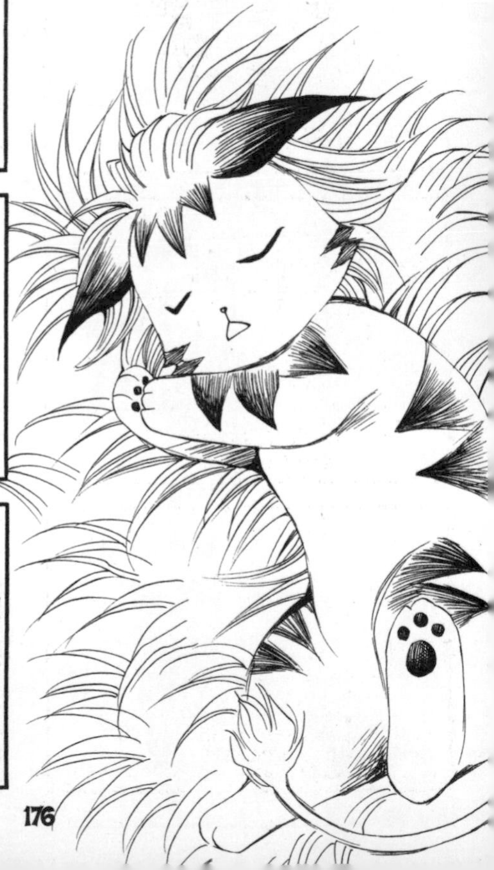

Hi again!

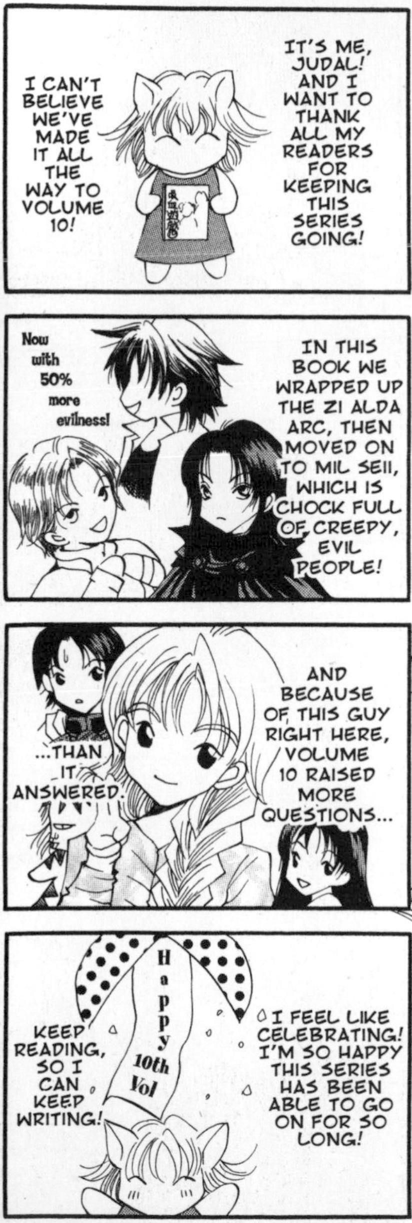
IT'S ME, JUDAL! AND I WANT TO THANK ALL MY READERS FOR KEEPING THIS SERIES GOING!
I CAN'T BELIEVE WE'VE MADE IT ALL THE WAY TO VOLUME 10!
IN THIS BOOK WE WRAPPED UP THE ZI ALDA ARC, THEN MOVED ON TO MIL SEII, WHICH IS CHOCK FULL OF CREEPY, EVIL PEOPLE!
Now with 50% more evilness!
AND BECAUSE OF THIS GUY RIGHT HERE, VOLUME 10 RAISED MORE QUESTIONS...
...THAN IT ANSWERED.
I FEEL LIKE CELEBRATING! I'M SO HAPPY THIS SERIES HAS BEEN ABLE TO GO ON FOR SO LONG!
Happy 10th Vol
KEEP READING, SO I CAN KEEP WRITING!

About Sharlen

THIS IS THE VAMPIRE SHARLEN.
HE USUALLY LOOKS ABOUT 25 YEARS OLD.
25?
WHY DO I LOOK YOUNGER THAN HIM?
RELAX!
YOU'RE BOTH ANCIENT, SO WHAT DIFFERENCE DOES IT MAKE?
AN-CIENT?!
ははは

About Valentine's Day

THANKS AGAIN FOR ALL YOUR LETTERS! MOST OF YOU WANTED TO KNOW...
IS YUJINN...A SWITCH HITTER?
YOU ALSO WANTED TO KNOW...
WHO DOES DARRES LIKE?
BUT NO ONE COULD HAVE PREDICTED THAT...
...JILL WOULD HAVE THE BEST VALENTINE'S DAY!
AND THAT KRAI...
...WOULD END UP WITH A BROKEN HEART. AWW...

Home Page

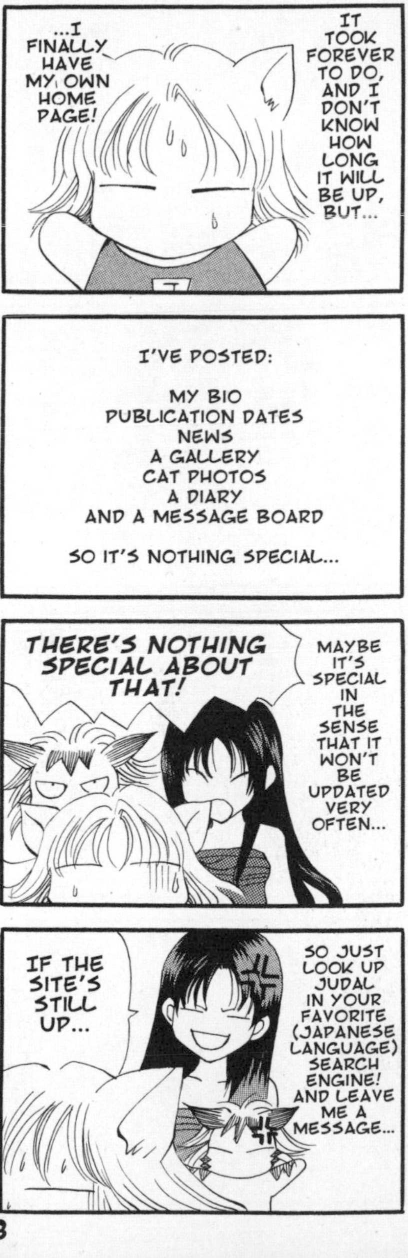
IT TOOK FOREVER TO DO, AND I DON'T KNOW HOW LONG IT WILL BE UP, BUT...
...I FINALLY HAVE MY OWN HOME PAGE!
I'VE POSTED:
MY BIO
PUBLICATION DATES
NEWS
A GALLERY
CAT PHOTOS
A DIARY
AND A MESSAGE BOARD
SO IT'S NOTHING SPECIAL...
MAYBE IT'S SPECIAL IN THE SENSE THAT IT WON'T BE UPDATED VERY OFTEN...
THERE'S NOTHING SPECIAL ABOUT THAT!
SO JUST LOOK UP JUDAL IN YOUR FAVORITE (JAPANESE LANGUAGE) SEARCH ENGINE! AND LEAVE ME A MESSAGE...
IF THE SITE'S STILL UP...

Finally...

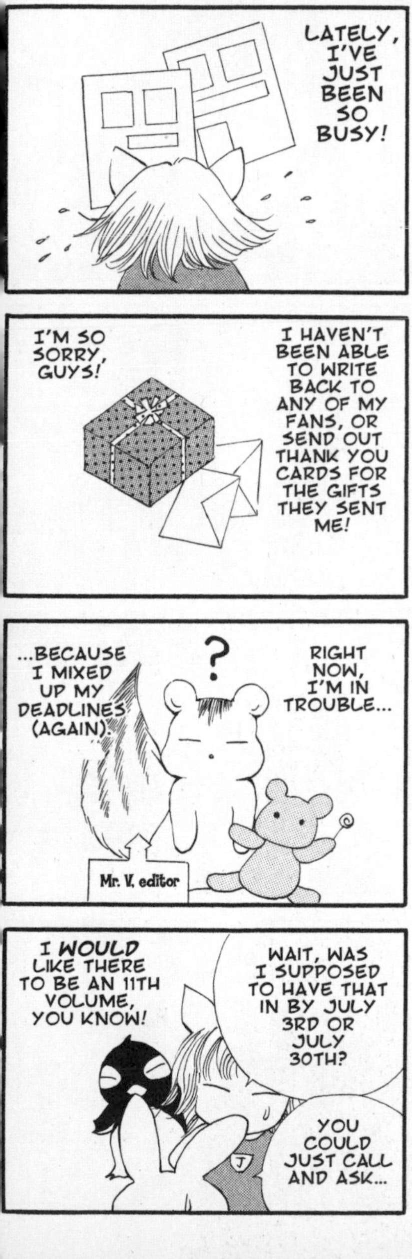
LATELY, I'VE JUST BEEN SO BUSY!
I HAVEN'T BEEN ABLE TO WRITE BACK TO ANY OF MY FANS, OR SEND OUT THANK YOU CARDS FOR THE GIFTS THEY SENT ME!
I'M SO SORRY, GUYS!
RIGHT NOW, I'M IN TROUBLE...
...BECAUSE I MIXED UP MY DEADLINES (AGAIN).
Mr. V, editor
WAIT, WAS I SUPPOSED TO HAVE THAT IN BY JULY 3RD OR JULY 30TH?
I WOULD LIKE THERE TO BE AN 11TH VOLUME, YOU KNOW!
YOU COULD JUST CALL AND ASK...

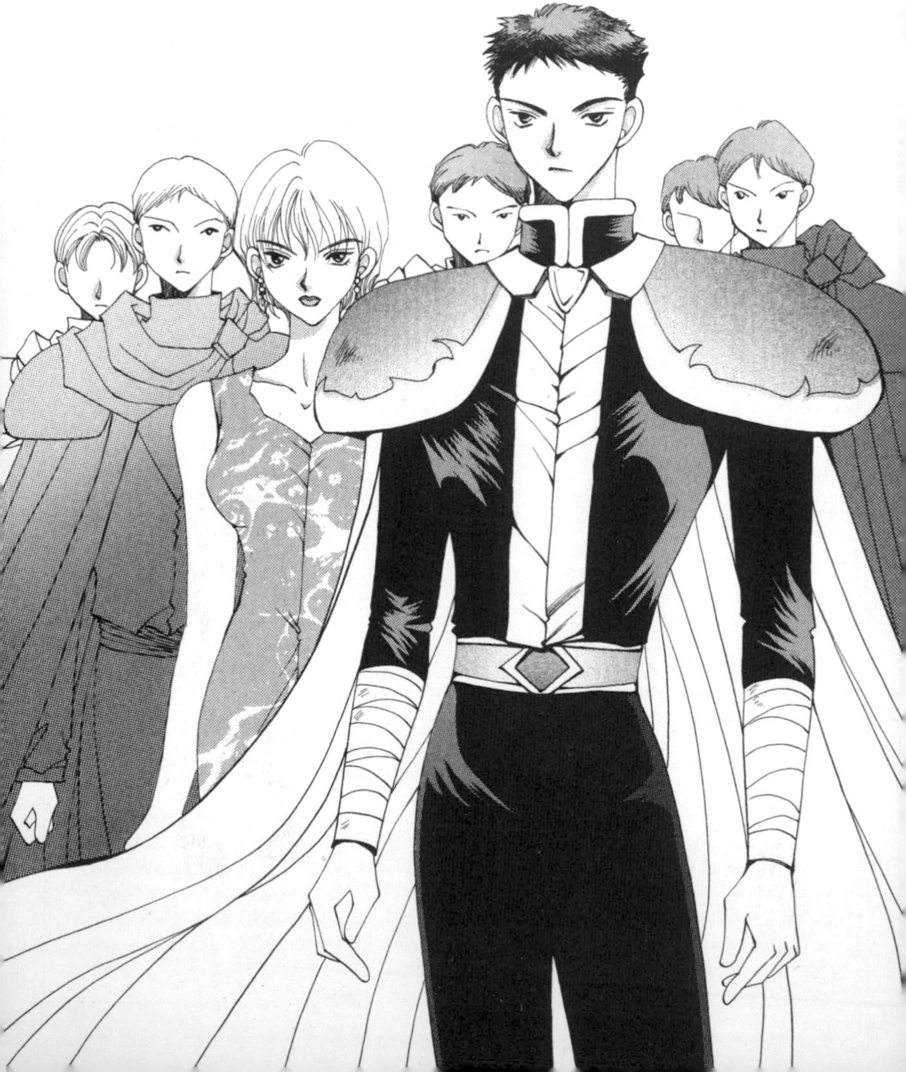

VAMPIRE GAME

Next Volume...

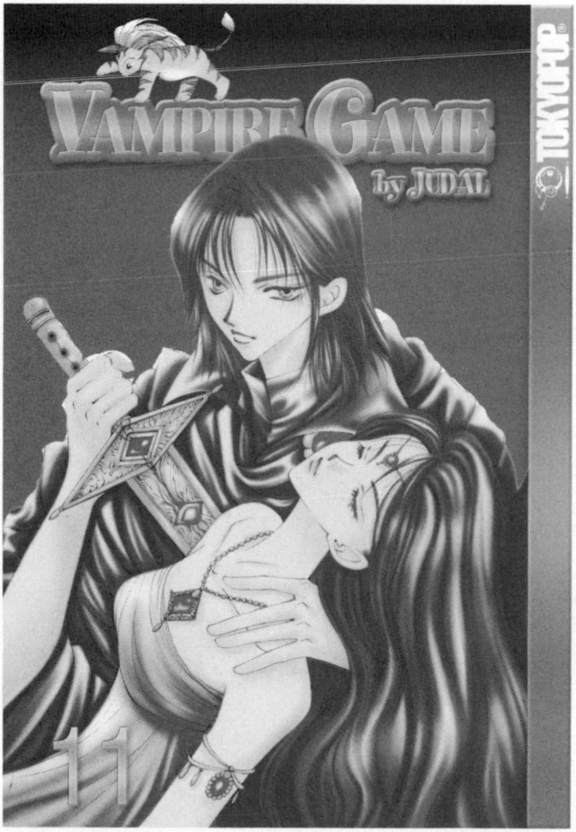
VAMPIRE GAME
by JUDAL
TOKYOPOP
11

Lassen of Mil Seii is Ishtar's cousin, and like most members of her family, is likely to become a powerful pain-in-the-neck. For starters, he's a master magician and poisoner. He also really seems to enjoy hanging out with vampires. Throw in the fact that he's been coveting Pheliosta's throne for a long time, and we've got a bona fide crisis brewing in Mil Seii. But danger's not the only thing in the air. Are those wedding bells we hear? Well, maybe not, for to prove that he's part of the royal family, Darres must pass a test. If he's truly a member of the Phelios' clan, Darres should have no problem unsheathing Sidia, the Holy Sword. The problem is that he's not really royalty...is he? Looks like we'll all find out together in the next volume of Vampire Game!

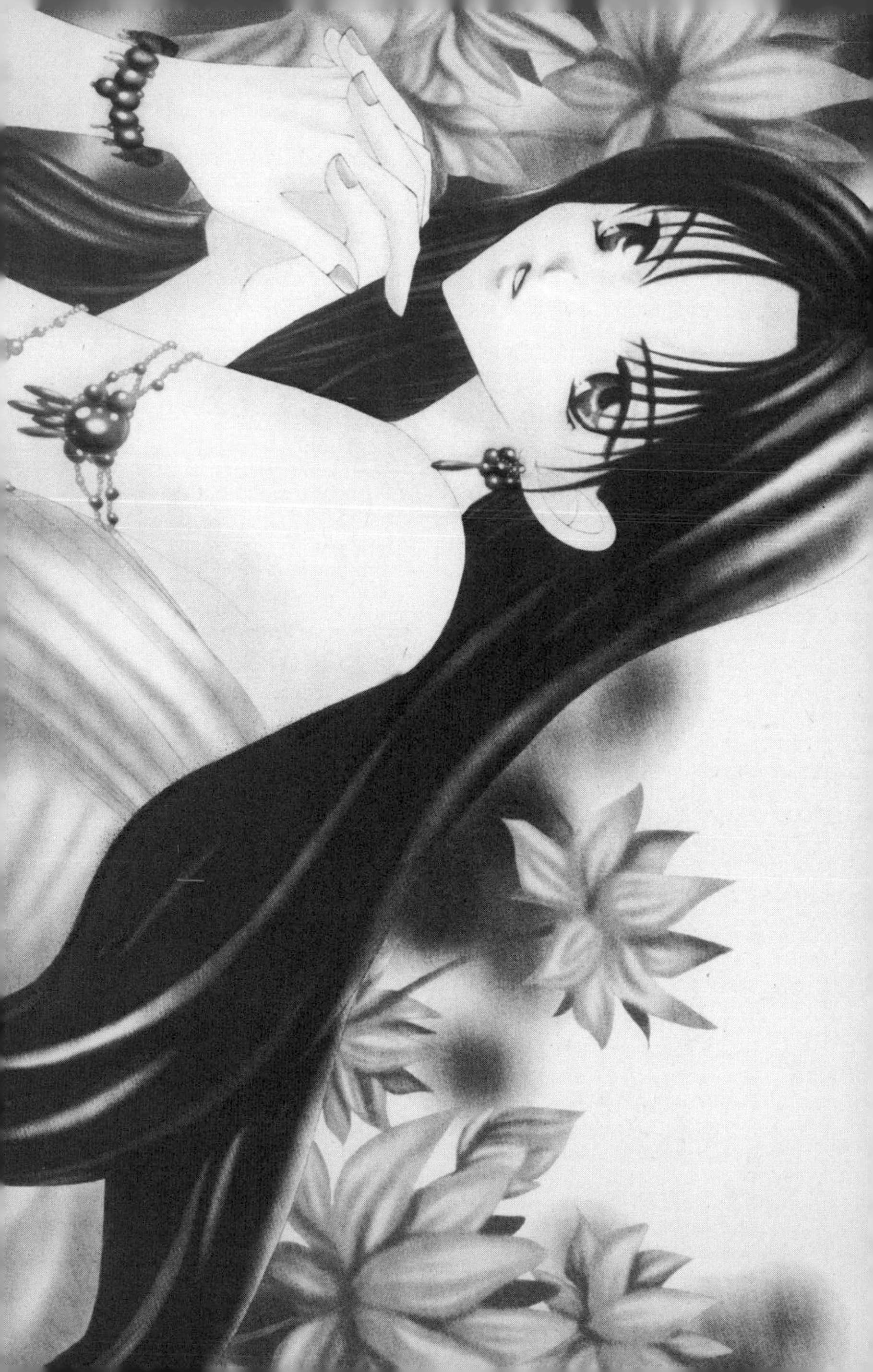

ALSO AVAILABLE FROM ◎TOKYOPOP®

You want it? We got it!
A full range of TOKYOPOP
products are available now at:
www.TOKYOPOP.com/shop

10.19.04T

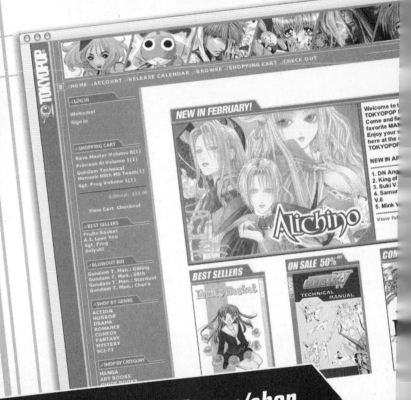

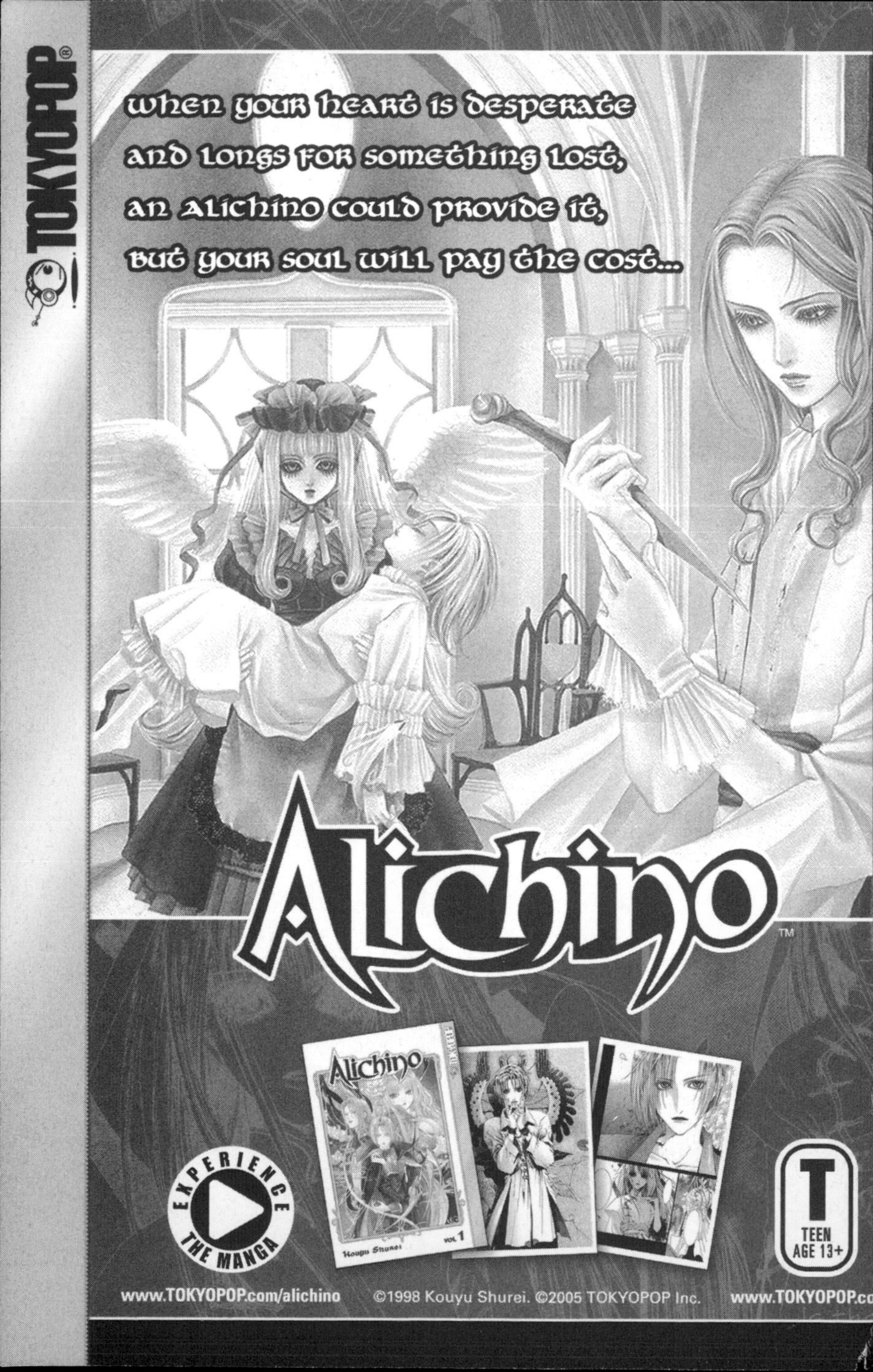

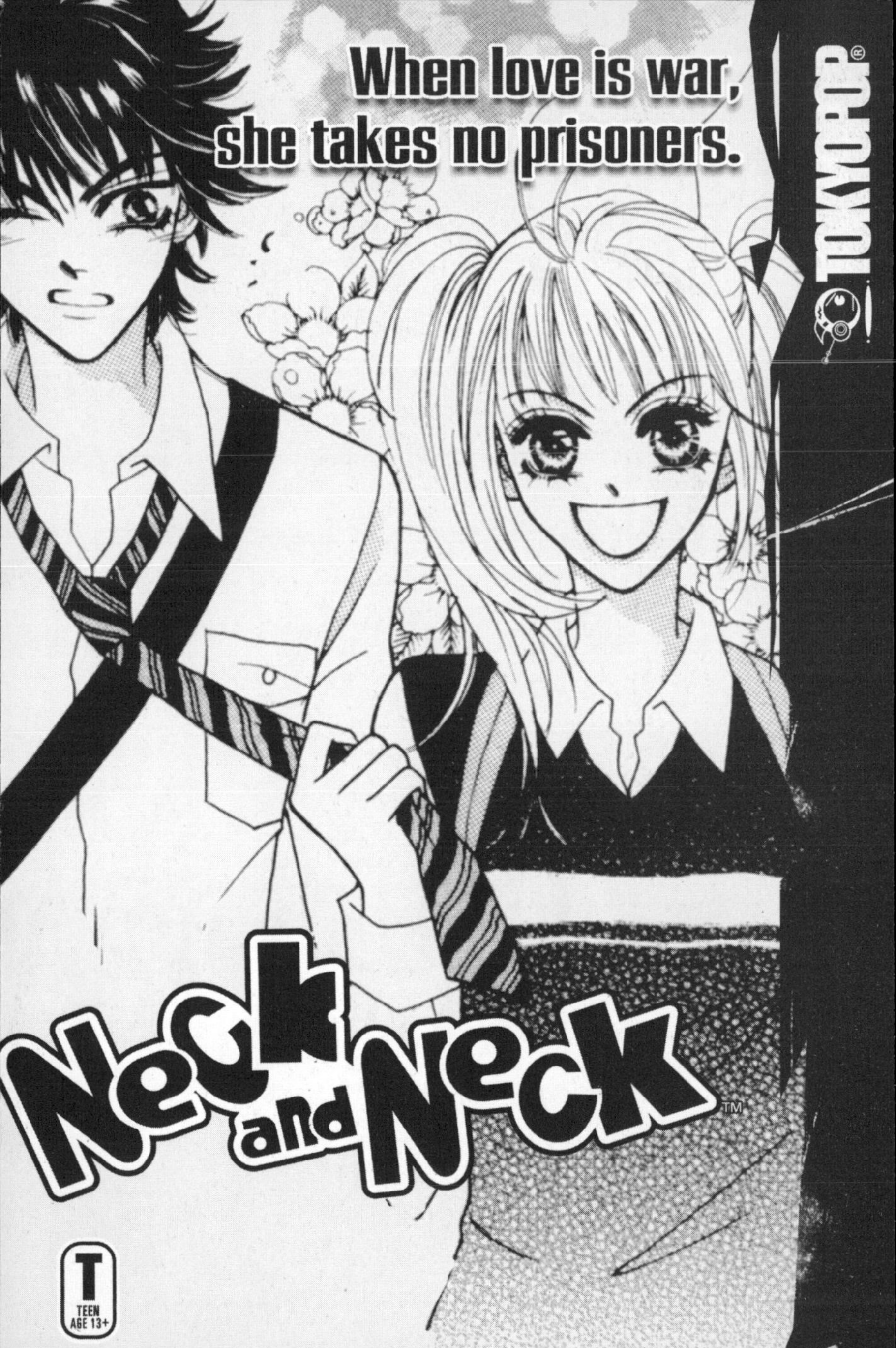
When love is war,
she takes no prisoners.
TOKYOPOP®
Neck and Neck™
T
TEEN
AGE 13+

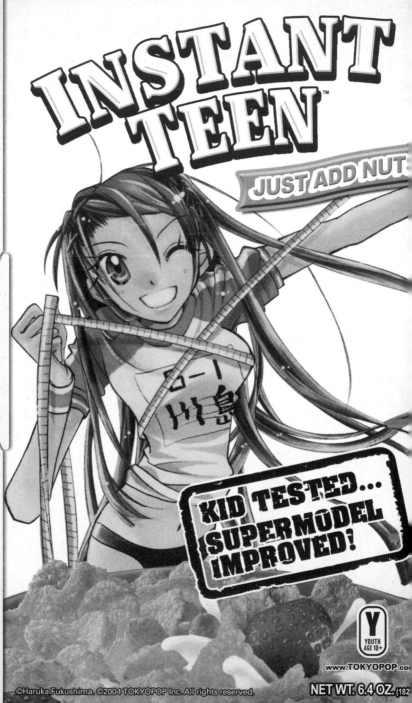

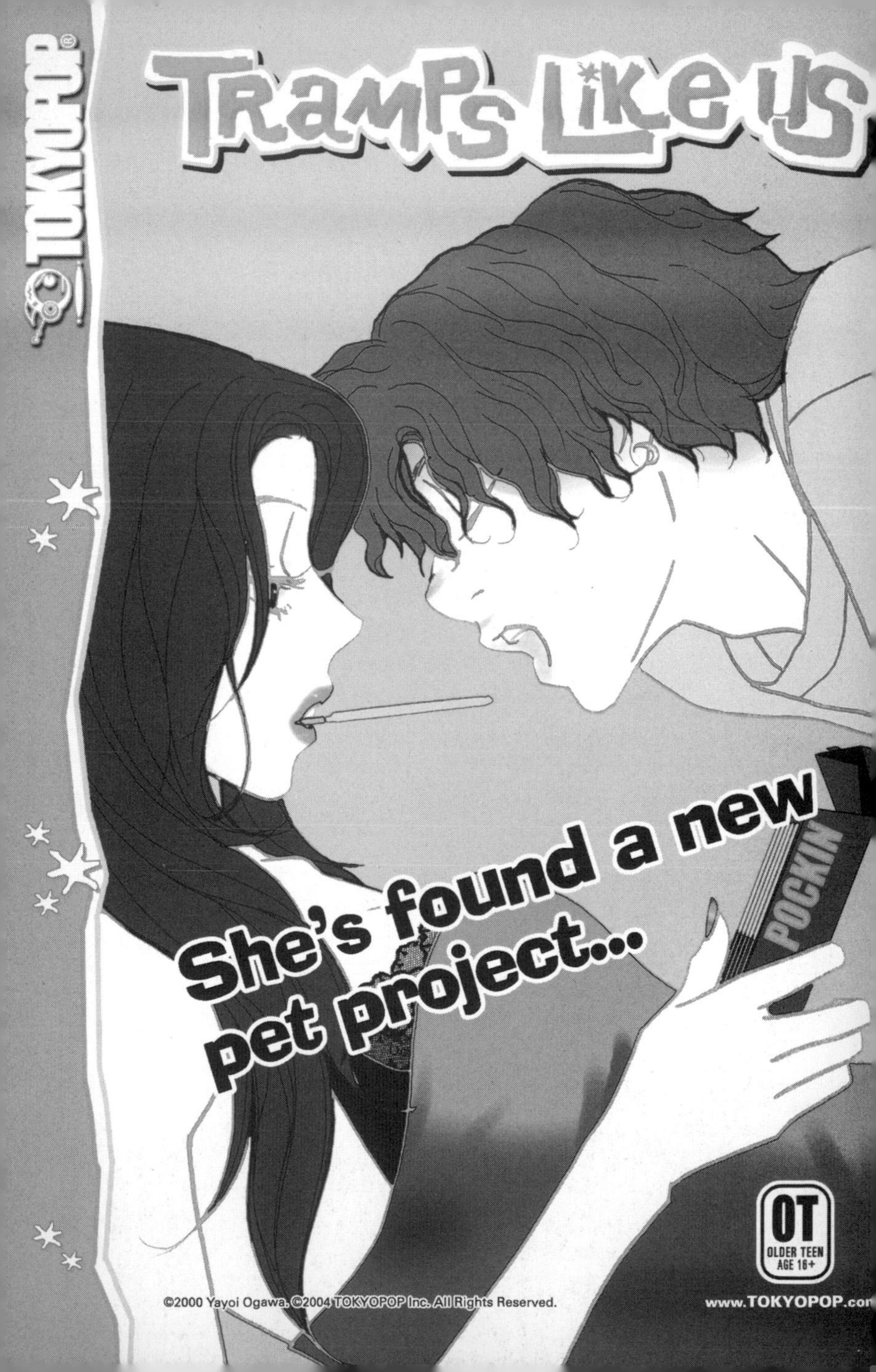
TOKYOPOP
TRAMPS LIKE US
She's found a new pet project...
POCKIN
OT
OLDER TEEN AGE 16+
©2000 Yayoi Ogawa. ©2004 TOKYOPOP Inc. All Rights Reserved.
www.TOKYOPOP.com

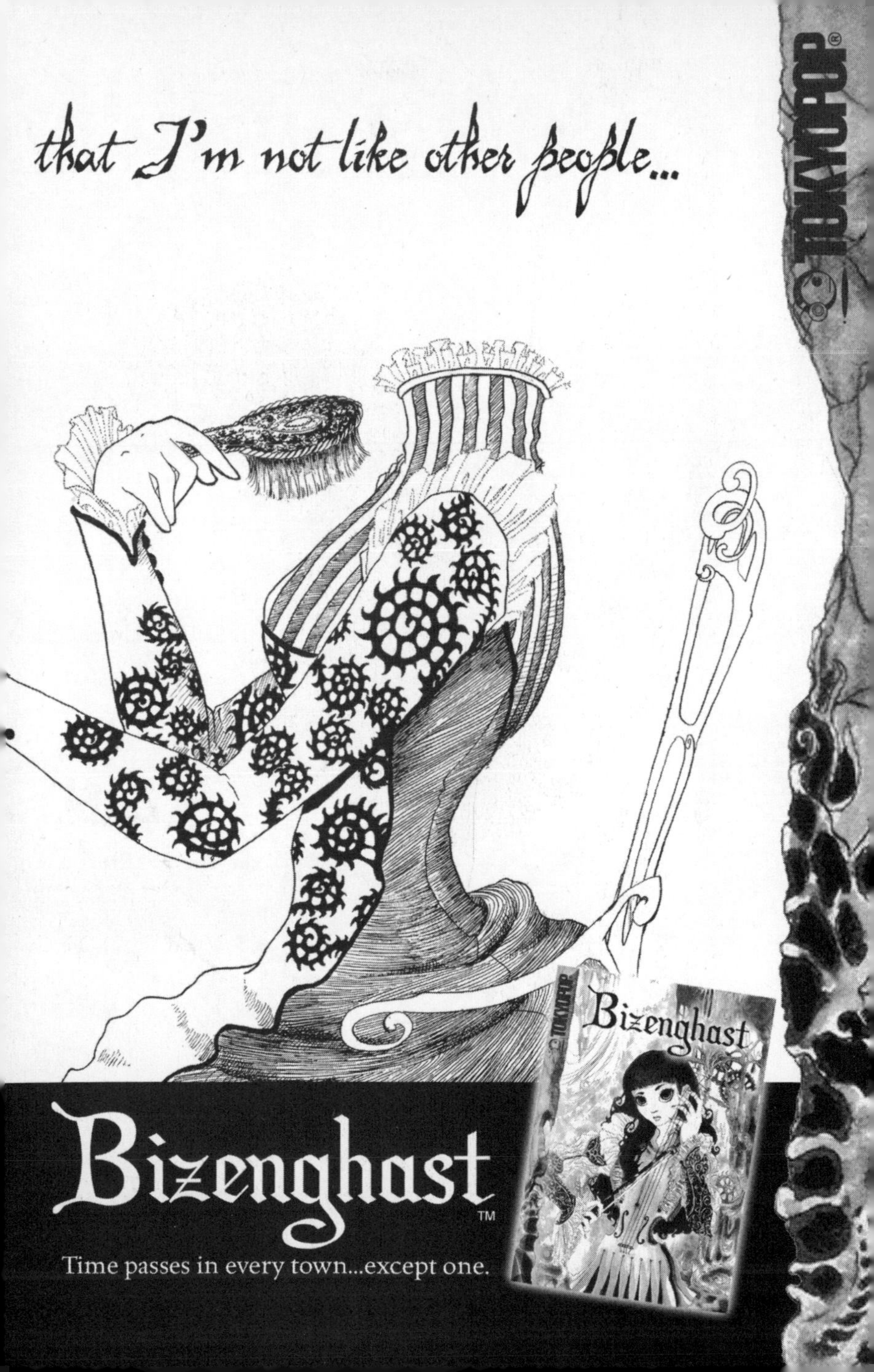
that I'm not like other people...
Bizenghast
Bizenghast™
Time passes in every town...except one.

Dear Diary,
I'm starting to feel

When a young girl moves to the forgotten town of Bizenghast, she uncovers a terrifying collection of lost souls that leads her to the brink of insanity. One thing becomes painfully clear: The residents of Bizenghast are just dying to come home.

STOP!

This is the back of the book. You wouldn't want to spoil a great ending!

This book is printed "manga-style," in the authentic Japanese right-to-left format. Since none of the artwork has been flipped or altered, readers get to experience the story just as the creator intended. You've been asking for it, so TOKYOPOP® delivered: authentic, hot-off-the-press, and far more fun!

DIRECTIONS

1
2
3
4
5
6
7
8
9
10

If this is your first time reading manga-style, here's a quick guide to help you understand how it works.

It's easy... just start in the top right panel and follow the numbers. Have fun, and look for more 100% authentic manga from TOKYOPOP®!